SUPERSHIP

NOËL MOSTERT

SUPERSHIP

M

SBN 333 17923 4

First published 1974 in the United States by
ALFRED A. KNOPF, INC.

First published 1975, in a revised and updated edition, by
MACMILLAN LONDON LTD
London and Basingstoke
Associated companies in New York Dublin Melbourne
Johannesburg and Delhi

A substantial portion of the material in this
book appeared originally in *The New Yorker* in
a different form

Printed in Great Britain by
WESTERN PRINTING SERVICES LTD
Bristol

IN MEMORY OF WOUTER DE WET

INTRODUCTION

My interest in writing this book was long standing, although the original intent was somewhat different. These huge, strange, unattractive ships struck me as a new and significant part of man's story on the waters. What I had expected to write was simply a profile of big tankers and the men who sailed them but, in 1966, when I myself first sailed in one of these ships their size and technology were advancing so swiftly that the vessel in which I travelled, a mere 50,000 tonner, quite clearly already was inadequate as the vehicle for my intentions. Everyone on board regarded her as belonging to the past. As ships got bigger, however, their owners and operators became increasingly shy about allowing strangers on board, and the entire venture might have died without the active, sometimes furious, encouragement of Derek Morgan of *The New Yorker* magazine, to whom I virtually owe the existence of this book. Without his persistent prodding and nagging I undoubtedly would have given up. I wish also to express my deep appreciation to Mr William Shawn, editor of *The New Yorker*, for his sympathetic interest and encouragement at a most critical point.

There could have been no book, however, without a ship, and I want to acknowledge the kindness, courtesy and great consideration of the P & O in allowing me to sail aboard their tanker *Ardshiel* in 1971. When those arrangements were made the concept of the book was still quite different – simply to draw a profile of a strange and fascinating class of ship. When I disembarked, however, I was already aware that the subject was much larger and more complex. I left *Ardshiel* asking myself far too many general and specific questions about the dangers and shortcomings of this type of ship to write merely a description of one curious transport. It took three years to attempt to answer those questions, partly because of the vast amount of research required, and partly because the matter under study itself kept changing. International concern about the environment and the various studies, debates and measures relating to this, as well as events such as the Middle Eastern War of October 1973, and, of course, changes within the tanker industry itself, often forced changes and revisions and new research. But it all remained set within the natural framework of that long voyage aboard *Ardshiel*.

At the end, my opening sentence for Chapter One and its fixing of the voyage in 'a recent June' was more than a lingering reminder of the original expectation of an earlier deadline: I kept it, and shall continue to keep it, because, in a very neat sense, it conveys the deadly seasonless mood of these ships. That part of it all, the ship and its life, its structure and the problems attendant upon these, the route and its hazards, does not change. *Ardshiel* continues to steam steadily to and fro on her ceaseless circuits, only the faces on board change from time to time; and even these not so much because usually there are one or two who have been aboard before. Sadly, I do not believe that this June is perceptibly different from another, except that the ship gets older.

Off the Cape, nothing has changed, nor I fear is it likely to, until tankers stop. Ships continue to line up for repairs to seriously defective machinery, to be found sometimes, usually after they have broken down, to be in a state of disgraceful neglect, or occasionally either to vanish or wreck themselves.

But, whatever my misgivings about the new race of ships of which she is part, *Ardshiel* herself had given reassurance that, though much had changed, much else hadn't. Her young officers need special commendation. I was daily conscious during the voyage of their high capability and intelligence and sensitivity, so explicitly conveyed in the taped conversations I brought from the ship, and, ultimately, as my dismay regarding supertankers increased, so did my awareness that in the high standards and calibre they represented (so reflective of those of the British merchant marine as a whole) lay perhaps our only hope.

Alan Ewart-James in particular struck me as a fine example of the new and necessary sailor, in whom a different, special skill must serve a different and special responsibility. Without his articulate response and fastidious explanations both during the voyage and again more than a year after, much of the value of the *Ardshiel* experience might have been lost. I am deeply grateful, as I also am to his other shipboard colleagues on that voyage, especially James Jackson and Peter Dutton, who both went to great effort to explain the vicissitudes of steam and automation.

It would be difficult to thank all those many others who at one time or another contributed to the detail and pattern of this book, but among those to whom I feel specially indebted are Mr M. W.

Richey, Executive Secretary, the Royal Institute of Navigation, London; Mr J. A. H. Paffett, Director, Ship Division, National Physical Laboratory, Teddington, England; Mr Per-Johan Borke Bogerud, of Det Norske Veritas, Oslo; Mr John Kirby, former president of the Chamber of Shipping of the United Kingdom and of Shell Tankers UK Ltd; Comm. E. W. Platt and Mr G. Sterry, British Petroleum; Mr I. P. I. Blom, of the Rotterdam Port Authority; Mr N. R. Knowles and Mr John Edmondson, Senior Pilots, Trinity House; Dr Alan Longhurst, The Institute for Marine Environmental Research, Plymouth; Dr Molly Spooner, The Marine Biological Laboratory, Plymouth; Sir George Deacon, former director, National Institute of Oceanography, Wormley; Mr Erik Gjeruldsen, division manager, Norcontrol, Oslo; the Chamber of Shipping of the United Kingdom; Lloyd's Register of Shipping; Mr Boyce Richardson, Montreal, for his indispensable assistance on Arctic environmental matters and the problem of tankers in cold waters; Mr Norman Pascoe, the *Montreal Star*, for technical assistance and help on all matters relating to the *Arrow* disaster; Mr Mahmoud Younes, Beirut, past chairman of the Suez Canal Authority; Mr Mashhur Ahmed Mashhur, present chairman of the Suez Canal Authority; Mr Maurice Cooper, president, Seabrokers, Inc., of New York; Mrs Brenda Gerolemou, for her considerable editorial assistance and her translation of Baudelaire's poem on the albatross; and to Mrs A. Westphal, of the South African National Foundation for the Conservation of Coastal Birds, for her great effort in providing material on the tragic struggle of southern sea birds against pollution since the closing of Suez. SANCOB has the highest success rate in the world for rehabilitating birds. It is a voluntary organisation of slender means, and its most difficult years may well lie ahead. In the event that this book should create a concern for the life of the great southern seas in any of its readers strong enough to require expression, then I unreservedly recommend that they make the South African National Foundation for the Conservation of Coastal Birds, Box 17, Rondebosch, Cape Town, the beneficiary of that impulse.

NOËL MOSTERT

SUPERSHIP

ONE

ON a warm but overcast morning of a recent June S.S. *Ardshiel*, a
British supertanker with a deadweight of 214,085 tons, a length of
1,063 feet, a 157-foot-9-inch beam, a capacity for some 206,000 tons
of crude oil, and flying the house colours of the Peninsular and
Oriental Steam Navigation Company, better known simply as P & O,
was the biggest object in sight in the Gironde estuary, through which
pours the sea trade of Bordeaux and south-west France.

Ardshiel had brought to the Gironde what remained of a cargo of
Persian Gulf crude, having discharged the bulk of it at Rotterdam,
where I had boarded her. Although I had often in the past crossed
the North Atlantic in the old Cunard *Queens, Queen Mary* and
Queen Elizabeth, and had imagined myself accustomed to mere size
in a ship, the short run down the English Channel and across the Bay
of Biscay had not yet accustomed me to the novelty of being aboard
a cargo ship vastly larger than either of the old Cunarders. Nor indeed
had it yet accustomed me to the company and special outlook of an
apparently new sort of sailor. Cut off from the sea itself by the very
size of his ship and from the shore by the different nature of her
voyaging, he was a man whose viewpoint seemed often to be the
likely one of someone on a space platform rather than that of the
seafarer as we have known him. In the Gulf, *Ardshiel* had loaded her
thirteen cargo tanks divided into five giant sections from a pipeline
terminal anchored about nine to ten miles off that desolate shore and
then, without stopping, sailed 11,000 miles to Rotterdam via the
Cape of Good Hope. She was on a long-term charter to Shell Oil and
this was her normal route.

At Rotterdam *Ardshiel* had discharged the first portion of her
cargo in just over twelve hours, from daybreak to sunset, but no one
had left the ship. There was no time for leave. The dials and gauges
that monitored the outflowing oil had to be carefully watched and
checked. Even those who might have found a spare moment or two

1

for going ashore entertained no thought of doing so. Oil tankers usually find their terminals surrounded by refineries and industrial acres and miles from anywhere. At Rotterdam anyone who might have considered going into the city for a mug of beer would have faced the prospect of an hour's taxi ride. On most voyages, the ship would have discharged her entire cargo and sailed as soon as the last drop of oil had been cleared, back along her monotonous route, with only the climatic variations offered by two crossings of the equator and a brief excursion through the southern hemisphere's winter to provide some sense of difference and variety. On this occasion, however, the diversion of half the cargo to the Gironde had brought the ship's crew a most unusual break in the normal pattern of their shipboard lives.

Ardshiel had berthed near the northernmost tip of the Médoc peninsula, whose chalky soil provides some of the finest vineyards of France. It was a short stroll from her berth at Pointe de Grave to the tiny village of Le Verdon, still so simple and rural and pre-1914 in manner and appearance that one could easily see it as the label illustration for one of the local châteaux and its vintages. It seemed on the face of it one of the unlikeliest places in Europe in which to find a *port petrolier* or to encounter one of the biggest ships afloat. It all made sense, however, when one remembered the proximity of Bordeaux with its industries and refineries which, like those everywhere else these days, have an insatiable demand for fuel. As the channels of the Gironde are too shallow for ships the size of *Ardshiel* to sail all the way to Bordeaux their berth had to be at the very entrance to the estuary, and Le Verdon became its site.

This is truly lovely country, with its dunes and pines at the sea's edge and forests of oak or orchards of cherry, apple, and pear interspersed with the vineyards behind. Opposite Le Verdon the large town of Royan with its wide, curved beach of white Atlantic sand is a popular summer resort. Fortunately therefore the installations that load and discharge a supertanker are so compact that they are relatively unobtrusive. Known as Chiksans, they are part of a simple steel scaffolding into which is built a row of sixteen-inch pipes as well as the embarkation ladder for passing to or from the ship; pipes and ladder are automatically adjusted to the slow rise of the ship as it empties, and to the rising and falling of the tides.

A small administrative bungalow was the only other structure on the jetty at Le Verdon. The large storage tanks close by into which the oil was fed had been skilfully painted, with typical Gallic sensibility one liked to think, some being in a wavy camouflage of forest colours and others in the light and dark tones of the encroaching tidal sands, so that they seemed of a piece not merely with their background but also with the blockhouses, now tumbling to ruin, which the Germans had built during the war. From these tanks, underground pipes took the oil away to the refineries at Pauillac, about eighty kilometres downstream. All told, the magnificent approaches to the Gironde did not seem unduly scarred; only the ship obtruded, and by no means unpleasantly.

Even to those of us who had descended from her, the sheer size of the vessel against the low wooded shore with its accompanying stretches of marsh and tidal flats was impressive.

Royan has not been spoiled by high-rise buildings and thus had a lot to say to one's memory of what large provincial towns of this sort used to be all over Europe. This was all the more remarkable because Royan was virtually flattened, mistakenly, by American bombers during the war. It restored itself to its former modest scale so that, coming back from an excellent lunch there, one confronted with some surprise the impact of *Ardshiel* upon the opposite shore, and it was easy to understand why busloads of sightseers had been coming down the rough road from Le Verdon since we'd tied up. For miles around, everybody's attention inevitably would be drawn to the gigantic ship, for she clearly had taken possession of a considerable portion of the estuary and its sky. Standing as a light frail vertical mark beside it, as though to provide a measure, the church steeple of Le Verdon was hardly noticeable.

Visually, *Ardshiel* was of course at her most impressive. Now completely empty, she was waiting for the tide to release her from her berth.

The sightseers climbed from their buses and cars, stood about in groups exclaiming about the size and impact of the ship, took photographs, and then got into their vehicles again and went back the way they had come, their sense of novelty satisfied; whatever their curiosity and surprise, it could not have been equalled by what was felt on board the ship itself, where the peace and rural beauty of the surroundings and the idea of walking down the ship's ladder and passing among gardens and trees weighted with cherries to any of the fine local restaurants with their tables set on green lawns and spread with crisp white linen was something beyond all normal expectation. Forgotten pleasures. A country stroll, different food, the sight of strangers.

Ardshiel's deck and engineering officers were British, but the seamen and stewards were a mixed bunch of Pakistanis, Chinese, and Indians, the latter being mainly Goanese, which meant they were Catholic in their religion and had Portuguese names. Many of the officers had not been on shore for months and some of the crew not for a year, or even more. The Pakistanis were mostly Pathans, the farming and fighting men from the area of the Khyber Pass, and their love of land and plants was normally assuaged only by the vases of plastic roses and carnations that many of them kept upon the bureaux in their cabins and fastidiously dusted before the captain's weekly inspection on Saturdays. In Le Verdon they walked about knowledgeably discussing the orchards and produce, sniffing the air, and occasionally stopping to wash their hands in earth, all with that spontaneous joy of difference that the landsman feels when he himself comes from the interior down to a salty shore.

Although I had been on the ship for only three days it already had enclosed me within its general mood of isolation and endless voyaging, so that I understood their pleasure and was affected by it.

Sitting on an old stone bench at the edge of Le Verdon, beguiled by the hot summer stillness and its cursory human interventions – the *trrrrring* of a bicycle bell, a woman sweeping her doorstep and talking to someone inside the house, the steady scrape of a rake on gravel – the thought of the imminent journey to the Persian Gulf and back, and the sight of the outsize vehicle for it so improbably sitting at the end of the orchards, gave me a disturbing feeling of loss and forfeit that I'd not known since the war. It seemed incomprehensibly long and far to go.

Ships at least provide their own reassurances, and their snug appearance of self-containment is one of the principal of these. Despite her bulk, *Ardshiel* when I returned to her shortly before sailing time conveyed that charged air of special community that is the mark of a ship about to put to sea. 'Shipshape' is the word that comes to mind, and in that pleasant alliteration the mind's eye sees a vessel that suddenly has rid itself of the dust and commotion and informal coming and going between ship and shore that settles upon it with the activity of loading or unloading. It has cleared its decks for reunion with its element and dressed itself with the flags and pennants proper to the occasion. In an older ship it means hatches battened and covered in canvas; winches, tackle, and other working gear secure; and the Blue Peter, a dark blue flag with a square white centre which is worn as an indication of intention to sail, snapping from a signal halliard above the bridge house. Tugs are standing by. Visitors who were welcome quite suddenly aren't. The brief kinship with the shore is over and short shrift made of its untidy influences. Both litter and gangways have been removed and stowed with the fervour and obsessive exactness of puritanical standards renewed.

The mood is consciously aloof; there is no lolling about, everyone is at some appointed place.

Boiler suits and overalls have been replaced by uniforms white and starched. Everyone has his cap on. And to those of us on shore who

4

might be watching, the gap between ship and shore becomes the unbridgeable moat between ourselves and all wish fulfilment.

This whole business of a group of sailors shaking off the shore and its entanglements while assuming, as though for brief appearance's sake, the stance and flair of high mission, whether on coastal collier or battleship, has always attracted me as being one of the most extraordinary of our reasonably commonplace experiences. It is the original act of dropping out which has been dressed, one feels, with mock solemnity, and which, satisfying so many of our baser needs – arrogance, self-pity, sentimentality, and sheer irresponsibility – seldom fails to be anything but thoroughly enjoyable.

With oil tankers things are a little different. Their intimacy with the shore is so much less than any other ship's. Usually they are alongside their berths too briefly for departure to provide any companionable sense of social or sentimental leave-taking, or even to bother about flying Blue Peter. Their berths are too remote and well guarded anyway to allow for visitors except those on ship's business; and the actual job of loading or discharging is so neatly and invisibly done that it brings little disarray to the decks. Even so, they have to gather themselves to some degree for the sea, securing what gear has been in use and breaking out the necessary flags; and Ardshiel, being P & O, a company where traditions die hard, was as formal and correct in getting away as a cruiser on a flag-waving run. Uniforms were certainly white and starched, and caps most definitely on.

When the blower called 'Stations fore and aft', a terse command from the master that made Ardshiel seem even more like a warship moving against an enemy pacing into gun range, I went to the bridge, which, since I was a supernumerary, was to be my emergency post during the voyage. Like everywhere else on the ship, its principal characteristic was space; the bridge house itself was as wide across as the width of a medium-sized liner. Beyond its doors, the bridge wings reached out in long promenades, the ends of them hanging out above the water. Ranged beneath the large angled windows that looked forward over the main deck was a bank of shiny consoles containing the buttons and switches for the complex electronic gear upon which modern ships increasingly depend, while the after end of the bridge house contained a screened-off chartroom area, all of it looking as immaculate as a space control centre. To a stranger such as myself, however, the main impact upon arriving here came not from such a familiar air of clinical control but from the spectacular forward view of the ship.

We were five decks and forty-five feet above the main deck and, being in ballast, sat one hundred and thirteen feet above the water; from the main deck to the sea alone represented a height of sixty feet, which put it at about the same level above the water as the promenade deck on either of the former *Queens*.

The prospect forward was of a great acreage of red-painted steel, with a raised catwalk amidships dwindling all the way toward the bows, which were almost a quarter of a mile away; small indistinguishable figures moved busily to and fro up there, handling the lines to the tugs and bringing in those loosened by the shorehands. Their urgent disembodied cries of advice and response to orders crackled continually on the portable Very High Frequency radios that all officers carry and that are an essential form of communication aboard such a big ship, especially between deck and bridge.

Gathered on the bridge were *Ardshiel*'s master, Basil Thomson, fifty-six years old, appreciably more than six feet tall, and of course even taller with his cap on; the first officer, Alan Ewart-James, twenty-nine; a navigating cadet, Stephen Davis, twenty; a Pakistani General Purpose Rating First Class, Haroon Rashid, thirty, who was at the wheel; and the French pilot, who was calmly detaching the ship from the jetty, an operation scrupulously observed and checked by Thomson, who moved around with the restless questing manner of dispossessed authority, uneasy as all masters are about not having his ship obedient to his own discretion.

Ardshiel, even though empty and riding light, still had a ballasted draught of thirty-one feet, only eight feet less than a fully loaded *Queen Mary*, and she could move from her berth and out to sea only on the turn of the tide, not a moment too soon, nor any thereafter. The Gironde currents are strong, and imprecise handling could put such a ship on a mudbank where she could be settled for days, at huge cost to her owners and her charterers. Even though a pilot is nominally in charge, the master is generally considered to bear ultimate responsibility for anything that goes wrong. It takes an exceptional situation, however, before he is likely to interfere with or take over from a pilot, certainly nothing less than a belief that his vessel is being placed in imminent danger by the other man's orders, a circumstance that seemed scarcely possible with someone as cool and assured as our Gironde man appeared to be.

The ship had lain at the jetty as she'd entered, with her bows pointed up the estuary and her stern to the sea. The currents that had pinned us to our berth before the turn of the tide could, once she got off the berth, start playing all sorts of tricks with the big hull. But the French pilot, a stocky, dark, youngish man, took us away with a cheerful joy, frequently patting the rail where he stood as though in affectionate encouragement of such a lumbering though obedient beast. He called out his commands in a clear, full voice and they were repeated across the bridge, by First Officer Ewart-James,

6

who stayed constantly at the pilot's side, and then by Rashid as he adjusted the ship's wheel accordingly. Cadet Davis stood beside one of the consoles with the Bridge Movement Book before him, recording each detail of departure and the precise time it occurred.

'The wheel twenty degrees starboard,' called the pilot.

'Starboard twenty,' Ewart-James cried.

'Stop her!'

'Stop her!'

'Midships.'

'Midships.'

It was a litany of persuasion slowly, distinctly sung by priest and acolytes, without tremor of doubt, in fullest conviction, even though the ship was swinging without any natural aptitude, with a feeling of huge and reluctant weight. Like Mass in the southern lands, where ritual is familiarly scarred by chatter and other more fluent purposes, our litany was accompanied by fragments of casual conversation, reprimand, and the homilies and bits of comment that sailors are prone to offer either to each other or to no one in particular, merely as a matter of by the way, when they stand around on these occasions. In this instance these verbal bits and pieces came mainly from Thomson, who stayed inside the bridge, an intimidating figure except when he suddenly sat down in one of the high so-called captain's chairs placed at both the port and starboard sides of the bridge house, and when his great frame seemed to fall slack, his eyes fixed upon some remote introspective point within himself. He would just as suddenly rouse himself and resume his pacing to and fro. For all his restlessness, his body seemed simple and slow in its movements. His eyes were everywhere at once, however, and his voice when it sounded was small and querulous: he was one of those men in whom height and size appear the passive but willing servants of a diminutive, shrill master set somewhere atop it all, like a child driver upon an elephant's back.

Having set himself down in lassitude in one of the captain's chairs and then abruptly back into motion again, he suddenly paused in anger beside the Bridge Movement Book. Cadet Davis had committed an error, having used the abbreviation 'V'L', meaning 'vessel'.

'What's this?' Thomson demanded.

'Vessel,' Davis replied. He was a slender, pale youth, of delicate features and expression.

'Vessel? This is a ship, a bloody ship! We're turning, we're moving. Ship! Like ships that pass in the night, except that this time we're reluctantly passing in daylight. A vessel could be an urn, a ruddy vase. No abbreviations in this book, m'lad, except those already in use

7

and which you see before you, if you take the trouble to look back and see what's previously written.'

The pilot called, 'Slow ahead.'

'Slow ahead, sir,' Ewart-James repeated, and worked the engine-room telegraph.

'Slow ahead it is,' he advised.

Our bows were swinging perceptibly faster now, along the low green shore and then across the distant, pretty, abandoned city of Royan.

'Tell them to be ready to let go.'

Ewart-James gave the order to the bows on his VHF and then watched the response there through a telescope.

'Starboard. North, three-six-oh.'

'It is quicker to go than to come,' Thomson said with instinctive rhyming response and a lingering hint of reproach to the pilot who'd brought us in the previous day and who, according to him, had been late.

'Steady.'

'Steady.'

'Half ahead.'

'Half ahead, sir.'

'We're round now,' Thomson said. 'Start to let go.'

The figures on the bows moved like men in a panic as they worked the lines.

'That's the starboard tug gone.'

'Three-four-five.'

'Port tug gone.'

The tugs paused in the water one by one as they were released, lying briefly exhausted, emptied of strain, without resource. Then, with a farewell toot, they drifted back toward the jetty. The whole bay itself was still revolving. Finally it stopped.

'Full speed ahead.' This was manœuvring speed.

'Pilot?' Thomson asked. 'Do you want to get off the starboard side, or port?'

'Probably port.'

'All right now,' Thomson said, addressing Ewart-James. 'Tell them up forward that they can secure and pipe down aft and get their lunch. There should be nothing else we need now. You can leave me and go and get your own lunch.'

Ewart-James said 'Aye,' and went below, replaced on the bridge by Third Officer Stephen Tucker, twenty-three.

'Three-four-two,' the pilot called.

'Three-four-two,' Thomson repeated, and asked: 'Like some coffee?'

'*Oui*, yes. Or a cup of tea, no? I would prefer a nice cup of English tea.'

Thomson, examining the paintwork on the bridge wing, was saying, 'On shore they have no idea when you order supplies for a ship this size. To paint one of these ships, the office estimate is five thousand quid. But they never ask us. It's never less than twelve thousand, and that's doing it pinchingly. You can work it out in square feet, how much paint it takes, but they still set a budget which isn't possible.'

'How often do you paint her?' the pilot asked.

'Every two years. We're doing it this trip.'

'Port.'

'Port.'

Thomson, as if in afterthought, went over to the blower and said into it, 'Attention please, the pilot's getting off the port side. I want someone there to see him off.'

A tray arrived and the pilot accepted his tea.

'But that's not much good to me,' Thomson said to the steward, lifting his cup to reveal a puddle of brown liquid in which it was resting. 'Go into the pantry and clean that saucer!'

'When is the summer coming, pilot?' he asked, when the cup returned.

'Next year, now it's too late.'

'At least the weather's better at Wimbledon than here,' Thomson said, addressing the bridge at large. 'But tennis isn't the same any more. It's all hotted up. If you put somebody against a man like Rod Laver he's lucky to send back two balls in a game, or even a set. All those tantrums too, Virginia Wade throwing rackets about. I think of tennis as an afternoon recreation for ladies and gentlemen. Now they play each other with vindictiveness. I used to play a reasonably fast game myself, but that's all gone. High blood pressure. Can't even swim any more.'

'No swimming, never?' inquired the pilot, politely, adding, 'Two-seven-oh.'

'Two-seven-oh,' Thomson repeated. 'No, I'll never go into the water again, unless it's to get off this ship. I was lying under a mis-fired gun at Aden during the war, a three-inch Ack-Ack, trying to clear it, when someone pressed the trigger. The old ears were never the same after that.'

'That's for sure,' said the pilot. 'Two-six-five.'

'Two-six-five.'

'Nothing's the same,' Thomson said. 'Take these ships, the more comfortable they are, the more time they all have to think out moans and groans.' He broke off, and demanded, 'What's he doing

9

down there?' He indicated a Pakistani working on the deck below. 'That APO's turning out the wrong accommodation ladder,' he told Tucker. 'Tell him the pilot's leaving from the port side.'

'No,' he said, resuming the conversation. 'The more you give 'em these days, the more miserable they all seem to be. During the war I came home from Cape Town via Freetown in the old *Britannic*. Six men in what used to be a single-berth cabin, with one air blower. There was a washbasin with a tap that ran for an hour and a half each morning. We all took it in turn getting out of our bunks to wash and shave. But it was a happy voyage. It was the same before the war aboard so many ropy old ships; the ropiest were often the happiest; conditions were terrible on some, just a fan to keep you cool in the tropics, not much food and none of it any good, but you didn't hear them moaning the way they do today. Junior officers now earn as much as a cabinet minister did before the war and they live in luxury, but they don't want to stay at sea. When I ask them at the office why these people go ashore and give up the sea they can never give me any reason. Perhaps people like myself are partly to blame. Sometimes officers object to the standards I insist upon. Some of the young men complain that I don't call them "mister". I call senior officers by their first names, but the junior ones and the cadets I address by their surnames. That's how it was in the navy. When I was in the office they once asked me to change my attitude on this. But I told them that, after thirty years, it's difficult to be someone else, or to change my ways.'

'Two-seven-five,' said the pilot.

'Two-seven-five.'

'We can start slowing down now for dropping the pilot,' Thomson told Tucker. 'It's just over half a mile.' Thomson himself relayed this to the engine room, however, and stood watching the fast-receding shore. We were far out now, the coast very low, Royan too low to be seen, and the Corduan light, a lonely offshore tower at the entrance to the Gironde channel, was the only distinct visible reminder of the place we'd left.

Thomson began talking more hurriedly, as though wishing to complete his line of thought before the Frenchman left. 'They think I'm too strict but they should have been with P & O forty years ago. We had a fleet commodore who spoke to nobody and nobody addressed him, except to say "Yes, sir, No, sir, three bags full".'

A launch had detached itself from a large pilotage vessel that lay just ahead and it now bobbed toward us.

'Dead slow.'

'Dead slow, sir.'

'Do you want to go down now?' Thomson asked the pilot.

'Yes, sir.' He pulled on a pair of light plastic waterproof over-trousers over his suit, said a graceful good-bye to each of us in turn, and then went down to the main deck. A ladder, air operated, hissed down from there over the ship's side. The pilot went through the gate and vanished. As the launch pulled away Thomson went out onto the bridge wing, waved, and sounded several long blasts on the ship's whistle. The pilot ship responded.

Re-entering the bridge, Thomson said to Tucker, 'Take the pilot's, the explosives, and the French flags down but leave mine up. Chop her off this chart and put her on the other one. Full away at three. Stream the log and don't forget to zero it at full away.'

He rang the engine room. 'Full away at three, chief.'

Tucker synchronised the clocks, set the log at zero, worked out his position and, as the clock approached three, called the engineers, gave them a time-check, and waited, phone in hand, for the hands to touch the hour.

'Fifteen hundred,' he called, started the log, made an entry in the Bridge Movement Book, and cried, 'We're off!'

The voyage had begun.

TWO

Oil tankers, a once obscure and largely unremarked race of ships, have established themselves during the past fifteen years as the dominant vessels of the age and, arguably, of all time. They qualify in both respects merely on grounds of size. They are the biggest ships that have ever been, their dimensions being one of the technological audacities of the century. Most of all, however, they qualify because no other ships have ever been so universally important, none more political. They were the harbingers of that new manifestation of global strategy and national self-interest, the energy crisis; it was to keep them moving that Britain and France landed their troops at Suez in 1956. Much broader and more subtle implications now rest upon their safe voyaging. They have become indispensable to so much more of the world than at the time of Suez that they are now pivotal to global peace and economic survival to a degree that could not have been easily visualised even then.

The fate of much of mankind often has been affected by ships of various kinds, usually fighting ones, and the survival of individual nations occasionally has been dependent upon shipping as a whole, as Britain's was for periods during the Second World War, but there never was a time when the viability of life for millions in both hemispheres was inextricably linked to the daily unimpeded passage of any one class of merchantmen. Oil tankers are the first to hold this perilous distinction, because they are quite simply the principal means of carrying the world's oil from where it is to where it's needed. Without them, much of the world would simply stop, and it is a circumstance that will remain with us until oil has been replaced as a principal source of the world's energy and fuel, which no knowledgeable authority supposes to be possible before the end of this century. When that time comes, these monster ships, like the dinosaurs, will swiftly vanish.

Meanwhile, they are still in their ascendancy. They get steadily bigger, and their influence upon our lives and well-being waxes proportionately. In fact, one of the most astonishing aspects of these ships is the very rapidity with which universal dependence upon them has grown.

For nearly a century oil has been so much taken for granted in the United States as an easily available and widely used fuel that it is easy to overlook how very new those same assumptions have been elsewhere, particularly in Europe and Japan.

In the early thirties coal still supplied 75 per cent of the world's energy. Oil accounted for 15 per cent, and most of this consumption was in the United States. By 1950, oil already accounted for 25 per cent of world energy consumption. By 1965 it was 37 per cent. In the industrial societies of the non-communist world, which are the main users of energy, oil is now far and away the dominant fuel. It really owes this position to what probably was the most important economic change after the war, the conversion of Europe and Japan from coal-based to oil-based energy: during the sixties alone Europe's oil demand trebled, while Japan's increased sevenfold.

In Europe's case, the shift from coal to oil was necessary to save it from an energy crisis caused by the wartime ruin, neglect, and dislocation of the coal industries. In 1951 only about 15 per cent of Europe's total energy requirements came from oil, and these amounted to some 73 million tons. Five years later the proportion was rising toward 25 per cent. By 1968, oil finally had replaced coal as Western Europe's principal source of energy, accounting for 56 per cent, which meant an annual importation of some 500 million tons of oil. This was rising at an annual rate of 8 to 10 per cent. About half the oil came from the Middle East.

Japan shifted even faster. Encouraged by America, she had reluctantly turned to oil when it became apparent that her coal industry would not be able to cope adequately with the future pace of the country's development. The Japanese coal mines lie mainly at the far ends of the archipelago, on Kyushu and Hokkaido, and are therefore remote from the main industrial production centres on Honshu. The mines, like Europe's, were run-down, and increasingly unproductive besides. In 1950, coal supplied 60 per cent of Japan's energy requirements and oil a mere 7 per cent; by 1960 oil was as important as coal. Today Japan is the world's largest importer of crude oil. She consumes more than 300 million tons a year, 90 per cent of which has to be imported, and 80 per cent of which in turn is brought by ship from the Middle East via the shallow Malacca Straits between the Malayan peninsula and Sumatra.

In 1972, a depressed year for all consumers, the world's oil consumption was 2,600 million tons, 55 per cent of which had to move by sea in tankers; aside from Japan's 90 per cent, this included 60 per cent of Europe's oil and 60 per cent of Australasia's. Seventy per cent of tanker tonnage was used on voyages from the Middle East, which makes it only too clear why the fourth Arab–Israeli war in October 1973 had such a swift and shattering economic effect. When the oil tankers started arriving with only 60 per cent of their normal capacity on board as a result of the oil cuts, Europe and Japan began to see themselves in real peril. Japan obviously could not survive without her Middle Eastern oil deliveries. Their temporary reduction was sufficient to stop the legendary economic miracle which, even if it fully recovers, will never be quite the same, at least so far as blithe, assertive self-confidence is concerned. Without any tanker deliveries, the Japanese social fabric would quite simply be rent apart.

The position of Western Europe is only marginally better, notwithstanding oil discoveries in European waters, and it was the shortfall of tanker deliveries from the Middle East to the American east coast, which has become increasingly dependent upon them, that helped to make the energy crisis something more than a phrase in much of the United States in 1974. In oil, one shortage cannot be alleviated without creating others, which was why countries such as Britain and France, favoured by the Arabs, didn't do as well as they had hoped in avoiding an oil shortage: oil that should have gone to them from non-Arab sources such as Nigeria and Iran was diverted to those under Arab boycott. Oil tankers of course were the essential pawns in the game. By simply deploying and redeploying them in their huge traffic-operations rooms literally hour by hour, exactly as convoys were routed and diverted in the Admiralty map and operations centres during the war, the oil companies maintained complete control over the world's oil distribution. While they hold complete control over the oil ships, it will ever be so.

In that third crisis involving the world's dependence upon oil ships, the United States was a new and embarrassed recruit to the community of the afflicted. It was a novel situation. In 1956 the United States could assure plenty of oil (at a price) to those in need, and even in 1967 this still was possible. The United States is still the single biggest oil producer in the world (followed by Russia, Saudi Arabia, and Iran), but its considerable reserves are now running down and, anyway, they have long since become incapable of coping with galloping American demands. The United States was self-sufficient in energy for so long that it easily and complacently began to overlook the fact that it had come to depend upon fuel imports for a third of its supply. The delusion was not difficult because the imports were largely from immediate neighbours, Canada and the Caribbean.

According to the United Nations, American oil consumption per head in 1970 was the equivalent of 7.4 tons against a world average of 1¼ tons, and a British one of 3.6 tons. The United States in 1972 consumed 776,200,000 tons of oil, which was 70 million tons more than Western Europe's entire consumption, and more than double Japan's.

The pressures of such demand, coupled with the fact that neighbouring suppliers could no longer guarantee fulfilling it, made the United States an inevitable customer for Middle Eastern oil. American Middle Eastern imports were only 24 million tons in 1972, but they already were significantly higher for 1973 when the October war abruptly reduced them. Before the October war and its embargoes had shaken the smooth predictions and calculations of all concerned, it had confidently been supposed by the oil experts that, even with Alaskan oil in full flow, the United States by 1980 would be dependent upon the Middle East for at least 35 per cent of its oil, and of course upon fleets of supertankers to bring it.

Those fleets of superships represent a problem that often seems commensurate only with the very fuel crisis that has created them. Coping with the phenomenon of bigness in ships involves an entirely unprecedented maritime relationship and, as Europe and Japan principally have discovered during the past decade, it is not an easily assimilable matter.

Oil tankers are hardly new to American waters. The prototypes of the modern tanker were designed a century ago to carry American oil overseas. But oil ships such as *Ardshiel* have taken maritime matters not only into a new physical dimension but also into a bewildering, complex, and even sinister new experience. Mere comprehension of the world's fleet of oil ships, whether singly or collectively, requires some effort of the imagination. In the simplest terms, it means that at this moment hundreds of ships each several times the size of the old Cunard *Queens* and entirely filled with oil are sailing around the seas.

On 31 December 1973, there were 388 ships of 200,000 tons deadweight or over in service, and 493 more under construction or on order. Of these, 119 were in the 260,000 to 280,000-ton class, and 26 were of more than 400,000 tons deadweight. *Ardshiel*, with just over 200,000 tons, was, on that summer's day of her departure for the long voyage to the Middle East and back, a quite ordinary and unexceptional unit among the 3,359 tankers engaged in the business of delivering the world's oil and petroleum products.

The entire world tanker fleet in mid-1973 stood at just over 200 million tons deadweight, which accounted for more than half the tonnage afloat. The 45 million tons of supertankers under construction and scheduled for delivery in 1974 alone were the equivalent of the world oil fleet in 1957. The American Committee for Flags of Necessity, an organisation of American shipping companies which put ships under foreign flags of convenience, estimated in a recent study that an international fleet of 350 million tons deadweight, or approaching double the present fleet, would be necessary by 1980 to handle the world's oil imports. Thirteen per cent of this huge tonnage would be needed to handle American imports alone. These ships undoubtedly would all be supertankers of varying sizes.

The October war and subsequent American determination to attempt to achieve self-sufficiency in oil again through various forms of economy and new intensive offshore oil exploration may affect those predictions. But not, so far as one is now able to judge, to any profound degree. While it may not be drawn upon as greedily as originally assumed, oil imported from the Middle East will flow in steadily increasing amounts into North America, which means that year by year the fleet of supertankers handling it will expand.

Superships are the product not only of expanding oil demand but of a need to haul oil over long distances, as Europe and Japan have to do. This explains their absence from North American waters up to now. Most of the United States' imported oil arrived either via pipeline from Canada or was brought as refined spirit in small tankers from the Caribbean, where American refinery interests had concentrated their investment. In the future, supership routes will touch all shores. They will bring Alaskan oil down the west coast, and deliver Middle Eastern crude to the Gulf and to additional points along the east coast from the St Lawrence to Delaware. And, as their bulky shapes finally become familiar to all, they will present as well their many special problems, and occasional disastrous difficulties.

There are tankers and supertankers and year after year it becomes more difficult to define which is which: yesterday's supertanker becomes today's humble workhorse. Hundred thousand tonners now operate the feeder services from the terminals of 300,000 tonners to the ports that the bigger ships can't enter.

For most of us, the old Cunard Queens, Elizabeth and Mary, remain the handiest comparison for judging size in ships. For two generations they symbolised the ultimate achievement of marine engineering and, until fairly recently, most seamen accepted that nothing bigger would ever be built. They were right in a sense. In terms of visual bulk, nothing will ever equal the Queens because the days of the passenger liner, which as a class gave us our towering ships, are now fast coming to an end. In any event, when big ships such as the new Queen Elizabeth 2 are built, advanced technology

17

allows them to carry the same number of passengers within more modest dimensions.

What the marine prophets failed to imagine, however, was a cargo carrier on the scale of the old *Queens*. That scale was passed by supertankers a decade ago, in the early sixties.

To compare a supertanker such as *Ardshiel* to the old Cunard *Queens* actually is a tricky business because, where a giant passenger liner climbs into the sky, a tanker spreads itself below the water, rather on the principle of the iceberg. Eighty per cent of the ship is below the water, which is what one must remember should one happen to see a supertanker in the vicinity of *Queen Mary*, which now lies permanently moored as a museum on the fringe of Long Beach Harbor in California. *Queen Elizabeth*, once the largest liner afloat, was sabotaged by fire in Hong Kong harbour in 1972 and was completely destroyed.

All ships express their size through tonnage and any comparison between the *Queens* and supertankers is further confused by the fact that tankers describe themselves in deadweight tonnage while passenger ships do so in gross tonnage; before the Second World War it was standard for most ships. Gross tonnage is a ship's enclosed cubic capacity, a gross ton being equal to one hundred cubic feet of permanently enclosed space, making it by far the most effective measure for a passenger ship, whose gross tonnage rises rapidly with each cabined deck added to its superstructure.

Deadweight tonnage, on the other hand, is the actual weight in tons of cargo, fuel, stores, and ballast that a ship can carry before submerging her load line, or Plimsoll mark. Since fuel, stores, and ballast make only a fractional difference to how deep a tanker sits in the water, deadweight becomes a rough description of how much oil the ship can carry, although this can vary somewhat from season to season and with different grades of oil.

Laid alongside the old *Queen Elizabeth*, *Ardshiel* would be thirty-three feet longer and thirty-nine feet wider. The *Queen Elizabeth* normally drew thirty-nine and a half feet of water; *Ardshiel*, fully laden, draws sixty-three. Her gross tonnage is 119,677 tons against the 83,673 tons of the old *Queen Elizabeth*, which, to avoid confusion with her successor, *Queen Elizabeth 2*, should perhaps be identified as *Queen Elizabeth 1*.

It is when supertankers ride high and in ballast however that visually speaking they truly match the old Cunarders. Empty of cargo, as she was alongside the jetty at Le Verdon at sailing time, *Ardshiel's* hull sides were virtually as high as those of *Queen Elizabeth 1* once were: a smooth steel cliff the more formidable for being unbroken by portholes and embarkation ports.

Big as she is, *Ardshiel* is less than half the size of the world's largest tankers, the sister ships *Globtik Tokyo* and *Globtik London*, which are regularly employed between Japan and the Persian Gulf, and which have an approximate deadweight of 476,000 tons, a length of 1,243 feet and a draught of 91 feet 11 inches.

The evolution of the supertankers moved at an astonishing pace. When the Second World War ended, the largest tankers had a deadweight of 18,000 tons. In 1950, a 28,000-ton ship was considered important enough to be launched by Princess Margaret. By 1956 tankers of 45,000 tons were sailing the seas and plans for a 100,000 tonner had been announced. The first ships in the latter class were being saluted with all manner of superlatives in the early sixties, and these praises were extended in turn to the 150,000, the 170,000, the 200,000, and the 250,000 tonners which all followed fast upon each other. By 1968, however, when the first of a sextet of 326,000 tonners entered service on charter to Gulf Oil, all exclamations of amazement had grown limp from repetition. The novelty was over. There was a weary concession that anything was now possible at sea. In any event, public wonder already had turned to consternation as a result of the wreck of *Torrey Canyon*, a 120,000-ton Liberian supertanker which, fully laden, had run herself onto rocks off the Scilly Isles early in 1967 with devastating results for the adjacent coasts of the English Channel and which as a result has become the symbolic warning of the environmental threat that supertankers generally represent.

The title of the biggest ship in the world has become as ephemeral as Miss World's. Even now, who of those who ever saw them could forget *Aquitania, Berengaria, Leviathan, Normandie, Rex, Bremen,* and *Conte di Savoia* as supremely big ships, despite the fact that it is decades since their demise? Supertankers unhappily have no true distinction to preserve them from anonymity once the mere novelty of their size has been superseded. I doubt that any tanker sailor could recite the successive titleholders since the first 100,000 tonner hit the water. I would bet on the other hand that any AB on *Queen Mary* in 1939 would, if pressed, have been able to give a pretty accurate summary of the Atlantic Blue Riband competition since 1907, when *Lusitania* and *Mauretania* began the big-ship high-speed era, together with the speed and times of crossing between Ambrose Lightship and Bishop's Rock.

Be that as it may, when in 1972 the 372,000-ton *Nisseki Maru* succeeded the 326,000-ton Gulf ships as the biggest vessel in the world, the event passed virtually without remark, and the commissioning of *Globtik Tokyo* a year later was an event noticed mainly by the industry. *Globtik Tokyo* itself will fall back in line when several 550,000 tonners now ordered are completed, and they will be eclipsed eventually by a 750,000 tonner which *Globtik Tokyo*'s owners have announced. Japanese and British shipbuilders have been busy for some time with the designs and dockyard preparations for what must surely be the penultimate in vessels, a million tonner, although some shipping men already have started talking about a 1,250,000 tonner.

For the moment, however, a million-ton tanker is enough for anybody's imagination, not to speak of peace of mind. To most people, sailors included, such a ship is too improbable to imagine: not merely a vehicle whose dimensions are ignoble for their distortion of conventional maritime scale, or any scale for that matter, but a thing without normal sense of reference.

Such a ship would have a length of 1,640 feet, which is 620 feet longer than the old *Queens*, a breadth of 274 feet, and a draught of 100 feet. Almost any of the great cathedrals of Western Europe would easily be fitted into one of her five major tanks. Loaded, it could enter no existing port in the world or even venture close in along the offshore shelves of most coastlines. If it broke down, the only drydocks in the world to which it could be taken for repair would be in Europe, the Persian Gulf (under construction), and Asia. A long tow would be in order if this happened anywhere removed from these. The prospect of such a ship helplessly adrift *anywhere* while waiting for tugs doesn't bear thinking about, least of all if it were full of oil and close to some coast.

In those other epochs that forged the sea experience as we know and understand and romanticise it, the sea was a free emptiness that, by subsequent international agreement, began three miles offshore; beyond that limit, ships went about their business outside all jurisdiction except that of the flag they flew, and they were beholden to no one on the coasts off which they might sail or steam; any presumption upon these most ancient rights was a warlike act, or one of piracy. Any idea of the landlubber being inquisitively intrusive upon the sailor and how he should run his ship was unthinkable to both. But as the equivalent of outsize floating balloons that, if punctured, could release in whole or in part upon the water up to half a million tons of crude oil, supertankers have brought a complete rethinking and revaluation of the seas and shipping and the relation that these bear to society as a whole. What is principally recognised is that the old notion of the freedom of the seas is no longer viable, for these ships represent a break in the business of sailing those seas that offers very little comparison with anything that has gone before. Their size alone has changed the look, the aesthetics, the design and construction of ships, thereby affecting the whole conventional sense of them, and the threat that they pose is in turn affecting the navigation and handling and operating principles of ships to such a degree that, all told, even the change from sail to steam begins to seem a lesser event.

Aesthetically, we are very much the losers. Supertankers by and large have assumed a look of such brutal and uncompromising functionalism that they strike the observer as being not so much ships designed to carry oil as mere tank barges fitted with engines and a place in which men can bunk and steer. In fact, even the operators and the sailors themselves now seem to have an aversion toward calling them ships. They address them simply as VLCCs, Very Large Crude Carriers. The term applies to ships over 200,000 tons, and even it is outmoded, with a new designation, ULCCs, Ultra Large Crude Carriers, being used for vessels over 400,000 tons. The old idea of the ship as 'she', with the possessive marriage to the sea and its moods that the term implied, is all but gone, certainly so far as these craft are concerned. They have brought monotony and a feeling of loss to the maritime horizons and, as a result, a certain dispirited mood to those such as myself who like to sit upon a seashore and doze and dream and watch the ships go by.

Offering so little charm in their profile and practically no speculation about their purposes, they plod past in endless procession, dimming the seaward imagination. Or so it goes for much of the time. I live above the Straits of Gibraltar, with a view over this passage from Tangier's Vieille Montagne, and if I scan the sea there at any given moment through my glasses there is a good chance that every vessel of the twelve to twenty that may be in sight is a tanker. I do this many times a day when I am home, and I feel elated when the sweep of the deeply laden or ballasted and high-riding oil carriers reveals in its midst a 'three-island' merchantman at least forty years old, imperceptibly moving at eight to ten knots and blowing smoke in such quantities that one knows her to be a coal burner: a three-island ship is one with the traditional balance of a forecastle, a midships bridge and accommodation structure, and a poop. The ship I might see very likely is Spanish but, this being the entrance to the Mediterranean, she could be anything – Portuguese, Greek, Turkish, Cypriot, Maltese, Algerian: hand-me-down tonnage that was probably built on the Clyde or Tyne, holds five or six changes of name to her credit in Lloyd's, has tramped at one time or another through every trade in the world and is now reduced to coasting at arthritic pace in the Med, with Casablanca, Lisbon, and the Canaries as the limits of her endurance beyond.

Such a vessel does at least open every sort of conjecture, and exposes one to a lot of sentiment and nostalgia. She looks like a ship, sits upon the sea as though fitted to it, adaptable to all its caprices because, first of all, she has sheer, meaning that her lines from stem to stern flow with an upward slope at both ends; and she also has rake, which her two tall masts and single funnel give her, rake being that fine and nicely calculated angle at which masts and funnels lie from the perpendicular.

Rake, where it still exists, and most elderly passenger liners and freighters have it, is the steamship age's last lingering inheritance from sail: the rake of the great masts of a square-rigger helped diminish the tremendous strains put upon them by full canvas and the pitch and lurch of the ship. In composing the raked balance of the masts and funnels of the passenger liners of the North Atlantic, marine architects often achieved a memorable beauty and one only has to return to photographs of ships such as the old Cunarders *Mauretania* (1907) and *Aquitania* (1914) to confirm this. When these and any of the big liners of the thirties used to sail down the Hudson and then slowly stand out on their course for the Narrows they went with a stateliness and serenity that seemed strangely poignant for such vast and powerful structures, and this was especially so when one watched from the Jersey shore or the Staten Island ferry and saw them against the perpendiculars of Manhattan; passing before the arrogant uprightness of the skyscrapers the delicate slant of their masts and funnels implied acceptance of the essential fallibility in all man's works, the very set of them so distinctly conveying a respect for and a concession to their element.

So when I see one of these three-island relics from the near past of merchant shipping dawdling through the Straits of Gibraltar what I am looking at and really admiring are the aesthetic qualities that not so long ago distinguished practically all ships, from the grandest to the humblest. These are the qualities that supertankers, or VLCCs, as perhaps one now should refer to them, mostly lack.

Of rake and sheer they have none. Just about the only lines these ships have are straight ones: the bows might have a slight protective upward tilt for taking the seas, but the hull runs back to the stern like a wide solid straight steel pier. The stern itself, instead of gracefully closing off the hull with some form of curve or fold, is often flattened, as though sawed off. The lofty slanting masts of yesteryear are replaced by some type of steel tower atop or about the bridge; it is mainly intended for aerials and radar scanners which, of course, do the job once left to the man in the crow's nest, that lonely lookout barrel that was set halfway up the foremast.

These huge and complex oil ships represent an entirely new seafaring experience, yet one of the curious things about them is that they support so many reminders of the past. The anomaly lies in their routes and the great length of their voyages, which are a throwback to the days when much of seafaring was a long, tediously slow process of there and back. They go eastward around the Cape of Good Hope, as Europe's trade did before the opening of the Suez Canal and, like the East Indiamen and China clippers, may take aboard fresh supplies; then, within sight of Good Hope itself, they slowly wheel through that historic sequence of course alterations that nearly five centuries ago told Bartholomeu Dias that he had found the seaway to the east. Beyond the Cape, the tankers in fact follow precisely along the Carreira da India, the route the Portuguese used for three centuries in sailing to and from monsoon Asia. It is one of the oldest and most evocative trade routes of the world and, despite their gross proportions, the tankers make use when possible of many of the same natural phenomena, such as the south-west monsoon and its drift, and the Mozambique and Agulhas currents, the way the Portuguese did. These can be surprisingly important to ships, saving fuel and time when the vessel is running with them; a big tanker in ballast, sitting lightly in the water and with a height of some sixty feet between its main deck and the waterline, and with perhaps forty feet more of housing above that, offers a great spread of steel structure to the wind, which, some sailors believe, can add a knot or so to the ship's speed. The hours thus gained can be balanced against those lost when returning against the same forces; anyway, to fly a little faster in a VLCC seems to give those aboard a certain elation, and again for the same reason that it once affected men in sail. They hold, briefly, the illusion of losing the weight of their apparently interminable journey and of making time toward its conclusion. For the supertanker voyages are the longest unbroken sea journeys that sailors have been employed upon since the days of sail. In the heyday of the tramp steamer men stayed away from home for much longer, of course, but there lay ahead of them always the mystery or familiarity of the next port, a few days, at the most a couple of weeks, away. There was always an experience just over to talk about and one ahead to anticipate.

The two routes for which supertankers were principally designed, between Europe and the Persian Gulf via the Cape and between the Gulf and Japan through the Straits of Malacca, are long ones anyway. On the former, for example, the distance between London and Abadan at the head of the Gulf is 11,300 miles, so that fetching a cargo from there means a voyage roughly equal to a circumnavigation of the globe. It is, moreover, a painfully slow trip because of the modest speed which is the most economical for these ships, usually something between fourteen and fifteen knots (the most illustrious clipper of all, *Cutty Sark*, often ran seventeen knots and easily did fifteen, and could have outflown a VLCC, as she did sixteen-knot passenger mailships of her day; many modern freighters average eighteen to twenty knots, and the last Blue Riband holder, the *United States*, was said to be capable of forty knots. She won the Blue Riband by hitting an average of 35.59 knots); this means that a round-trip voyage between Europe and the Gulf requires at least two and a half months, occasionally more. The voyage between the Gulf and North America takes roughly as long.

During the voyage there are no stops. The mail and fresh supplies taken aboard at the Cape are delivered either by a helicopter, which drops its packages onto the deck while the ship is under way, or they are brought by launch to a rendezvous point twelve miles off Cape Town harbour. When the ship reaches the Gulf loading often takes place from sea rigs up to fifteen miles offshore. It is all done in twelve to eighteen hours, and the ship starts the long haul back to its European destination, which may change several times during the voyage, being dependent upon the prevailing pattern of European demand (an early autumn cold snap in Norway, a winter thaw in northern Italy, or blizzards in the Ruhr can bring a general reshuffling of routes and destinations for dozens of ships lumbering toward the continent).

Such changes of orders are only of brief interest to the ships themselves, however, for it makes scarcely any difference to those on board whether they wind up in Bantry Bay, Eire, or Taranto, southern Italy, unless of course they are getting off and going home on leave; if they are not, the activity of discharge is too brief and intense to offer much chance of getting ashore, assuming there would be anywhere to go if they could, the tanker berths as a rule being the farthest reach of any port. An increasing practice anyway in European waters is to moor tankers to offshore pipeline buoys, so that a ship travelling between the offshore stations of the Gulf and those of Europe is permanently removed from the shore, forever at sea. Such is likely to be the practice too in the future for ships trading between the Gulf and the American east coast.

Supertankers, like jet aircraft, operate on the principle that they are too expensive to be kept idle. Until recently, rough assumption was that a ship spent a third of its time in port, loading or discharging or waiting, and the rest at sea. A tanker spends less than 10 per cent of its time in port. Estimated costs of tanker operation are based on a ship's being at sea three hundred and forty days a year. Strenuous efforts are made to increase even this where possible, and tanker masters must account for literally every minute of delay: Shell Oil once calculated that cutting one hour in port on the thirteen thousand or so port calls made by its tankers in a year could save two million pounds a year. It costs between six and eight thousand dollars a day to operate a VLCC (these are running costs, but most companies allow from $30,000 to $50,000 a day when including depreciation and other book costs) whose profit can be as much as four million dollars on a voyage; thus any idleness, enforced or otherwise, becomes an anxious matter.

What all this means so far as the tanker sailor is concerned is that, once aboard the ship, he seldom gets off again until his immediate period of service in the vessel is done; it is not uncommon for men to stay on board ship for a year or more without setting foot on land, and one often hears of much longer periods. The chief engineer aboard a Shell tanker in which I sailed in 1966 told me that he'd once been twice around the world, through the Mediterranean, to the Far East, across the Pacific, to Fiji, through Panama to Curaçao, South America, and all sorts of other exotic and interesting places, and 'seen nowt of the lot of 'em; nowt but the bloody engines and the bloody bulkheads of me cabin, and the back of the old man's gin bottle'.

These days, the big oil companies and all scrupulous tanker operators make great effort to give their supertanker crews a fixed rotation of service and leave. Few expect to do less than two consecutive voyages, which means at least five and more likely six months on board. The leave period is from six weeks to two months, and then back for another bout. Even this can prove too much for some. In 1971 three young British tanker sailors were sent to jail for trying to set fire to their ship, *British Hussar*, while she was discharging at Trieste. They were said by the prosecutor to be so fed up with life in the ship that they had planned to set it on fire in hope that the crew would be paid off and flown back to Britain. They at least got their wish.

As supertankers get bigger, so do their problems. Indeed, if there were a ratio between problems and size it probably would show a proportionate increase with each advance in size. Navigation of these ships is virtually a new skill, even to the extent that they involve forces never before seriously considered in relation to ships: their size makes them the first of man's surface vehicles likely to be affected by the earth's own rotation.

Large masses moving on the earth's surface are affected by the global spin. This effect is known as the Coriolis force, named in honour of a nineteenth-century French mathematician who first described it accurately. It causes a clockwise drift in the northern hemisphere, while south of the equator a moving object is pulled to the left of its course. Coriolis force has been important so far in considering winds and currents: it exerts such considerable influence upon a mass such as the North Atlantic that it causes a slope in the surface of the ocean, which in mid-Atlantic is as much as forty-eight inches above the level of American coastal waters. Its effects upon supertankers have not yet been adequately defined, but they have been sufficiently established to show that they may have to become a part of practical seamanship in future, especially in dangerous waters: if a particle of sufficient mass moves eastward, increased centrifugal reaction causes it to move toward the equator; if it moves westward, lower centrifugal force moves it toward the pole.

Conning these ships means a revised set of judgments and reflexes for what such a long, wide vessel can or cannot do in harbour or in an emergency such as a collision situation. The whole experience is so completely different and dangerous that the Esso Oil Company trains its masters aboard miniature exact-scale models of VLCCs on an eight-acre lake near Grenoble, France, whose facilities include scale models of piers, sea berths, loading buoys, and typical narrow channels; and at Delft, Holland, tanker crews can be trained in a simulator similar to those used for flight crews and offering the facsimile bridge of a 250,000-ton tanker. It is the only one of its kind and it gives men the exact experience of taking these ships into port and docking and undocking them in all sorts of weather, as well as in various situations that might arise in the open sea. It is a comparatively lucky few who are sent to Grenoble or Delft to train – usually the masters for the big oil companies. Most VLCC masters have to learn on the job, which can be a terrible ordeal of caution and doubt.

Guiding and steering a ship from a bridge set nearly a quarter of a mile from the bows is frightening enough to a man unaccustomed to it, but he also is one hundred feet above the water and has to walk one hundred and fifty feet from port to starboard to see what is happening on the other side: even on the *Queens* the bridge was reasonably close to the bows, and anyway moving one of those ships in or out of dock was normally a huge joint effort of ship and shore and fleets of tugs.

Even on the open water supertankers need plenty of sea room. They cannot respond to split-second timing. It takes at least three miles and twenty-one to twenty-two minutes to stop a 250,000 tonner doing sixteen knots: overlong hulls create different forces of momentum, giving the effect of a lower resistance to the water, despite the awkward blunted shape, and sheer weight seems to augment this and to keep them rolling on and on and on. The Ship Division of the National Physical Laboratory found that a 100,000 tonner may lose only one knot per minute while attempting to stop. At very low speeds such as those advisable in fog mammoth ships may be unable to manœuvre at all. Between four and five knots a 30,000 tonner easily loses its steerage way and starts sheering off its course, unless helm and engines are skilfully used. Under these circumstances, trying to stop or manœuvre a VLCC on the open sea is tricky enough when attempting to avoid collision or to retrieve a man who has gone overboard, these being the most common of emergency manœuvring situations, but in confined and crowded and shallow waters it is infinitely more so, and sometimes impossible.

Anchors don't stop these ships. Where an ordinary merchantman would drop its anchors in an attempt to hold its motion, putting down anchors to stop a 200,000 tonner even slightly underway would simply mean having their cables wrenched from the deck. 'We were in the Rotterdam waterway when the ship's power failed,' Ardshiel's first officer, Alan Ewart-James, told me in recounting an experience aboard another 200,000 tonner in which he'd served. 'We started drifting on the current, toward a sandbank. We got one anchor down, but it wouldn't hold. You don't put two anchors down on these ships: they simply get tangled or you stand the chance of losing them both. We managed to jam the cables to stop them paying out, otherwise they would have pulled the deck apart. Luckily we got power back on the ship and got her out of there, but it was a close shave.' Experiments with braking flaps and even underwater braking parachutes have not offered any practical solution to the problem because of the strong sideways sheering motion of tankers when stopping.

In a technical article on ship steering published in the September 1973 issue of Safety at Sea International, the principal research officer of the British Ship Research Association, D. Clark, pointed out that the number of ship lengths required to stop a ship did in fact increase in proportion with increase in ship size itself. 'When considering the magnitude of some of the quantities involved it is easy to appreciate the difficulties,' he wrote. 'In the case of a typical quarter million ton tanker, the displacement is about 300,000 tons, the ahead resistance at service speed only 250 tons, and the propeller running astern can generate in the region of 120 tons. Recalling Newton's second law it can be seen that the best deceleration that can be hoped for is about 0.001g, which is very small compared to the 0.5g required by law for motor cars. These figures illustrate a problem which is inherent in this type of ship and it is not possible for the naval architect to do much about it, unless some type of auxiliary brake flap or parachute type of device is adopted.'

Supertankers, like all ships, sail according to an international set of rules of the road which substantially are an inheritance from the nineteenth century. They have served shipping well until now but for supertankers they have proven to be often impracticable, or downright dangerous. The sort of thing that happens was recently experienced by the master of a fully laden 200,000 tonner passing through the Straits of Dover to Rotterdam. Confronted by an oncoming ship whose course lay in collision with his own, he found that none of the prescribed procedures was going to do him any good because, unable to stop in time, the only alternative was to put the helm over, which would have taken the long hull out of its depth and put it hard aground. He was left entirely dependent upon the savvy, courtesy, and vigilance of the other ship, a smaller conventional merchantman, who fortunately recognised his plight and acted accordingly.

Similarly, the riding lights prescribed by regulations to identify a vessel and its course at night have caused confusion, which can be fatal. Some instances have been reported of smaller ships trying to steer *between* the forward and after lights of a supertanker, on the understandable assumption that the great distance between them indicated two different ships.

The size of supertankers places such distance between their sailors and the sea that tanker crews may not even be aware that they have run down a smaller vessel. The inexplicable loss of trawlers and coasters has sometimes been attributed to these ships. The South African trawler *Harvest del Mar* was lost with all hands through just such an incident in August 1973, when she was run down by the Spanish tanker *Mostoles*. The trawler was trampled into the sea without the crew of the tanker even being aware. When the master of *Mostoles* eventually realised because of slight damage to his bow that he had struck something, he reported that he had hit a 'semisubmerged object'.

To help supertankers, and those around them, the maritime regulations and rules of the road have been extensively revised. The big ships will have priority and right of way in restricted waters and they will be expected to show specific lights; they will also be allowed to give light and sound signals to indicate their manœuvres. Unfortunately, however, the new rules are not to become effective before 1976.

Changes to the international rules at sea always involve a lot of time. The supervisory body that controls these matters, or attempts to, is the Inter-Governmental Maritime Consultative Organization, generally known as IMCO, which is a specialised United Nations agency based in London. IMCO is the only international organisation with any sort of maritime jurisdiction, but any law that is put on the books must be ratified by the domestic legislature of those proposing it, and this takes years even for a handful of IMCO members.

Supertankers enter shallow waters at great risk simply because of their draught. Fully laden, many cannot enter the Baltic at all, and they have to be taken with extreme delicacy along some of the passages they most frequently use, such as the North Sea, the Straits of Malacca, and the Straits of Dover.

The shallowness of these and other similar waters has always been a caution to sailors but never in the disturbing fashion it has become for the VLCC master, who finds that the charts and sailing instructions that have been faithfully and dependably used for decades and even, in some instances, for more than a century no longer can be relied upon. They don't always tell him what he most wants to know, such as the actual look of the seabed, which super-tankers have brought much closer to our concern and fear than it has been before. For one thing it is far more changeable than it hitherto was assumed to be, and it has become apparent that any-thing more than mere surface use of the sea by ships, which is more or less what the position has been up to now, involves far more than the information we have been getting by on, and something more sophisticated than the tools we have been using. Technically, the problem is that the supertanker has to be treated as partly submarine and partly surface craft: the deep hulls of the big ships have added a new dimension to the sea by extending subsurface navigational requirements to depths that previously had been considered only the concern of submarine captains. The experience of submarines, how-ever, has been of little use here because they are rarely operational in some of the waters supertankers use, such as the English Channel, which has never been considered safe for submersible craft.

In many inshore areas supertankers sail with a clearance of as little as two to three feet. The danger of striking even the most modest obstruction on the bottom is increased by the fact that supertankers tend to squat by the bows, and in ships over 200,000 tons this can be by as much as three to four feet; this squat is worsened by quite ordinary wave effects, tidal surges, and currents. The Ship Division of the National Physical Laboratory has also found that these ships are affected by shallows even when they have what appears to be more than sufficient water under their keels. Their manoeuvrability is sharply diminished once the water under their keel becomes the equivalent of forty feet of their draught. When, say, a ship of fifty-foot draught still has twenty feet of water under her keel her turning circle is doubled; that is, when her helm is put over the turn is only half as tight as it would be in deeper water. The danger of this is that the ship's compass itself indicates that the ship is turning normally when in fact she is making a far bigger circle than her master might suppose. When water under a VLCC is down to three feet, the ship is virtually unsteerable, the Ship Division of the National Physical Laboratory has found. Touching bottom on the sandy Straits of Dover is not quite as dangerous as doing so in the Malacca Straits, where the seabed is granite. On one occasion two Japanese VLCCs within the space of one week holed themselves inexplicably on the floor of the Straits, when they had supposed that they had sufficient water. On 12 March 1973, the 160,000-ton Italian oil–ore ship *Igara* struck an uncharted rock in the South China Sea near Singapore and became, it was later said, the largest single marine insurance loss ever. The ship was a year old and was being navigated, it was said, from charts prepared from surveys which were at least sixty-five years old, made only by lead and line, and which didn't indicate the reef on which she foundered.

When *Queen Mary* faced a similar draught problem during the war extraordinary measures were taken to avoid the ship hurting her bottom. To pass over the shallow water above the Hudson Tunnel at slack tide with 15,000 troops on board meant that every soldier wherever he was had to stay perfectly still until the tunnel had been cleared, to prevent the men crowding the rails on one side and thus giving the ship a dangerous list, in which case she might have scraped the tunnel.

In a report published in 1970, Rear-Admiral G. S. Ritchie, Hydrographer of the Royal Navy, declared: 'With the present state of the science of hydrographic survey and with the shallow and changeable seas round north-west Europe cluttered with wrecks of two world wars, anxiety is felt at the minimal below-hull clearances accepted by tanker companies.'

Another urgent warning was made in 1974 by Rear-Admiral Ritchie's successor, Rear-Admiral G. P. D. Hall, in his report covering the previous year. He said: 'Increasing concern has been felt over the continued risks taken by deep-draught shipping in calculating their under-keel clearance in relatively shallow waterways by reference to predicted tide levels – and over the possible consequences to the coastal environment from the stranding of giant tankers as a result of actual levels being lower.' He continued: 'Predicted levels take no account of meteorological factors – and these can cause "surges" which raise or lower the levels by amounts possibly exceeding the calculated under-keel clearance. In the latter case (i.e. a negative surge) results could be catastrophic.'

'When the Hydrographer feels constrained to such commentary it would seem that the shipping world in general – and probably tanker owners in particular – should feel the need to listen and possibly to worry,' *Tanker and Bulk Carrier* stated in an editorial in its issue of June 1974. It added: 'A meeting of marine technologists in Washington in 1973 was told by a Lloyd's broker: "I doubt very much if any of you would be happy to take off from Dulles Airport knowing that the navigator's map was made before the Wright brothers first became airborne." But this may well seem to be just a similar situation to that in which the big ships of today, and those much bigger tomorrow, may find themselves – unless somebody does something.'

Shell Tankers UK Ltd, the single largest operator and charterer of tankers and consequently a pace setter in these matters, in 1967 declared that its own policy was to allow a minimum clearance of two feet for its ships. Commenting on this in an article written for the June 1971 issue of a specialist maritime monthly, *Safety at Sea International*, Commander M. B. F. Ranken, a British marine engineer and maritime consultant, remarked, 'While this may be sufficient in well-maintained dredged channels with a sand or mud bottom, it certainly isn't in open sea conditions, more especially if the bottom is rock or coral, if there are any wrecks in the area, if the weather is stormy, or if there have been few chances for accurate position-fixing.'

The Admiralty's hydrographic department estimates that there are 3,500 charted wrecks in the English Channel alone, and certainly many more that haven't been charted. Seabeds also are well strewn with submarine cables. But the most disturbing new element in the situation is the discovery, as a result of this closer scrutiny of the seabed, of huge shifting, changing sand waves or ripples which move along the bottom in certain areas, often as high as twenty feet, and even reaching fifty feet. Large areas of these mobile undersea dunes have been found in the English Channel and North Sea, at least three of them athwart the main tanker routes; the Admiralty has received at least one report from the master of a 200,000 tonner who touched bottom where the charts indicated he had twenty feet of water below him.

The reason for such an important omission from the charts of the seas is carefully explained by Commander Ranken in his article in *Safety at Sea International*:

Until about forty years ago all bottom soundings were measured by hand lead line or sounding machine, and echo sounders have only come fully into their own in quite recent years to measure depths vertically below the vessel's track. Although these enormously increase the rate of surveying, large numbers of parallel sounding lines are needed to establish the bottom topography, and even then there are bound to be unsurveyed areas between each pair of lines, in which obstructions could be hidden. Although these 'unseen' areas can be swept with a wire dragged along the bottom in a similar manner to minesweeping, this is a laborious, enormously time-consuming and therefore a costly operation.

Further along in the article, he adds:

Hydrographic surveying involves accurate position-fixing in three dimensions, and the operation of very large ships in shallow seas increasingly requires navigation to almost equal degrees of accuracy. The present low accuracy of many existing charts in relation to these very large vessels, and the danger of grounding which this introduces, needs to be appreciated by shipowners and authorities alike. This is no reflection on the surveyors who prepared the charts, maybe as little as ten years ago, when fifty feet draught was exceptional; many deep water soundings have not been checked since the last century, even in some busy shipping lanes.

To cope with this, the seas and their routes will have to be resurveyed and the charts revised. The navies of the world have always seen themselves as custodians of this task, the Royal Navy especially, since the British interest for more than a century was self-interest; but navies, including the Royal Navy, no longer have generous access to the purse strings – the British Hydrography Office already has been cut down – and the great and costly effort required to ensure the proper accuracy for big ships will not easily be achieved. The British government meanwhile has sponsored new sonar equipment that will give a more thorough picture of the sea bottom. But the dangerous impermanence of the sand waves would mean that any charts it produced would have to be constantly revised to ensure that a supertanker master proceeding up the English Channel or through the Malacca Straits would always be absolutely sure of what lay on the seabed under his ship. Of even more use, possibly, will be a new acoustic system that warns of underwater obstructions by using long-range sonar beams that probe ahead. It has been developed for the United States Maritime Administration.

Merely getting these ships into port and alongside a jetty became a serious problem as supertankers continued to grow. The normal procedure in a port is to put the ship parallel to the jetty and then to nurse it alongside with tugs and the use of the vessel's engines. This requires minimum motion, which is extremely hard for a master or a pilot to judge when standing one hundred feet above the water and a quarter of a mile from the front of the ship. A 250,000-ton tanker fully loaded has an actual weight of between 300,000 and 310,000 tons (its deadweight plus the actual weight of the steel and fittings in the ship) and if its impact speed is merely a quarter of a knot, that is, slightly more than twenty-five feet per minute, ship and jetty will be badly knocked about, with the chance too of either oil leakage or, worse, an explosion. Some tankers have been equipped with side thrusters to help manœuvre them, and jetties have been banded with strong springs to catch and deflect the weight of the ship. Sonic mooring devices also have had to be installed. These measure movement down to four feet a minute and the distance off the jetty down to two feet. At Rotterdam, traffic signals of red, amber, and green help give immediate visual warning of the diminishing or accelerating approach speeds of a supertanker.

When they were first emerging from the yards VLCCs were ships virtually without havens. Fewer than a dozen ports in the world could handle them. Even now, very few harbours in the world can accommodate ships drawing more than sixty feet, which is the draught of a loaded 200,000 tonner. Their size forced a new pattern of port development wherever they sailed. The Dutch have spent many hundreds of millions of dollars deepening the North Sea and providing facilities at Rotterdam, which is now the biggest oil port in the world. Once undertaken, such effort becomes virtually ceaseless, until tankers stop growing. After preparing for draughts of nearly sixty, then sixty-two feet, channels had to be deepened to accommodate ships of sixty-five feet, and work is now under way to allow ships drawing seventy-five feet to enter. In Rotterdam's case, this must be the limit because the North Sea itself won't allow ships sitting much deeper in the water. The French undertook the same task at Le Havre, where they too are once more digging and dredging, to bring in the new race of 500,000 tonners. On the whole, however, the best solution has been to build new ports at places where sea commerce could never otherwise have been expected, or else ships are sent to man-made offshore islands or loading buoys, as they do in the Persian Gulf.

In the case of new ports, deep water influences the choice of site, and since in Europe deep inshore water often goes with some of the finest and most spectacular scenery – such as the bays of Ireland, the lochs of Scotland, and the fjords of Norway – that is where one might now expect to see the biggest giants: solemnly sliding into the lee of some of the grandest cliffs and finest seaward faces of the area.

The risks to such places were well conveyed by the spill of more than two thousand tons of crude oil which suddenly spread over the surface and along the shores of Bantry Bay on 22 October 1974. A valve in one of the tanks of the 80,000-ton Liberian-flag *Universe*

Leader, on charter to Gulf, had been left open for some thirty minutes. Twenty-two miles of coastline were affected, and rocks and beaches were coated.

Gulf chose Bantry Bay, one of the most beautiful places in Ireland, as the terminal for its sextet of 326,000 tonners. Bantry Bay is in effect an oil transit port: from there the crude is reshipped in 100,000 tonners to refineries in Wales, Denmark, Holland, and Spain. This entrepôt concept has become central to all plans for handling the very biggest of ships, anything above the 300,000-ton range; it is the one that has been applied too to the initial installations for VLCCs in North American waters.

While VLCCs have actually been built in the United States, none is able to enter an east-coast American port while fully laden. The shallow continental shelf keeps them firmly away. Inshore deep water starts at Maine in the east and Puget Sound in the west. There is plenty of it along the Canadian shores, both west and east, and so far it has been mainly the latter, the coasts of New Brunswick, Nova Scotia, Quebec, and Newfoundland, that have welcomed the construction of the first VLCC terminals. True to form, all this northern deep water lies beside some of the finest scenery and most handsome unspoiled country in North America. Nova Scotia already has learned to its cost the price of hospitality to tankers. The first massive dousing of crude oil from a wrecked tanker experienced on the North American east coast came on 4 February 1970, when the Liberian tanker *Arrow*, running at full speed with good visibility toward Port Hawkesbury, N.S. (which, incidentally, now holds the dubious distinction of having received the largest ship ever to dock in North America, the 326,000-ton *Universe Japan*), ran aground in Chedabucto Bay in the Canso Straits and spilled 11,000 tons of oil.

The United States itself narrowly averted a far worse disaster in January 1972, when the 92,000-ton Japanese tanker *Kaiko Maru*, with about 90,000 tons of crude oil aboard, and drawing forty-seven feet, ran aground off Delaware. *Kaiko Maru* is about the largest of supertankers that at present could approach an American east-coast port. As it was, she was scheduled to be lightened of much of her cargo before actually docking to discharge the rest.

The entrance to Delaware has two channels, one with a depth of forty-five feet and the other of fifty feet. *Kaiko Maru* chose the wrong channel and went aground while still in open water. Even in the deeper channel she would have had only three feet of clearance, and would have required delicate handling. The ship's master had died and she was in the charge of the chief officer.

The ship was not holed, but gale warnings were forecast and, had she broken up, the disaster could have been of the order of *Torrey*

Canyon's. The vacation beaches of Delaware and southern New Jersey would have been inundated. That the United States then did not suffer possibly the worst incident of tanker pollution on its record was entirely due to the swift action and expertise of the Murphy Pacific Marine Salvage Company, which lightened *Kaiko Maru* and got her off in freezing temperatures and deteriorating weather. The Murphy Pacific salvors have indeed saved American waters from disaster on several occasions in recent years. One other such episode was that involving the Panamanian tanker *Alkaid*, which ran aground in the East River at 42nd Street, in the shadow of the United Nations building, in 1960, with 22,000 tons of Kuwaiti crude oil aboard. The East River currents might have broken her, but Murphy Pacific got her off in time.

That there will be other, perhaps less successful, incidents of this sort in the future there can be no doubt. It is for this reason that attempts to extend the Canadian range of deep-water ports to Maine ran into strong resistance. The proposals are for deep-water VLCC havens at Portland and Eastport. In the case of the latter, the Canadian government itself has opposed the project because the approaches are through narrow, tricky waters, which mainly lie within Canadian jurisdiction. But one way or another provision for these monster ships and their smaller brethren has to be made on a very large scale if America is to meet its energy requirements during the rest of the decade. The shallow continental shelf would have made medium-sized tankers the ideal vessel for American deliveries. New, advanced terminals for these ships could have been distributed from New Orleans to Quebec. But the prospect of massive American imports through the seventies and into the eighties was one of the major reasons for the massive upsurge in tanker orders in 1973 that, in effect, more than doubled the existing fleet. The oil and tanker industry's interest in protecting this investment will make it lobby for the establishment of reception facilities for VLCCs along the American coasts. By European standards, the United States already is eight to ten years behind in planning the reception and handling of these ships. John I. Jacobs and Co. Ltd, a British firm which publishes specialist studies and statistics on tanker operations, recently predicted that lack of deep-water facilities on the American Atlantic seaboard would result in 'unprecedented traffic congestion' by the 1980s, with all consequent environmental risks. Too many ships will be fighting for berths in too few ports, or circling around aimlessly and dangerously until they can get in. For the conservation-minded, there would seem therefore to be no gain whichever way one turns. The ultimatum would seem to be surrender more or suffer more.

The likeliest solution for American east-coast ports, these being the reception points for American imports of Middle East crude, would be the solution adopted in the Persian Gulf; that is, a string of man-made port-islands moored in deep water far offshore, probably about fifteen miles off, where the depth runs to one hundred feet. These would not only keep the tankers away from the coast but facilitate distribution, which would be a problem if all the imports were to pour in mainly through closely clustered north-eastern terminals. These islands would lie offshore at intervals down the east coast. Particularly massive ones have been proposed for off the Delaware and Louisiana coasts. Whichever way the problem is solved, what cannot be solved is the damage any form of tanker unloading causes. A three-year research programme undertaken by an oil pollution research unit of the British Field Studies Council found that small quantities of oil escaping from refineries during normal operations caused greater long-term damage to the ecology of the shore than one major inundation from a wrecked tanker would. The main trouble, the report said, came from apparently insignificant traces of oil discharge in refinery effluent, and from the small amounts splashed overboard from time to time during loading and unloading. This chronic pollution caused long-term damage to marine life, and even caused deterioration of the sand and silt in which marine organisms live. The deep-water ports where super-tankers tie up clearly will be more severely affected by these circumstances, but the persistence of slicks around any man-made islands equally clearly will not benefit sea life in the immediate vicinity, or upon adjacent shores; and may be expected to play havoc among seabirds, unless effectively controlled.

Aristotle Onassis, ever inventive, has carried ship and entrepôt concepts to what seems likely to be their ultimate practicality. The design plans for the one-million-ton ship he proposes to build are for a vessel with four 250,000-ton tanks which are detachable from the ship itself. The million tonner would come up to an offshore terminal as one piece and then tugs would take its tanks away, leaving the mother vessel looking exactly like a filleted fish, the bow section linked to the after section by a backbone with giant cross-sections into which the empty tanks would reslot.

Surveying such a ship will require a new technology not yet devised. Surveying an ordinary VLCC alone is a formidable new task, for which experience is limited as the ships are so new. The surveys are essential to detect hull or tank damage and faults. In the case of the tanks especially, corrosion is what the surveyors most anxiously search for. A 25,000-ton tanker has about 400,000 square feet of plating in her tanks. A 350,000 tonner has around 3 million, and the tanks themselves may be 100 feet deep. F. N. Boylan, deputy chief ship surveyor of Lloyd's Register of Shipping, and F. H. Atkinson, senior principal ship surveyor, have described the survey task on a VLCC as being 'roughly equivalent to climbing Mount Everest and still having another 6,000 feet to go.' Physically, it means travelling a distance of 35,000 feet to examine 257 miles of various kinds of riveting. This is not the only complication that size has brought to ship survey. The surveyors are not yet sure how corrosion affects such large tanks. In small tanks it tends to be uniform. 'In a very large tank it would be difficult to extrapolate this type of uniform corrosion. The rate and type of corrosion occurring may differ greatly in various parts of the tank', a recent article in the Lloyd's house magazine, 100A1, declared.

At Lloyd's, all tankers are assigned a class known as '100A1 Oil tanker'. To keep a tanker in this insurance category, the rules at Lloyd's are that the ship must be inspected in dry dock approximately every two years. In the case of VLCCs, the main survey problem was the same as the main repair problem: Where did one do it? At the end of 1972, there still were only twenty-one repair docks in existence to handle them, and ten of these were in Japan. Another ten were in Europe, two of them in one place, Lisbon. One was in Greece. This meant that if they broke down anywhere between these points they had to be towed thousands of miles by tug to the nearest dock. There was no dock for them even in the Gulf, and none will be operational there until the end of 1975. By 1976, it is estimated, about forty-two large docks throughout the world will be able to serve them, and these will be well distributed along their principal routes.

As things stand at present, on the long haul between the Persian Gulf and Europe crippled supertankers have practically no refuge nor means of repairing themselves. Cape Town, the principal point of succour on that route, will handle only VLCCs riding light, and in any event won't take in anything bigger than 260,000 tons. To diminish these anxieties some tanker operators are now considering adapting maintenance of their ships to the styles used for aircraft: that is, automatic replacement of various parts at the end of a fixed 'life', whether they are faulty or not, so as to help avoid unexpected breakdown. But this still doesn't solve the problem of a big, fully laden ship that has broken down or been wounded and needs to be dry-docked, but is remote from one. Even where there are docks, ports often don't want to let oil ships in if they are leaking. Wounded tankers can in fact find themselves knocking at door after door, begging to be let in and dirtying the sea as they go. Even if they are let in, no fully-laden tanker can enter dry-dock. So the first problem for any disabled, loaded VLCC is to get rid of its cargo. But this might be difficult, as sometimes happens at the Cape, where bad weather or lack of smaller ships into which oil can be pumped might delay the operation for weeks.

What will happen when such a deep-laden ship is crippled off Maine or Nova Scotia in winter? It could happen in any season, and if not this year, it will be the next, or the one after – some day soon. It cannot be avoided. In the controversy over whether oil ports should be built this appears to be the one urgent issue that has been overlooked. The north-eastern seas are not friendly ones in winter. A laden 200,000 tonner could approach no dry dock on the east coast if hurt in a collision or otherwise. If she remains afloat she will either have to be lightened at sea, which is hard to imagine in a real blue-nose storm, or she will have to be towed across a stormbound winter North Atlantic, which is just as hard to imagine. Both are sobering prospects. But, apart from collisions and other accidents, tankers also get into frequent trouble through mechanical failure. When they do so, they are apt to lie helpless, and the consequences can be disastrous.

In February 1971, a 70,000-ton Liberian supertanker, Wafra, owned by Getty Tankers of Wilmington, Delaware, broke down from a relatively minor fault: a twenty-eight-inch intake pipe between the engine room and the ship's side burst. The ship was fifty miles off Cape Agulhas, southernmost point of Africa. The ship's chief engineer expected the preliminary flooding of the engine-room deck to remain at the same level, but the water continued to rise until the ship's machinery and power failed. She finally ran onto a reef near Agulhas, spilling nearly half her cargo of 63,000 tons of crude oil into the sea, which in that area happens to be one of the principal breeding grounds for many of the bird and penguin species of the Antarctic seas. One thousand penguins were removed from Dyer Island, a particularly important breeding area, to save them from the oil; and in Cape Town volunteer workers cleaned thousands of seabirds of the oil that clogged their feathers and pores.

However serious all the many technical problems of managing and navigating supertankers can be shown to be, in the long run they all prove to be merely aspects of the real and overwhelming worry about these ships, which is how to prevent them doing irreparable harm to the oceans and coastlines – that is, to avoid having them do any more than they already have done. On the face of it, it seems a forlorn wish.

THREE

IN May 1970, the 50,380-ton Norwegian tanker *Polycommander*, carrying a full cargo of crude oil, ran aground and burst into flames at Muxieirio Point, on the Spanish Atlantic coast near Vigo. The oil spillage amounted to about sixteen thousand tons, or one-third her cargo; it caught alight on the sea, and the flames created by this burning oil were so fierce that they caused a 'fire storm': a heat disturbance of such intensity that it raised hurricane-force winds in the immediate vicinity of the stricken ship. The winds whirled aloft a huge amount of oil, spraying it into a fine mist, and bore it up to high altitudes. The mist condensed into drops and some days later a black rain began to fall upon the coast – upon its farmlands and upon the villages of Panjón and Bayona. Damage to homes, gardens, and crops was extensive and cattle died of eating oil-covered grass; it all would have been much worse had it not been for the fact that most of the black rain fell on uninhabited bush and hill country.

As tanker and pollution accidents go, the Vigo incident was comparatively minor, though not of course to the inhabitants of Panjón and Bayona. *Polycommander* itself was a small ship compared with the general run of tankers these days, and not to be classed in the VLCC category. The startling and horrible results of the fire, however, made the accident unique. The damage caused, conservatively calculated to be in the region of $480,000, was scarcely comparable to the devastation caused by *Torrey Canyon* and other similar accidents, but it certainly added a new dimension to the general concern, not to say apprehension, about tanker disasters, all of which must henceforth be projected to include the consequences of the same sort of thing happening to the biggest of ships. Who can visualise the consequences of a *Polycommander*-type fire storm rising from a ship ten, twenty or even thirty times larger upon the green pastures and forests of Scotland, south-western France or Newfoundland? It would of course require some extraordinary circumstance to break the entire frame of such a vessel, but it is not unreasonable to suppose that at least two of its giant tank-sections could be torn open and set ablaze in a collision. God knows, the fire ball created by just one of them is more than the mind can grasp.

The means that tankers have of causing havoc upon the sea are many and varied, ranging from spectacular mishaps such as *Torrey Canyon*'s to the insidiously accumulative effect of constant leaks, spills, and irresponsible dumping of tank slops at sea. Every tanker, however well managed, drops some of its oil into the sea in some form or another; badly managed ships are ceaseless polluters and, like garden snails, can often be followed by the long iridescent trail of their waste.

The subject of pollution of the oceans has become a vast and complex one since it involves such an enormous variety of effluents going into the sea from rivers, coastal towns, and cities, indiscriminate dumping of noxious commodities, and leaks from offshore oil rigs. Examples are legion. West Germany and other Rhine countries send half a million tons of waste chemicals down the Rhine every year for dumping in the North Sea. In 1969 some twelve thousand seabirds as well as thousands of fish and seals died mysteriously in the Irish Sea. A plankton and fish survey conducted in 1970 revealed that plankton throughout the entire Atlantic Ocean already contain unsuspectedly high levels of an industrial pollutant related to the pesticide DDT.

Oil, however, remains the single biggest pollutant and tankers the single biggest dispenser of it.

Nobody knows how much oil is going into the sea every year. Official estimates tend to be conservative against those of marine conservationists, but they are disturbing enough. An estimate of the amount of petroleum products going into the oceans was presented to the Ocean Affairs Board of the National Academy of Sciences in Washington in May 1973. This analysis, based on available official estimates, indicated that about 1,370,000 tons of oil are discharged into the sea every year during routine operations of tankers and other ships; in addition, accidents dumped another 350,000 tons. On the conservationist side, there have been many warnings during the last few years about the depletion and ruin of the oceans, but one of the most forceful was that of Professor Jacques Piccard, the Swiss oceanographer, on the eve of the United Nations conference on the human environment, held at Stockholm in 1972, when, speaking on behalf of the Secretariat, he said that many experts now believe that life in the seas could be extinguished within the next twenty-five to thirty years unless man stops polluting them. His own estimate was that something between 5 and 10 million tons of petroleum products were going into the oceans every year, with tanker dumping being responsible for at least 1 million tons of this. If, in the absence of definite figures, we accept the true amount of dumping as something between Piccard's estimate and the American one, the position is serious indeed, because most of the oil is being dumped in estuaries, offshore waters, and other areas where the true fertility of the sea is concentrated.

Plankton is surface matter. It is the basic life of the sea and consists of phytoplankton, the 'grass' of the sea, that generates through photosynthesis at least one-third of the world's oxygen, and of zooplankton, the minute organisms that form the lower animal life of the sea; the phytoplankton convert the water's nutrients into the sugars, starches, and proteins upon which all sea creatures ultimately depend through their intertwined cycles. Zooplankton feed upon the phytoplankton, and those that feed upon the zooplankton in turn feed others. Seabirds fall from the sky and feed selectively upon this thriving cycle. As Professor Piccard himself pointed out, all that needs to be done to disrupt the marine cycle fatally is to destroy the phytoplankton, which oil skim so easily does.

To what degree and how often do we have to bruise this delicate living surface of the oceans with oil and other pollutants before the whole system collapses or is destructively and irreversibly diminished?

There are many areas of the oceans where the surface life of the water now seldom has a chance to remain free of pollution for more than a few weeks, or even days. Considering how far the Atlantic plankton already appear to be polluted, the general diminution of life over big stretches of the open and apparently unscathed seas might be far more advanced than we could suspect. If it is, then it would represent, certainly, man's single most calamitous act.

That the very seas should be considered a wasting asset must surely be the essential nightmare of the whole business of the despoliation of this planet which daily is perpetrated before our eyes, about our ears, and inside our nostrils. It is simply that the salt seas are for almost all of us the perpetual assurance of an accessible freshness and cleanness; and, I suppose, there is in this as well the remnant of an atavistic instinct defensive of our remote origin, a much-needed conviction of their inviolability, that whatsoever other havoc we wreak, however deeply we pile the ashes, the seas still will rise and fall and safely breathe in their depths. But their wastage is happening so fast in the Mediterranean around where I live that it has become almost a visible phenomenon; certainly the condition of this sea deteriorates perceptibly season after season. The Baltic is worse, already scientifically dead over much of its bottom, useless as a fish source where once it was the home of the herring and the source of the Hanseatic fortunes; and, although it means less to me personally as a sea, as I have crossed it only once and then through fog and ice, its condition strikes me as a terrible augury for the whole body of our waters.

There are whole stretches of the Mediterranean where I no longer will enter the water. A lot of the reason for this is local sewage and industrial-waste arrangements. Seventy-five per cent of Italian sea waters are more or less seriously polluted. Spain's Costa del Sol, where I have happily bathed during the past decade, no longer tempts. One often feels that hepatitis is as endemic there in summer as the common cold in Britain during the winter. But it is the oil that really creates feelings of violence. Local self-interest and the value of the tourist industry might clean up the sewage, but one can't see it doing much as regards the oil. One of the finest beaches in southern Spain used to be the strip of clean white sand between Gibraltar and Algeciras, the rim of the Bay of Algeciras. Five years ago a large refinery was built and the sea surrounding it in the bay sometimes is thick, sluggish and iridescent with oil. The Straits of Gibraltar, which half a decade ago were virtually as unspoiled as in the days of Homer, are now constantly and densely polluted and the fast currents carry this mess either deep into the Mediterranean or out into the Atlantic. The Moroccan fishermen have seen their catches dwindle and I myself have watched the gull population in the area diminish year by year to vanishing point. And it becomes an angry pain when I come down to the Moroccan coastline more or less opposite the seat of this havoc, that is to say between Cape Malabata and Ceuta, where some of the best beaches in the world are to be found, only to find the sands and rocks blackened by oil or to see a miles-long slick moving along on the offshore currents, like an endless loathsome serpent seeking a likely place to come ashore and leave its offal. There are times when the water seems to be of that full blackness which promises to be our ultimate reward: a viscous shroud spread along every shore and reaching to all horizons. If this seems far-fetched one only need return to the million-tonner idea and ask oneself what the actuality would be if one of those behemoths-to-be lay wrecked and breaking upon any of our shores. One ship could spill in one place what Professor Piccard now estimates the world's tankers and other vessels do over the period of a year.

The position is disastrous enough simply as a result of the casual spillage that now goes into the sea everywhere. There is not an ocean in the world that at this moment of my writing, or your reading, does not bear countless slicks distributed across its entire surface ranging in size from a few yards to many miles. In his log aboard his raft *Ra*, the Norwegian explorer Thor Heyerdahl reported that drifting black lumps of oil were 'seemingly never ending' across the Atlantic. In 1970 the yachtsman Sir Francis Chichester, after a Mediterranean voyage, wrote this letter to *The Times*:

I have just returned from a 4,600-mile try-out sail in my *Gipsy Moth* V to the Mediterranean and back. Time after time we sailed through patches or slicks of oil film on the surface. Seas coming aboard the yacht left clots of black oil on the deck and stained the sails. I noticed signs or effects of oil at intervals all the way from the Solent to Gibraltar and in the Mediterranean itself between Gibraltar and Majorca. I mention this because I think it is probably more noticeable from a small low yacht than from a steamer. Does it mean that in time, if it continues to increase, the oil effect will kill life in the sea?

In a report on sea pollution in *Science* in 1970, three marine scientists, M. H. Horn, J. M. Teal, and R. H. Backus, said:

Taken all together our observations indicate that lumps of petroleum exist in surprisingly large amounts on the sea surface. These lumps form a chronic type of oil pollution which may significantly affect the marine ecosystem. It is evident that a concerted research by interested oceanographers from around the world will be required to assess quantitatively the distribution of oil on and in the ocean, to understand the physical, chemical, biological and microbiological processes involved in its dispersion and eventual disposition, and to estimate the effects upon the marine ecosystem. ...

We are still very far from even beginning to understand the effects of oil, but at least our assessment of the *quantity* of it is improving. A recent American survey has found that at least 80,000 tons of *indestructible* tarry residues are to be found floating upon approximately 10 per cent of the total oceanic surface of the earth, including the Arctic and the Antarctic, a permanent legacy of the millions of tons of oil that have gone into the sea in recent years and disintegrated or been absorbed. The concentrations vary. They are estimated at twenty kilogrammes per square kilometre in the Mediterranean and one kilogramme per square kilometre in the North Atlantic.

International concern about pollution at sea is already fifty years old. The contamination of the seas by oil during the First World War disturbed Congress so much that it proposed an international conference, which was held in 1926. *Torrey Canyon* may have initiated the first intensive study and concern about the effects of oil pollution but it also brought its own confusion to the matter because the detergents used for cleaning up the seas and coasts on the British side of the Channel caused as much damage as the oil itself, sometimes more. There is not enough data by which to assess the effects of pollution accurately because we haven't yet begun to explore the full range of its interactions in the sea. We do know that all crude oils are poisonous to all marine organisms, but we need to know at least to some extent the degree to which they are poisonous to the different flora and fauna and, above all, their long-term consequences.

Crude oil is one of the most complicated natural chemical mixtures on earth; its components vary from locality to locality. It has so many chemical and physical properties, so many agents of solubility, volatility, and toxicity, that its interactions with the sea's own abundant range of salinity, temperature, and other changes pose seemingly limitless possibilities. What we do know is bad enough. Oil poisons, smothers, burns, coats, taints; among many consequences, it can start carcinogenic processes in sea animals, affect reproduction, and cause genetic change; it affects respiratory organs and clogs the filtering mechanisms of fish; it affects, as we have seen at the Cape, the balance and independence of a bird such as the penguin; it causes imbalance in the cycles of plant life, when it doesn't kill it altogether; its degrading process consumes large quantities of dissolved oxygen, which is vital to the life in the sea.

The uncertainties that exist about oil pollution were indicated after two big American spills in 1969, the one at Santa Barbara and the other at Falmouth, Massachusetts, when there appeared to be strong scientific disagreement about the effects on marine life. Dr Dale Straughan of the University of Southern California's Allan Hancock Foundation said in her report on the biological effects of the Santa Barbara spill that tests had failed to reveal any effects of oil pollution on the Santa Barbara channel's zooplankton and phytoplankton and that, similarly, sea plants and the production of fish and larvae were not lastingly affected. The principal reason for the low animal mortality rate, Dr Straughan said, was that toxins are the lightest components of oil and can rapidly evaporate. This conclusion was, however, apparently contradicted by Dr Max Blumer of the Wood's Hole Oceanographic Institute in Massachusetts after he had studied the results of the spill off West Falmouth, where he found that the toxic elements of the oil were actually the most persistent.

These contradictions were not quite as confusing as they seem. Experience of oil spills shows that they vary enormously, and capriciously, in their effects. 'Each spill will have its own characteristics, its own family of problems', the Canadian report on the stranding of the tanker *Arrow* off Nova Scotia in 1970 declared.

In the first place, the oil that is being spilled on the sea is of many kinds; even crude oil is of many different types. Of them all, the crude oil that was spilled off Santa Barbara is, in the short term at least, less obviously devastating than refined oils, which were spilled at Falmouth. This latter spill involved between 160,000 and 170,000 gallons. Three days after the spill oceanographers trawled the area and found that 95 per cent of their catch was dead. A year later, life on the seabed was still dying.

The toxins in refined oil and crude seem to be quite different in their effect and action. If, as Dr Blumer found out at Falmouth, the toxins of refined oil are more persistent at the area of spillage than crude, it does not necessarily mean that those in crude oil are less dangerous. In fact, the very swiftness of their dissipation may make them even more dangerous under certain circumstances in that they not only evaporate from the surface but also dissolve quickly into sea-water itself. Crude oil is most toxic soon after it is spilled, which is the main reason for burning it in a wreck or sinking the vessel with the cargo inside or at least getting the crude out as soon as possible. At this point it contains a large amount of aromatics, including benzene, which are poisonous. The oil's naphthenic acids are highly poisonous as well and have the effect of coagulating a fish's protein. Long after beaches have been scoured and cleaned these toxins may lie in the sediment of the sea bottom and seep out slowly through the action of water movement and currents, thus maintaining a flow of poison over a protracted period. This is a danger that Santa Barbara may yet have to confront: the area experienced the heaviest rains in forty years at the time of the spill, and silt that washed into the sea stuck to the oil and sank with it to the bottom; the silt thereby became one of the main cleansing agents. But if most of the oil now lies in the sediment at the bottom of the Santa Barbara channel, some of its effects may well be long delayed. In the *Torrey Canyon* affair, the French were congratulated for doing better than the British in disposing of oil before it struck heavily at their coasts. They dropped chalk on the oil, which had the same effect as the Santa Barbara silt and carried the oil to the bottom of the sea. It has been reported that the oil occasionally returns to the surface, but this is hard to verify because of the persistent pollution in the English Channel. At any rate the oil is still at the bottom and will only be very gradually dispersed over many years. It was for these reasons that chalk, which is one of the cheapest and easiest ways of disposing of oil on the water, was not used by the Canadians during the *Arrow* clean-up. In their official report on *Arrow*, the Canadians gave as their reason the fact that they were afraid of damage to sea-bottom flora and fauna and the possibility of the oil's coming to the surface later; they concluded: 'It is believed that further work is required on the fate of oil treated in this way before serious consideration is given to the use of sinking agents in future spills.'

Again in the case of *Torrey Canyon*, there was some early belief that the effects of oil pollution were not as lethal as first supposed and one of the arguments was that shellfish in areas that had not been treated with detergent fed on the oil and so helped clear large stretches of coast. But in her evidence to the Canadian inquiry on *Arrow*, Dr Molly Spooner said that laboratory experiments on fish that had ingested sublethal amounts of oil indicated that the oil might be having carcinogenic effects on them. Elsewhere, experiments with oysters showed that when water-soluble fractions of oil were introduced into their water, the amount of water filtered by the oysters decreased from between 207 and 310 litres a day to between 2.9 and 1.0 litres after eight to thirteen days. It is hard not to wonder therefore to what degree the Cornish shrimp actually benefited from their diet of *Torrey Canyon* crude.

Both *Torrey Canyon* and *Arrow* carried crude oil, but even these two experiences can't really be compared because *Arrow*'s cargo was of a type known as Bunker C, which is relatively non-toxic compared to other forms of crude. Bottom life in Chedabucto Bay was not affected by the spill. The lobster season opened on schedule and the catch was normal. The herring catch was above normal. Clamming, however, was closed down. Three months after the accident there was a 25 per cent kill of clams because of suffocation caused by plugging of their airholes by oil. The principal victims of *Arrow* were more than seven thousand seabirds, the majority of them killed on Sable Island, off the Atlantic coast of Nova Scotia and 125 miles from the wreck. It was *Arrow*'s slick of course that killed them. The Canadian report on *Arrow* concluded that 'despite the relatively large amount of oil released from the wreck, the overall or lasting effect on the wildlife and fishlife of the bay was not significant'. What it did not, and could not, account for was the damage done by *Arrow*'s slick on its way to and beyond Sable Island.

There has been an understandable tendency in all oil spills so far to regard the limits of the catastrophe as roughly the area visibly contaminated by oil, as well as its underlying depths. What any given locality suffers when oil comes ashore is very much determined by local tides, currents, winds, temperature, and other weather and climatic phenomena. In the Persian Gulf, much of the toxicity of spilled crude is removed by the swift rate of evaporation in that region's heat, which also helps the disintegration of the oil on the surface. What afflicted areas in more temperate climates usually look for is similar help from local weather conditions to save their beaches and tidal zones from inundation. Sir George Deacon, former director of Britain's National Institute of Oceanography, has said that 'instead of the *Torrey Canyon* oil drifting inevitably to our coasts there was at any time only a fifty-fifty chance, depending on the wind'. This is probably true for most coastal communities where wind and tide conditions are strong and where, if pollution threatens, the hope invariably is that the oil will change course and head somewhere else, out to sea, and the response always is relief if the slick finally is seen travelling toward the horizon. By and large, I suppose, we all live for today.

One might feel somewhat more sanguine about this if some way had been found for dealing with slicks at sea. None has that one could call truly effective. Practically all ways of dealing with oil spillage concern handling it on beaches, offshore, or on reasonably accessible areas of the sea. Nor are any of these fully effective. When they were working on *Arrow* the Canadians found that, on the beaches and in the shallows, straw and peat moss served as the best and safest absorbents. On the water the device they found most useful was the so-called slick-licker, a sort of conveyor belt that literally licks up the oil from the surface. The use of these contraptions is limited by weather and circumstances: it would take an awful lot of licking to remove from the sea's surface a slick such as *Wafra's*, which was thirty-five miles long, several miles wide, and several inches thick. All manner of other devices have been invented or improvised for damming, scooping, or holding spilled oil, but each has its limitations, and none would be of any practical use on a major slick on the open sea, least of all on a troubled sea such as that around the Cape, or off Maine and Nova Scotia in winter.

The best answer of all is to burn a slick, but oil floating on rough or choppy water picks up large quantities of seawater and there is little hope of burning slicks that have been exposed to weather for more than a few hours, which was another conclusion made by those working on *Arrow*. A possible solution is one now under investigation, namely to provide bacteria that feed on oil and themselves die when they have consumed it all. Until something like it is found no one perhaps should feel too grateful that any threatened pollution by oil slick has vanished seaward under propulsion of wind and tide. If the beaches are saved, what else is doomed?

It is virtually impossible to document the incidence of slicks, but the British Advisory Committee on Oil Pollution of the Sea in 1973 reported that in the previous year the length of the British coastline

47

polluted by oil had increased by a quarter. Twenty-one slicks came ashore in the area near the Straits of Dover in 1971. Sixty miles of coastline in Lancashire and the Irish Sea were hit by thirty-three slicks in 1972. Probably most of this sort of thing comes from the flushing out of ships' tanks as they head for the Persian Gulf or wherever to fetch another cargo after discharging their last. Some wait until they get to the deeper ocean; many don't. In the long run, one might well ask, What difference does it make? After the *Torrey Canyon* disaster there was a sharp increase of reports of ships seen discharging oil in the English Channel off the British and French coasts even though it was an offence punishable by a fine of up to one thousand pounds (since raised to fifty thousand pounds); the British coastal authorities believed that these were all ships taking advantage of the disaster and hoping that *Torrey Canyon* would be blamed for their own sludge. The same happened after the *Arrow* disaster off the Nova Scotia coast. Tankers cleaned out their tanks at night in the vicinity of the wreck to enable them to get rid of their oily swill without detection. With such scruples, what hope have we got? None, it would appear, if we have to depend upon much of the modern maritime conscience.

There is no effective international or even national means of dealing with such a problem. Enough oil clings to the sides of a ship's tanks after they have been emptied to form up to one per cent of the cargo which, in the case of a 200,000 tonner, means as much as two thousand tons of oil, though in practice it is usually something between one thousand and two thousand tons. Unscrupulous masters might flush all of this into the sea and, without question, often do, causing destructive slicks.

There is still no blanket international law against dumping oil at sea, but there is one against pumping out off coastlines. IMCO, the Inter-Governmental Maritime Consultative Organization, is of course the instrument for pushing these measures into existence. Even when it finally gets a total prohibition against dumping of all oil at sea, however, the force of such an international law will be an elusive thing. There is no effective means of enforcing it upon the seas. Any vigour it might possess must depend upon the zeal of individual governments, which is a variable quantity, to say the least. As it is, judging from the time it takes to get any legislation on the sea generally approved, one feels that the vigour and survival of the oceans has a low priority with most members of IMCO.

In 1954 IMCO suggested to its members that a ban should be imposed upon dumping sludge or any other form of oil fifty miles off any coast. It took eight years to get this ratified.

By that time, however, the major oil companies, ever prudent of

48

their image and in face of gathering public dismay about the state of the seas, had voluntarily introduced a simple system called 'load-on-top' to eliminate most of the oily sludge left in their ships' tanks without emptying it into the sea. In this system the seawater used for washing all the tanks is pumped into special 'slop' tanks where the oil eventually rises to the surface. This oil is mixed with the next cargo and the residual water only is put into the sea. Great precaution is taken even with this water, whose oily content varies. In 1970 IMCO put up a fresh proposal, which suggests that no tanker be allowed to dump more than one-fifteen-thousandth of its total cargo capacity. This would amount to about thirteen tons in a 200,000 tonner, which would cover the oil content of residual water. IMCO's proposal is that this water should never be of a strength greater than one hundred parts oil to one million parts water, and that it should never be dumped at a rate of more than sixty litres per mile. Given the rate of increase in world oil consumption, IMCO feels that even this is too much and wants, by the end of this decade, to have in effect a complete ban on any oil whatsoever going into the sea. Considering that world oil consumption will have almost doubled again by then, it would seem to be a brave but wishful hope, particularly since the performance on current measures has not been impressive: by mid-1974 only twenty of IMCO's members had approved the residual water measure.

Tanker specialists in London, including spokesmen for the Chamber of Shipping of the United Kingdom and for Shell, which initiated the load-on-top principle in the mid-sixties, believe that 80 per cent of the world's tankers are capable of using the system (that is, that they have the tank space to use for slops) but estimate that probably only about 50 per cent actually do so, which means that their oil goes into the sea.

In the end, much depends upon the vigilance of coastal states themselves. All British ships keep oil record books, in which every drop of oil on board, whether fuel or cargo, must be fully accounted for to British inspectors. The United States Coast Guard runs air patrols one hundred miles off the coast to watch for offenders, who are easily traced simply by following a slick all the way up to the very wake of the ship. If an offender puts into port it can be penalised under national laws but if it is spotted dumping oil at sea and continues on into international waters the only recourse is to make a complaint to the nation whose flag it flies. The IMCO rules specify that the owner nation must apply penalties. Unfortunately a large proportion of the world's tankers fly one or the other of the so-called flags of convenience, which means that they are registered in small non-seafaring nations such as Liberia, Panama, Costa Rica, Honduras,

Lebanon, and Cyprus. Any flag of convenience master choosing to dump oil sludge would not feel unduly perturbed about the punitive consequences at his home port, whose conscience and standards on these matters might be questionable, and which anyway his ship probably never has visited, nor ever is likely to.

As the Field Studies Council report on devastation around refineries indicated, small steady slicks do more damage than one big spill if they are persistent in an area. The steady dumping of sludge, tank washings, and other forms of oil upon the open sea might be having the same effects there. There is certainly no reason to suppose that the effects are less. There is indeed some evidence to suggest the contrary. Slicks have become so persistent in British offshore waters because of the tanker traffic that great anxiety has been expressed over the future of British seabirds. A breeding survey financed in 1970 by the Torrey Canyon Appeal of the World Wildlife Fund and the Royal Society for the Protection of Birds found that guillemots, razorbills, and puffins are threatened by extinction around British coasts unless something is done about oil pollution; and most of the damage to the seabird communities was found to have been caused long before oil slicks actually reached the British shores.

The steady pollution of the southern seas off the Cape of Good Hope since tankers stopped using Suez similarly has threatened the extinction of at least one species of penguin, the jackass penguin. Tens of thousands of penguins and seals and seabirds, belonging to species that breed in the mild waters and rich feeding grounds off the South African coasts, have been wiped out by steady oil spillage and by accidents such as that of Wafra.

So far the world has not seen an oil tanker spill bigger than Torrey Canyon's, although there have been many devastating lesser ones. The worst of these, second only to the Torrey Canyon spill, and perhaps finally even more serious in its consequences, involved the 206,000-ton Shell tanker Metula, which went aground in the Magellan Straits on 9 August 1974. Fifty thousand tons of oil, one-quarter of the ship's cargo, spilled out into those waters, so rich in Antarctic fauna and flora. Seventy-five miles of Chilean coast were fouled, with oil up to three inches deep. Metula was pumped empty of the rest of her cargo by United States Coast Guard salvors and towed to port. She was the second VLCC to come close to creating the superspill that everyone fears and expects at some point. In the autumn of 1970 the British VLCC Esso Cambria, with 241,000 tons of crude oil in her tanks, ran ashore in the Persian Gulf. She fortunately ran onto a shoal instead of rocks; even so, two of her tanks were broken and she spilled 1,500 tons of oil, which she'd loaded the previous day.

In recent years safety at sea has been deteriorating steadily. The rate of ship accidents has been rising to an alarming degree, and tankers are very much part of the problem. In 1971 tonnage totally lost by the world merchant fleet was the highest in civil times since records were first kept in 1891; it amounted to just over one million tons, and was the equivalent of one-sixth of the losses in the Atlantic in 1942, the worst year of the war for U-boat activity. Tankers accounted for one-third of the tonnage lost: twenty-two in number, totalling 328,337 tons. Casualty figures since have remained close to these levels.

In the four years 1969 to 1973, according to the Tanker Advisory Center, New York, whose data are obtained from Lloyd's List, there were 82 total tanker losses, together amounting to 3,299,000 tons deadweight, and in which 451 men died. The calculated spillage caused by these accidents was 719,000 tons. Thirty of these losses were through weather or stranding, twelve through collisions, twenty-seven from fire and explosions, and five from flooded engine rooms.

In the two-month period November–December 1972, for example, the 12,440-ton Romanian tanker *Ploiesti* sank in the Straits of Messina after collision, with the loss of three lives; the 100,000-ton Liberian tanker *World Hero* collided with a Greek warship, which sank with a loss of forty-four lives; the 8,816-ton Singapore tanker *Cosmopolitan* was extensively damaged by fire in its home port; the 12,000-ton Norwegian tanker *Texaco Britannia* was extensively damaged by an explosion at Keelung that killed eleven men and injured forty-two; the 12,000-ton Italian tanker *San Nicola* exploded off Brindisi, killing three men; the 200,000-ton fully laden British tanker *Fina Britannia* was taken in tow in the Indian Ocean after breaking down; the 63,000-ton laden Korean tanker *Sea Star* caught fire, exploded, and sank in the Persian Gulf after colliding with the Brazilian tanker *Horta Barbosa*, with the loss of twelve men; the 1,500-ton Swedish tanker *Nova* sank off Ystad after colliding with a Greek freighter, with one man lost; the laden 26,000-ton Italian tanker *Bello* exploded and burned out in the Mediterranean; and the 85,982-ton Spanish tanker *Alvaro de Bazan* caught fire in the engine room in the Persian Gulf, was left drifting and powerless, and eventually towed to Bombay, which offered the nearest dock. A total of seventy-one men lost their lives in this dreary but by no means unusual record of calamity and destruction.

In the first quarter of 1974, according to the Tanker Advisory Center, New York, there were three hundred and twenty-six tanker casualties throughout the world compared with three hundred and twenty in the same period of 1973. One ship, a 133,000-ton Italian

51

tanker, was a total loss after an explosion in her tanks. Included in these casualties were eighteen tankers disabled by fires and explosions, twenty-nine which suffered weather damage, twenty-nine which stranded, and fifteen involved in collisions. Twenty-five persons died or were missing and nine were seriously injured in all these incidents.

The main danger to ships throughout the ages of sail was shipwreck, either through stranding or bad weather. Steam allowed ships to choose the most direct routes, which meant that on busy trades they were choosing the same track and were in much closer proximity than sail had brought them. Collision therefore became the main risk at sea, especially off headlands and in narrow waterways where many routes converged. Since the late fifties the rate of collision has been climbing steadily. The fact that such a high proportion of these, indeed of all accidents, happens to tankers has made the casualty phenomenon at sea an international menace and a matter of critical concern beyond merely maritime circles.

A British survey of tanker accidents published in 1973 showed that during the ten-year period 1959 to 1968 a total of 11,501 ship accidents occurred in north-west European waters; 2,749 of these involved tankers. During that period 13,379 accidents occurred to tankers throughout the world. The total tanker population during that time was 50,559. It is this high rate of accidents to tankers that makes safety at sea an international problem going beyond merely maritime circles. Most of the big oil spills that have occurred since the loss of *Torrey Canyon* have come from ships that collided with each other or went aground.

In a detailed study of fifty recent ship accidents published at the end of 1972, the British Chamber of Shipping said that most of the collisions involved were attributable to appalling seamanship and could have been avoided if alertness and prudence had been shown, while all the groundings were directly attributable to bad navigation. Shell Oil, in a detailed study of forty serious tanker accidents that involved pollution, found that the common link between all was that 'people made silly mistakes'.

A very large number of the mistakes seem to be made by ships flying one of the flags of convenience. These countries, together with others such as Greece, Formosa, and the Philippines, have dominated the marine casualty lists for some years; each year for the past five years Liberia has had the biggest total losses of any country.

Twenty years ago world shipping was largely a Western European business, with Britain firmly in the lead as the biggest owner and operator of ships; outside Europe, America and Japan were the only major shipping nations. Liberia now has the world's largest merchant marine, followed by Japan and Britain, and her lead is rapidly increasing; flag of convenience fleets have regularly grown at rates more than twice those of world fleets as a whole. Liberia and Panama together now own, on paper, nearly a quarter of world shipping. Tankers dominate these expatriate fleets.

Thirty-five to 40 per cent of the Liberian tonnage is American-owned, and an additional 10 per cent of it is American-financed, which helps explain where the American merchant fleet, in steady decline since the end of the war, has taken itself. According to law, American-flag ships must be built in the United States and must be three-quarters manned by Americans. American shipbuilding costs used to be double those elsewhere (inflation abroad has helped make them competitive again), and American seamen's wages are still higher than elsewhere. American users of the flags of convenience, and they include Gulf, Esso, Texaco, Getty Oil, Tidewater, and Union Oil, have argued that they act not for convenience but out of necessity. Their plea has been that without the flags of convenience the American merchant fleet would have substantially vanished by now, because of costs. They have pleaded in fact that theirs is a patriotic stance in that they ensure the survival of a merchant fleet that would be vital in a war. How this squares with the fact of fewer trained American seamen, or how they would ensure the loyalty of their foreign crews and continued possession of their ships in such an emergency has never been explained.

Flag of convenience operators often say that their ships, especially many of those under the Liberian flag, are among the largest, best-equipped, and most modern in the world. This may be true. But ships are only as good as the men who run them, and the record is not impressive. Old ships traditionally have a higher casualty rate than new ones. Liberian losses between 1966 and 1970 not only averaged twice as high as those of the other major maritime nations, but, contrary to the rule, the ships they were losing were on the whole new ones, certainly newer than the ones lost by the other principal merchant marines: the average age of Liberian losses in that four-year period was 8.7 years, while that of the Japanese and Europeans averaged 12 years.

To a disconcerting degree, oil cargoes have been delivered in recent years by improperly trained and uncertificated officers aboard ships navigating with defective equipment. One of the biggest of all tanker accidents involved an American-owned Liberian ship which was in the charge of an officer who had no certificate whatsoever.

After the Liberian tanker *Arrow* ran ashore in Chedabucto Bay, a three-man committee of inquiry, which was led by Dr P. D. McTaggart-Cowan, executive director of the Science Council of Canada, found that *Arrow*, owned by Aristotle Onassis, had been operating with almost none of its navigation equipment serviceable. The radar had ceased to function an hour before the ship struck; the echo sounder had not been in working condition for two months; and the gyrocompass, which is used to steer by and to keep the ship on course, had a permanent error of three degrees west. The officer on watch at the time of the accident, the ship's third officer, had no licence. The commission of inquiry said none of the crew had any navigational skill except the master, 'and there are even doubts about his ability'. In its final report the commission said: 'We are well aware of the fact that no form of transportation can be 100 per cent safe but from the record available to us the standard of operation of the world's tanker fleets, particularly those under flags of convenience, is so appalling and so far from the kind of safety which science, engineering and technology can bring to those who care, that the people of the world should demand immediate action.'

If one judges the record, it often seems to make little difference aboard a flag of convenience ship whether it has the newest equipment or the oldest; too often those in charge of an ultra-modern bridge don't know how to use what's there, or don't know how to repair anything that breaks down, or, worse, don't even bother to report a fault when they get to port. Even in the case of well-qualified men commanding ships of the highest standard, as was the case with *Torrey Canyon*, their judgment, responsibility, and seamanship in the long run can be affected and impaired by terms of service that would not be tolerated on any ship flying the British or American flag, or that of any of the other major maritime powers. When *Torrey Canyon* went aground off the Scilly Isles, the ship's Italian master, who had behind him an outstanding reputation and record as a seaman, already had served 366 days on board.

As the British and French governments discovered when they sought to find someone to hold responsible for the accident, the task of trying to pin down a flag of convenience ship within any accessible frame of legal jurisdiction is wellnigh impossible. *Torrey Canyon* was owned by the Barracuda Tanker Corporation, a financial offshoot of the Union Oil Company of California, which leased the ship and had, in turn, subleased it to British Petroleum Trading Limited, which was a subsidiary of the British Petroleum Company. The ship, built in the United States, and rebuilt in Japan, was registered in Liberia, insured in London, and crewed by Italians. For an international lawyer any suit involving such a vessel must, one assumes, be the sort of stuff of which dreams of eternal litigation are made. The British and French, however, took a simple course. They pretended they weren't looking and, when one of *Torrey*

Canyon's sister ships, *Lake Palourde*, ambled into the first port where the law was held to be firm, they pounced and had her arrested until the insurers, the only accessible body with responsibility, paid up $7,500,000 as a settlement for damage.

Starting with *Torrey Canyon*, most of the major oil spillage calamities of the past six years have involved Liberian ships. These have included *Ocean Eagle*, whose wreck fouled the beaches of San Juan, Puerto Rico, in 1967; *Arrow*, which coated sixty miles of Nova Scotia shoreline in 1970; and *Juliana*, which in 1971 gave Japan its worst oil spill when it broke in two after hitting a breakwater off the port of Niigata. In October 1970, two fully laden supertankers, the 77,648-ton *Pacific Glory*, Chinese owned, and the 95,445-ton *Allegro*, Greek owned, both flying the Liberian flag, and between them carrying 170,000 tons of crude oil, ran into each other off the Isle of Wight. *Pacific Glory* suffered a violent explosion and was burnt out; fourteen of her crew died. Most of the oil in their tanks fortunately remained intact. The third officers of both ships were on watch at the time; *Allegro*'s third officer, a Greek, had no certificate whatsoever. Two of her engineers, Greek as well, had no certificates either. Two of *Pacific Glory*'s engineers also had no certificates. This was, at the time, the worst maritime collision on record, but it lost this distinction in August 1972, when two Liberian-flag supertankers, the 95,000-ton American-owned *Oswego Guardian*, fully laden, collided with the 100,000-ton Greek-owned *Texanita* north-east of Cape Town in the Indian Ocean. *Texanita*, which was empty, exploded with such violence that it rocked buildings and woke people forty miles inland from the coast, which itself was twenty-three miles distant from the accident. *Texanita* broke in two and vanished within four minutes. Thirty-two men died with *Texanita*, and one aboard *Oswego Guardian*. Both ships were travelling at high speed through fog so dense that the master of *Texanita*, who survived, couldn't see the masts of his own ship; although they had observed each other on radar, neither ship reduced speed. *Texanita* made only two attempts to plot the course of the approaching ship, the second when it was only four miles off, and *Oswego Guardian* made no attempt whatsoever to plot the other ship.

The chief officer of a Norwegian freighter, *Thorswave*, later provided what might be the first electronic eyewitness account of a major maritime disaster. His own ship was in the vicinity and he had watched the accident develop on his radar screen. 'I saw these two ships coming closer together,' he told the *Cape Argus* in Cape Town. 'Then the two dots came into one. Just then we heard this terrific explosion and felt our own ship shake twice. I thought there was something wrong with our own ship because the explosion was so loud. A minute or two after this I saw the two dots coming away from each other. Then one dot suddenly disappeared from the screen.'

Immediately after the collision, the master of *Oswego Guardian* ordered his ship at full speed away from the scene. No attempt was made to pick up survivors, who owed their lives to other vessels in the area including *Thorswave*. *Oswego Guardian*'s SOS call gave a wrong position, which was not discovered until six hours after the accident; no correction was ever sent out. *Texanita*'s master lost his licence for eighteen months; the master of *Oswego Guardian*, a Chinese, had his revoked.

Half the ship collisions in the world take place in the area bounded by the Elbe and the English Channel. Most of these are head-on and by far the majority of them occur in or near the Straits of Dover where, at any given moment, some forty ships usually are moving. Dodging this situation as well as the many wrecks and sandbanks in the area has become the principal nightmare for all supertanker and VLCC masters; and it is one they constantly confront because Rotterdam is the main tanker terminal for Europe and the most common destination for tankers inbound from the Persian Gulf. Tankers, as one might expect, are the ships most commonly involved in accidents there, especially flag of convenience ones, and usually because of appalling seamanship and standards aboard them.

Between October 1970 and April 1971, for example, ten tankers carrying between them some 300,000 tons of crude oil were involved in serious accidents in the area. Half of them were Liberian and they included *Pacific Glory* and *Allegro*. On 3 March 1971, the Liberian tanker *Trinity Navigator*, carrying 32,000 tons of oil, ran aground off Berry Head, Torbay, and was refloated after five hours by a British channel pilot who later said that the ship's radar was out of order and that she had no VHF radio for local communication. The Chinese crew in any event spoke no English, the international language of the sea as much as it is of the air. Coast guards and a pilot boat that signalled to her by lamp advising that she was on a dangerous course got no reply. On 4 April 1971, the Liberian tanker *Panther*, carrying 25,000 tons of oil, grounded on the Goodwin Sands and was freed two weeks later by tugs. Her radar too was reported defective by the pilot who boarded her. A Trinity House master mariner, Captain W. L. D. Bayley, writing in *Safety at Sea International*, in its issue of December 1969, said that supertankers with faulty VHF or radar were so numerous that channel pilots had ceased to report them. A further instance of almost total inadequacy was provided when the Greek-owned and Cyprus-registered tanker *Aegis Star* ran aground on the Swedish coast in November 1972. A surveyor who boarded her after she had been refloated found that her gyro-compass, echo sounder, radar, automatic log, speed indicator, and rudder indicator were all out of order, according to a report in the *Cape Times*.

A senior Trinity House channel pilot, Captain N. R. Knowles, told me recently that, far from improving, things were in fact getting worse, and described an incident involving a Liberian vessel inbound for Dunkirk which had been advised that she would have to stay outside because no berth was available. As pilotage is not compulsory and many ships, flag of convenience ones especially, avoid taking aboard pilots for the English Channel run because of the extra expense, the ship in question had not asked for a pilot when she made the approaches. Fighting a gale off Dunkirk, she searched for anchorage by steaming north, and then back down the Channel to Beachy Head on the English side. Her fifty-seven-year-old master finally sent an urgent appeal for a pilot to show him to safe anchorage on the English coast. He was near exhaustion when the pilot boarded. He was the only officer on board with a mariner's certificate; his first officer had been at sea only three and a half years. Aside from the threat that such an improperly manned ship presented to tanker traffic in the area, Knowles said, she herself was typical of many tankers he'd boarded.

The menace of such vessels and their substandard operation was one of the principal factors behind the introduction of two-lane traffic in sixty-six busy maritime areas throughout the world at the beginning of this decade. Ships now are required to move in these double lanes of one-way traffic when laying course through these areas, which include the English Channel, the Cape of Good Hope, the Malacca Straits, the San Francisco and New York harbours, the Baltic, the Straits of Gibraltar. It was felt that this system would at least help minimise the risks to heavily laden supertankers. Unfortunately the lanes are ignored by many ships (referred to as 'cowboys' by those who stick to their proper lane) and the results can be tragic.

On 11 January 1971, a 12,000-ton Peruvian freighter, *Paracas*, entered the English Channel and, instead of using the north-bound lane off the French coast as she was supposed to do, took the shorter and more convenient down-bound lane along the English coast. She struck the Panamanian tanker *Texaco Caribbean* and the resulting explosion shattered windows five miles away in Folkestone. Nine men went down with the ship.

The British coastal authorities marked the sunken *Texaco Caribbean* with three vertical green lights as a wreck warning. The following day a German freighter, *Brandenburg*, outbound for North America, hit the wreck and sank with the loss of more than half her thirty-one-man crew. The British added a lightship and five light buoys to the green lights on the site, but on 28 February a Greek freighter, Niki, struck the two ships and herself went down, taking her entire crew of twenty-two. A second lightship and nine more buoys were added to the collection of wrecks, but on 16 March an unidentified supertanker ignored a barrage of rockets and flashing lamps from the guard ships, ran through one row of buoys and, to everyone's surprise, got away with it and vanished. Within a two-month period, sixteen ships were reported by British coastal authorities for having ignored the elaborate arrangement of lights and signals and entered the area of the wrecks, which have since been demolished. In February 1974 the *Daily Telegraph* reported that about thirty ships a day, including supertankers, were still ignoring the 'keep right' rules in the Straits of Dover.

It is a situation that can only get much, much worse as world trade and world fleets expand. Today's run-of-the-mill superships, the 200,000 tonners, will be tomorrow's traders of low degree. The write-off life of a VLCC is about 10–15 years. Most of the first wave of 200,000–250,000 tonners already have seen half that. Superships aren't built to last. As they get older they begin to fall apart, to break down, and repairs and maintenance, not to speak of long tows, become too expensive to justify their retention in the service of any well-managed fleet. As the next big wave of investment starts creating the next plateau in tanker size, probably with the 500,000 tonners, the older ships will be handed down in job lots to the next generation of newcomers seeking a fortune in oil ships. So it presumably will continue, with demand and profits waxing and the oceans, alas, waning, unless some extraordinary international effort is made to control standards at sea. There seems a strange sinister touch of alchemy about it all – of black gold turned to golden gold and the lot ending up as purest dross, which will be the quality of the environment, and of life within it, we eventually will be left with.

FOUR

SUPERTANKERS belong among the true emblems of our epoch, the conveyors, so regardless of the ultimate cost, of the well-being of the nations of affluence: Russia, China, Eastern Europe, and the underdeveloped societies, representing nearly four-fifths of world population, use only about 25 per cent of world oil production. These ships are as indecently symptomatic of the consumer societies and their gross and potentially destructive appetites as the trampships were of the lean and commercially slack thirties, when they trudged from port to port bidding for depression-rate cargoes, steaming at four knots to save coal and looking as shabby and dispirited as the time.

Oil tankers by contrast are vaunted creatures, probably the last true darlings of old-fashioned tycoonery, which alone makes them in many quarters objects of a certain admiration and respect; for, as it was with the westward rails and their freight trains a century ago, almost nothing nowadays can make money faster and more easily when the circumstances are right than an oil tanker, except the oil well that fills it. Although the fourth Arab–Israeli war brought some shocks, there's certainly no reason to suppose, an occasional slump or two notwithstanding, that anyone plying tankers on a reasonably businesslike basis is going to find himself on his uppers until the oil runs out. It is no accident that the richest individuals in the world seem to be in tankers, starting with Paul Getty himself.

During the past fifteen years the new tycoons, who are for the most part Greek, Chinese, American, or Norwegian, have made money of an order that certainly hasn't been even visualised since the old free-booting days of nineteenth-century laissez-faire. Their finest period might well have been that between the Arab–Israeli war of 1967, which closed the Suez Canal, and the early days of the war in October 1973. They made or enlarged their fortunes by building tankers and chartering them, either on short or long term, and usually a skilful mixture of both. These operators are known as the independents, and they include the two most famous Greeks, Onassis and Niarchos, lesser ones such as Minos Coloctronis (who began business in 1964 with five ships worth $1,200,000 and now operates a fleet valued at very many times that). Aristomenus Karageorgis, the Hong Kong magnates C. Y. Tung (who owned *Queen Elizabeth* when she burned) and Y. K. Pao, the Norwegian Hilmar Reksten, and the Indian Ravi Tikkoo. What they mostly have in common, other than a desire to make money, is an original modest speculation with second-hand ships. Shipping lines such as the P & O which have formed their own tanker-operating subsidiaries are also counted among the independents.

Their charters are made with the big oil companies such as Shell, British Petroleum, Esso, and Mobil, who have their own fleets, but these account for only about 35 per cent of all tanker tonnage. There are good reasons why the oil companies leave so much of the business of moving their product to the independents. It releases capital for other requirements and does not tie it down uselessly when oil demand slackens and some tankers go idle. The independent spreads his fleet across the market and thus suffers less from fluctuations and often also is in business with ships other than tankers. After the 1967 crisis, British Petroleum alone chartered five million tons of tankers, which at that time represented nearly 5 per cent of existing fleets.

Playing this charter market is a complex game requiring cool instincts and a quick eye for chance. The essentials are first of all to get your ships as cheaply as possible, and then to know precisely what you are going to do with them. Supertankers have been amortised after a few voyages through skill and good fortune, and for the big boys the real game has been to acquire these huge and immensely expensive toys (these days a 300,000-ton ship can cost between $70 and $80 million) without putting down too much of their own cash, or, preferably, if it can be managed, without putting down any at all, except briefly on paper. Hundred per cent financing with payments over twenty-four years, now available in the United States, amounts to the same thing: the shrewdest form of making money with someone else's money. Anyway, putting all these parties and opportunities together in the proper sequence and producing a ship that pays for itself virtually before the first payments fall due from anybody is what has given the tankerman's manipulative art its highest polish. Buying somebody else's unwanted ships at the right time also is helpful. Minos Coloctronis bought his five ships in 1964 when tanker fortunes were slack, but then quickly began building his own fortunes three years later when Suez was closed by the Arab–Israeli war.

Once he has his ships, the independent tankerman has a choice of five forms of tanker charter. Four of these are long term, and the fifth is 'spot' or single voyage. Tanker rates soar when oil demand is high (a bad winter in Scandinavia can make a conspicuous difference), and they fall when it isn't (warm winter in Scandinavia). Long-term charters protect the independents against such fluctuations, though the rates for them are lower, sometimes half those for spot contracts. Most independents, including Onassis, prefer to work mainly with long-term charters, but they make brilliant use of single-voyage ones when the market is good and they have ships free. When Onassis got early delivery of a 200,000-ton tanker in 1970 he chartered it to Shell for a single return voyage to the Gulf, which gave him an estimated profit of just over four million dollars, or the equivalent of just under one-third of the cost of the ship.

The charter rates by which tankermen live and make their fortunes are based on something known as Worldscale, which, physically, is a book containing thousands of rates for different combinations of ports throughout the world. All the rates in this book are known as Worldscale 100 and they represent the cost per ton of carrying oil in a 19,500-ton tanker travelling at fourteen knots. They take into account all operating costs and depreciation and allow for what the oil industry calls a 'fair margin of profit'. The bigger the ship the cheaper it is to carry oil. So the owner of a 200,000-ton ship knows that he might accept a rate at something less than Worldscale 100 and make money because his operating costs are not very much more than a 19,500 tonner's while his freight revenues needless to say are vastly greater. In actual practice, the break-even rate for a 100,000 tonner might be well below Worldscale 100. Before the Arab–Israeli war of October 1973 Worldscale was fluttering at around 300 for spot charters to the Gulf. The outbreak of the war took it up to 450, the highest ever. The break-even point for a 100,000 tonner at this time was between Worldscale 25 and 35, which in cash terms meant its owner was making a profit of some $3,600,000 on every voyage between Europe and the Gulf. But in one week the spot-rate charter for tankers fell from Worldscale 420 to Worldscale 80. The cause was the Arab oil embargo, which sharply cut the need for tankers. At one point it fell as low as Worldscale 47.5.

This precipitate descent was typical of the opportunities and disappointments that can make or mar a tankerman's peace of mind; but this particular line between boundless expectation and stony disillusion, between the state of mind of 1973 and that of 1974, is an important one to consider.

The year 1973 will remain an astounding one in maritime history. There will never be another like it. The prospect of continuing, rising profits from oil ships prompted a shipbuilding spree without precedent. In effect, the tanker operators ordered a doubling of the world's tanker fleet, which already was colossal. Ships in operation at the end of the year totalled 212 million tons, while on order or under construction at the time were 1,279 vessels totalling 194 million tons. More than half of these were being built in Japan. Nobody in the business seemed prepared to believe that the prodigious levels of energy consumption in the industrialised nations might be checked by some circumstance. American dependence upon Middle Eastern oil imports in any event was regarded as the brave new frontier for tanker investment and profit.

As an example of the giddy rise and fall of the tankermen's hopes during this period there is the case of the British firm of Ocean Transport & Trading Ltd, which ordered a 260,000-ton ship in Japan in 1972 at a fixed contract price of $37.5 million. The ship's value started rising almost as soon as the contract had been signed. Demand for tankers had created a backlog of orders, and prices for them anyway were rising because of inflation. Ocean Transport therefore found that it could expect a price of $65 million for the contract (construction hadn't even started) if it put it up for auction. Its dilemma was whether to take this immediate cool speculative gain of $27.5 million or to accept a four-year charter for $50 million, with the ship still available as a valuable asset at the end. Ocean Transport took time to decide, and by the time it did the October war had changed things and the price it negotiated for its tanker contract was $10 million less than it might have got earlier. It decided to sell. A few weeks later, however, the prospective buyers pulled out of the deal, in fear of a world tanker surplus, and Ocean Transport found themselves back where they had started, except that they had lost the charter contract as well.

Once the shortages caused by the October war were made up, oil and tanker demand began to slacken. Oil stocks in consumer countries were plentiful, and the industrial societies were in any case sliding toward recession. The profit for tankermen lay with small ships, which could take oil directly to where it was needed, particularly on the American east coast. Fortunes that had held the prospect of apparently limitless expansion mere months before suddenly trembled. Where they had been 'making out like bandits', to quote a phrase used to me in the spring of 1973 by one American broker, tankermen found themselves fighting to maintain profit margins on their big ships. But they continued to make a profit, although many of the independent owners found themselves with liquidity problems: they had to pay for vessels whose earnings they'd assumed would be so big that the building price was virtually immaterial when they were ordered. In the industry, it was clear that the ships that would be most in demand in the immediate and foreseeable future were smaller ships. 'The ship of the future is the 60,000 tonner, to carry petrol from the refineries the Arabs are bound to establish in the Gulf,' a spokesman for Mullion Tanker, London tanker owners and brokers, told me in November 1974. But, having ordered the previous year 194 million tons of shipping, 70 per cent of which would be unable to use the Suez Canal (30 per cent alone consisted of ships of 300,000 tons and over), the industry clearly was not going to write off its big ships; these therefore will continue to dominate the seas, and our futures.

The actual economic principles upon which the staggering profitability of VLCCs originally were based are themselves one of the most remarkable inventions in the history of commerce. To call them a proposition would probably be more accurate, but the swiftness of the design and realisation of mammoth tankers, essentially within the decade of the sixties, was certainly inventive.

There was no single architect or innovator of these superships; they belonged to no vision or dream, as their only truly comparable predecessor, Isambard Kingdom Brunel's giant iron vessel *Great Eastern* of 1852, had done; but, while there was no Brunel behind them, there was at least a theory and it probably was first propounded in a report published in 1948 by the Society of Naval Architects of New York, which showed that if the cost of a ton-mile of carrying oil in a 12,000 tonner at twelve knots was taken as 100, the cost of transport in a 50,000 tonner at seventeen knots would be only 60.

This idea of the economies in maritime size does in fact hark all the way back to *Great Eastern*. Brunel believed that his single massive unit would monopolise the bulk of the business to India and Australasia. The *Great Eastern* was five times as large as the largest steamship of the day; but the idea then, like *Great Eastern* herself, was too far ahead of its time.

As a ship type, oil tankers are less than a century old and, because of the different nature and risk of their cargo, have always been somewhat experimental craft: in this century, they have introduced most of what has been truly radical in marine architecture. Since before the First World War most oil tankers have been built on what is known as the Isherwood Longitudinal System, which simply reversed the traditional vertical strength of a ship's hull and made it a horizontal one instead, allowing long, flexible hulls capable of sitting deep in the water and holding great weights.

The ancient Greeks carried bulk petroleum as offensive equipment, and the Chinese during the eighteenth century shipped oil from Burma to Russia in specially designed junks with a deadweight of fifty tons, but modern sea transport of oil began after Colonel Edwin Laurentine Drake drilled the first oil well in the United States, at

Titusville, Pa., in 1859. The circumstances then offer a curious parallel to those that prevailed a century later. Because of a declining whaling industry, newly industrialised and mechanised Europe had begun to fear a shortage of lubricating oils for turning its machines. Without a new source of oil industrial development might have been seriously affected. The first shipload of barrelled oil went from Philadelphia in November 1861, aboard the 224-ton brig *Elizabeth Watts*. Business picked up so rapidly that by 1864 the United States was exporting a total of 31,750,000 gallons of oil. The development of the oil tanker as a distinct type was bound to follow. Cargo tanks replaced barrels, and in 1886 the first specially designed tank steamer, the 2,307-ton *Gluckauf*, built on Tyneside for the German-American Petroleum Company, entered service. She had her engines aft and her bridge amidships and supplied the prototype profile for practically all tankers that followed her right up to the early 1960s.

At the start of this century oil tankers already were among the biggest ships in the world. The Anglo-American Oil Company's *Narragansett* of 1903 was 12,500 tons deadweight; her gross tonnage was 9,196, which compared well with the 14,350 tons of the North German Lloyd's *Kaiser Wilhelm der Grosse*, then the largest ship in the world. In 1907 an early attempt was made to move truly sizeable quantities of oil across the Atlantic. The tanker *Iroquois* was designed to operate in tandem with the tank barge *Navahoe*. Each had a deadweight of close to 10,000 tons. Known among shipping men as 'the cart and the horse', they continued their strange but successful partnership until 1930.

It is reasonably safe to say that three men pushed the oil business into supertankers. These were a Texas oilman, Daniel K. Ludwig, who owns one of the biggest private tanker fleets in the world; Aristotle Onassis; and his fierce rival, Stavros Niarchos. Ludwig however must be considered the true father of it all, and certainly the Japanese give him that credit because he brought big-ship building to them after the war.

All three men were operating ships of forty to fifty thousand tons in 1955 and in that year Ludwig ordered an 84,000 tonner, *Universe Leader,* which gives him reasonable claim to be the real pioneer of the very big superships. *Universe Leader* (later to hit the headlines in the Bantry Bay spill of October 1974) already was in the water when, late in 1956, Onassis ordered the first 100,000 tonner. Niarchos topped this by ordering a 106,000 tonner, and Ludwig outdid them both by asking for *four* 100,000 tonners.

They might have remained a trio of eccentric gamblers on big ships had it not been for the first Suez crisis in 1956 and the general political instability of the Middle East that followed, for their experiment was sceptically regarded by much of the shipping world, including other tanker owners. The closure of the Suez Canal after the Anglo-French landings of November 1956 had threatened to stop Europe's transport and much of its production, hampering its painful reconstruction and thereby threatening its very survival. Britain alone imported 65 per cent of its oil through Suez, France 45 per cent. Since the Anglo-French political collusion and joint military operation with Israel had failed to stabilise the Suez passage, it was left to the tanker operators to secure their independence of that fateful ditch as soon as possible. Although Europe had bought oil from the United States and South America as an interim measure while Suez was closed, this was more expensive than Middle Eastern oil and, quite as important, required scarce hard currency. Any solution had to be based upon sending oil around the Cape in an emergency, which meant almost doubling tanker capacity: the Cape route added twelve days each way to the voyage and a tanker fleet that had been delivering about 95 million tons on the 6,000-mile route through the Mediterranean could only handle about 50 million tons if it had to go around Africa, a distance of 11,300 miles. In numbers of ships, this meant that about seventeen tankers would be needed on the Cape route against ten using Suez.

The choice was to build more ships, or fewer and bigger ones on the model provided by the two Greeks and Ludwig. It was a difficult decision, and the oil companies and independents found it hard to make up their minds. The weight of counsel was against superships. A 100,000-ton ship would be cheaper to build and to run than four 25,000 tonners, or three 33,000 tonners, and it would carry oil for half the cost of the smaller ships, even when it sailed via the Cape; but it was widely felt that these advantages had been oversimplified.

Four months after Suez, in March 1957, the shipping correspondent of The Times, commenting on the advent of the 100,000 tonners, predicted a questionable future for them, and said: 'By the size and roundness of the figure the 100,000 tonner was bound to be something of a landmark in shipping development; and yet ... it has already diminished, like the four-minute mile, to its proper place in the scheme of things – a point along a line of progress.' He added: 'These vessels will never form more than a small proportion of the world ship-building programme, and, with perhaps three or four exceptions, British yards might be wiser to leave them to others to build.'

Basil Mavroleon, chairman and managing director of London and Overseas Freighters Limited, a major independent company, concurred in this view in a subsequent letter to The Times: 'Quite apart from the scarcity of dry-docking facilities, the potential cost and loss of earnings time could be enormous if a long tow proved necessary from the scene of a major breakdown or mishap to the nearest dry dock. On the other hand, one 25,000 tonner out of four being put out of action in similar circumstances could be more quickly restored to service at a port nearby, and while the ship was under repair the other three would continue trading.'

Whether in fact mammoth proportion was the essential solution or whether fleets of smaller tankers would have done the job quite as well is becoming at this remove steadily more difficult to prove or disprove, though independent minds will continue to wonder, especially when they weigh the risks to the environment that size involves. The tanker industry has never presented a convincing case. The usual defence is altruistic, that these ships were built to save us money by carrying oil more cheaply, and to save our coasts by reducing the number of ships and thereby the risks of collision. But these are justifications that came after the event and they scarcely hold up. The ships were built as a speculation against Middle Eastern politics and with the prospect of immense profit, no more, no less.

Without question smaller ships would have made their owners and operators quite rich enough; but the superships promised so much, much more, an excess beyond all prevailing notions of profit, and, as the energy consumption of the industrial nations became steadily more profligate, the case for them was regarded as obvious. In 1966, nine years after the shipping correspondent of *The Times* had advised British yards to leave the big ships to others, at least one of them, Harland & Wolff of Belfast, builders of the *Titanic*, had applied for patents on the design of a 1,000,000-ton ship. After the June war of 1967 the case for them was regarded as irrefutable. The big leap forward, not so much in actual size as in numbers ordered, really dates from then. As a result, the seas, the shores, shipbuilding, the entire geography of commerce, the shape of all cargo ships to come, and the structure of fuel demand and supply have been adapted to them or influenced by them. By the time the Middle Eastern war of October 1973 began the commitment to them was so far advanced that there appeared to be no going back.

The final arguments for the leap into size were extremely persuasive on all counts. While the economic advantages of a 100,000 tonner over a fleet of 25,000 tonners were considerable, the best sums of all appeared when one began working with multiples of the 100,000 tonner itself. The model that most operators settled for was the one in the 200,000 to 250,000-ton range, to which *Ardshiel* belongs. This is what the tankermen and oil companies now refer to as the plateau in supership construction. More supertankers have

66

been built in this class than in any other in recent years. They now account for more than one-quarter of the tanker tonnage afloat.

In 1967 it cost three dollars and twenty-nine cents per ton of oil in an 80,000 tonner to make the round trip from Rotterdam to Kuwait at the head of the Persian Gulf and back, going through the Suez Canal both ways. A 200,000 tonner could carry the same oil between the same points but via the Cape for less than two dollars and forty cents a ton, making the longer route considerably cheaper than the traditional shorter one, and making problematic the future of the Suez Canal even if it did reopen.

Shipbuilding costs didn't rise in proportion to size. Part of the attraction of these ships was that an increase of 25 per cent in dimensions provided an increase in capacity of something like 95 per cent: the sixty-three-foot draught of a 200,000-ton ship is only ten to fifteen feet more than the draught of a 100,000 tonner, so the weight of steel required proportionate to each ton of cargo carried is therefore much less than the bigger ship. The capital cost of machinery falls as well. The hydrodynamics of the bigger ship, which moves more easily through the water, means that it requires commensurately less propulsion.

To travel at sixteen knots, a 20,000 tonner requires at least 10,000 horsepower; for the same speed, a 37,000 tonner needs about 14,000 horsepower, and a 100,000 tonner only 21,000 horsepower. A big tanker requires no more crew than a small tanker, often less, and here there is no possible comparison with a passenger liner such as a Cunard Queen. A supertanker might have a crew of anything from twenty-nine to forty men against 1,285 officers and crew aboard, say, Queen Mary, most of whom of course were stewards attending the needs of the passengers, A 200,000-ton ship costs less to run than two 100,000 tonners – one crew, one set of bills. On top of it all, one ship instead of two or three saves on port charges, pilotage, and general administration.

It is nonetheless doubtful whether supertankers would have become the phenomenon they now are without the promotion and fanatic dedication of the Japanese, whose commitment to these ships was one of the most powerful factors behind their creation. Tankers would certainly have got bigger, but not so soon, nor so quickly.

The Japanese shared with Onassis, Niarchos, and Ludwig (all of whom had built small supertankers in Japan before 1956) a conviction that these were inevitable ships and that the trend toward them would not be reversed. Their own growing dependence upon oil and the long route between their country and the principal source naturally helped convince them, but they also had been searching, as they recovered from the war, for major technological and industrial opportunities and had settled upon shipbuilding as one of these, with an emphasis on supertankers. With determined pace-setters among the independents, as well as a low, fixed price and a firm delivery, they saw no reason to suppose that they wouldn't carry the shipping world with them, and they were right.

Some of the early 100,000 tonners were built in the United States but the Japanese thereafter made construction of superships practically a national skill and resource. Since the late sixties Japan has accounted for about half the new tonnage built every year throughout the world. In an ordinary year the yards of Mitsubishi and Ishikawajima-Harima Heavy Industries together build more than the combined output of heavy shipbuilding nations such as Sweden, West Germany, France, and Spain. Ship sales compose the second largest category of Japanese exports, amounting to about 9 per cent of the total. Supertankers were entirely responsible for this supremacy. Japan built the first 200,000 tonner, and most of its sisters; it built the 326,000 tonners, the 370,000 tonners, and the 470,000 tonners. (France, however, undertook the first 530,000 tonners.)

To build these big ships at the speed and price at which they were offered required new formulas and technology and these were produced under great pressure. The reasons for Japan's being able to do so were interesting. Japan had ranked behind only Britain and the United States in world shipbuilding before the war and built the world's largest battleships, *Yamato* and *Masashi*. Under pressure of a worsening war situation Japanese skills were pushed into new semi-automatic and standardised production and assembly methods which were matched only by those the Americans were using to build vessels such as the Liberty ships, which were delivered with steam up ten days after their keels were laid. But the Japanese postwar initiative got its main start from the curious fact that, despite the systematic and wholesale bombing undertaken by the Allies, her dry docks and shipbuilding facilities escaped undamaged. The Japanese still don't know whether this was intentional or not. It was especially curious in the case of the big Kure naval dockyard, which was entirely destroyed except for its shipbuilding facilities, dry dock, and shops. It was the survival of the dry dock, in which the battleship *Yamato* had been built, that allowed the Japanese to get their lead in building mammoth ships. It was capable of allowing construction of a 150,000-ton ship. General MacArthur had imposed severe restrictions on Japanese shipbuilding and the Japanese consequently didn't know what to do with their yards or their pool of idle but highly skilled designers and engineers. The solution for the latter was to spend their time on finding ways of building a ship as economically as possible and tying this to designs for new specialised vessels. In 1952 their genius and vision were joined to Ludwig's. The American tanker-man leased the Kure shipbuilding yard from the Japanese government. Ludwig brought with him the advanced technology of American prefabrication and standardisation methods used during the war. The yard began planning and building ships far larger than those projected anywhere else in the world, and the age of the VLCC was under way.

The traditional way of building a ship is to do so methodically from keel to truck on an inclined slipway, down which it eventually slides into the water. A keel plate is laid from which structural frames slowly grow. Upon these, steel plates are laid to form a steel shell. Before the war, the plates were sewn together by rivets. This was the way in which the Cunard Queens and the Normandie were built; the latter, for example, needed thousands of steel plates ranging from eight to thirty feet in length which had to be riveted together in sequence, more or less one after the other. About eleven million rivets were used, the weight of which alone was a colossal addition to the ship's structure.

The Japanese technique is to build the vessel in huge welded sections, such as the whole of the bows, stern, superstructure, and various tanks, and these are assembled inside a dry dock, placed in position there by giant cranes; once in position, they are welded together, after which the dock is filled and the ship floats out, ready for her trials. It took twenty-one months to prepare merely the basic unequipped steel shell of the Normandie for launching. Mitsubishi Heavy Industries takes seven months to convert the blueprint for a 260,000-ton supertanker into a vessel ready for her maiden voyage.

In 1969 there were thirty yards around the world able to build ships of 200,000 tons or more. As others followed the Japanese into giant tankers, they introduced their own variations on these prefabricated principles. The idea always was to turn the ship out as fast as possible. Dutch yards built 200,000 tonners in two halves, launching these separately from a slipway and then welding them together in the water. German and British yards were still disposed to use a slipway on which the prefabricated parts of the hull were put together and then sent into the water in conventional style. A Swedish yard passed steel through one end of a line of sheds, rather in the fashion of an automobile factory, with complete sections of a ship emerging at the other end, ready for assembly in a nearby dock. Admirable and inventive as all this was, supertankers, wherever and by whomever and whatever method built, unhappily began to reveal unusual stresses and strains, and a high and dangerous rate of structural failure.

They had grown too big much too quickly, without commensurate

69

knowledge of the forces created by their enormous hulls. As it took only six years for ships to grow from 100,000 to 300,000 tons, this meant that, initially, even though they were patently quite different from anything else, they were always growing faster than any proper experience of their sea qualities or their wearing qualities, and to some degree were therefore being built blind. No one truly knew how they would behave.

The long hulls had shown a great deal less than their estimated strength. They had a propensity to buckle and crack under certain pressures, sometimes even in dock or on the slipway while still under construction. Some incurred serious damage when launched, others returned from their trials or their first commercial voyages with their internal strengthening members buckled. In 1968, when about two hundred supertankers of 150,000 tons or more were under construction in various parts of the world, most of them were delayed for varying periods because of modifications.

A number of tankers simply tore apart in heavy seas, reminiscent of the way that many prefabricated American ships broke up during the war, when they cracked their hulls at a rate of five thousand feet per second and vanished as swiftly as if expunged by explosion. The American wartime ships cracked because of an insufficient richness in the manganese content of their steel, which became brittle in cold temperatures, especially on Arctic convoys to Russia, causing the ships to split and hurling their crews to an instant death in those frigid waters. It was the price paid for haste and innovation in an emergency. Yet it seemed to have made no impression upon the architects and builders of the first truly mammoth tankers, even though they were dealing with a grossly enlarged, infinitely more sophisticated, and untried version of the techniques that produced those wartime ships.

The first penalty of haste is workmanship itself. In October 1972 the Japanese Ministry of Transport censured two of the biggest shipyards in the country, Ishikawajima-Harima Heavy Industries and Kawasaki Heavy Industries, for negligence in construction and for the cracking of ships soon after they had started trading. The ministry's inspectors for some time had been thoroughly examining Japanese-built superships whenever they returned to Japan for overhaul and had found a high rate of defective workmanship in vessels built between 1962 and 1969, which were the years of most intensive supertanker production. Some ships had been sailing with vital parts of their structure not welded at all, or imperfectly welded. A 58,000-ton tanker built in 1964 had four ribs without any welding whatsoever. A 60,000 tonner built in 1967 had hull cracks caused by faulty welding. The two yards said the welding was done by workmen employed by subcontractors, and they recalled fifty-five super-ships built for Japanese, British, Greek, Liberian, Panamanian, Yugoslav, Formosan, and Dutch owners for repairs.

Haste and innovation, so characteristic of everything involved with the emergence of superships, have always been entirely alien to the seagoing experience, taking our concept of this as, say, that which Conrad so splendidly defined, and which really has persisted to the present day as the one whose images of the sailor's life and of seacraft we generally live with: one in which the sea dominates as an element whose perverse and unpredictable nature so intimidates the well-foundedness of even the finest of vessels that seamanship remains the utmost development of man's vigilant, precautionary, and intuitive self. Seafaring's standards of consistency and exactness have been seen always as the exemplary, orderly way of doing things, and the taut singing power of its idiom the finest for linking command to action.

This respectful tribute from the landsman to the sailor is as old as maritime venture, and the very source of our pride and pleasure in ships: an accolade that grew steadily through the five centuries of maritime development that followed Portugal's initiation of the search for the sea route to the east, that crucial and pivotal western impulse that finally set man upon systematic navigation of the deeps.

The sea's horizon was the awful edge of the proven universe, and of the unproven beyond. The ship – so perishable upon those infinite and unknown waters – was the true microcosm, and sailors the most fateful of men, confronting from their decks, unprotected by the myriad shades, niches, and succours of the land, the fullest view of the whims, confusions, perversities, and sheer helplessness of existence. Once a ship was drawn into itself out upon the wide ocean only two things could bring it through: the stoutness of the ship itself, and seamanship with its appreciation of the monumental power of water, the caprice of wind and current, the devious interactions between sea and shore, and the limiting strains of the vessel's fabric.

Any voyage was combat without quarter, requiring all the virtues and disciplines of the battlefield: courage, loyalty, obedience, steadfastness, teamwork; as well as a capacity for hardship, deprivation, brutal suffering, and the constant prospect of some particularly dreadful form of death. Understandable that for so many centuries shipwreck struck man as the epitome of irony and despair: the failure of himself at his proven best, within a rope's throw of salvation.

Against such an adversary nothing ever could be taken for granted, and rarely was. Only the tried and true could be depended upon. Innovation whenever it appeared was regarded with suspicion and treated with reservation, not as a matter of principle but out of wary knowledge that, inevitably, there would be some cost to pay, usually in sailors' lives. This had to be the mariner's outlook throughout the long ages of sail, when ships had to follow the wind, which often meant the worst of routes, particularly in the southern latitudes when the course bent around Cape Horn. Here, anything insufficiently tested by local circumstances could prove fatal. When, for example, wire began to replace rope in the rigging of mid-nineteenth-century square-riggers, it took some time, many dismastings, and a few total losses, before it was realised that, for all its apparent strength, a sudden jerk could part wire stays and braces as neatly as though snipped by giant scissors.

Ships evolved at such a gradual pace before the advent of supertankers that they remained recognisably the same from age to age, century after century: vessels comfortably shaped to sit upon or between the waves. The ships of Trafalgar were not so very different from those of the Armada.

The shift from sail to steam was so gradual that, except for Brunel's *Great Eastern*, which was an isolated freak, there was no point during that whole epochal century of maritime transition and overlap when anyone could say that the ships of the day were remarkably different in appearance or behaviour from those of the generation before.

Size in ships was so gradual in its approach that *Queen Mary*, set upon the drawing boards in the late twenties, was the natural descendant of Samuel Cunard's *Britannia* of 1840, with a perfectly logical progression of scale from one to the other. At the beginning of this century, eighty years after the introduction of steam power on the Atlantic crossing, quite sizeable steamers still were equipped with sail-bearing yards on their mainmasts, in case of engine breakdown. Even in the 1920s there were freighters similarly fitted, and commercial square-rigged vessels continued to be launched. This meant that until fairly recently the commanders in steam were substantially sail-trained. They kept their traditional cautions and inculcated these in their juniors, who form our present senior generation of mariners.

Steam thus quite naturally extended the sea's continuities, outlook, and habits. Ships, however massive and powerful, remained vulnerable and the sailor's demeanour before his element therefore still could only be the abiding one of humility. Any deviation from this, or any scornful over-confidence of the sort indispensable to the landsman's vision of progress and indeed accepted by him as a virtue, would soon enough exact some retributive balance, as Captain Edward J. Smith of the *Titanic* might have affirmed as he regarded the sudden fatal slope of his warmly lighted and apparently impregnable decks.

Titanic represented a lapse of those old, chastened views of the sea and not one of actual seamanship, for she was probably better run than most ships afloat today; but she was not unsinkable. Her tragedy was enlarged by presumptions about her buoyancy and her high speed along a dangerous routing. These were mainly conceived by her shorebound owners and operators. For seafarers, however, the moral of her sinking lay in the unhappy concurrence, obligatory or otherwise, of her officers. The reforms she brought principally sought to ensure that when a vessel went down those aboard would lack nothing that might help save them; but so far as seamanship was concerned, her loss reasserted with renewed vigour all the old deference and humility of sailoring, and the sea stayed deeply conservative in practice and spirit, more settled in its ways and unswerving in its customs than any other calling. Nothing seemed likely to change fundamentally, neither ships nor the ways of handling and operating them: the temper and unpredictability of the sea after all were never going to be any different.

That these precepts remained valid even for *Titanic*'s eventual mighty successor, the 83,000-ton *Queen Elizabeth*, was borne out when she too came close to an appalling tragedy during the war. Off Greenland, with thousands of troops on board, she was very nearly overwhelmed by seas in a manner all too reminiscent of the days of sail, during which ships foundered sometimes through being simply blotted into extinction by immense solid masses of water falling atop them.

The *Queen Elizabeth* incident is as illustrative as anything can be of the power and surprise of the sea. Moving through a storm, her bows dropped into the trough below a gigantic wave that fell upon them, burying them deep. A second huge wave piled atop the first, shoving the bows even deeper, so that the ship seemed to be set virtually upon its nose. The officer of the watch staring from the bridge toward where the bows should have been found himself gazing past the crow's nest, normally well above his head, obliquely down toward the bed of the ocean.

Such an experience upon what was the biggest ship in the world might have been considered beyond belief, except that the bridge, ninety feet above the waterline, had its thick plate-glass windows shattered by the water, which washed the quartermaster from the wheel as though he'd been on the open poop of a wool clipper rounding the Horn, and washed another sailor from the wheelhouse itself out to the wing of the bridge. *Queen Elizabeth*'s staff captain, shaving in his cabin immediately below the bridge, was knocked down by a block of plate glass from his own shattered windows and, dazed, found himself sitting waist-deep in water. The ship's foredeck had

73

been hammered six inches below its normal level, and all equipment there was out of action; all anchors were jammed. The world's biggest ship was in dock for nine weeks undergoing repairs during a critical period of the war when her services were badly needed.

Another great passenger ship was to suffer the same terrifying encounter before the age of the transatlantic liner was over. In April 1966 the 46,000-ton Italian liner *Michelangelo* met a similar freak wave during a heavy storm. The water smashed in the forward structure of the ship below the bridge, which was wrecked, together with the officers' quarters and twenty first-class cabins. Two passengers and a member of the crew were killed. One woman had to be rescued from the debris of her stateroom by crew members who first had to hack a hole in the door with axes. The *Michelangelo* entered New York with her flag at half-mast.

It is against this background that the hasty evolution of the supertankers must be considered. Sixteen months of tests with models in tanks were undertaken merely to determine the hull form of the *Normandie*. For *Queen Mary*, there were more than eight thousand tests using twenty models, which travelled a distance of more than one thousand miles up and down the testing tank of her builders, John Brown's yard on the Clyde.

The stresses upon the huge supertanker hulls were at first calculated theoretically, using as a basis the measurements and basic hull design which had served reliably in tankers since construction of the *Gluckauf* in 1886. The scantlings (the measurements of the 'bone' structure of the ship) of the first 200,000 tonners thus were mere enlargements of the standard 18,000 tonners of the immediate postwar period, even though just one of the five tanks in these big ships would hold the full cargo of the latter. Furthermore, before the behaviour of the ships was fully experienced or understood, widespread attempts were made to economise even on these hulls by building lighter structures and thereby using less steel, which is the costliest item in such enormous craft.

It was soon discovered that building a bigger ship by simply enlarging the dimensions of a smaller one wasn't enough; to have structural integrity, it had to be a different ship altogether, with compensation for weak points created by new stresses. Structural analysis using computers has helped strengthen succeeding generations of tankers, but the sea has no pattern to its moods, even where it is most predictable in them, and its caprice is generally so variable that the fullest strain and stress upon a new form of hull or gear might not be properly assessed for many years. It took ten years of intensive postwar research to discover why the American wartime ships cracked.

It is going to take much longer, despite computer analyses, to know in reality the true limits of the biggest of the supertankers.

This point was raised when a member of Lloyd's Register of Shipping, James I. Mathewson, discussed the structural failures of large tankers before a meeting of the Honourable Company of Master Mariners in London in the spring of 1969. The development of the very large tanker over a very short period of time had been one of the more spectacular events of marine history, Mathewson told his audience, and went on to discuss in technical detail the problems and shortcomings of the giant hulls, with a concluding observation that service experience of 200,000 tonners was still very limited.

A member of the audience, a Captain Watson, asked: 'There are over a hundred 200,000 tonners on order for delivery by 1973. Surely we are going to get the experience?'

Mathewson: '...the critical service period for tankers...was generally eight to twelve years after build, depending upon the cargoes carried. The present longitudinal strength standards are based upon experiencing the maximum permissible stress on a probability of once in twenty-five years, so that it may be that in, say, a five-year period the probability of experiencing high stresses may be so low that true service experience is lacking.

'Statistically speaking, it appears that the service experience to date is too small a sample to draw significant conclusions applicable to the total population of tankers.'

In this light, the *Queen Elizabeth*'s encounter with her own maximum stress – in her lifetime she experienced no worse occasion than that partial submersion off Greenland during the war – is perhaps relevant. The total bending stress of her hull had been designed for the maximum possible conditions for her anticipated route. The highest wave ever recorded was 112 feet. There were no estimates of the size of the sea that piled atop the *Queen Elizabeth*'s bows, its arrival having been too precipitate and violent in its consequences. In any event the strain it imposed must have been close to maximum.

There can be no doubt that a ship of lesser strength would have fared very much worse, and might not have survived. When designed, the chances of the ship meeting such seas as those which nearly swamped her had been considered remote, but wartime sailing orders from time to time sent the Cunard *Queens* along northerly tracks they would not normally have used.

Supertankers and VLCCs are now sailing through the one area of the world's seas where such waves, or holes in the sea, as they have been called, are endemic. These waters, off the Cape of Good Hope and along the South African coast, are among the most dangerous in the world, and they have taken a dismal toll of tankers so far. This state of affairs was immediately apparent after Suez closed in 1967 and the oil ships had to travel between the Persian Gulf and Europe via the southern hemisphere winter. The experience was a shock to seamen as well as insurers. Ships cracked; some survived, others didn't; some vanished without trace. One of those that broke apart and sank was the 46,434-ton *World Glory*, one of the earliest supertankers and once the pride of the Niarchos fleet; when built in 1954 by the Bethlehem Steel Corporation at Quincy, Massachusetts, her principal dimensions were exceeded by only five passenger liners in the world, the two *Queens*, *United States*, *Liberté*, and *Ile de France*. She snapped in two in a storm off the South African coast in 1968; sparks from the splintering steel touched off an explosion that shattered the vessel even further and left her remnants blazing. She was only one of many either lost or severely damaged in those waters during the first seasons of navigating the Cape; since then huge numbers of tankers have been smashed, disabled, or lost, to remind one that Cabo Tormentoso was how the Portuguese first were inclined to describe that headland. The apocryphal story is that Bartholomeu Dias, after discovering the passage to India round it, properly named it Tormentoso for the rigours he experienced there, but was subsequently corrected by his mentor, Prince Henry, who suggested Good Hope as an augury for the riches to which it laid access. It is now believed that Dias himself called it Buena Esperanza; anyhow, the Portuguese sensibly have always credited it with *both* its identities.

Possibly the most astonishing aspect of all this is that, during the southern winter, every loaded tanker rounding the Cape is more heavily loaded than was formerly thought safe, and is therefore breaking one of the oldest, and in all other circumstances, most rigorously applied rules of marine safety: that a ship should be loaded according to the climate of the seas through which she will sail. The world's seas are divided into tropical, summer, and winter load zones; tropical seas are allowed the heaviest loads, winter ones the least. If she is too heavily loaded for winter seas, the effort of countering them can strain a vessel's plates and frames and spring leaks, so that she can even start sinking from the damage. On a voyage from the Persian Gulf to Europe that starts during the northern summer, as ours did, a tanker passes from tropical to winter, back to tropical, and then into summer. The winter passage, around the South African coast, is a matter of three to five days. Originally this meant that for the brief portion of the journey around the Cape the ship had to be down to her winter marks. She therefore had to load less oil in the Gulf to comply. In *Ardshiel*'s case, for example, this would have meant loading about 4,000 fewer tons of oil: a lot of oil, and a lot of profit to sacrifice. In 1966, when the advent of the VLCCs meant that the Cape passage was becoming a fixed calculation in the tanker business, IMCO was asked to reconsider the matter, and it did. The Load-Line Convention was amended and in July 1968 tankers were allowed to round the Cape on summer marks. They already had been given sanction to load more cargo as well. They paid a price in punishment from the weather, and the coasts and those waters also paid a price. The master of one Swedish tanker described watching one wave advance over his decks from the bows at sufficient height to smash and flood his bridge. When a tanker is deeply loaded it has very little freeboard and, as in the case of that Swede, the water smashes over it as it would over a low-lying reef. Some of the worst slicks in that area have been attributed to cargo dumping by masters who feared for the safety of their ships.

But storm has actually been the least of supertanker fears. Their overlarge oil tanks are the seat of frightening and still incompletely understood forces when empty. Three 200,000 tonners were torn by tank explosions so severe that their long decks rolled back as though opened like cans of sardines. One of them, the Shell tanker *Marpessa*, sank on 15 December 1969, and achieved the unhappy distinction of becoming the largest vessel ever to founder. She lost this distinction in 1973, however, when the 216,326-ton Liberian tanker *Golar Patricia* also exploded and sank off West Africa. Supertankers thus altered the maritime scale in disaster to the same outlandish degree that they have affected it in everything else.

FIVE

Ardshiel sailed away fast across a humidly silver sea; the day was the twenty-fifth of June and, as the Gironde coast vanished into the haze, I had the unhappy feeling of the whole summer being folded away with the horizon. It was, as I discovered, a feeling of sudden intense disappointment I shared with the entire vessel. The flowers and rural greenness of Le Verdon had been deeply unsettling to all those who'd been on the ship for some time, as well as to those who'd boarded in Rotterdam. In its place they could now look forward to two crossings of the equator, one week of southern winter and two of northern summer recurring every five weeks.

The ship seemed very different as I descended from the bridge after our three o'clock departure. I was for the first time fully aware of how huge the interior was. This was because it was suddenly so empty. All activity had died. No commands on the blower. No slamming doors or distantly ringing bells. No hurried steps. No traffic on the stairs.

On the way down from Rotterdam *Ardshiel* had seemed as crowded and noisy as a liner. The relieving officers had boarded in Holland but, since the voyage officially ended only at Le Verdon with full discharge of the cargo, those they had come to relieve remained on board until we got to the Gironde. We'd had two chief officers and two chief engineers at the master's table for all meals. Some of the wives of officers who were not getting off had joined the ship for the short run down the Channel. All young and modish, they'd filled the ship with chatter and colour. Their absence now extended the feeling of a bright season lost.

The wardroom, where they'd danced nightly under flashing discothèque lights to a noise so loud that it seemed propulsive of the vessel itself, was empty. From its windows the main deck looked even more abandoned, and the catwalk running all the way forward and dwindling into distance suggested a path that one day one might follow for a solitary walk into the unknown. But it was a listless thought.

For such a general and disturbing sense of anticlimax and depressive introspection there is truly only one remedy at such an hour: the British ritual of afternoon tea. And, sitting in my cabin wondering about so many weeks and even months of sea and ship, the companionable rattle of tea-things on trays began to break the silence of the passageways outside, imposing discipline upon the emotions and a more comforted and reassured state of mind. It is a delicious sound upon afternoon quiet, declaring the arrival of strong brew for the end of reverie, though without any tone of forcefulness; implying rather an imminent homely intrusion, something nicely fussy to give one a sense of domestic encouragement to help one prepare for and contend with the two or three difficult hours that remain until twilight and more concrete refreshment. And the tray when it came was worthy of all expectation: shiny porcelain and silver arranged upon a starched cloth, hot tea, hot water for replenishing the pot, and hot crisp toast soused in melting butter. There was a strainer for the leaves and when poured the liquid properly was the colour of teak. The ship was rolling very slightly and the cabin windows shifted bars of hard and brittle light upon the floor. It scarcely mattered. Nothing else can so adequately defend one against the harsh quality of afternoon light as an English tea-tray, unless it be a Scottish one, laid with hot oatcakes. This P & O tray had quite sufficient of the substance of tradition, however: Thank God you're on a British ship, it appeared to say. Or was it I myself doing so?

'Strong enough?' the cabin steward asked.

'Yes, thank you.'

'More hot water?'

'No, thank you.'

'Would you like some more toast?'

'No, thank you. Well, perhaps I shall.'

Such moments, one feels, become the true hinges of survival.

Many of them would seem to be necessary on a supertanker, and the big tanker fleets make a point of providing them. For all their outward austerity supertankers often are remarkably well fitted and provisioned, and *Ardshiel* fortunately was one of these.

Supertankers are cheaper by the dozen so they usually come in batches, with whole clusters of ships, so to speak, pressed from the same mould. *Ardshiel* was one of four identical ships ordered by P & O from the Japanese yard of Mitsui Shipbuilding. Her keel was laid on 18 February 1969, she was launched on 4 August, and delivered on 1 December, which put her in the first generation of these ships.

On the water, *Ardshiel* looked a lot better than most supertankers. She had a large, elegantly raked modern funnel instead of functional, reedlike engine-room uptakes as so many tankers do. Her superstructure, too, looked shiplike instead of resembling a high-rise utility apartment block. Anyone with an eye for ships might have guessed to whom she belonged because old-established shipping lines have a penchant for architectural continuity even in their most revolutionary vessels; whatever the newfangled technology may bring, they like at least a hint of the way they have always done things in the past. P & O has the largest passenger fleet in the world; therefore it is not surprising that the influence of that experience should have affected the tanker tonnage. *Ardshiel*'s superstructure conveyed the multi-windowed suggestion of a passenger liner, and it was astonishing to regard the four principal decks upon which all these windows were arranged and to realise that they were mainly for the occupation of fourteen officers and, occasionally, their wives. The entire accommodation, from the portholed crew's deck below the main deck up to and including the bridge, covered seven decks. These were connected by wide stairways in a colour scheme of yellow and black, as well as by a lift which, rising from the bottom of the engine room to the bridge, had a shaft of about one hundred and fifty feet.

The foremost impression inside this superstructure was of the prodigious amount of space allowed merely by the beam of the ship. Alleyways running across the vessel seemed as long as the fore and aft ones on many passenger liners; they were as wide as halls.

As in a passenger liner, every deck in *Ardshiel*'s superstructure was named. The topmost was the Bridge Deck, where the bridge itself was situated. This deck had one especially agreeable feature. The rails surrounding it were of traditional teak; all others, except those encircling the swimming pool, were of metal. It was a small touch, but a human one; and one found oneself instinctively moving to this deck of an evening, or whenever one was disposed to view the sea, simply for the pleasure of leaning one's elbows upon a broad, comfortably warm, old-fashioned wooden ship's rail, the way one would on a passenger liner. To the degree that pleasures are relative, this texture gave that area the quality of a garden; and the pleasure was strengthened by the view over the green waters of the large swimming pool and its sunning area.

The ship's grandest accommodation was spread out on the deck below, the Captain's Bridge Deck. Three considerable suites accounted for practically all the space on this deck. These were the captain's to starboard, the chief engineer's on the port side, and the owner's in between. The chief engineer's and the captain's suites were identical: office, dayroom – with a refrigerator for drinks and snacks – bedroom, and bathroom. The owner's suite was a big open-plan room impersonally furnished and decorated in that softly upholstered, heavily carpeted and densely curtained manner of airport hotels. It was rarely used.

The Upper Bridge Deck and Middle Bridge Deck housed the rest of the officers as well as the petty officers. The two second engineers and the first officer, occupying the former, had suites virtually identical to those of the master and the chief engineer. My own cabin on the Middle Bridge Deck was typical of the accommodation provided for the junior officers. A small entrance hall gave separate access to the shower and toilet. The apartment itself was dominated by two large windows overlooking the sea and set close to the double bed (all beds were double for when wives exercised their option to accompany their husbands). The opposite end of the cabin was devoted to a living-and-work area: a long sofa, coffee-table, armchairs, and a wide desk with strong lamps. Like the rest of the accommodation in the ship it was carpeted wall-to-wall and air-conditioned.

The crew was just as well housed. Their quarters below the main deck were ingeniously arranged along wide, enclosed blue-tiled promenade decks running inside the ship's hull on both the port and starboard sides and illuminated by rows of closely set portholes. Their cabins, mostly single, were furnished with bed, desk, wash-basin, cupboards, carpets and chairs: large glass windows allowed their occupants to gaze out onto the promenade and to benefit from its natural light. Living in these quarters were four Hong Kong Chinese, ten Indians, most of them from Goa, and twenty Pakistanis. On the main deck just above they had their games room and mess, a handsome room stretching the width of the superstructure and with large windows overlooking the stern and the wake.

The Lower Bridge Deck between the main deck and the Middle Bridge Deck was the social centre of the ship containing a cinema-scope theatre, games room, hospital, and the officers' wardroom, library, and dining saloon.

There was very little on this deck to suggest shipboard life as experienced by any previous generation of mariners. The swimming pool and cinema are no longer regarded as luxuries but as indispensable items of supertanker life; and of the two the films are probably the most important. The main feature changed twice a week, selected from boxes delivered to the ship at the terminals and when passing the Cape. The films are seen over and over again, good or bad; even when, as sometimes happens, a ship drops a box only to find that it has been replaced by another containing films only recently seen.

82

The principal social centre of the ship was the officers' wardroom, a smart clublike room with teak-panelled bulkheads. 'It's only veneer,' Basil Thomson had remarked in answer to my approving comment when he first showed me around, with the dismissive tone of a man who had formed his sense of shipboard panels amid solid teak, mahogany, and walnut. Nonetheless it gave the room, and other parts of the ship where it was used, a pleasant hint of forethought, warmth, and solidity which formica and plastic, the usual dress of tanker accommodation, and indeed very much in evidence aboard *Ardshiel*, could not render. In the wardroom this panelling was complemented by an imaginative use of black, orange, and oatmeal tones. Long black leather sofas and easy chairs were grouped around white coffee-tables at one end, while at the other was a bar with stools. The room was carpeted in black, and at night orange curtains covered its long row of forward-looking windows. It contained also a two-hundred-volume library (changed at the end of every voyage) which offered a well-balanced selection, including Scott Fitzgerald, Solzhenitsyn, Robert Ardrey, John O'Hara, V. S. Pritchett, Waugh, Graham Greene, Tolstoy, Conrad, Agatha Christie, Hemingway, and Len Deighton, as well as various items of history, travel, biography, and autobiography. For further diversion there was a dartboard, short-wave radio, tape recorder and record player, and television. Some tanker companies send boxes of television tapes, especially of notable sports events, to their ships along with the films.

The oatmeal and orange tones of the wardroom continued into the dining-room next door which one entered through double doors of frosted glass. A P & O master appears in the wardroom only for coffee after dinner, unless otherwise invited; but in the dining-room his writ runs large: that is, if he wishes it to. For him, it is a place of public appearance second only to the bridge and therefore a natural extension of his style, preferences, and caprice. In a P & O master these can be considerable, and with Basil Thomson they often were.

The P & O has always made much of the fact that it gave the word 'posh' to English idiom. The word began life as a booking clerk's term in the late nineteenth century; it meant Port Out – Starboard Home, and a wise traveller of the day stipulated this formula when booking his cabin to the east and back for it put him on the shaded side of the ship both ways, away from the fiercest heat of the day on the passage through Suez and the Red Sea. Posh became a word that did for the whole style of passage by P & O, and it was the sort of style which the North Atlantic, so vulgarly competitive on various levels of ostentation, never really achieved, except perhaps in the White Star ships, which in their day were much more the gentleman's way than even the genteel though less fashionable Cunarders were. They were floating country houses rather than floating hotels, offering the same impeccable protocols and mannered informality, and this was very much the tone of the P & O.

Such strong identities are fading in the maritime world as fast as they are on shore; the individual shipowner, who once set his stamp upon whole trades, is becoming a thing of the past, his whims and fancies now lost in take-overs, mergers, and regroupings. P & O was founded by a partnership between two London shipowners named Wilcox and Anderson, who involved themselves in the Portuguese civil war of 1832 and later the Carlist wars of Spain; the word 'Peninsular' in the company's name commemorates the original Iberian services, which were extended to India in 1840, when the full title of Peninsular and Oriental Steam Navigation Company was incorporated by royal charter. Thereafter P & O was as potently symbolic of the British Empire and its mercantile hegemony as the Royal Navy itself, and perhaps even more so, for if the navy suggested power P & O conveyed the realities of it. Kipling seemed never able to keep the company out of his verses, and small wonder. It was the imperial connection: and there was nothing more persuasive of the fact than the sight of a big P & O mailboat on its aloof way through Suez, its black hull and black funnels separated by stone-coloured upperworks, white uniforms and plenty of gold braid on its bridge, its inevitable blue ensign dipping solemnly to the warships met en route, and bugles imperatively advising its first class to start dressing for dinner. It would not have occurred to any viceroy, governor, military commander, maharajah, or nabob to choose any other means of coming or going. Stanley began his journey to find Livingstone aboard a P & O ship, and Florence Nightingale began her mission on one as well. The commodores and masters of these ships themselves stood high in the upper imperial ranks, and often had considerable renown for their way with their ships, many of which were run with the high-handed style and flair of a feudal barony.

The P & O is still Britain's biggest shipowner. Aside from tankers and passenger liners, its diverse operations include freighters, salvage tugs, offshore oil rigs, liquid gas carriers, container ships, and car ferries. Through this position of strength P & O has managed to retain much character and even eccentricity where elsewhere a lot of the flavour has gone from shipboard life. Much of this retained flavour in P & O undoubtedly is due to the company's continued tradition of employing Indian and Pakistani crews under British officers, so that its ships reflect that oddly cosy mixture of Simla east and Cheltenham west that remains stamped upon so much of India itself.

There were moments aboard Ardshiel when I felt that I was on one of those very old-fashioned mailboats moving east of Suez a good many decades ago, and never was this more so than at night when, punctually at seven thirty, Basil Thomson led a small procession of his senior officers down from the evening's sundowner's party, or 'pour-out' as they preferred to call it, to the dining saloon, all dressed for dinner in 'Red Sea rig'. An informal dinner dress for warm climates which dispenses with tie and jacket while retaining the decorum of proper change for the evening, the ensemble consists of black dress trousers, silk cummerbund, and white short-sleeved shirt with gold-braided insignia of rank worn on the shoulder tabs. We moved into a dining-room where the Goanese stewards awaited us in stiff white jackets, grouped around their tables of fresh linen, silverware, and individual printed menus in silver holders.

Dinner chimes were broadcast throughout the ship at seven, but these were for the junior officers, who were expected to have finished by the time the captain's party arrived. Cadet Davis, a slow eater apparently, occasionally was still munching when we came in. 'Since you're still there, you'd better bring your plate over here,' Thomson would say sharply, with the tone of a man whose sense of order had been disturbed, and later, when Davis finally had finished, 'You can excuse yourself now!'

The dinner courses came and went silently, arriving upon salvers and served upon hot chinaware. Not much was ever said, except by Thomson, who, as masters are wont to do, exercised the right of monologue.

The food was exceptional, whether breakfast or dinner. A normal breakfast menu might be stewed apples, cornflakes, oatmeal, smoked cod in milk, sausage mince cakes, fried potatoes, cheese or plain omelettes, eggs to order, rolls and toast, tea or coffee. Lunch always featured a curry: birianis, keftas, Madras, dry mince and Deil sauce, vindaloos, Sally Mutton; and it was always served with chutney, popadoms, diced tomato, onion, coconut, and currants. A typical dinner could be mock turtle soup, grilled sole Tartare, roast veal and stuffing, baked and boiled potatoes, cauliflower, peach Melba, and that essentially English course, the savoury, such as bloater paste on toast.

After dinner, the party moved to the coffee-table in the wardroom. 'Who is going to be mum?' someone invariably asked, and whoever was nearest to the coffee began pouring, while others handed around the cups, the milk, and the sugar. Thomson usually dominated the conversation, and recounted to the juniors tales of his past experience, to which they patiently listened. These were stories they'd heard often enough, and would hear many times again before they left the ship. It was not however a lengthy ordeal. After half an hour

85

or so, the master would suddenly announce, 'Well, I suppose I'll go up and do my book of words,' and vanished. As a rule, he was followed by the chief engineer.

The departure of the two most senior officers brought a distinct lightening of atmosphere to the room; but, however much it lightened, the mood of the wardroom always remained somewhat formal and well-mannered. There was seldom any horseplay or ribaldry. One was again aware of the social lassitude of long confinement: that quality of desultory and inactive converse that is not listlessness but rather that emptiness of real mutual interest that settles upon men who have heard each other out too often. And one was aware not so much of the remoteness of the world at large but of most of the ship itself; it was the feeling of being inside a walled-in community upon one end of an otherwise uninhabited island whose opposite shore few ever bothered to visit and some scarcely knew, and which one actually had to wonder about from time to time.

The wardroom in *Ardshiel* was used a great deal more than it was in other tankers, so they all said; on other ships one apparently could seldom expect more than two or three people to be gathered in it at night; yet it struck me that activity in *Ardshiel*'s wardroom died soon enough. They seemed to prefer gathering in each other's cabins, as if in retreat from the huge and impinging emptiness of the ship; and there, in a fog of smoke and a growing litter of beer cans, the hubbub, ribaldry, affectionate jeering, and repartee absent from the wardroom asserted itself.

When people started to drift from the wardroom one evening I decided to follow the path to the other end of our island and went down and started along the catwalk to the bows. The night was overcast and very black, and the farther one went the stranger and lonelier and more frightening the experience became. The front of a ship's superstructure is always dark, all windows heavily curtained, to avoid spoiling night vision from the bridge, so that one walked from a façade that showed no hint of light; but there was at least the sheltering comfort of its towering proximity. After a while one lacked even that; it was distant and only faintly discernible, and still the steel path ran on into the dark as far as one's straining eyes could see. Ships had always had great appeal for me at night, when their peace and detachment seem greatest. I felt quite different on *Ardshiel*'s main deck, and what I felt was close to the fringe of fear, or even terror if one allowed oneself to be impressionable about it, which would not have been too difficult.

An unpleasant loneliness grew from this apprehension of the ship's gloomy distances. One felt the arid metal acreage spreading invisibly all around, and its impact was one of menace: a mechanical desert of indefinable purpose imposed upon the sea's own emptiness, and with forms and shapes that had no reassuring familiarity; it was filled with wind signs, not those of masts and rigging but of abandoned structures upon a plain, and there was no comfort even from the sea. One did not even feel its presence amidships on that path over the somnolent pipes and obscure fittings; the sea lay somewhere a long way below the remote and unseen edge of the deck on either side, and what saltiness reached one's lips had the taste of steel.

The overpowering impression was of desolation and severance from that vague far-off castle one had left; but when I returned there I found it entirely abandoned as well. Those who had been drinking and talking when I left had gone, presumably into the cabins, and, as aboard the *Mary Celeste*, only the fragments of their recent presence lay about: half-emptied glasses of beer, the open magazines, full ashtrays, and cups of cold untouched coffee. One passed from wardroom to dining saloon, to cinema, games room, hospital, emergency room, up the stairways and along the deserted alleyways, encountering no sound or sign of another human. And when, on sudden compulsion, I took the lift down to the engine room as well, the melancholy surrealism of the experience seemed complete, for the engines are switched to automatic controls at night and over the weekend and left running on their own. The engine room consequently was as fearful as the deck. It was disturbing to follow those narrow fly-overs, suspended sixty feet over the pounding machinery, and to find one's imagination susceptible once more to aloneness in a mechanical world, especially one of such ceaseless and unaccountable activity.

I returned to the lift and went up to the bridge, the only place where one knew one would find someone without having to knock on a door, and, as it slowly ascended, felt that I could well understand why, as First Officer Alan Ewart-James had informed me, Stanley Kubrick's 2001 had been so unpopular in the theatres of these ships when it was shown.

'You often suddenly get that feeling of ghosts or a presence when you stand alone up here at night,' Third Officer Stephen Tucker remarked when I recounted my various journeys. He had been sitting in the starboard captain's chair gazing into the darkness when I arrived, and he offered it to me. The old man had been gone only ten minutes, he said. He came up every night at ten for his cocoa, which Tucker brewed, checked how things were, gave his orders, and then retired. Once he'd left he never came back unless called, and Tucker then felt he could safely sit in his chairs. On another ship they used to bring the two captain's chairs together and sit and chat the hours away. Tonight he'd been sitting here thinking about that.

There were times, he said, when he felt that one could go round the bend on these ships.

Tucker began calculating distances. Did I know it would take a car travelling sixty miles an hour twelve seconds to travel the length of the ship? A sprinter would need five seconds to dash across the main deck! He added, with suddenly diminished spirit, 'I was in good form at dinner and we all had a good giggle at our table. But it's always the same; around half past ten I begin feeling what's the use of it all, this life.'

The all-aft structure of supertankers began appearing in the early sixties. Before that, the standard profile of oil tankers had been that of the old *Gluckauf*, with engines aft and bridge amidships. Ships as big as 100,000 tons were still built on this pattern. These old-style tankers had conventional masts and funnels, a certain degree of rake and sheer, and, after the Second World War, showed a lot of pride in their design and appearance. This was especially true of many tankers built by the Greeks Niarchos and Onassis who, acknowledged as masters of the business in the fifties and the sixties, responded with flair and showmanship, and good taste. Their flagships had lovely lines and nice colours. They were ships that other sailors admired and envied. Word that a new Onassis ship was passing could bring the crew out on deck, the way a new candidate for the North Atlantic Blue Riband would during the thirties.

Torrey Canyon was a good example of the last ships of this type, and when she wrecked herself even the dreadful pollution spilling from her tanks couldn't diminish the grief one felt on seeing the dramatic photographs of this ship broken almost completely in half and the two halves folded into a V shape by the seas. She clearly had been a very handsome vessel, beautifully kept, and one assumed an owner's pride in her as an individual.

Those ships not only looked very different but they had as well an entirely different culture and pattern of living. The crew and engineers lived aft, above the machinery. The dining saloons and galleys and recreation rooms were also placed there. The master and other navigating officers lived in the midships structure, below the bridge and, in effect, the ship consisted of two communities connected by a catwalk. This maintained more emphatically even than on other sorts of ships the traditional rivalry between deck officers and engineering officers. Segregated aft with the crew, albeit convenient to their machinery, the engineers on the old tankers felt that the living arrangements merely enhanced the deck officers' traditional sense of higher caste and overall superiority. It was a quarrel as old as steam propulsion.

Whatever it did to aesthetics, the all-aft principle of construction (introduced for economy, and because it was felt to be safer in the event of explosions) changed entirely the social structure of tankers, putting the engineers and navigators together, with the chief engineer and the ship's captain finally and unequivocally sharing status and the same deck. But automation has carried these changes even further. Where once there were only two castes, navigators and engineers, there now is another, the electronics men; and they, it already is assumed, will be the future masters: in many ways they already are.

Only a decade ago the ship's electrician was a petty officer who changed the light bulbs and fixed the fuses. He is now called the electrical officer, and he is accepted on the master's and chief engineer's level of seniority. Behind the resentment the engineers used to feel was the belief that ultimately it was they rather than the navigators who were the least dispensable in the running of the ship, but even they now probably stand behind the electronics men when it comes to dispensability; for the electrical officer's brief is the complex and beautiful maze of coloured wiring of the multitudinous systems that control these ships.

There are supertankers already in operation whose navigation, cargo-loading and discharge, engine operation, crew's wages, and even medical diagnosis are handled by computer. The computers receive a ship's position from satellites and steer it accordingly; they avoid collision by monitoring the radar's reports of surrounding ships and then initiate the necessary manœuvres so as to keep clear of them. While such installations are too costly to be general (Ardshiel herself was automated only in the engine room), they represent the trend, and the unmanned ship sailing the seas by remote control is now considered the inevitable and natural progression of it all, though the more likely event, probably within a decade, will be the management of ships by a small team of technician-navigators no larger than the flight crew of an airliner who will surrender command and control to the terminals they are approaching. Such revolutionary experiments undoubtedly will start with Japanese, American, and West European-owned vessels, not only because they are the ones who can afford them but also because they are the ones who have the biggest problem in finding crews for their ships.

These changes and prospects dominated much of the conversation aboard Ardshiel, and there was general acknowledgment that this was the last generation of sailors and seamanship in the old-fashioned sense, and that the traditional supreme authority and overlordship of the captain was so to speak over. One British company, partly owned by P & O, already had dropped the title of captain and was calling the ship's master 'manager', while the ship itself was being run by a 'committee' consisting of navigation, engineering, and electrical officers. If there had been recrimination before between navigators and engineers, any dispute now was academic; or so it appeared. Both sides now sat regarding, with a dispassionate sense of common cause, the gradual simultaneous demise of its own kind. Basil Thomson's summarising rejoinder to the others was invariably the same: 'Well, I've only got two years to go so none of it worries me.'

Ardshiel was a ship that reflected as much as any vessel could, one felt, the very turning point of all these momentous events at sea. She sailed with the past and its conventions on her bridge, and the semi-automated present in her engine room; and the future had its proper symbol in the presence at the master's right hand at table of Dave Haydon, the electrical officer. There was everywhere a knowledge of difference; not just the literal one created by the ship's size, but more impressively that distinct social and psychological one as well.

With other ships in other days, a voyage began and it ended. It had the identity of a single experience and could be a whole distinct memory. Only disaster or near-disaster can do the same for supertankers. Otherwise each voyage is indistinguishable from another. The voyage in fact never really ends. Life aboard them revolves continuously and repetitiously. All crews overlap; at each terminal there is somebody or other whose time stint is up, and he is relieved by another, who waits on the dock as the ship ties up. The relief man walks into a routine that hasn't even paused. As Alan Ewart-James remarked one day, 'In the old days you came aboard a ship in dock, looked around, found your cabin and the lay of the land, got to know the ship, chatted to people sitting around in the saloon or standing about on deck, and slowly settled in. On these ships you come aboard and you're handed a boiler suit and you're right down to it. You resume where you left off two months ago on the other ship.'

When they are built in batches supertankers are so similar, even in their decorative schemes, that anyone getting off one ship and returning to another of the same class two months later when his leave is up might easily suppose it is the vessel he left. In time, a whole class, such as Ardshiel and her three sisters, Ardlui, Ardvar, and Ardtaraig (a fifth was built but P & O dropped its option on it), is regarded in reality as one ship. 'These ships', they tend to say even when discussing some domestic matter aboard Ardshiel. Sentiment is difficult to evoke when a man comes back to the same dials, the same accommodation layout, the same room and, if unlucky, the same batch of films and books.

This repetitious environment and circumstance make some feel as though they are aboard a modern form of the *Flying Dutchman*, destined to pass to and fro around the Cape for ever more; but such standardisation has distinct advantages. Alan Ewart-James for one preferred this system to the old which he had described. It meant, so far as he was concerned, that when a man came aboard he had no time to dwell upon what he'd left behind because he was on the job immediately and, once the ship was away, was so settled into the whole routine once more that the worst part of the loneliness and sense of separation from the shore was over.

The common international practice for all merchant ships such as *Ardshiel* is to carry, besides the master, at least three watch-keeping navigating officers (passenger liners usually have double this number or even more). In the case of Britain, the chief and second officers would hold a certificate of competency obtained after stringent written and oral examinations supervised by the Department of Trade, which is the British government department in charge of merchant navy matters, and the third officer is often certificated as well. These officers stand watches in rotation on the bridge, four hours at a time; thus each of them does two four-hour watches within every twenty-four-hour period.

The most junior of them, the third officer, has the two eight-to-twelve watches, finishing at noon and at midnight. The second officer has the succeeding twelve-to-four watches, and the first officer (or chief officer as he more often is referred to) has the four-to-eight watches. The master does not stand a watch, unless he voluntarily relieves one of his juniors. The engineers would have a similar system on ships that weren't automated; on a vessel such as *Ardshiel*, they go down in a body for a normal full working day, with one of them delegated to answer automatic alarms from below during the night.

In British ships the navigating side usually comes from the southern or western parts of the British isles while the engineers as a rule are from the north; they are either from Scotland or they are Geordies, from the industrial and coal-mining area of Newcastle upon Tyne and its satellite towns. South-of-the-border Scotsmen I one day called *Ardshiel*'s Geordies, to their horror, but it is a description that nonetheless serves the outside world, to whom they sound virtually indistinguishable from the real thing.

Basil Thomson lived near Brighton. Alan Ewart-James was from Southend, at the mouth of the Thames, while Second Officer Alfred Hattrell and Stephen Tucker were from the Greater London area. None of them had had any relations or friends in common before meeting on the various company ships. The engineers on the other hand often gave one the impression of being members of the same clan. The Geordies provided the essential warmth and gaiety aboard.

Geordieland, as they themselves called it, remains one of Britain's depressed areas. Their collective memory was of hardship; most either had worked in the coal mines or had relatives doing so; yet the communal mark of it seemed to be an attitude of gentle, reproving humour. It was helped by the fact that most of them came from the twin towns of North or South Shields and were constantly discovering friends, neighbours, or relatives in common; that is, if they hadn't in fact known one another or about one another since childhood. It was obvious that North and South Shields had provided generations of engineers to the British merchant marine, and in addition to the ceaseless joyful discovery that they had shared the same schools, pubs, girl friends, or cousins by marriage, they took one deeper into the ramifications of their complicated social structure by discovering that uncles, fathers, and grandfathers had served on the same ships, or were torpedoed together on the old so-and-so in the last war. They were unaffected, lacking entirely the southerner's inviolate sense of class and social levels, and there was sudden disapproving silence when, after dinner one evening during a discussion of football and the salaries that modern British footballers got, Thomson leaned back and cried, 'It's all very well, but when a man so highly paid and captain of a team opens his mouth on television, it's a pity that so often he can't even speak decent English. They've got dreadful accents. When you consider the English they speak, it's a terrible letdown.'

The Geordies sat looking into their coffee cups until James Jackson, the chief engineer, said, 'Well, I don't know what accents have got to do with playing football.'

'It spoils the image,' Thomson said. 'It definitely does.'

Jackson, his two principal subordinates, Harvey Phillips and Peter Dutton, both of whom were second engineers, and the two third engineers, Graham Allen and Charlie Bradley, were all from either North or South Shields. The junior engineer, Graham Chalmers, and the engineering cadet, Eddie Ronnie, were Scotsmen.

There was a cordial, easygoing relationship between Jackson and his engineers which was markedly different from that between Basil Thomson and his navigating officers, who anyway were on less obviously intimate terms with each other than the engineers. Thomson, an often cantankerous disciplinarian, was not a popular master to sail with. He was strict on rules: the normal seagoing ones, company ones, and his own, many of which were simply arbitrary and some of which were decidedly strange. It was on the bridge, of course, that his whims were most apparent. Every officer taking over a watch during which Basil Thomson was likely to appear on the bridge (the only one in fact during which he made no regular appearance was the second officer's midnight to four in the morning) made an immediate check of a somewhat intricate mental list of Thomson's idiosyncrasies to be sure that none was being violated. Stephen Tucker had sailed with him as a cadet and had rueful memories of the experience; as the most junior and therefore most vulnerable of the navigating officers he was particularly meticulous in seeing that Thomson's major and minor edicts were all complied with.

When he began his watch, say the eight to midnight, he passed slowly around the bridge setting right anything that was not as Thomson wished it to be. The two captain's chairs had to be precisely six inches from the bulkhead, the binoculars lying in their canvas bin on the console had to have the viewing ends pointing *inboard*, thirteen switches on the console had to be adjusted to give the exact strength of illumination Thomson preferred on their dials.

When I arrived on the bridge one evening he was setting the ship's log book dead centre on a shelf in the chartroom. 'Not port or starboard but *amidships* it has to be,' he said. 'Bas wants things just so, and no deviation, otherwise it's a rocket.' No books, except those immediately in use, were allowed on the chartroom table; no charts either. When the ship was on automatic pilot there was no need for charts to be lying around, Thomson maintained. With every course change the charts should be taken out and, when the work was done, folded and set back in their drawers. This, Tucker agreed, was a reasonable enough request. 'But if I overlook a pencil whose point hasn't been sharpened, that's a rocket too.'

When, that very evening, he did appear on the bridge Thomson's eye missed nothing. He picked up the telephone, set it just so, moved the port captain's chair half an inch back, checked the row of Admiralty Pilots to see that the volumes were all there and in sequence, touched the binoculars, glanced at the switches and, finding nothing amiss, began taxing Tucker with making too much noise above his head on the earlier watch. 'The starboard door was jammed, sir,' Tucker said.

'You don't have to take the ship to the breaker's yard to unjam it!' Thomson cried.

'I'm sorry, sir.'

'That ship we were overtaking, have we passed it?'

'Yes, sir.'

'When?'

'Half an hour ago, sir.'

'What was her name?'

'It was too far to make it out.'

'You didn't talk to her on the lamp?'

'No, sir.'

'You didn't call her up?'

'No, sir,' Tucker was emphatic. Thomson did not allow his officers to talk to passing vessels on the radio-telephone, unless there was good reason.

'What line was she?'

'She looked like a Clan boat.'

'What do you mean "looked like"? There's no mistaking two red rings on a black funnel, which is what every Clan ship has, and has had for donkey's years. Anyway there's no Clan ship so slow these days that we'd overtake her. Did you look up her markings in *Flags and Funnels?*'

'It wasn't light enough to really see, sir.'

'Not light enough to read *Flags and Funnels*, or to see her colours?'

'Not light enough to see her colours, sir.'

'Perhaps you'd better have your eyes checked before you sit for your next examinations!'

Regardless of his irritability or whims there was one point which everyone saw markedly in Basil Thomson's favour: he was not a man who sprang unfair surprises. He laid down his routine and stuck to it. If he was due on the bridge at seven he arrived on the dot, not a moment before nor one after. That way, Ewart-James remarked, they all knew where they were, unlike other masters who liked to sneak up on their officers to catch them off guard.

Thomson's daily routine began when he relieved Ewart-James for the last hour of his four-to-eight watch. His emergence from his suite was to all intents and purposes the beginning of the ship's day as well. 'Before seven,' Ewart-James told me, 'I can dance the hootchy-kootchy, swing from the rafters, sit in the old man's chairs, leave things scattered about, but at seven the bridge must be the way the old man wants it, with everything just so and so. It's a fair bargain.'

The hard part of the bargain began for everyone else as well at that hour. Thomson went down to breakfast at eight, when Tucker appeared on the bridge for the eight to twelve, and his descent, as always, was a critical examination of all points en route: the tidiness and polish of the alleyways, stairs, the wardroom and, finally, the dining-room itself. At nine he met his officers for a conference on ship's business. When they had left he sat at his desk doing whatever paperwork there was; at sea, this was mainly of his own creation – orders, memoranda to individuals, revised instructions to various departments, items for the notice board clipped from the various maritime and safety publications he received. The paperwork that he himself generated in this manner was often considerable and, as he insisted upon stamping every item, the steadfast sound of the master stamping papers was the one most likely to be heard as one passed his office, which was also the main entrance to his suite (even letters which he forwarded after I'd eventually left the ship each bore his small oval stamp and red-ink signature).

After the day's stamping, and approval of the menus brought to him by the chief steward, he would perhaps make one of his regular inspections of different parts of the ship. He lunched in his quarters and, at two, went to the bridge to relieve the second officer for an hour and a half on the twelve-to-four watch. This gave him, he said, the chance to do his daily exercises, light arm-waving calisthenics, which he performed as he strode to and fro from one bridge wing to the other; as he did so his eyes were never still, as intent and curious as those of a slow-circling gull, missing no flick of movement of surface life on his decks; and, watching him thus, his physical domination of his world appeared complete: even if one were watching from the bows, distance appeared to enlarge rather than diminish his bulk, so that it seemed as he strode out to port or starboard that he was quite likely to tip down the far ends of that solid structure.

These appearances on the bridge were of course entirely voluntary, and much appreciated by those he relieved; the morning's relief allowed Ewart-James to go down to his cabin to wash and change into uniform before going to breakfast (the night and dawn watches are traditionally given latitude for informal dress on these ships), while in Hattrell's case it left him free to enjoy at least part of the middle of the day which he otherwise might not have had.

Thomson himself obviously enjoyed these interludes; they helped break the long reach of the days at sea by providing two periods of fixed occupation around which the rest of his day was built and they brought him out of his quarters where, as he himself said, he either would have had to twiddle his thumbs or find something else to do, presumably more paperwork and stamping. Or brooding, the unhealthy preference of many masters, according to Ewart-James, who was more defensive of Basil Thomson's ways and methods than the more junior officers appeared to be. While many young men preferred not to sail with Thomson if they could avoid it, he himself had deliberately chosen to do so to get to know the man; he'd seen it as a challenge, and was pleased that he had found his own way of handling him. 'When I'm expecting him on the bridge,' he told me one dawn when I found him hastily tidying up in preparation for Thomson's imminent arrival at seven, 'I check everything, and if I see nothing that he can grouse about then I leave one of the thirteen switches wrongly adjusted. He blows up, has a good grouse, and then he's happy and I don't hear from him again.'

Ardshiel's day had two clear lines of demarcation. These were the noon chit, and pour-out. The former was a small composition read over the ship's speaker system during lunch and prepared by Hattrell during the morning. This is an old P & O passenger-liner custom and there was the same respectful hush in the saloon as there would have been in a mailboat when the loudspeaker punctured the general hum of conversation and luncheon orders with its sudden expectant crackle of static, followed by Hattrell's solemn call, 'Your attention please, your attention please. This is the second officer speaking.' The severe formality of this introduction was one of Basil Thomson's strictures; perhaps because, as on any ship on a long voyage, the noon chit became, like mealtimes, one of the occasions of the day to be looked forward to and therefore deserving of form and some respect. Its essential function was to give the ship's mileage steamed since the previous noon, its speed, and its estimated time of arrival at its destination, but it was embellished by ship's notices such as lifeboat drill, announcements of royal birthdays and anniversaries, those of the Thomson family ('Today is the birthday of Betty Thomson'), crew birthdays, a Thought for the Day of the Christmas cracker kind, provided by Basil Thomson, and the relative position of Mecca ('Mecca is two points on the port bow') to enable the correct positioning of prayer mats by the Pakistani ratings, who were of course Moslems.

The principal diversion of the day was sundowner time, when the working day was over for most, enabling the juniors to gather in the wardroom and the seniors to start their pour-out in one or the other of the ship's several executive suites. Pour-out had been suspended on the voyage down through the strains and stresses of the English Channel to Le Verdon and my own first acquaintance of it came on the evening of our departure from the Gironde, when there was an unmistakable relief that the ship was free again and running – no tides or pilots or bloody Frogs and such to depend upon for another thirty days or so; the wider sea ahead, with hopefully fewer strains from surrounding traffic; a greater ease in everybody's manner, a certain cosiness in the sense of the ship gathered in upon itself once more, perhaps even a sort of joy; and yet, underneath it all, a wistfulness, a hint of the forlorn, as they retrieved the familiar communion of the hour and sought to get the conversation going.

But it came desultorily, and there were frequent silences as they sat with inward expressions, nursing their glasses; and we all listened gravely to the hum of the bottles as the vibration of the ship jarred them into contact on their tray. 'Oh ay,' James Jackson would say, leaning forward to pour out another gin, the movement and tone like a sudden resigned assertion of an accepted point of view. There was implicit concurrence in the attentive shift of their eyes as they watched him. Generous dollop of gin. Ice. Sprinkle of bitters. Tonic.

Lemon. 'Well, yes,' Basil Thomson agreed, as Jackson leaned back with his full glass. 'There we are, so it goes.'

Those present, aside from Thomson and Jackson and myself, were Harvey Phillips and Dave Haydon. Ewart-James was on watch and the only other officer eligible, Peter Dutton, had excused himself permanently from pour-out.

We sat in the deep chairs and sofa that were arranged in the master's dayroom around a long coffee-table on which the drinks were set. The evening was still bright but then Thomson's steward, Diaz, came in and drew the curtains along the two windowed bulkheads, encircling us in more soft material and shutting off the outside entirely, and we sat in opulent isolation, with the space beyond the coffee-table having an air of untenanted luxury and unwonted extravagance.

They began talking, as they frequently did, about the past; for most of them, that is for Jackson, Phillips, and Haydon, this meant the recent past of other ships and of those with whom they'd not so long ago sailed, but Thomson preferred the deeper prewar past, when to his mind P & O was still P & O. 'When old Sir William Currie was chairman he knew by name every one of the thousand or so officers serving on his ships. Every sailing, he came down the day before to make his own inspection, to see that the great P & O liner was as it should be. All the officers were assembled in a formal parade in order of rank in the first-class entrance. Sir William was piped aboard by the bo'suns' whistles and met by the captain and staff captain. He greeted every one of the officers lined up by name. When he'd inspected the ship he usually went up to the first officer's cabin for tea and toast. He liked his toast an inch thick, hot, with slabs of butter on it. When I became first officer I thought I'd test his memory to see if he was just memorising the names of the officers by rank before he came down from London, so I mixed them all up in different order; but Sir William greeted them all by the proper names, and, when he'd done, he said to me, "When I come up to your cabin for tea later mind you don't get my toast all wrong as well." After he'd gone, the public rooms were locked up again and everyone went over to the Tilbury Hotel to join the wives who were waiting there and who'd been shooed off the ship before the official party came down.'

'They were a fine lot, that generation,' Harvey Phillips said.

'That they were,' Thomson said appreciatively.

'Oh ay,' James Jackson said.

'Well, I dunno,' Dave Haydon said. 'Sometimes the good old days look better from a distance than they did then.'

'Well, we weren't spoiled the way this lot is today,' Thomson said.

'And I think we were a lot better for not being spoiled. When I started, a fourth mate's salary was nine pounds ten a month. A mess kit cost one month's salary and had to be bought. You couldn't get out of it. So, in fact, an officer got only eleven months' salary.'

'The Norwegians used to put British ships to shame the way they treated their seamen, there was a time when their wages were just about double ours,' Dave Haydon said.

'Hold on,' said Thomson.

'I heard they were a pretty grim lot to sail with anyhow,' Harvey Phillips said. 'No humour.'

'Well, you didn't get the stewards dressing up in drag and giving a show the way they do on British ships, I'll grant you,' Haydon said. 'But they had their moments. On that Norwegian ship I sailed in once between Louisiana and Le Havre – well, she was a dry ship, and one night I was telling them about the parties and good times we'd have on the P & O tankers. Her old man was a real sour humdinger, a regular Captain Bligh. But he listened to me, and then starts questioning me about the parties and how we ran them. Then he says, "All right, now we have a party. That's an order!" It was an order, all right. Everybody had to be there, cabin boys, stewardesses, the cook, deckhands, all the officers; the lot. He opened up the liquor store, laid it out in the saloon, and yelled, "Okay, you bastards, drink!" It was "Skol," and away you went! Five o'clock the next morning it was still going on. Bodies everywhere, and the old man chasing the chief steward with an axe because he'd chased somebody else. The officer who'd been on watch when it started was still on the bridge.'

'Well, I think that's overdoing it a bit,' Thomson said.

'They never stopped talking about it for months,' Haydon said.

'Well they might,' Harvey Phillips said.

'It reminds me of the trip I made once in an old cargo liner,' James Jackson said. 'She was a two-funnelled job. They built some of them like that after the war. The Greeks got her a long time ago. We took her out of Liverpool to St John's, Newfoundland, and Halifax in December. One of the worst trips of my life. The ship was in a terrible state. The crew nearly walked off. We had to keep the watertight doors closed because the stern gland was leaking. The radiators also leaked. It was warm enough when you went to bed but it all froze up during the night. One of the engineers jumped out of bed in the morning and went flat on his backside. The deck was one sheet of ice from the radiator leakage that had frozen. We were alongside in St John's for Christmas. The second steward was queer and had spent forty quid on a new wardrobe for the trip, new dresses and gowns, golden shoes, even silk underwear. When he was all done up you couldn't tell the difference. He went down to entertain the lads, but there was nothing on hand for us. So we phoned the matron of the hospital to ask for some nurses and she said, "Well, you better send someone up so we can have a look at you!" The third engineer and the second officer went. But there wasn't one under forty of the lot they brought back!'

'Charming!' Haydon said.

'You wouldn't be so fussy these days,' Harvey Phillips said.

'Reminds *me* of that trip in the old *Ellenga*,' cried Thomson, smacking his hands upon the arms of his chair. 'Remember, James?'

'Do I!' Jackson said. 'That was another.'

'Oh yes, but what a time.'

'Rust,' cried Jackson. 'Rust everywhere, you should have seen the hull, she was just a ball of rust. When Dorothy, my wife, came down to join us the taxi driver who'd brought her to the ship asked, "You going in that?"'

'That's because she'd been on the Atlantic run,' Thomson said. 'I don't know how long. She was like a ruddy submarine, with the funnel just sticking out the water. There had never been a chance to paint her. I joined her in Rijeka and the mate had finally painted her. When we got to Canada it was forty above but when the pilot came aboard he warned us that there was going to be a big drop in temperature. By the time we got to the berth it was thirty below. A seventy-degree drop in an hour and a half! After that, she just crumbled to rust. All that new paint just went. But she was a nice ship. I did eighteen months in her. She was the only tanker except this one in which I have served more than twice; being on her was one of the happiest times I've had.'

SIX

Two ships converge upon a clear sunlit empty sea. There is nothing in sight except these two vessels and the blue sky, a bluer sea, and a horizon of absolute clarity within whose arena this perverse little game of the gods is being determined. It is a game best played without distractions, upon a flat and unoccupied sea and with total visibility, so that only the essentials, the two ships and their ordained occupants, are involved. Will they or won't they?

It is one of the most common, dangerous, and strangest of situations at sea. We had rounded the north-west corner of Iberia and passed from the Bay of Biscay into the Atlantic, whose long slow even motions folded toward us and then away toward the land. We were back in the main shipping lanes, but the vessel we had sighted was the only one we had seen all morning. She was a tanker as well, much smaller, and she had appeared to be on the same course as ourselves; but then she was seen to be crossing. 'He's on a crossing course on my starboard so it's my duty to keep clear,' Stephen Tucker explained. 'He's on 210, we're on 244. I've brought her around thirty degrees, so his nearest approach point will be about a mile and three-quarters.' Without such precautions, we probably would have collided.

The other ship closed in and passed well ahead, as Tucker had predicted. She was about 25,000 tons, riding light, wearing Spanish colours, and, compared to *Ardshiel*'s calm progress across the beam swell, she was plunging and rolling to such an extent that one moment we were gazing at an expanse of wet underwater plates and the next at the whole panorama of her decks.

The episode reminded me of a similar but more dangerous one I'd experienced a few years before when I was a passenger on a Spanish freighter sailing from Seville to Montreal. It too had been on a blue, sunlit, and empty sea. A bulk carrier first sighted on the horizon at midmorning and ostensibly on a course parallel to ours gradually drew closer until it was clear that she was crossing, which she did, passing so close forward of us that our bows came up level with her stern almost the moment she cleared our path and, for a moment, the ships ran virtually alongside each other! I could have lobbed an orange onto her decks without much strain, or so it seemed. She was a Swedish ore carrier inbound for the St Lawrence, and everyone on board shook their fists at us; which they had every right to do because the Basque commanding my ship had taken no evasive action as Tucker had done. 'He must have been a real cowboy,' Tucker observed when I recounted the incident.

It is the quality of the inexorable in these encounters that makes them so strange and so disturbing. How can it be, one feels, that the courses of two ships, the only visible objects upon a vast sweep of ocean, should converge so relentlessly toward mutual peril? How is it that the human mind, alone and methodical and alert, aloft in the disciplined confines of the ship's bridge, should with the sharpest-pointed pencils and other fine, delicate instruments be drawing the straightest of straight lines upon the finest and most expensive parchment extending it beyond the horizon to meet at some predetermined point of this limitless sea the advancing straight line of another?

Tucker had no answer. He was a good-humoured young man. Noon was imminent, a bright, unclouded one at that, and he was about to go off duty. There was no shade upon the day that invited abstractions. Winking and with an elaborate ballet with his fore-finger he pressed a button and the ship's whistle blew one long extended blast. Picking up the blower, he gravely pronounced to the ship's company, 'Twelve hundred. *Twelve* hundred!' It was his final chore on the eight to twelve. Then, bouncing his hands together, he turned to greet his replacement, Hattrell: 'Alfie, old bean, why do ships collide?'

Hattrell shook his head. 'Search me,' he said. 'Because they're cowboys.'

Lunchtime was always the wardroom's most convivial hour, probably because lunch itself was an informal meal, without the master's presence; uniforms were worn, of course, but the atmosphere was lighter, the drift to the tables was casual, and talk was more un-inhibited, though decidedly familiar: this ship, other ships, other shipmates. Talking shop; it is any ship's principal form of leisure activity, the most common conversational currency. The exchange is usually a bland one: boyish gossip, recollection and anecdotes. Rarely malicious or personal – much nicer for it, of course, but obviously duller. *Ardshiel* was no exception. That strong natural conservatism of the sailor, which in a way is a mark of his almost total dissociation from the press and overlap of events and shifting opinions on shore, was pronounced. Opinions huddled to the safe and tried, which usually made them sound like the stereotyped attitudes of the world twenty-five years ago. 'I personally am cut off. I always have been; that's my way,' Ewart-James said. 'This is the first time in the past five years that I've had a radio at sea, and only because it's part of the cabin furniture. I could quite happily throw it away. I think, really, that most people here are like me; they are cut off and quite happy to be isolated, if you come down to it.'

Sport was one of the few continual lifelines ashore: they had to know the scores in soccer, and the results of golf and tennis championships. But there seldom were arguments; here, as in most other matters, the consensus ruled, or appeared to. If anyone thought otherwise he seemed not to feel a need to be assertive about it. 'You can't afford to be obnoxious, you've got to live with people a long time, and it's too small here for ill feeling,' Tucker said one night on the bridge when talking about the ship and its life. He could have been any sailor talking on any ship over the past five hundred years – or thousand years for that matter.

Blandness has its price. Board of Trade acquaintances, they call each other. There are few real friendships at sea. At the end of a voyage they exchange addresses and make tentative arrangements to meet again with the same earnest futility of bar and table companions on a passenger-cruise liner, and with as little faith in what they are saying. Only rarely does anything come of it all. They wait to meet again on some other ship, or never.

As *Ardshiel* slid down the west coast of Iberia the various personal accommodations were made and the living pattern of the ship established, such as it was; those who were to be temporary confidants, wardroom mates, and table-tennis partners, or whatever, sorted themselves out, and the loners defined their privacy. It was a curious thing to watch, though to describe it as something actually observable is hardly accurate for it simply happened without any apparent conscious thought or effort or even awareness upon anybody's part. People knew beside whom they would sit to think and say nothing, or accompany to the cinema, where the idle choice of seats for the first film performance we all saw together once the ship was away seemed to become set for all shows thereafter. Even when all of us attended we filled fewer than half the seats in the cinema, but we went back to the same ones night after night, and became bound by our social partnerships there: whose turn it was this time to get up during the change of reels to fetch drinks from the wardroom. Almost half the ship's complement was new, so these adjustments were necessary after Le Verdon, but the swift and unobtrusive ease of their accomplishment was impressive, as if by instinct.

In these arrangements, all of them merely casual and without intimacy, there was an immediate defence against the natural tensions and hazards of boredom and confinement – quick durable shelter for politeness and ease; and their effectiveness was perhaps the oldest quality aboard the ship itself: sailoring manners directly drawn from the sensibility of a sailoring nation.

There was too the common cause provided by Basil Thomson, who inspired unity of a sort through irritation, occasional anger and dismay, and, fairly often, good-humoured mockery. Much of the time they didn't take his temper seriously. He was the stranger in their midst, the visitor from another era. He himself was dealing with something he didn't fully understand. He lived with many of the discarded notions of yesteryear, when civil disciplines were sharper. What he seemed to mourn was not so much the diminishing exercise of discipline as the absent wish for it for its own sake; and when he carried about the ship his gift of chronic rebuke, whether irate or benign, he often seemed like a lonely man mumbling over the loss of his own defences.

These fusions were too functional to make Ardshiel a happy ship, which is something not easily defined: a vessel in which the quality of wit and humour has an existence larger than mere mutual tolerance, and flourishing perhaps because of one man's personality or because of a climate of controlled permissiveness, perhaps because of something in the very nature of the ship itself; each case has its own character. Yet Ardshiel was not an unhappy ship either. However fussy and fiddlesome he might be, Thomson prompted no running tensions. Whatever anger or irritability arose quickly lapsed. 'I'm a sentimental man,' he would say, 'I like a good cry in the cinema,' and cry he did. I sat near him in the cinema and, in touching scenes, my companion would lean over and whisper, 'Bas is dabbing his eyes.' When the lights went up at the end of the reel, Thomson would sigh and say, 'Well, I liked that scene. It was a jolly good scene that. It's what I call acting.' Then: 'I only wish you wouldn't laugh so loud in the funny bits, electrical officer, I can't hear half the words on the screen when you laugh like that. It's not normal.' Recrimination built upon bathos could not easily incur the deepest of offence, and if by and large our days ran with a comparative if somewhat dull serenity it was due possibly to an overall sense of the ridiculous in life rather than of the bitter.

One was now aware of the almost permanent emptiness of the main deck. Sometimes one looked forward and to one's surprise noticed a figure moving about somewhere up around the bows and one wondered, as one would about likely trespassers, What's he up to? Yet one was briefly happy to see activity there; it gave life and meaning to the entire expanse of brick-red deck.

On ordinary ships the faintest roll or pitch gives the tip of every mast or derrick or ventilator some small rhythm in its set against the sea and horizon. On *Ardshiel* they simply moved implacably, inflexibly onward against the water, fixed to the sky, borne along by a hull which trampled down the squally waves as heedlessly as an elephant would the underbrush. The wide beam and tremendous length, all of it so deeply embedded in the sea, even when the ship was light, gave one that sense of conquest by size that men for so long have sought on the water but never quite realised, except perhaps Brunel, whose *Great Eastern* bore the same relation to other ships of its day that supertankers bear to the old *Queens*; but by conquest men really meant achievement of some state of the imperturbable over perturbation, and this neither *Great Eastern* nor the *Queens* achieved, all three having been extremely tender to the sea, bad rollers and steady pitchers. The *Queen Mary* was said to have once gone through a roll of thirty-two degrees.

In supertankers there is at last comparative solidity upon the waves; they bash through, which is their danger. They can roll, of course, when riding light, but it requires a massive beam sea to do it. For the most part, this world at sea gives the quality of shorebound steadiness more readily than anything else ever has afloat. The loss of intimacy with the water that such proportions entailed cropped up from time to time, especially in conversation with Ewart-James, who liked to talk about the pleasures of dinghy sailing when he was on leave and which brought him closer to the sea than when he was on these ships. The others weren't quite so keen to retrieve contact with the sea when on leave but they felt an occasional need to do so on the ship itself and the only place for this was at the bows, where one could stand looking down at the big curling foaming wave that the ship pushed steadily before it. It broke and sported ahead, tumbling and ricocheting like the whirlers, clowns, and acrobats that preceded solemn medieval pageant. Nothing royal about a supertanker, but standing up front like that and watching the unbroken sea flow toward the ship and yield to it one at least could hold fleeting communion with that instinct that once set figureheads upon ships; that mythology of the sea, its fates and furies, that made sailors proffer in brief advance of their vessel some emblem of serenity or propitiation, or of strength and defiance. No figurehead for *Ardshiel* but, in keeping with the other features that made her distinct from the general run of supertankers, she wore on her bows a remnant of the figurehead instinct, a plaque emblazoned, appropriately enough, with a large trident. That other traditional decorative feature of a ship's bows, the ship's bell, was a more pronounced absence. 'Who's going to walk a quarter of a mile to ring it?' Ewart-James said.

Ardshiel was steaming southward at sixteen knots and the empty hull established a vibration of increasing ferocity. On the bridge the binoculars hopped in their bin and, sometimes, Tucker said, it was impossible to write on the chartroom table. In the cabin it was often impossible to read comfortably. Any glass or plate left untended on a smooth table top began travelling at once, singing as it went. Vibration is a major supertanker problem. It can reach sufficient pitch to raise stress levels in the hull and crack it. At one point it was feared that vibration, which increased proportionately with size, on its own would set a limit to the continued growth of these ships; its control, however, has become partly a matter of supertanker seamanship, and although impossible to eliminate, its accumulative power can be diminished by slight alterations in speed, thereby putting the pulse of the machinery on a less intense level; or through equally slight changes of course, which break the rhythm pattern established by seas regularly striking the bows. Needless to say, it requires a new instinct, or an attentive awareness of the degrees of vibration, to ensure that these changes are made when necessary.

Ardshiel was ballasted by sixty thousand tons of salt water, which had been taken in as her cargo was discharged. This still left nearly three-quarters of the ship empty. 'Wait until the loaded passage,' someone always said when the vibration was mentioned. 'You don't even feel the engines, they're buried too deep. Everything still and steady. Oilberg!'

Those sinister humming caves below our decks were about to be cleaned. They were, suddenly, the main topic in the ship, and an unwelcome one: no one liked going down into the tanks to inspect them, the most dangerous and unpleasant of all tasks, which followed the automatic cleaning by spray machines. Some said they would not go down at all, others that they wouldn't do so unless ordered. One who had to go down was Alan Ewart-James, who was responsible for the inspection and who, as the ship fell toward the south, was busy preparing for the job.

On all ships, the man who really runs the vessel is the first officer: his is the most effective daily authority on the ship, that which is most active. The mate, as he was known in the days of sail and even for much of the age of steam, is the one who must ensure that things are shipshape, that they get done, that the ship and its gear are in good running order, that the cargo is efficiently loaded and discharged, and that the crew is under control and doing its job. For the latter task, muscle was once mandatory, especially in the days of sail. It was common for a sailing ship to sail 'with blood on the lid of her'; that is, with her decks stained with blood after the mate had been forced to thrash a new, truculent, and usually drunken crew into submission, and it was apposite to wonder as one sat in Ewart-James's panelled and carpeted office what those men of iron might have made of such a seat of operations, surrounded as we were by a computer, technical volumes and drawings, graphs and diagrams, and multicoloured schedules of various kinds.

Ewart-James himself appeared to be the only one aboard aside from the master who was a sailor by vocation. Going to sea was something he'd intended to do since boyhood, and he frequently indicated his pleasure in being where he was. He was more resilient, therefore, and not as vulnerable to Thomson's outbursts and quirks as the others. 'I can't account for my feelings about the sea,' he said. 'It's just the way it is. I mean, I really do like the sea. I feel quite happy being on this ship, although the run is very boring. If I were completely bored, I'd just quit.

'Oh now and again you get depressed, you say, "Oh I'd like to get ashore and have a shore job!" You feel life disappearing. You are stuck on a ship and it's all happening without you. But after a few days you think, "Oh well, it's not such a good idea after all." But why? That's something else, I really don't know, except that I made up my mind about coming to sea when I was about nine, and I never changed it.'

When he was eighteen he'd entered the Southampton School of Navigation on a one-year course, which taught him basic seamanship. He then went as an apprentice to Furness Withy, one of the biggest British shipping groups; his first ship ran between Britain and the west coast of North America, the next to the Mediterranean and North Africa. He'd sailed in his first tanker, a 20,000 tonner, in 1963, and had joined P & O's tanker fleet in 1964 as third officer; at the end of 1969 he'd got his master's ticket. The present voyage, however, was his first as first officer, a promotion which had just recently come through.

Young as he was, Ewart-James's nautical background made him a somewhat old-fashioned figure among his contemporaries or near-contemporaries in supertankers because there already exists a whole race of officers who have served on no other sort of ship and have no real knowledge of the sea experience as it is lived in ordinary merchantmen; and they would listen intently and with envy in the wardroom as Ewart-James recounted the way it was in 'the old days' when he was a cadet and, while there was no money in it, how nice it was to go ashore in the different ports and 'just walk around looking at the shops'. He had a store of experiences of a sort unlikely again to come the way of a serving tankerman, including a spell in the early sixties as a member of a maintenance crew aboard a laid-up ship, an episode reminiscent of the 1930s, when whole fleets swung at anchor for years. It had been exactly like camping, he enthusiastically told his audience one evening: no power on board, they used a diesel oil pump to flush the toilets, there were only hurricane lamps to read and eat by, and they kept a dinghy alongside in which to sail ashore when they wanted to get off.

Ewart-James was sure that he was among the last supertanker seamen to know both worlds. It had become unlikely, considering the size and specialisation of the ships, that anyone except those who had made their careers in them would serve in them. Ewart-James estimated that it would take at least six months for a man drafted from an ordinary merchantman to get a general conception of what was going on. Even then he would not really be able to cope if things started going wrong. No major tanker operator was going to take such chances with such costly ships, he believed.

Ewart-James's day was far longer and busier than anybody else's. It began at three forty-five in the morning with a call from the second officer on the bridge, and at four he took over the watch. 'The second makes me a cup of coffee, so when I walk through the door it's already there, which is what we all do for the next person,' he said. 'The second tells me what ships there are around and what they are doing; if we're near land he'll advise me of any points of interest. I check the position he put down at four o'clock, just to make sure we're all right. I'll ask him whether the engine room is manned or unmanned, and I like to know how much weather there is, and how many ships he's had over the past four hours. That gives me an indication of what I myself can expect over the next four hours. If we're in open waters, there's nothing much to do until it comes to taking the stars to find out our position in the morning. Before that, I'll check the error on the compass; this is standard practice you do on every watch.

'I like the four to eight when the sun rises about six in the morning. Dawns can be very very attractive, and also in the evenings sunsets can be nice too. So the four to eight is rather nice at times. There's always something of interest, a ship, a bird, perhaps an albatross, an unusual dawn. The other night we passed a Liberian tanker and her Greek captain called me up on the Aldis light and asked me to go on the radio, which I did. Then he was asking me questions about the size of the ship and where we were going, and then he told me that he was the captain of the ship, a sixty-thousand tonner. I told him I was the chief officer on here. He wanted to know how long I'd been on the ship. I told him about six or seven weeks since coming back from leave. He wanted to know how much longer I had to go, and I said I was hoping to get off in about three weeks; and then he said, "Oh well, I've now been in continuous service on this ship for three years, but I hope to get off in four months' time, in October, to go and see my wife and daughter in Greece." After hearing that, I didn't think anyone here had anything to grumble about. But what seemed strangest to me was that he, the captain, should have been standing watch; and at that hour. That's what it seemed like anyhow.

'At eight o'clock in the morning, after my watch has ended, the chief petty officer reports to me here in the office and I give him his jobs, which he distributes among the crew. There are fourteen crew members on this ship against, say, twenty-five deckhands on a small conventional cargo ship. Like everything else on these ships, these seamen are quite different to anything before. They are known as GPs, general purpose seamen, which means that they shift between the deck and the engine room. You no longer get, at least in these ships, a man who goes to sea as either just a greaser or as a deckhand. He's got to do both things. The idea was very unpopular when first introduced by P & O. Nobody wanted it. Those on deck didn't like going down to the engine room, and those in the engine room didn't want to go up top. Most of those men left the sea rather than do what they didn't wish to do. What we have now are the new men who have adjusted to the pattern. What it means for the chief officer is that he has to balance the needs of the engine room against the deck and divide them accordingly. I still find it strange, when they're all down in the engine room, for example, to see this ship sailing along during the day with not one man in sight anywhere on her decks doing a job of work.'

After breakfast he did a general inspection of the ship which included the decks and accommodation and engine rooms. 'On these rounds I make lists of things that have to be seen to. For instance, looking at my list here, I see that I've got to check the wires that lower the lifeboats, and the mooring ropes forward. I understand from the second officer that one of them seems to be on the point of breaking. Those are the sort of small attentions that keep the ship going, and which I make a note of every day. But the overall maintenance is directed from the shore, from head office, according to that big plan you see there,' and he pointed to a large coloured diagram of the ship set upon one of the bulkheads of his office and decorated with small triangular red flags and red circles. 'It's called the planned maintenance system. They've divided the ship into various sections and in head office they decide how often these various sections should be looked at and maintained. The system is tailored for these ships. Each little triangular flag there tells me which section should be done in which month of the year, and when I do a check and survey on one of those sections I cancel it out with one of the circles, so that at a glance I can tell exactly what's been done and what hasn't. When a new chief officer comes aboard he comes in here at once and just looks at that and says, "Oooh, he did this last month, so this has got to be done this month!"

'The outward passage in ballast is always busier than the loaded passage back from the Gulf. We've got to clean the tanks first of all, the biggest job; and when they're clean we go down to overhaul the various bits of machinery down there which you can't get at when loaded because they're submerged in oil. When we come back from the Gulf we're going to be painting the entire ship. It will take most of the voyage to do it, and, since it's polyurethane paint, they expect it to last five years, though I myself doubt that it will.

'Now that so many decisions on the actual running of the ship are made on shore, it means of course that we're loaded with paperwork. Our charterers, Shell, for example, have time sheets for loading and discharging. Every single operation involved in taking these ships into port, unloading or loading them, and then getting them out again, has been tabulated and given an allowable time known as the target time. So when we throw the ropes over the side, connect the pipes, and start things rolling, it's all got to be done within the specified time that Shell now reckons each operation should take, and if you are longer than this Shell wants to know why. The old days of dawdling into port and taking your time about getting alongside and putting the gangplank down and so on, well, they're gone for good. These systems started with tankers, but the day'll come when they'll apply to all ships.'

Ewart-James was also the ship's doctor and when the rest of his chores were done he usually found that he had a patient to see to. 'Generally it's a matter of aspirin,' he said. 'But yesterday just as I was settling down at the pool for a doze before going back on watch the cadet came and told me that a Chinaman had something in his eye.

'He had been mending a leaky steam pipe and a spark from the metal flew into his eye because he wasn't wearing goggles. I immediately gave him an eyewash. I could see there was something in his eye but it was too sore for anyone to go probing about. I did what we always do, looked up the diagnosis in the *Shipmaster's Medical Guide*, which is our medical Bible. I gave him an eye anaesthetic in drop form. This deadened the eye and I opened it, removed the fragment, put in some antibiotic drops, some antiseptic ointment, and gave him an eye shade to wear.

'The only other serious case I've had so far was eczema. It appeared to be from an allergy, and, from the questions I asked, I assumed it was from paint we'd been using, the polyurethane paint, so I gave him some anti-allergy pills and told him to lay off painting.

'At the moment we're supposed to have the St John Ambulance Brigade first-aid certificate, which is very elementary, to say the least. I myself went along to the casualty department of my local hospital when I was home on leave, purely off my own bat, knowing full well that I might meet some unexpected cases at sea. I spent a day or two there. Most of what I saw was broken bones. What I was mainly interested in, however, was stitching. This is a thing I have never done and don't feel I would like to do, but I thought it better to see how it was done. Luckily they had two or three patients with bad cuts that had to be stitched up and I was shown how to do it. At the moment if a shipboard medical case is really serious we either radio the symptoms to a shore station for advice, or send out a call to see if there are any ships around with a doctor on board. As passenger ships disappear from the oceans, that becomes more and more difficult to do. The Japanese already carry doctors on their tankers. Our people are now talking of new men doing a proper hospital course before they get their master's and chief officer's certificates.

'Well, aside from the unexpected such as a medical emergency, my ship's day really ends with the four to eight. I actually come down just before eight, to join the dinner party in the saloon. I might stay in the wardroom a bit after dinner, or see part of a film if they're showing one, but usually I come up here, do some paperwork, and then turn in. I like to read, if there's something interesting: lately I've read Solzhenitsyn's *Cancer Ward*, which I found a bit boring, and Albert Camus's *The Outsider*, which I liked very much.'

The Canaries approached, hidden inside a long featureless Saturday dusk, and they passed after dark as a loom of distant light above the horizon, releasing us toward the great southern Atlantic, and a tropical Sunday. Weekends were an ache, affected by a sudden feeling of void in ship life, which intruded more perceptibly than usual. This was apparent in Stephen Tucker, whom I found sadly watching the fading of that distant glow as though it were a vanishing promise.

'There'll be lots of package tour people there now, swilling down the old vino and having a ball,' he said. 'Probably I'd even find somebody I know from my own street.' He turned moodily to the various phenomena surrounding the duller business of our own progress into the night. In the dusk, in the same quarter as the islands, a large supertanker paced us on a parallel course. There was scarcely a moment on the run down past Iberia, off the Straits of Gibraltar, and along the passage toward the Canaries when one of these ships wasn't in sight: empty ones on the same course as ourselves usually lay to starboard, laden inbound ones to port.

After returning the glasses to their bin, neatly, in the required position, Tucker resumed the task of switching on the ship's riding lights, the various deck floodlights; and then, carefully, set the exact strength of dim stipulated by Thomson for the clock dimmer, which regulated the illumination of all clocks on board; and finally arranged the bridge console's various switches.

Ardshiel was quietly sailing into the onrushing night, falling south-westward with the wind, whose sizeable disturbance ran equably alongside. It had settled in behind us off the Straits of Gibraltar: a powerful Levanter. From the bridge one could smell the crests as they curled and broke. We stood at the bridge rail and quietly talked in a soft windlessness, while the water crashed below, sounding like breakers heard from a height on a still evening.

An approaching tanker, its hull low from its weight of oil, battled toward us against a howling gale, its main deck continually awash from the spray that exploded upward as solid white walls and then collapsed in deluge over the bows and decks. Nobody could have ventured forward there and lived. She was an Esso ship and Tucker, grateful for the diversion, called her on the telephone.

'Esso ship passing, good evening, sir. What is your name? Is that the Esso tanker north-bound, please? Over.'

The telephone rang and Tucker answered. 'Okay, yes, thank you very much. Esso *Skandia*, are you? This is *Ardshiel*, south-bound. You're heading for Le Havre? We've just come from Rotterdam and Le Verdon. Thank you, sir, and I wish you a good trip.'

'I've seen him before,' Tucker said, and we went out to watch the big ship fall away behind. She vanished into the dark, a dwindling sequence of faint white soundless explosions. 'Another Saturday gone,' Tucker said as we watched the ship disappear. 'It's the one day I enjoy when I'm home. I prefer it to Sunday, which gets a bit ragged; I mean, you lie in bed all day reading the papers. But everyone's in a good mood on Saturday, even people who have to work; oh aye. You go out shopping, and then to the pub; Saturdays in pubs, lunch-time; it's great, really great. I like the spirit. You feel you've got all the time in the world ahead of you. I say to the girlfriend, "Shall we have a bite somewhere? Or go off in the car to visit friends?" Then in the evenings we sit reading, make spaghetti, go off to a show, or to the pubs before closing.'

There had been a party in the wardroom before dinner to celebrate the promotion of one of the engineers, Graham Allen, a Geordie of course, from junior to third engineer. It had continued briefly in the wardroom after dinner and, finally, around ten, the survivors had transferred themselves to the newly promoted third engineer's quarters, which were now declared to be in a state of open house for the rest of the night, or until whenever.

Graham Allen's wife, Pat, was the only woman on board. They were a decorative couple, both just over twenty. She was a fresh, clear, and pretty girl and her husband had that dark olive-skinned handsomeness which in Scotland or Ireland one supposes to indicate Armada descent (a myth that has little probability, according to Garrett Mattingly in his *The Defeat of the Spanish Armada*). They had been childhood sweethearts, and an adolescent obsessiveness still clung to their intimacy which, because it was the only one on board, drew longing toward it. Their cabin was next door to mine on the Middle Bridge Deck and it was a favourite rendezvous for the other junior officers, who trekked constantly from the distant corners of the ship to enjoy a taste of feminine company. Tact and manners on both sides were admirable. She was a young woman of great self-possession and she handled with natural discretion and grace a situation that many others her age might understandably have regarded either as an opportunity or an embarrassment. She moved through this company of bored and restless men without any hint of provocation or coquettishness and they for their part regarded her with an admiration that was open and forthcoming and never sly.

They were frank about their bliss. He had always been very religious, Graham Allen said, and still was as a matter of fact; but it had meant that they'd never done anything before their marriage, whatever the temptation. They'd only done heavy necking, all of which caused a lot of tension and unhappiness. Now they were making up for it, which was why it always seemed to others that they were on a permanent honeymoon. It was all still very exciting to them.

'Why do you want to talk about these things in public? It isn't done; it isn't interesting to anybody else,' the radio officer said. He and Tucker had joined the party after Tucker had come off watch at midnight.

'It *is* interesting,' Graham Allen insisted. 'It's *very* interesting, and you bloody well lie if you say it isn't.' He burst out laughing, a wild engaging laugh, and kicked up his heels.

'What's also interesting is all the wild oats sown in other directions, as I'm bound to tell if pressed,' Graham Chalmers said.

'You're not,' said Allen.

'Tell us about Quinn's Bar in Tahiti for a start,' Chalmers went on.

'I'll tell you what happened in Aruba,' Allen offered.

113

'It reminds me—' Chalmers said, but he was cut off by Pat Allen, who interrupted, 'It reminds me that it's time you all went to bed. Finish up, everybody.' To her husband, she said, 'I'm putting *you* to bed.'

'You're too rough,' Graham Allen complained. 'You don't put me to bed nice and gentle like me mum used to do.'

'Come on now,' Pat Allen cried, collecting glasses. 'Drink up and out, the lot of you.'

'Good night,' Graham Allen gaily called. 'Good night.'

Graham Chalmers shook his fist, and they went out one by one, gazed a moment at the door that shut so firmly behind them, and then moved off in a disconsolate group toward one of the other cabins.

The main difference that indicated Sunday on board was the solemn hoisting of Basil Thomson's blue ensign at eight in the morning on the dot. It would remain aloft, fluttering from a halliard abaft the funnel, until struck at sunset. The blue ensign was not flown on weekdays, except in port. The normal flag of the British merchant service is the 'red duster', a red flag with the Union Jack set small into the upper left-hand corner. The blue ensign – blue where the other is red – is the flag of the Royal Navy Reserve and, as a former serving member of the Royal Navy, Thomson was privileged to fly it on his ships instead of the red ensign. It is an honour much esteemed among British masters.

Instead of going up in the clear light of a tropical morning, however, the ritual now coincided with sunrise.

One of Basil Thomson's more confusing habits was that he didn't set the clocks back to accord with the time zone through which we were moving. If we'd changed clocks we would have been doing ten days of it south-bound, half an hour a day. On that Sunday morning we already were more than two hours ahead of the sun; we had been rising in blackest night and breakfasting at dawn and Hattrell, to his chagrin, had been doing his noon position at two in the afternoon, suntime. 'We all like noon at midday but we never get it,' he had been plaintively crying as he did his sums. What it also meant was that the morning swim around the pool, which should have been accomplished in the first strong warmth of the tropical sun, was done instead under the stars; it was a disconcerting exercise, which I soon gave up.

'On the passenger ships they change the clocks for the passengers, who want to know when the sun rises and when it sets,' Thomson remarked at breakfast. 'On these ships it's no skin off anybody's teeth that I don't set the clocks back.' He was in a good mood and,

114

as though to account for it, said: 'I enjoy Sundays, and I'll now go and find my church service.

'I twiddle the knobs on the radio until I get what I want. Then I lean back with my pipe and enjoy the old parson. It may not be the proper way, but I believe that religion should be a thing of joy, light and free. I don't think Jesus would have minded.'

He added, after a brief reflective silence, 'None of us can even tell what God is like, whether he is black, white, blue, or yellow. Whites like to think he is white, the blacks that he is black, but we're all equally ignorant.'

For the navigating officers Sunday was just another working day. They continued through their normal round of watch-keeping. But the engineers, who switched their engines to automatic control at midday Saturday, were free until Monday morning. Sundays they spent at the pool, or raced about the decks before lunch on the bicycles which all supertankers keep on board as one means of defeating the distances of the main deck during working hours. Sunday's curry lunch was somewhat more elaborate than the weekday ones, and at teatime in the afternoon there were special cakes called tabnabs instead of Huntley & Palmer biscuits. None of these diversions was sufficient, however, to appease the restless energies of the engineers and, at the heart of a long humid tranquil tropical afternoon that Sunday, there lay a small pocket of violence in the swimming pool. The junior officers were playing in the water with a polo ball. They played ferociously, long and tirelessly, hurling the ball at each other as though it were a weapon. The pool itself was like a cauldron and the area around it was sodden from their splashing. Graham and Pat Allen sat in deck-chairs, good humouredly watching, oblivious to the stinging showers that drenched them from time to time. Their deck-chairs were raised to give them a better view of the arena and its combat, and they lay with their palms cradling their heads, their arms and elbows spread like small open resting wings and their bodies slack with ease and satisfaction from their own appeased energies.

They all brought into the wardroom that evening the taut skins and glowing alertness set upon them by the day's sun and salt water. They looked very young, healthy, and expectant of something more yet from the day. The barman had been let off to go to the movies, so they had at least a mood of Sunday domestic improvisation in the wardroom itself, a general sense of lending a hand. Harvey Phillips was barman, playing the role of publican, taking orders, serving them with mock flourish, wiping his counter and setting things straight. Pat Allen was behind the bar with him, washing and drying glasses. Graham Chalmers collected empty beer cans and took out the 'gash'; Graham Allen emptied ashtrays.

As they finished their chores they came over one by one to join the after-dinner group at the coffee-table, where the master himself was lingering over his coffee, watching it all with his benign expression. Harvey Phillips was last, bringing over a tray of drinks. 'I've enjoyed meself,' he said as he served the orders individually. 'Lawrence should go to the pictures more often and leave us to it. It passes the time. It's a change, like on one of the other ships where Sunday nights was always Night Club dinner. It was a good way to finish the weekend.'

'What exactly did that mean?' Basil Thomson asked.

'Well, not too much if you come to think about it. They had the saloon lights off and a candle stuck in the centre of every table and you sat there trying to see your food. But it gave a sort of a mood. It was different anyways.'

'If it's just a question of a candle stuck in the centre of the table, I think we can manage that,' Thomson said.

'Actually, there was more to it. They had a cabaret. It depends on the talents you've got aboard. They had some good acts so they could do it. One of the officers was a magician. He dressed up in the clothes of one of the wives on board and then did his magic. It was the star turn.'

'On the *Garonne* they used to do pub lunches on Saturdays,' Graham Allen said. 'A regular buffet was laid out in the wardroom. You could go and help yourself while drinking at the bar, just like in a pub.'

'Was old Peter Simpson chief engineer on her when you were there?' Basil Thomson asked.

'He certainly was,' Graham Allen said. 'He's one of the nicest blokes I've ever met on these ships.'

'Oh yes, a fine man,' Thomson agreed. 'A charming chap, and so is his wife.'

'Yes, what a lovely person,' said Pat Allen. 'A *really* lovely person.'

'So are their children,' said Thomson. 'And they've certainly got enough of them. Six.'

'Oh no, it's five,' Graham Allen corrected.

'No, six,' said Thomson.

'Then they must have had one very recently because Pat and I know them well and we saw them last time we were home,' Graham Allen said. 'We spent some time with them and she wasn't pregnant then.'

'All I can tell you, young Graham Allen, is that they've got six children,' Thomson said. 'I *know* it's six.'

'In that case, as I say, they must have had another just recently because it was five when we last saw them,' Graham Allen said.

'Well, all I can say to you, Graham Allen, is that I'm glad at least that you admire him; I hope then that you'll take him as an example and not become one of these what I call professional third engineers, and I'm thinking of one in particular who's been on this ship and who said he wasn't interested in further promotion, he was going to stay third engineer and not bother about advancing himself because a chief engineer only got forty pounds a month more than he did, after paying taxes, and he didn't think that so little extra money was worth the responsibility.'

'I plan to study for my second's ticket as soon as I can, so that's not my view,' Graham Allen said. 'But funnily enough, and I don't want to seem disrespectful, but I can understand that point of view, especially since junior officers don't get the perks that a senior officer gets, so they wonder if the life is worth so much extra bother to get another promotion.'

'What perks? How am I better off than you?' Thomson demanded. 'I don't even travel first class on the planes. When I go to the office I'm not treated as a captain, not like in the old days. I don't get any better food or drink. Only my quarters are larger, and those I don't need. Now let me remind you of something, young Graham Allen, which is why I mentioned this in the first place; you yourself once told me that if your wife didn't come aboard then you would quit. You said you would leave the ship and the company if you couldn't have her with you. Don't start thinking that that's forgotten, because it's not. It's down in my book of words. It's no use denying it now, it's there.'

'I'm not denying it,' Graham Allen said.

'You couldn't if you wished. I put it down when it was said, so it's there; unarguably there. You said that if your wife couldn't be with you, then you yourself were going!'

Silence settled over his words. The alertness that the sun had fastened upon all of them had crumpled to lassitude. Normally there would have been the sound of Lawrence the barman quietly doing something or other behind the bar, with the bar itself a vacant brightness at the far end. Nobody moved, except occasionally to pick up his glass to drink. Thomson finally rose to go, and the others followed one after another.

'Good night.'
'Good night.'
'Good night.'

Out up the empty stairs, along the empty passages, and out onto the decks for some air; not quite deserted, however. Peter Dutton, the other second engineer, was sitting in a deck-chair near the swimming pool listening to Charlie, one of the Chinese donkeymen, playing his pipes. They were an inseparable pair. Dutton, who had been on the ship for three months already and whose wife had been among those who'd joined *Ardshiel* for the short passage from Rotterdam to Le Verdon, was one of the ship's loners. He kept to himself, never joined pour-out, and seldom lingered in the wardroom. Nobody knew how long Charlie had been on the ship. Some thought he had been aboard since *Ardshiel* came out of the yards. The pipes, slender Pan-like reed ones, were his solace and one often suddenly heard them playing somewhere or other; in this big ship one could never be quite sure where he was playing. They were like an agreeable ghostly presence that constantly shifted its habitation around us, always calling from somewhere different, and they were particularly pleasing to the Geordies and Scotsmen since the lament that lay at the heart of the notes reminded them of their own pipes. 'Charlie's playing his pipes again,' one of them would say, and they would become thoughtful, their heads half turned toward the suspected direction of the sound.

When one heard the pipes thus during one of the long silences of the wardroom they could bring to the room a feeling of great melancholy, but the charm of the music could never make one regret listening. Now, confronting them from the shadows of the deck, visible at last beside the calm green surface of the floodlit pool, one *could* feel a spasm of regret, as though having unwittingly stumbled upon an unsought revelation; but the notes out here were so much freer and clearer and sweeter, and the tableau of the two men, the blond young Geordie and the elderly Chinese, sitting in such quiet and harmonious attachment, was itself so sustaining that one didn't really mind after all.

SEVEN

SUPERTANKERS are the biggest moving things ever built by man, and also the most dangerous. To the public mind, tankers are dangerous because of their inflammable cargo; although a fully laden *Ardshiel* would have aboard as much compressed passive thermal energy as a hydrogen bomb, she, like all these ships, is safest when her tanks are brimming with oil.

If its cargo tanks aren't breached and remain securely sealed, a laden tanker can be swept by flames and have its accommodation gutted without touching off the cargo. A notable instance was the spectacular collision of the *Pacific Glory* and the *Allegro* off the Isle of Wight in October 1970; although torn by engine-room explosions and ravaged by a fire that destroyed her superstructure and spread across the surrounding sea, the 77,000-ton *Pacific Glory* kept her cargo of Nigerian crude intact, and it eventually reached its destination in Europe.

It is not the oil itself that burns or explodes but the gas given off by it. Hydrocarbon gas has a very low flashpoint and burns or explodes even at temperatures as low as minus forty Fahrenheit. The gas lies in dense possession of the tanks after the oil cargo has been discharged and therefore it is when tankers are empty, travelling in ballast, as we were doing, that they are most dangerous.

This gas is not easily controlled or got rid of. Hydrocarbon gas is so potent that mere puddles of oil can generate a hazardous atmosphere, and an empty supertanker has a great deal more than puddles inside her hull. After the cargo has been pumped out pools of thick residue lie at the bottom, where the main pumps can't reach, like dregs in a gigantic cup; and the walls of the tanks are covered by a thin layer of an oil-wax mixture. If a film one millimetre thick covered all the steelwork in the tanks of a ship such as *Ardshiel* it could amount to some two thousand tons; normally tank cleaning retrieves at least 1,200 tons of oil. Until the tanks are cleaned all of it continues to exude gas, thus thickening considerably the concentration left behind by the cargo. This mixture of hydrocarbon gases can be touched off by the faintest spark, the risk naturally being greatest when any sort of activity occurs in or near the tanks, which of course makes tank cleaning the most critical event of all: however cautious, the whole business involves countless possibilities of sparking the gas and blowing the ship apart.

The obvious aim of tank cleaning therefore is that it should be done in a non-explosive atmosphere. Hydrocarbon gas can't explode if it is 'overrich', which means when it is so dense that there's insufficient air present to sustain combustion. Nor can it explode if it is too 'lean', which means when the gas has been so dispersed by air that it cannot ignite.

Tankers hitherto have mainly used either an overrich or a lean atmosphere to clean their tanks. The overrich one was a natural preference because tankers are in an overrich state right after the cargo has been discharged. The concentration of fumes left by the oil remains densely overrich for several days (it is the overrich condition of laden tankers that makes them so much safer). Once this overrich condition becomes doubtful in an empty tanker, those cleaning tanks have to create a lean atmosphere by blowing so much air into the tanks that the amount of gas left is too thin to be dangerous.

No equipment has yet been devised to ensure the stability of either of these atmospheres when they are being put to such practical use. In each case there is constant danger that somehow the balance will be upset and the atmosphere will become explosive.

A third atmosphere, now generally regarded as the safest, can be created for cleaning tanks. It involves use of the flue gases from the ship's boilers. These are the so-called inert gases, such as nitrogen and carbon dioxide, which are non-combustible. They are drawn from the ship's funnel, cooled and purified, and pumped into the tanks simultaneously as the oil is pumped out, so that, theoretically, there should at no stage be an explosive mixture in the tanks. The system is costly to install, so it has been the least commonly used for cleaning tanks.

Whatever the system used, the actual business of tank cleaning is highly automated in a supertanker. The tanks are sealed and fiercely hosed by high-pressure water jets built into the tanks. The principle is that of immense garden sprays, spurting water with the same eccentric motion, that is to say both vertically and horizontally. They can clean one of the main central tanks in about eight hours, flinging lumps of water the size of buckets with practically the speed of a bullet and cleaning out oil from every surface, crevice, beam, or strut.

Tankermen using an overrich atmosphere inside the tanks know that the very act of washing is bound to affect the stability of the mixture and that there is *always* a moment, as the gas-producing oil is washed away, at which the gas level inside the tank falls within the explosive limit. Overrich gas can also contain pockets of oxygen, much as a viscous liquid does, and these, once liberated into a less turgid atmosphere, can also bring it all within an explosive range. Over the past decade the majority of explosions aboard tankers at sea in ballast have occurred when the overrich method was being used to clean tanks. The overrich atmosphere also makes empty tankers doubly vulnerable in a collision which might tear open an overrich tank whose atmosphere, upset by the inflow of air, could be exploded by sparks from the crash.

The lean gas method with its circulating air currents can be equally unpredictable because, if an unsuspectedly large amount of oil has been left behind from the cargo, the high-velocity washing jets could churn loose sufficient gas to raise the explosive limit into the dangerous range.

Explosion can only come from a spark and the art of tanker safety therefore lies not only in maintaining the atmospheric balance in the tanks at safe levels but also in avoiding any chance of a spark reaching them should they become unsafe. It seems on the face of it incredible that a spark so faint as to be to all intents and purposes invisible could blow up a 200,000-ton ship by travelling from its open decks into its sealed tanks, yet it can happen. The low flashpoint of hydrocarbon gas means that an ignition as infinitesimal as a boot grinding a grain of desert sand on a steel deck could touch it off. So could a worn wire grinding against another, or the switch of a non-tanker regulation flashlight, or the static of a nylon shirt. The gas, of course, is only too often there. Runnels of gas possibly trickling from any of the many tank openings that lie level or almost level with the deck could flash a spark to the tanks; or it could travel by gas that, on a windless night, might fall from the mast-high vents on the main deck.

The varieties of gas seepage are as limitless as the possibilities of causing spark, and everything is done to avoid either, but especially spark. No smoking is ever allowed on deck and, when the tanker is loading or discharging, only in designated places such as the ward-room. Strict rules are enforced on materials, tools, and tasks that might inadvertently cause a spark: on P & O tankers, for example, artificial fibres, which are critical producers of static electricity, are avoided if possible, and under no circumstances allowed inside a tank. Decks are chipped only when a ship is loaded, and even then only when all sand and grit have been washed off them and when there is a wind of not less than five miles an hour blowing across them.

Oil tankers have been blowing up since the earliest days of the species; the first major inquiry into a ship lost by presumed tank explosion was held as early as 1905. During the last fifteen years there has been an average of fourteen explosions a year on oil tankers, many of them fatal to both ship and crew. Apart from shipboard sparks, lightning can explode tankers, as happened in Le Havre harbour in August 1972 when the 33,000-ton Greek tanker *Princess Irene* was torn apart when petroleum fumes were ignited during a thunderstorm. The common causes of tanker explosions, however, are static electricity or human negligence and usually a combination of both. Whatever the cause, the consequences are always terrifying.

In October 1958, the 17,000-ton *Stanvac Japan* blew up in the Indian Ocean with such violence that the forward accommodation structure of the ship holding the navigating bridge was torn bodily from the ship and hurled into the sea. Everyone inside it perished, except the second officer, who was on duty, and whose escape remains one of the most remarkable stories of survival at sea.

Stanvac Japan was a tanker of the old type, with two accommodation areas. The second officer had been gazing forward and then decided to go into the chartroom, which faced aft. The explosion threw him to the deck and when he got to his feet he found himself gazing down at the ship, which was sailing away from him, minus its bridge. The 400-ton superstructure had reversed itself as it was thrown into the air. The second officer stepped into the water from the deck of the bridge as it sank below him, and was picked up by his own ship.

In 1968, a 20,000-ton Argentinian tanker exploded at her loading berth, where she sank; the explosion damaged two 25,000-ton ships at adjacent berths, and they too exploded and sank. The incident passed almost unnoticed, as do most tanker explosions as a rule, except in the maritime world, and even there tanker explosions have become such a matter of course that nobody really regards them as extraordinary.

It required something vastly more spectacular for the shipboard dangers of hydrocarbon gas to gain public impact, or, for that matter, to raise real maritime concern, and this was provided during a momentous eighteen-day period in December 1969, through another chain of triple tanker disaster.

On 15 December 1969 the 206,000-ton Shell tanker *Marpessa* sank off Senegal on her maiden commission, after a tank explosion that killed two men. On 29 December, a sister ship, *Mactra*, also 206,000 tons, also owned by Shell, suffered an equally violent tank explosion in the Mozambique Channel, again killing two men. The next day, off Liberia, the 220,000-ton Norwegian tanker *Kong Haakon VII* was similarly torn open by tank explosion. The *Mactra* and the *Kong Haakon* managed to reach port, having suffered less critical weakening of their structures than *Marpessa*.

One such explosion might have been accepted as just a big accident, two might have passed for coincidence, but three suggested something more, and the maritime world ever since has regarded the triple sequence as one disaster, especially since the consequences, notably increases of 25 per cent and more in insurance premiums for supertankers and a hovering mistrust of them as a species, became general.

Just the sinking of *Marpessa*, at that time the biggest ship ever to founder, was a historic event, but taken collectively the explosions form the greatest maritime loss of civil times.

Mactra and *Kong Haakon* had to be almost totally rebuilt: the bill for each was more than the original cost of the vessel.

Exhaustive investigations into the explosions began almost at once. There was at that point no clue whatsoever as to what had caused them. Although it was not ruled out, there was no apparent negligence in the three ships, whose officers and sailors were all experienced tanker hands and therefore fully aware of the risk to themselves and the ship if they dropped their guard. All that anyone really knew was the obvious: that to set off the explosion there must have been *both* an explosive atmosphere in a tank and a spark to ignite it. To the maritime world, it was a crisis of quite staggering proportions.

Obviously, and fortunately, a disaster of this nature can never match in story and human impact any tragedy of the great passenger ships, like the *Titanic*; nonetheless it was a measure of the gravity with which shipping regarded the event that the London inquiry into the *Mactra* explosion, which in effect became the definitive inquiry into all three accidents, was the first since the *Titanic* inquiry in 1912 to have a High Court judge sitting as Wreck Commissioner. Indeed, nothing since the *Titanic* provoked such international maritime alarm, or raised a more exhaustive concern about safety at sea. If one disregarded the emotional factors involved with the foundering of the White Star liner, the tanker explosions indubitably had much profounder implications both for shipping and society as a whole than *Titanic* had.

There was, of course, the disturbing parallel in these two epochal maritime tragedies of the fallible mammoth (*Marpessa* too was on its maiden commission). But *Titanic* was a self-contained tragedy, a compound of arrogant assumptions, human errors, and horrible ironies and therefore largely accountable and remediable in its omissions: her sinking established standards and conventions that were overdue, but it left no technological mystery, it did not challenge the projected shape and trend of ships or the fundamental substance of maritime planning and evolution, nor threaten the proposed economics of half the world's seaborne trade, as the VLCC explosions did.

The explosions brought international shipping as close as it probably ever has been to a collective trauma. Where an accident such as *Titanic's* involved only the White Star Line's investment so far as actual loss was concerned, the VLCC explosions affected anyone who owned or was building big tankers, and at the time that meant practically everyone who was anyone in the shipping business. The possibility that these ships, technologically speaking, had been pushed too far too fast already had been ominously suggested by the serious buckling that many of them had incurred before or after launching, or on sea trials. That they should be fatally flawed as a species, as many now began to feel, had really not occurred to anyone before, for no one had supposed that the ships might offer an entirely new and incalculable set of fire and explosive hazards as well.

The suspicion that this was now so appeared well founded. In the six months previous to the *Marpessa–Kong Haakon* sequence of disasters, two 100,000 tonners had exploded at sea under similar circumstances. There was in any event a striking unity in the December explosions. All three of the tankers were new ships, all were about the same size, all were in ballast, all were cleaning tanks at the time, all were steaming in the tropics, and all were using similar mechanical systems for tank washing.

That something quite unforeseen was implicated seemed clear too from the fact that while the explosions and circumstances were similar the tank atmospheres were not. The *Kong Haakon* had used the overrich method for cleaning tanks, while the two Shell vessels had used the lean gas method. Shell especially was convinced that some entirely new element was involved because it had not suffered a tank-cleaning explosion on any of its ships for twenty-three years, which it had long considered a tribute to the relative security of the lean gas atmosphere. It immediately stopped cleaning operations on all its VLCCs. So did many other operators of the superships, and when Shell called an international symposium in London on 16 January 1970, to discuss the accidents to its ships and to canvass ideas and speculation, it found the event attended by the chief executives and technical experts of practically every major supership-operating management in Europe, America, and Asia.

It was quite apparent to everyone present that profound gaps remained in their knowledge of the workings of hydrocarbon gas and the mechanics of tank cleaning inside such vast structures. Andrew

Sinclair, senior technical adviser to the Salvage Association (which advises underwriters), declared his scepticism of the big ships at a special meeting convened at Lloyd's in 1970, and expressed his belief that there was a direct link between size of tankers and the explosions.

But it was unthinkable that the new superships should or, in the case of those already afloat, could be written off: sixty-three tankers of 200,000 tons and over already were in service and, in the biggest shipbuilding boom in history, at least three hundred were under construction in various parts of the world, especially Japan. An additional hundred or so were in the planning stage. These ships represented, the owners and designers claimed, the economic equation whereby Europe and Japan, and anywhere else dependent upon large long-range imports, not only would get their oil in the future at a pace commensurate with their needs but at a low and stable delivery price.

There was no practical alternative to them that anyone could imagine, or rather was prepared to imagine, yet every VLCC afloat, building, or projected had to be recognised as a potential bomb of terrifying power (in *Mactra*'s case, it was estimated that about 4,400,000 cubic feet of gas exploded to wrench open almost the width of the ship for a distance of nearly half its length). If superships were going to continue blowing up at such a rate no one would be prepared to finance them, insure them, or even have them in port; no one would wish to serve in them; and, alas, they would shatter the biggest prospect of maritime profit ever entertained.

Probably far more cash and time were subsequently spent on unravelling the mystery of the explosions than were ever spent initially on models, experiment, and general research before the prototype VLCCs were built. It was the first and most serious attempt made to understand the true nature and character of these ships, and it certainly was the single most cohesive international programme of maritime research ever undertaken.

What practically everyone was looking for was a spark. One can wonder whether any other ignition has ever initiated such an exhaustive hunt. Elaborate and multitudinous experiments were conducted ashore and afloat by all concerned; research programmes were sponsored at universities in Japan and the United States; NASA, the American space agency, gave data on static gathered from shooting rockets through clouds; and international conferences and symposia were held, including one in Sweden which brought together the world's leading experts on static. Huge sums were spent by Shell and the other big oil companies, as well as by individual governments and shipping organisations. Shell alone spent more than one million pounds on its own research. The official British inquiry into the

Mactra explosion, which ran from October 1971 to March 1972, was one of the most technically difficult on record and the longest of all British maritime inquiries; it was eleven days longer than *Titanic's*, which previously had been the longest on record. Yet for more than two years it all seemed to be getting nowhere.

The origin of the fatal spark was narrowed to three possible sources: static electricity, an object that broke loose and fell to the deck, or the release of a static field from the explosion of a gas bubble when it was slammed against the steel sides by water. The most popular theory was that the spark originated with the washing machines, and Shell itself followed two main lines of investigation: whether the strength of the water jets caused parts of the giant nozzles to break loose and fall to the deck, causing a spark; or whether the jets of water themselves caused an electrostatic field. Shell took several superships out of service for use in experiments. An American company, Chevron, undertook similar experiments.

While practically everybody else searched for a spark, Gulf Oil sought instead to find out what could make the atmosphere inside a supership's tanks explosive. It used its own fleet of 326,000-ton superships for its investigations and what it found out was a shock to its own personnel, for the experiments showed to Gulf's satisfaction that the overrich system, which Gulf itself used, could be highly dangerous unless more skilfully monitored than it traditionally had been. Tanks that had been registered safe by its conventional monitoring system were shown to contain explosive mixtures when monitored with more scientific instruments; the gas vapours lay stratified in safe and explosive layers to a far greater degree than hitherto suspected. As a result, Gulf switched from using the overrich system and now uses the inert-gas system.

Shell's own experiments convinced it that static electricity caused by the high-velocity water nozzles had been the cause of the explosions aboard *Marpessa* and *Mactra*. What happened inside the tanks, it believed, was rather similar to the creation of thunderstorm conditions.

What first had to be accepted was that static was the probable cause of the spark. Long and detailed experiments in Dutch laboratories led Shell to suppose that it was; it then slowly began putting together the likely circumstances that actually touched off the static, and these were seen to be as follows: as the water emerged from the nozzles of the washing machines, it expanded into huge chunks and, as the washing process lengthened, these were flying through the thick clouds of spray that gradually accumulated in the tanks; static electricity present in the spray was absorbed by the lumps of water and these, in their brief flight from nozzles to tank sides, could become as charged as a thundercloud and, when striking some metal projection, were capable of drawing a flash, somewhat like lightning.

None of this was conclusive, although it is a theory that remains widely accepted by VLCC operators. Their sailors, however, including of course those aboard *Ardshiel*, continue to feel that the forces locked inside those empty VLCC tanks are enigmatic and undependable. Tankers, including VLCCs, have continued to explode since the *Mactra–Marpessa–Kong Haakon* sequence. In 1973 a 216,000-ton Liberian VLCC also exploded and sank off West Africa, and took from *Marpessa* the distinction of being the largest ship ever to founder. The sailors' suspicions anyhow appear to be borne out by a report published early in 1974 by the International Chamber of Shipping in London concerning explosions aboard a new class of ships known as OBOs. These are giant vessels designed to handle three different sorts of cargo: ore, bulk freight, or oil. They too have become prone to explosions but, unlike the explosions in the VLCC tankers, the OBO explosions have *not* been associated with tank cleaning. Preliminary investigations indicated that high static voltages were developed because of strong slopping movement of oil-contaminated ballast water. The water itself is believed to throw off minute sparks as it sloshes, and those could touch off any gas pockets created by the small amounts of oil floating about. At any rate, since nothing can be taken for granted, the only insurance against disaster is an unequivocally non-explosive atmosphere for tank cleaning. Naturally the insurers of superships share this view since tanker disasters in recent years have cost them so many millions. Insurance premiums now amount to as much as 54 per cent of the cost of operating a VLCC. They rise to more than 70 per cent in the case of ULCCs.

At present, inert gas is considered to be the only safe atmosphere to have in a supership's tanks when cleaning them. There have been no explosions on ships properly employing this system of using the non-combustible waste gases from the ship's own engines. Ninety per cent of all new superships are being equipped with it, and insurers are actually offering reduced rates for those who have it.

As most tankers do, *Ardshiel* cleaned tanks as we slipped down toward and into the tropics. The work took six days; it began off the Canaries and it finished the day we crossed the equator. After each tank was cleaned it had to be inspected; for the tankermen this is the most dangerous, feared, and generally abominated task. For the Geordies especially, it brought to the ship the same perils and dreads they knew from their generations of experience in the Durham coal mines.

The three VLCC explosions were a frequent subject of discussion on board, but only as a curiosity of the business, shop talk; any apprehension expressed was over having to go down into the tanks. Although gas may not remain in explosive quantities after a tank has been cleaned, enough of it may lurk to kill people, and the danger of the descent into an apparently scoured and air-blown tank is that pockets of gas might yet be floating around the bottom like invisible balloons which, if punctured by a man's passage, could overcome him with their contents; or that a lethal cloud of hydrocarbon gas might be stirred into the atmosphere merely by walking through any sludge that hasn't been washed away. A group of men moving through puddles of oil on their inspection of the bottom of a tank can quickly create areas of concentrated gas which then lie about in the tank atmosphere like traps suddenly sprung for them. If the concentration of gas is high it requires only two or three inhalations to render a man unconscious. Sensations are blunted, the skin becomes numb and movements clumsy; a feeling of elation follows, and then, as the vital centres of the brain become affected, a drowsy sleep. It is all horribly swift. Once he is overcome, a man has to receive oxygen within four minutes to avoid permanent brain damage; a minute or so more would mean that he is dead, which would be more merciful.

On the face of it, there would seem to be little survival chance for anyone overcome at the bottom of a ninety-foot-deep tank with an entrance a quarter of a mile from the main part of the ship unless a warning were sounded the moment he was seen to stumble and fall – that is, seen by a rescue party waiting with full equipment on the deck immediately above.

Gassing is in fact the most common accident in tankers, and the matter was very much alive aboard Ardshiel as a result of a traumatic incident on the previous voyage when a group of men had been briefly lost and presumed missing at the bottom of number four centre tank, one of the largest in the ship. They finally had emerged safe and well.

The party had consisted of the then first officer, Donald Watson, who had been relieved at Le Verdon by Ewart-James; a cadet, who had also left at Le Verdon; Graham Allen, who of course was still aboard; and one of the Pakistani seamen.

After an accident had been suspected and the alarm had been sounded, things went wrong with the rescue attempt, which was seriously delayed for a number of reasons. Equipment wasn't where it should have been, and misunderstanding was rife.

Watson's wife was on board Ardshiel and her agony, though brief, was intense and terrible – that of a pithead wife, seaborne. Summoned to the bridge by the emergency signals, she watched Basil Thomson take charge and co-ordinate the rescue, saw the rescuers running up the long deck toward the aperture where just a short while before her husband had descended, and knew that if he had been gassed, he almost certainly already was dead or beyond recovery because of the delays.

The misery over the confusions that had delayed them in attempting to reach their companions, the bitterness and guilt they felt even as they struggled to make a rescue, knowing that in all likelihood their efforts already were too late, their shame in knowing that Watson's wife was desperately watching and depending upon them, their own frank fears about descending into the fumes, and then the extraordinary emotion of mingled consternation and relief when the men they were afraid for were seen emerging from the tank, were all gone over time and time again, as though they still couldn't credit an outcome that none of them at the time was prepared to believe possible. What they were expressing underneath it all was the true dread in these ships: that, unsuspectingly, in a matter of moments, one could be turned into a vegetable or snuffed out. There was no fear of the ship as a dangerous entity, nor even of the gas as an explosive power; only of this spectre forever lurking within its caves. It was a topic that recurred constantly throughout the voyage and, if they lived that tale of terror too often, it was because it involved the personal rather than the abstract and so contained all the essentials of the tragedy and drama they themselves were likely to encounter in these ships; false though the alarm was, the fear, the shame, the remorse, and the relief were not.

The story was that Watson and his small party had gone down into the tank (which was right forward) after it had been cleaned to inspect various valves. All four descended the long ladder together as far as the last flight of stairs, where Graham Allen was to stay with a portable VHF radio. A system of whistle signals had been arranged between Watson and Graham Allen to indicate when valves were to be opened and shut in the cargo control room and Allen was to relay these orders by VHF to Graham Chalmers, who was on duty in the control room. A cadet was to be on watch on the deck immediately above the tank.

Watson and his two companions continued down the ladder and vanished into the gloomy depths of the tank. Recounting the experience later, Graham Allen said, 'The cadet who had been left on deck, Roscoe, had orders to keep the chief officer's party in sight by following them from manhole to manhole. But after they'd gone I smelled gas and got a bit worried, so I radioed Roscoe to lower down a fresh-air mask. He did so, and then went back along the deck to spot the chief officer's party, but radioed back to me to say that he couldn't see them through any of the manholes. Then I heard a lot of whistling and shouting inside the tank. When you're inside one of those tanks sound gets distorted out of all proportion. I couldn't make out what it was about. It didn't sound like the signals we'd agreed upon. I couldn't see them, of course, and I couldn't move because my oxygen line wasn't long enough. Those tanks are so huge and inaccessible anyway, you just can't get around them. I always feel fear down there, and I did then a lot, because I couldn't understand their signals and because of the gas all around me. So I sounded the alarm. It was one of the worst moments of my life.

'I could hear the alarms going on the ship's horn and on the VHF. I was on the first landing on the ladder so I moved down to the bottom of the tank to be out of the way when the emergency party came down. I knew that those people were going to have to run from aft all the way up forward and that by the time they got to the tank top they would be out of breath, and the men they were going to rescue weren't at the bottom of the ladder with me, they were way over in some silly corner of the tank. They were going to come hurtling down that ladder, ninety feet, and then go searching through all those halls and bays, and over all those stringers to wherever the men were. It had never occurred to me how hopeless the whole business really was.

'The worst feeling was to stand there thinking all this and not be able to help those blokes in the same tank. It was a terrible feeling of helplessness. I got an awful feeling in my stomach; I was alone in that big tank, all alone with three dead men, or dying men, waiting for the emergency party to come; waiting and waiting.'

Graham Chalmers was in the cargo control room where he was to open and shut valves according to the instructions relayed by Graham Allen on the VHF. It was he who pressed the actual alarm bell within the ship itself. 'I was listening in on the VHF to the conversation between Graham Allen and Roscoe and heard Allen ask for air,' he recalled. 'I rushed down the deck to help the cadet give Allen the air. I returned to my duty in the control room and then heard Allen say, "Help, the chief officer's been gassed." I went into the ship's office and pressed the alarm, and then grabbed the speaker and announced, "There's gassing in number four centre tank." I stayed in the ship's office until the whole emergency party had been mustered, but it took about three minutes before everyone had mustered.'

Peter Dutton, who led the emergency party, had been in the engine-room control room when the alarm went off. 'I was the second one into the emergency headquarters, after Alfie Hattrell,' he said. 'Hattrell was just shooting out the door and I said, "What's the matter, Alf?" He said, "I don't know, I think the mate's gassed down in the tank." There was no contact on the VHF sets and the panic started then. There was no contact; we didn't know what the hell was going on down there. I ran up to the tank top and looked down. Hattrell was shouting down. There was no answer, just echoes.

'It was bloody awful. It was the feeling I got when I saw a glider crash once. A horrible, horrible sense of disaster. Watson's wife was on board and you knew for a fact that you just weren't going to get anybody out of that tank alive. You had to get down there and find them for one thing. Four centre is a massive tank.

'What made it worse was that there was a fearful bloody tangle in trying to get the necessary gear. I had told a cadet to get out the Drager gear, which is the large-pack breathing apparatus the emergency team uses for going down into a gas-filled area. It was down in the pump room unfortunately. So we had to go all the way aft for it; when we eventually got the Drager gear to the tank top we couldn't get the darn thing connected up. There was an extension piece missing. I ran back to get a breathing apparatus, one you strap on your back; I was going to go down myself with the resuscitator.

'I was thinking all the time how hopeless it all was. When you consider that the time lapse when you're gassed is about four minutes in which they must get you back to the fresh air, you can see why we felt as we did. Allowing a minute for it to be discovered that you have gas, that leaves three minutes; and it takes at least two minutes for the emergency party to get to emergency headquarters from all over the ship, at least a minute to get to the tank if it's near the accommodation, a minute and a half if it's one of the forward ones. That leaves a minute or less for them to get to wherever you're lying. It's just not a feasible operation, whichever way you look at it. With all the delays we'd had, we were too late even by the time we'd got to the tank top.

'Even if I'd had a portable breathing apparatus right at the tank and gone down at once, it would have been a hopeless try. In the tank itself the transverse sections are so huge that you can't get over them, you have to crawl through a hole which is a foot and a half deep and a little bit less wide. You can get through by yourself wearing a boiler suit, but that's all; not with a breathing apparatus on your back. You've got to take it off and and throw it through or drag it through, and then put it on again, and in all that time you're breathing the tank atmosphere, which might be all gas. Then if you find your man, you've got to bring *him* back the same way. There's about twenty huge bays in a tank like that and you might have to go through half of them before you find the gassed man, and then back again dragging or pushing him through.

'When I got back to the tank top with my portable breathing apparatus I found Watson and the others coming up. What had happened was that the mate had wanted a piece of equipment lowered down to him from the deck and had been trying to attract the attention of the man on the deck. He was very upset when he realised the panic they'd caused.

'But it was a good thing in its way. We had a full inquiry on the ship. The whole episode had exposed the weakness of the system. We'd done a lot of training for tank rescues and that stuff, but it had all fallen down when it came to the real thing; and for all intents and purposes it *was* the real thing. Now the equipment is always at the tank top, thoroughly checked, before men go down, and anyway we also carry additional rescue equipment to avoid possible delays. We never have two working parties in gas areas as we had that day; and when a party goes down we have somebody at every manhole, or Butterworth plate as we call them, keeping them in sight all the time. But I think it's a terrible thing myself on these ships, to go down there, that they make us go down, when they know for a fact that they cannot guarantee that a tank's gas free, and that they cannot get anyone out of one. For us that day there were four corpses down in that tank, and that's the way we still remember it. There was a great sense of guilty conscience on the ship that night; we had failed, really we had failed.'

The entire episode, from the first warning from Graham Allen that the work party might be gassed until its emergence from the tank, had happened in less than ten minutes.

Approaching the equator we were now at the same point in the voyage at which the above incident had occurred. As each great tank was cleaned it was cleared of its inert gas and an inspection party, led by Alan Ewart-James, went down to examine the equipment and steelwork. As soon as an inspection was finished and the party had returned to the deck, the tank was refilled with inert gas. P & O had been one of the pioneer users of inert gas; the *Ardshiel* class of superships had been ordered to be fitted with it while under construction, even before the VLCC explosions. Thus the explosive power of the tanks caused comparatively little concern among my companions, who regarded the idea of an explosion on board as remote.

'We feel it is absolutely safe; well, at any rate safer than anything else available,' Ewart-James said on the morning of his final tank inspection, on which I was to accompany him. 'Very simply, when the engine burns fuel for the boilers the exhaust gases go up the funnel, but instead of going out as smoke, these gases are put through various bits of apparatus which take out impurities such as carbon and sulphur dioxide. What is left is a gas with practically no oxygen, and very few chemicals. It is then blown by fan along various lines into the cargo tanks. It displaces the air inside the tanks until they are completely full of inert gas. The oxygen content then is so low that you simply can't have an explosion. As soon as we start discharging cargo the inert gas system is in operation; it blows into the tank as the oil goes out. The only time that an empty tank is not inerted is when we go down to have a look, as we now are about to do.'

I had met him in his office, where he had laid out a boiler suit, Wellington boots, and gloves for me and, when I'd donned these, we went down to the cargo control room, where we were joined by the other members of the party, James Jackson and Harvey Phillips.

One of the things he looked forward to was the day when as master of a ship he would no longer have to go down into the tanks, Ewart-James remarked as we went forward up the main deck. It was a job he detested as much as the others, he said, and he could not understand why they had to go down at all as he couldn't see that much was accomplished by it: on such a cursory visit it was impossible to examine thoroughly a place the size of a cathedral. On some VLCCs they carry a rubber dinghy, the tanks are slowly filled with water, and the inspection teams row around inside examining the steelwork, which he thought made better sense.

It was a warm, sunny, tropical day, with the wind fresh across the main deck, and it was a long, pleasant walk forward to number one centre tank, into which the descent was to be made; the fumes from the open tank lid struck me as unpleasantly strong when we got there, but the apprehension I felt, and it was considerable, was for the actual journey down to the bottom; at that moment, the gas seemed decidedly less intimidating than the height, for which I've never had a strong head.

Ewart-James went first, vanishing like a potholer, the tank lid being very much like a subterranean entrance. It was large enough to take only one person at a time. I followed, then Harvey Phillips. James Jackson remained on deck, watching us through the Butterworth plates. A brief ladder went down through the lid onto a small platform, ninety feet above the ship's bottom, and from there another narrow ladder, with handrails, flew out across space, and then down; the narrowness of the ladder itself, the lack of protection between the steps and that thin handrail, all of it flying trapeze-like through the air, were terrifying.

Architectural curiosity requires a mood of dimension rather than mere sense of size and, in this regard, the tank was a surprise, not only among the biggest functional enclosures created by man, a hollow steel compartment to be filled with eighteen thousand tons of oil when required, but full of strange and interesting compositions, with a distinct life and expression of its own – a place for imagists, somehow indubitably of this age though somewhat mysteriously so. Illumination was provided by the open Butterworth plates, neat portholes of natural light, diminishing in size as we descended until they shone far above the lower darkness like a firmament of moons. In this faint light we began passing the washing machines, rising twenty feet from the bottom like weird pyramidal stalagmites. From the bottom itself, with the light falling in shafts from the remote Butterworth plates, the impression of height and size was far greater than it had been from the entrance at the top.

I hadn't expected quite such a mass of detail, of elaborate patterns of pipes and valves, so many flights of other ladders, so many beams and struts, platforms, nooks, crannies, and crevices. Most impressive of all were the transverse beams thrusting out into the huge emptiness, like transepts.

Even though there had been a slight sea movement on deck it was dead still and, more eerily, dead quiet down at the bottom; no ship sounds, no faint noise of sea strain or stress or creaking; just the clear, matter-of-fact voices of the two men and the unhurried scuffles of our boots on the steelwork. Although we were virtually at the bottom, the pipes and transverse frames were so huge that our path, which lay across the top of them, still carried us at a considerable height, perhaps twelve to fifteen feet, above the ship's plates.

When we reached the centre of this particular bay, the two men went down a series of handgrips to the lowest level, where they worked quickly by the light of their flashlights.

Standing on what I assumed to be the rider plate of the ship's keelson, which is the reinforcing steel stringer that normally runs the length of a ship's keel, I could understand the immense difficulties of trying to reach someone lying gassed somewhere in this complex gloom. An oxygen mask had been lowered down through one of the Butterworth plates and I had been told to stand as close to it as possible, an injunction which I selfishly appreciated and unhesitatingly obeyed. In any event we were at a point easily visible and were being closely watched. But to reach someone lying in the remoter regions of the tank, lost from sight and with only a rough idea where he might be, was tantamount, surely, to being told atop the dome of a darkened Gothic cathedral to descend an eighteen-inch-wide stairway pinned to its walls and buttresses and to find somewhere at the bottom among the naves, bays, chapels, colonnades, and apses a senseless form that had to be brought aloft, all within four minutes.

To pass from one bay to another, as Dutton had said, was a fearsome and claustrophobic as well as tiresome task; but the apertures through the beams couldn't be any larger, otherwise the hull-strengthening forces dormant in the beams would be considerably diminished: to puncture them to any great degree would be tantamount to cutting Samson's locks and the vessel might not be able to support its hefty loads of oil.

There was no strong smell of oil or gas inside the tank itself, no apparent trace of oil on the sides, none on the ladders; a remarkable cleansing job indeed. But everything was colourless in a distinctly sinister manner: the tank sides, the very steel of the ladder that one trod and touched, the pipes and beams – in fact everything in sight – was the terrible grey of things forever beyond sunlight and oxygen. If there was corrosion, as there usually is in tanks, it had none of the healthy colours of the open, the autumn reds of salted rust; everything had the look of ashes, which was fitting perhaps since this was the transient tomb for the oldest decease on earth, the primordial forests and vegetation, borne here portion after portion to their ultimate dissolution in their modern crematoria, the refineries.

Returning up the ladders to the main deck, I was again struck by that anomaly of these ships whereby they retrieve in so many curious ways some part of the experience of the great days of sail. The ascent and descent of great heights is a recurrent part of ship's routine aboard supertankers to a degree that hasn't been known since sail (on ordinary ships masthead painting or repair usually is done with the aid of a bo'sun's chair, and most modern ships anyway dispense with the foremast, preferring a steel structure for radar, radio aerials, and signal halliards abaft the bridge or funnel). The ladders we descended into number one centre tank ran in stages, angled to varying degrees, all of them steep; but in some tanks the descent is perpendicular, ninety feet of it, a test of head and nerves which few on these ships relish. But there the comparison ends. The sailing man went aloft into the sky, with exhilaration in fine weather and with a fierce sense of elemental combat during bad. Tank descent on the other hand involves removal from all that visibly matters: black holes in the sea.

It was a relief, a feeling of stunning exhilaration in reverse, to return to the surface of those shafts, back to the sun, to the sea itself, and to the ship with its sudden homely sense of place. For hours after

I could smell oil on my skin and clothes, which was the first time since I'd been aboard.

After tank cleaning, celebration! As it happened, the day of our descent was Basil Thomson's thirtieth wedding anniversary and the party had been planned since departure from Le Verdon. Fancy-dress parties are as popular on tankers as they are with the purser's entertainment committees of passenger liners, and preparations had become increasingly secretive and feverish, while conversation constantly recalled other parties on other ships, canvassing them for ideas.

Dressing-up entertainment is a very old part of the British sailor's life. Nelson himself promoted men who put effort into entertaining their mates in this fashion. Drag balls have always been a feature of life in the crew canteens of British liners, and glittering affairs they can be, often proffering the chief steward or urbane head waiter as Queen Mum. But such ribald lower deck vulgarity, which is the true tradition of these sea entertainments, was a long way away from ours. It was, without question, to be a sentimental, not an abrasive, occasion.

The juniors spent the afternoon decorating the wardroom and when the rest of us entered it that evening we found it handsomely festooned with flags, with prominence given to the blue ensign, which was mounted against the forward windows. All lights had been dimmed, tables and chairs set back and, on a small table in the centre of the room, rested a large anniversary card, made of old charts and sealed with ribbons and red sealing wax.

Lacking the fusion of coarser humours and self-mockery, the costume parade into the wardroom was somewhat self-conscious at first, with polite praise for all entries, until finally, encircled by vicars, bishops, fuzzy-wuzzies, astronauts, and toga'd Romans, Basil Thomson, dressed as a country bumpkin in bathing trunks, old shirt, old socks, and sporting cap, listened to a brief speech from James Jackson, who said that he'd been with Captain Thomson five years ago on his twenty-fifth anniversary, aboard the old *Ellenga*, now sadly gone, and he hoped that they might even celebrate the sixtieth together.

'Hello, what's this, then?' Thomson cried, accepting the card. Everyone had expected him to weep, which he always did, he said, when the occasion required, but he laid the card aside and said he would read it more appreciatively later in his cabin. 'Now let's enjoy ourselves and think of my good wife, Betty, and my two beautiful daughters, and know what a lucky man I've been!'

Thomson had a reputation of being a 'good feeder' and, on occasions such as this, of being a more than generous host. By the time dinner was announced the party had become noisy, and its decibel count rose vigorously after the tomato soup had been washed down by tumblerfuls of Bristol Cream sherry, the shrimp cocktail by Sauternes, and the chicken curry by Saint Emilion, and coffee by equal measure of brandy.

The Goanese stewards brought in their band and saluted Thomson with a thirty-verse tribute, each verse repeated, all in Goanese, both words and key, which was high-pitched and plaintive, and when they paused for breath, apparently before going through it all once again, Dave Haydon was hastily shoved forward to sing 'You'll Never Walk Alone' and 'Climb Every Mountain', both Thomson's personal requests.

'Bloody marvellous,' he kept repeating. 'Bloody marvellous.'

When Haydon had done, the Geordies, who had been deferentially quiet through the programme, rose in a body, set Pat Allen on a table, grouped themselves about her, and demanded that she sing 'I'll Take You Home Again, Kathleen'.

'Go on, then,' Thomson cried, when she looked to him for encouragement. She sang in a sweet, high unaffected voice of the sort that one properly associates with ballads and the Geordies kept shaking their heads, as though overcome by an inexpressible emotion. Then Charlie, the Chinese donkeyman, who'd been brought in to play his pipes, insisted on singing one of Mao's cultural revolution songs, which went on almost as long as the Goanese one, except that everyone, having had appreciably more to drink in the meantime, tried to sing it with him. When he had finished, he finally played his pipes, and the juniors rose one by one to dance to his strange, lilting tunes, each moving to his own rhythms, and together they formed a small, tight group in the centre of the floor, revolving dreamily before the long spread of the blue ensign.

EIGHT

THE tropics vanished overnight along with celebration and, as if in keeping with the more sombre spirit of its occupants, the ship itself entered a different mood, another sea. We were rapidly descending into the southern winter. The wind was rising and we'd begun to roll, which was no comfort for those whose heads were tender.

The party had left everyone distracted and restless. Their look and manner was as though they'd been celebrating their last night on board only to be told at breakfast that this unhappily had proved not to be the case. There was at any rate a sudden communal urge before lunch to have some sort of immediate promise of something positive to look forward to. An order book had been placed in the wardroom for those who wanted something or other from Cape Town. These orders were to be telegraphed to the P & O agent at the Cape and sent out by tender together with the mail and the ship's supplies. *Ardshiel*'s own shop was so thoroughly stocked with almost everything that anyone could want that the order page had lain barren of business. Now everyone wanted something. They hung over the book thoughtfully, pencil in hand, reflecting upon whim. None of what they finally ordered seemed truly necessary. The list for chocolate cakes was a long one, even though the ship's baker made cakes as good as any; but this was contact with the shore, a small gift to one's self.

During lunch itself the sound of Charlie's pipes far away in the crew's mess was like a faint receding echo of the night's festivities; as always, it fitted every mood, and now struck everyone as a sensible and soothing sound for the day after, for they listened to it appreciatively, without talk.

When the pipes finally stopped, Harvey Phillips quietly remarked that Charlie had had his own boatyard in Hong Kong. He'd gone bankrupt and come to sea. He'd been aboard *Ardshiel* for two years and hadn't seen his home in all that time. Yet, he was always happy and smiling. 'His mood never changes,' Phillips said. 'Always the same, the same old Charlie.' He shook his head in wonder, as if unable to match Charlie's responses to his own.

In the same speculative mood and speaking in the same tones of resigned weariness, Basil Thomson sat talking in the wardroom after dinner about an incident on a recent voyage when *Ardshiel* had broken down and drifted helplessly off the South African coast. It was an episode that frequently came up in conversation, usually raised by himself, especially during pour-out. It had great relevance as the ship approached those waters again, and anyhow the subject suited the introspective mood of the wardroom and, though familiar with its details, they all listened as carefully and kindly as though it were quite new to them.

Ardshiel had been on her way to the Gulf to load. Off Port Elizabeth the ship's power began to fail because of salt water contamination in her boilers. She was nine miles off the South African coast and Thomson had promptly warned all shipping that his vessel was having difficulties and asked everyone to stay clear of her. For four days she struggled to cover the 380-mile distance to Durban, to which *Mactra* also had limped after her explosion in 1969. The engineers managed to keep the engines turning, though with just sufficient power to keep her moving through the water. It was clear that if she broke down completely her position would be perilous, and Thomson had taken care also to warn the South African authorities of his difficulties.

The high incidence of tanker breakdowns off the South African coast since the closure of the Suez Canal has made it a worthwhile proposition for salvage tugs to station themselves permanently in those waters with their radios tuned to the passing traffic. The only tug available to *Ardshiel* in the event that she broke down completely was then lying in Durban harbour and, after listening to *Ardshiel*'s reports of her own distress, its master called up Thomson and asked whether he wanted the tug's services. Commissioning salvage tugs is a costly business which usually is regarded by owners as a final desperate resort; the salvage awards, calculated from the value of the ship as well as her cargo, can be enormous, and the inevitable litigation on the matter itself is a huge expense. A master must therefore have good reason for summoning a tug. Thomson, on the assumption that the tug would still be at its post if he finally did need it, declined the offer. To his surprise, however, the tug suddenly hove into sight some time later and, passing within hailing distance of the crippled tanker, its master advised Thomson that he was steaming south to undertake a commission on the coast below and that if *Ardshiel* required his assistance now was the time to say so.

Ardshiel's chances of making Durban under her own power seemed reasonable, although she had been stopping and starting; if the weather got bad, however, the ship would not have enough power against a seaway and if she broke down completely anyway, which she might yet do, she would be helpless. Thomson's dilemma was whether to risk a gamble on the frail engines and the weather, or accept a tow that might involve a claim for the full value of the ship (which, as it happened, was what the salvors eventually asked for).

'What was I to do?' Thomson now said. 'The weather was deteriorating and there disappearing over the horizon was the only tug that could help me if I needed help. If I'd let him go and then found that I needed him I would have been blamed. As it was, I was censured for calling him back. But what else could I have done?'

Normally at this hour, over the coffee, he might have been telling one of his anecdotes about the old *Ellenga* or life in the P & O in the past, and he would have been doing so while leaning well back in his chair, satisfied, with his hands slamming the arms of the chair for emphasis; but he now held his hands folded over his cup instead, his elbows resting on his knees, and he spoke slowly and heavily, as though his words held a weight of oppression. 'I was prejudged before I got to London,' he said. 'I got a letter of exoneration later, but it didn't make up for the feeling when I got to the office knowing that the issue had been decided against me in most people's minds. But how can anybody really know the pressures and circumstances of a thing like that if they aren't there at the time? I've never forgotten a board of inquiry on which I once sat. A British India Line master was up before us. His ship had been in a collision. They asked him why he'd given the orders he did when he saw the danger he was in, and he simply said, "I had thirty seconds in which to make up my mind and I did at that moment what I thought was best." There was no answer to that, and they let him go. When you've got half a minute you can't weigh up alternative courses of action, you just do there and then what you think is best, and you probably know that whatever you do isn't going to make much difference in all likelihood. Well, I myself had longer than thirty seconds, but it comes to the same thing. It's always easier later when you've got all the facts and figures and can decide leisurely at an inquiry what should have been done, but when the thing is actually happening, well it's all very different, which is what the BI master told them.'

They had listened gravely, watching him, but there was no comment when he'd finished. For once, however, their silence did not appear to detach their attention from him as it so often did when he'd finished some monologue; by so patently sharing the recollected weight of his despair they brought to the coffee-table a feeling of community which was not often there. Thomson's tone and resignation and their sympathy for him were all very much part of a general post-celebration depression and weariness. Apathy and irresolution sat upon all of them and made them captive to each other's moods. But it did not make their feeling for him any less genuine, and through this one felt that he was receiving the kindest gift of all so far. It was not often that they saw him for himself.

'It's time to go and do my book of words,' he said, but he sat a moment longer. 'Nothing is foolproof,' he suddenly began declaiming, somewhat disconnectedly but in more characteristic fashion. 'They lay on all those improvements to help you, but none is foolproof. There is only one perfect way of navigation, to know the error of your compass and to take two bearings on shore positions. Don't any of you ever forget it. Good night.' He was back in the past, with simpler ships and familiar tools.

Ships have always been liable to breakdown, either from the shattering force of the weather upon their hulls or means of propulsion, or because of mechanical failure, but probably no class of ship since the age of steam began has been more systematically prone to breakdown than supertankers. Nor has any class of vessel, whether in the age of sail or steam, been less able in the face of disaster to make do, mend itself a little, and perhaps get to where it is going through patchwork or improvisation.

In the days of sail the weather could be the only real cause of breakdown of a ship's physical equipment, unless it was all so aged and rotted that it collapsed of its own accord; even then, sailor's artifice could always make something new of what was available. The sailmaker and the carpenter were the most indispensable men aboard after the master and the mate. The sailmaker had to restitch and remake the sails blown and shredded by the winds. On a bad voyage a ship might have had to stitch an entirely new suit of sails for itself, and just one of these sails of brutally heavy canvas could hold as many as two million stitches.

If a sailing vessel was dismasted and otherwise damaged, a carpenter could hammer a manageable rig or steering gear from splinters, so to speak; improvisation was navigation's complementary art. It had to be, for such a vessel was entirely cut off, alone in its own unbeseechable eternity.

The age of steam and its mechanical breakdowns often required even greater resourcefulness from sailors. Lacking radio, early steamships often drifted for weeks, even months, while repairs were made to engines or steering gear. When, for example, the 5,000-ton British tramp steamer *Titania* lost her propeller during heavy gales in the

South Atlantic in 1900, the ship's head was held to the wind and sea by a sea-anchor, the forward holds were flooded to raise the stern and, lurching and pounding in this dangerous position, the spare propeller was swung outboard by cargo winches and then guided onto the wildly gyrating tail shaft, threaded onto it, and then sealed into place by a locknut. The whole business took several days and was supervised by the ship's master, who was suspended outboard in a bo'sun's chair which, with the motion of the ship, alternately swung him across the skies, then plunged him into the crests. Lloyd's awarded him its medal for Meritorious Services.

The sagas of make-do which have in this manner brought steamships and their crews to port against apparently hopeless circumstances are beyond counting. It still often happens during the North Atlantic winter: some flag of convenience Second World War-built freighter, perhaps a Liberty, whose cargo has shifted, whose power is faltering or gone, and which is lying almost on its beam ends, nonetheless manages to hold its head to the sea and, eventually, to make port. The two world wars, of course, provided scores of instances of skilful handling of disabled ships. When a torpedo in 1942 blew off the troopship *Llangibby Castle*'s stern and took with it the ship's rudder, she sailed 3,400 miles steering with her twin screws. Many of the greatest survival sagas of the last war involved tankers. A notable episode was that of the 8,000-ton British tanker *San Demetrio*, which was shelled and set on fire by the German pocket battleship *Admiral Scheer* when it raided an Atlantic convoy. *San Demetrio* was so badly damaged, her fires so uncontrollably raging, that she was abandoned. Twenty hours later, however, one of the lifeboats sighted the ship, still afire, and, since no other succour was in sight, its occupants manoeuvred alongside. They boarded the tanker with great difficulty, fought for two days to extinguish the fires, got the engines going and, although the bridge was one of the areas demolished by the flames, they conned the ship from aft. *San Demetrio* finally arrived with most of its precious cargo still intact.

One was always inclined to believe that nothing was impossible at sea, but it would be difficult to imagine too many such feats, or even opportunities for resourcefulness, in the case of supertankers. That, of course, doesn't preclude feats of seamanship or courage with them. It was seamanship of the highest order, notably calm manœuvring of the ship, that kept flames from engulfing the 206,000-ton *Mactra* after her tank explosion. Her master, Captain J. E. Palmer, turned the ship to keep the flames and thick smoke away from the accommodation area which, if it caught fire, would have meant abandoning the vessel. Her chief engineer, E. H. Edmondson, directed fire-fighting on deck for nine hours. But although much of her deck was blasted open, the working spaces of the ship were unharmed; no windows even were broken because the force of the explosion went straight up. Had her accommodation and bridge been burned out, however, and the ship been abandoned, it is hard to conceive that a *San Demetrio* type of salvage operation could have been carried out by her crew. Reboarding her sheer towering sides alone would have been a ferocious problem.

The mere size of the ship always emerges as one of the main restrictions upon the ingenuity of any supertanker sailor, however good he may be in an old-fashioned sense. The distance can be too great or access too awkward for practical solutions. If a supertanker loses a propeller it is virtually inconceivable that the spare that is carried right forward on the main deck could be manœuvred aft as it was on the *Titania* and fitted. It weighs between thirty and sixty tons. There is no practical means of handling such a weight for a distance of close to a quarter of a mile outboard along the ship's side, or even over the decks. It is there simply to avoid having to wait in a dockyard should a replacement be necessary. Anyway, on a loaded VLCC the propeller shaft is about forty feet under the water. Diving gear not a bo'sun's chair would be in order for any master wishing to supervise the task.

Such wholly new though understandable limits to shipboard resource and capability might have suggested, one would reasonably have supposed, that their design should have employed the fullest compensation where it was possible to do so: that is, whatever part of the ship could be made dependable, there no penny should have been spared. Quite obviously this would have been where their design and systems remained familiar and conventional and drew directly upon past experience.

One place where this should have been so was in the engine room. There was to be nothing revolutionary about supertanker propulsion. As the majority of them were to be steamships, it meant their propulsion systems were grown directly from a century of evolution and development. If there was to be any comfort for the pioneer navigators of these unwieldy ships, and for the rest of us, it should have been the knowledge that the most important part of the vessel, the engine room, the source of the ship's life and control, was the one area at least that remained heir to precedent and experience, and that, if the engines started to break down at all, as anything mechanical might do, at least it would be along a fail-safe route of reserve power and contingency units.

But economy dominated the concept, design, and construction of these ships and one's awareness of this grows with increased acquaintance. They lack that visual finish and feeling of workmanship that one traditionally associates with a ship of substance; this is understandable since the essential concept of them was of a functional, utilitarian unit, with the only extravagance that which the owner wished to provide as inducement for the crew – and some notoriously are not even concerned about that.

There is almost no aspect of these ships that hasn't been touched by price-mindedness; and it would not be such a concern if one were not so aware that much of the apparent deckside reflection of this is more than superficial and penetrates all the way into the sound, seagoing dependability of so many of the vessels.

No ships of VLCC size should have been built with single screws, as has been the case with the majority of them. No passenger liner would be without twin, triple, or quadruple screws. Although most cargo liners and freighters do have single screws, a great many have twin shafts. Anyhow they can hardly be compared with VLCCs. Twin screws are naturally more expensive to buy, install, and maintain, but they ensure better command of the hull, as well as better thrust. What makes them particularly essential for a VLCC is that they give much better slow-speed manœuvrability, which VLCCs so conspicuously lack because of their big hulls, and they make the ship less vulnerable to total immobilisation because of engine fault. No single-screw VLCC could do what *Llangibby Castle* did during the war and get herself out of trouble in a hurry or reach port when partially disabled by steering with her engines.

Such an outlandish hull manœuvred by one propeller and a single rudder is on the face of it ludicrous: relatively low drag allows supertankers to roll easily through the water, so the single-screw system is adequate for thrust, but it is wholly inadequate for emergencies, and hopeless as a means of braking the considerable momentum of the ship in a hurry. The advantages of the stronger system were proven by the Gulf Oil–Ludwig 326,000 tonners, which were given twin rudders and twin screws. As a result, these ships on their trials showed that they could crash stop from full power to full stern in about the same distance as a 50,000 tonner, about two miles, and that their manœuvrability and directional stability using twin rudders and twin screws was certainly as good as and possibly better than that of smaller tankers. Yet these ships are almost alone among VLCCs in being thus equipped.

Perhaps these economies make sense when one confronts the probability that supertankers are not built to last, which once was the only conceivable way to build a ship. Their write-off life is ten years, which is half of what has been considered normal up to now. In the case of P & O itself, the company declares that its write-off life for a tanker is 'from ten to fifteen years'.

145

That once apparently indestructible supposition developed through the ages that nothing could be left to chance in ships had of course been most manifest in the very construction and strength of the hull and of its machinery. There was an accepted life span for every ship: that is, an accepted period at the end of which the vessel might be considered to have reached the end of its commercial usefulness, to have paid for itself, earned profits, contributed to the corporate tax position and its own replacement value through depreciation, and finally even been able to earn a tidy sum through its scrap or resale value. As a rule, such a life span for a ship was held to be roughly twenty years. But invariably ships went on for much longer, because they were in fine fettle and were expected to be.

It is not uncommon for passenger liners to go on well beyond their fortieth birthdays. The record is probably held by the 3,167-ton Cunard liner *Parthia* of 1870, whose passenger accommodation was finally removed in 1941 although the ship itself continued sailing on the Alaskan coast until 1952, when its hull was converted into a barge and may well still be plodding faithfully along in those parts. Among the many vintage liners still doing very well for themselves under other names are the old Matson liner *Malolo*, built by W. Cramp & Sons of Philadelphia in 1927. In 1963 I sailed along the North African coast in a sixty-six-year-old Spanish liner, *J. J. Sister*, which had been built at the end of the nineteenth century for the Italians as the *Galileo Galilei*. She was when I boarded her undoubtedly the oldest passenger ship in the world, but her master was justifiably proud of her. 'Hombre! Todavia fuerte!' he protested when we set off from Ceuta and I expressed misgivings about the power of the engines against the strength of the Levanter gale outside. He was right, of course; she was still strong, and we reached Mellila and, finally, Almeria on the Spanish coast opposite at precisely the hours the schedule had said we would. Cargo ships used to go on even longer than passenger ships and, until recently, it was not unusual to find steamships of seventy or eighty years still trading around European coasts.

It was the superb engineering and the marvellous engines, with their immaculate workmanship, sound materials, and no cutting of corners involved, that gave that sort of stalwart service. Endurance and dependability were the qualities presupposed for ship's machinery. The shell and fabric of the ship had to be sound enough to deal with all that sea strain might impose upon it, but the engines had to be built for performance as well as strain. They had to give the maximum efficiency under the worst conditions, and they had to be able to do this for years, with as little trouble as possible. It was a tall order but, for the past seventy years or so, which roughly covers the

146

age of confidence and proven performance in marine engineering, it has been magnificently fulfilled in all major shipbuilding nations through all manner of ships.

Ship's machinery has not been infallible. The strains are too great. There can be duds, as happens with cars. They turn up from time to time. P & O itself had one in a recent passenger liner, *Iberia*, scrapped finally; her sister ship, *Arcadia*, still runs perfectly. But duds have been the exception rather than the rule. Probably no heavy-duty engines that man has developed have been more serenely successful than marine engines. Many conventional ships have trouble-free years, mechanically speaking. They go on steadily year after year without perceptible strain. Thousands of lesser vessels have qualified, and still do, for the sort of tribute paid in 1935 to the Cunard liner *Mauretania* (built in 1907) when she was sent to the scrapyard after an arduous career on the North Atlantic during which she had held the Blue Riband for twenty-two years. 'She was sound, fast, efficient to the end,' a British sea writer, Humphrey Jordan, wrote in an epitaph volume on the ship. 'When she was broken up, her boilers, the boilers of 1907, which had made steam to drive her across nearer three than two million miles of sea, were in excellent sound condition. She was not failing; she was past the fashion ... for the voyage to Rosyth [the breaker's yard] fifteen knots were ordered, but she would keep on working up to eighteen: that was herself.'

That emphatically is a tribute which no supership is ever going to earn, least of all for its boilers, which are the principal source of the considerable troubles they have. The evidence suggests that much of the time their power and propulsive systems are quite inadequate for the job, and for the responsibility that goes with the job, at least so far as those of us who worry from the shore about the damage these ships can do are concerned.

There was nothing unusual about the nature of *Ardshiel*'s breakdown off the South African coast. It has become commonplace among tankers, though not among those of the P & O fleet. Supertankers suddenly stop, all power gone, and lie helplessly adrift as they wait for a tow from another ship or tug, or, if they are off some coast, the hulk is set by wind and current toward shore as the crew resignedly watches. There are times when this malady, like a terrible inherent disease of the species, seems suddenly rampant among these vessels, with ships breaking down all over the seas, but with a frequency that somehow appears to be notably more pronounced in the waters encircling Africa, presumably because of the density of traffic on the run between Europe and the Persian Gulf; and also because of the violence of the winter seas at the halfway point, around the tip of southern Africa, and through which they have to pass twice on such a seasonal voyage, as we ourselves were about to do.

Tankers break down from many mechanical causes, but mostly because their power drains from them, and this, in rough order of incidence, is the result of boiler trouble, electrical blackout (itself usually a consequence of boiler trouble, though not always), or flooding of the engine room. Often it is an undefeatable combination of all of these.

The rate at which these troubles occur is extraordinary. When, for example, a British tanker, *British Comet*, broke down near Ceylon because of a flooded engine room, four other tankers answered her distress calls and were alongside her within twelve hours, but two of these themselves developed engine trouble and set off for the Persian Gulf in company so as to give assistance to each other if needed. The *British Comet* was taken in tow for Singapore by one of the other ships still standing by. Alan Ewart-James, who was aboard the only ship left free to continue its voyage unhindered by responsibility for another, told me that he would always remember the almost immediate appearance of four tankers around the disabled *British Comet* as being indicative to him of how dense tanker traffic really was on the high seas, while he would remember the sudden extension of distress within that small group of oil ships as being equally well reflective of the smart pace at which they can break down. In the first quarter of 1974, for example, there were one hundred and twelve tanker casualties involving machinery breakdown, according to the Tanker Advisory Center, New York.

The grave risk that this involves in the case of VLCCs was illustrated when, on 15 August 1974, the fully laden 250,000 tonner *World Princess* suffered an engine-room fire and broke down off Cape Town. The ship had come in to pick up mail and supplies. A sudden fire in her engine room caused complete breakdown and the helpless ship drifted to within a mile and a half of the coast. The weather, already poor, deteriorated rapidly during the next few days. Had she grounded she would have been lying fully exposed to the heavy battering storm swell. That she would have broken and spilled her oil under those circumstances can hardly be doubted.

Even while we ourselves were heading for the Cape, two typical tanker breakdown dramas were occurring upon *Ardshiel's* course ahead, one of them being a repeat under virtually the same circumstances of her own drama off South Africa.

A fully laden 40,000-ton tanker, *Simfonia* (which, as it happened, was a former P & O tanker, *Megna*, sold to Greek interests and now registered in Panama), had lost steam and power six miles off Danger Point, near Cape Agulhas. She was virtually at the same spot where the Getty tanker *Wafra* had broken down just five months previously. That meant that if, like the *Wafra*, she were to go ashore there, then that area with its various penguin, seal, and walrus breeding grounds would suffer a second inundation of crude oil within less than half a year. Furthermore, two months before the *Wafra* disaster, a 46,000-ton tanker, *Kazimah*, had lost power just outside Cape Town harbour and gone on the rocks off Robben Island in the centre of the bay before harbour tugs could take her in tow.

After two such deplorable incidents in their area within such a brief period, the Cape Town harbour authorities were understandably fearful of a third when they heard that *Simfonia* was in trouble. Fortunately, the prevailing wind and the lay of the coast gave *Simfonia* a longer drift than the six miles which was her actual distance off the coast and the tug dispatched from Cape Town reached her in time after a hundred-mile dash around Good Hope.

While this was happening, a laden 35,000-ton Niarchos tanker, *World Miracle*, was under tow for the Cape after her engine room had flooded. Engine-room flooding had been the cause of *Wafra's* disablement as well. In the first quarter of 1974, according to the Tanker Advisory Center of New York, seven tankers suffered flooded engine rooms or pump rooms.

The power failure and engine-room flooding in superships must be understood against the fact that most tankers are steamships. Engines are the single most expensive installation in a ship and the choice of machinery for their vessels has always been a difficult one for shipowners. In practical terms this means whether to build motorships or steamships. In operation diesels are by far the most economical form of marine propulsion (they use about a third less fuel than the steam turbine) but they can prove less attractive in other ways. They are more costly to buy and install initially than steam turbines, and they require a great deal more maintenance than steam, which is not only more compact but less fussy, and therefore easier to look after and to automate. In the case of tankers, these were the economies that seemed to matter.

Steamships make steam in their boilers, from where it is delivered to the propulsion unit, the turbines, which drive the ship, as well as to the alternators, which provide the ship's electrical power.

In the simplest terms, the whole apparatus depends upon two water systems, salt and fresh. The boilers use fresh water of absolute purity. A particular quantity of water is continually circulated through an arrangement of pipes. The furnaces in the boilers turn this water to steam, which goes into the turbines, propels them, and then, exhausted, this weak steam is delivered to the condensers, where it is condensed back into water, and thence delivered back to the boilers for another cycle. The cooling process in the condensers is achieved by cold salt water, which is drawn into the ship through an injection inlet well below the waterline and then circulated in condensing tubes enclosed in the large condenser chamber, into which the steam to be condensed is passed. The salt water then is ejected from an outlet above the waterline. It is principally when leaks or troubles occur in these two closed water circuits that tankers get into serious mechanical difficulty.

What happened with British Comet, Wafra, and World Miracle was that the condenser intake pipe began to leak or break and, as this grew worse, pressure of the water outside the hull forced sea-water in through the break. It is the equivalent of a hole suddenly punctured in the ship's side below the waterline. Water can rush in so fast that even by the time the leak is noticed the area around it is so flooded that the task of finding and sealing the break is difficult if not impossible. Aboard Wafra, mattresses and planks were brought from all over the ship and piled against the leak, but the water rose steadily and, as it did, it drowned the ship's propulsion and power, and she lay helpless. If a ship's tanks are empty, she will stay afloat because of the great buoyancy in the hull but if they are full she could sink; salt water is heavier than oil, and a large engine room filled with seawater could be sufficient weight to drag the rest of the vessel down.

If the ship is in deep water off a shore, sinking is probably the best thing that could happen; otherwise, as befell the Wafra, she's likely to go aground, break, and pollute the coast. In November 1972, fifteen months after World Miracle's breakdown, it all happened yet again in those waters when the 50,000-ton Greek tanker Gallant Coloctronis flooded her engine room north of Durban and went aground on the Mozambique coast. It is a particularly frightening accident: sudden, unexpected, inexplicable and, like a heart attack in a man apparently fit and well, it cripples swiftly, and often proves fatal. The main cause of it is believed to be the vibrations set up by the long hulls and the fact that the oscillations of these are not of the same frequency as those of the engine.

Serious trouble with the pure water system of the boilers, however, is far more frequent and cripples far more tankers than injection pipe failure. In most modern tankers breakdown of this sort is practically inevitable at some time or another and, if it already has happened, the chances are it will again. Boiler failure is an ailment as old as steam itself but, as they have done with everything else, superships have made of it a new and special tribulation, quite terrifying in its experience and consequences. In the past few years it has disabled dozens of VLCCs in the 200,000 to 250,000 class, not to speak of scores of lesser vessels, and time after time has put large oil cargoes into perilous circumstances, especially in the South Atlantic and Indian oceans. It would be a very rare occasion at Cape Town or Durban these days if there were not a cluster of tankers of various sizes, and always including some of the biggest, undergoing boiler repairs or repair of damage resulting from boiler failure.

Over the years, boilers have become increasingly more complex and fastidious, but insurance against trouble was always provided by the fact that a ship had several boilers, so that if one or two failed, there was always a third or more to keep the ship and its systems going. Ordinary merchantmen as a rule have seldom been fitted with fewer than two or three boilers, and often as many as six or eight. Passenger liners with their demand for speed and their huge domestic power requirements carry many more. The *Queen Mary* had twenty-four boilers for her main engines, three for her domestic services. Until the mid-fifties most tankers had at least two boilers and often three, but a common practice in the first generations of giant tankers and in a majority of the first VLCCs, especially Japanese-built ones, was to have only *one* high-pressure boiler. This practice, now somewhat less common than it was a few years ago, was one of the economies that helped make the original price of these ships so attractive to their buyers: the Japanese had experimented intensively to increase pressure and temperature in their steam systems to gain better fuel consumption, and when they achieved this, they offered what appeared to be an unbeatable combination of a steam engine that was more economical in its fuel consumption and also so compact that its cost, such a dominant factor in the overall cost of the ship, was conspicuously lower than most.

In practice, however, it has been an altogether different story.

If that one boiler starts to fail, the ship is in a desperate state, precisely as *Ardshiel* had been. Without steam, the engines go, and all electrical power as well. The electronic complexity of these ships is wholly dependent upon the main propulsive unit. As steam dwindles and the propeller stops turning, the lights fail, and so do radar, echo sounders, and all other modern navigating paraphernalia – the fire-fighting equipment, cargo handling and control, deck machinery, and all those marvellous new computers which are supposed to decide course, prevent collision, check wages, and diagnose illness. The lot goes. All blink, flicker, and die. All that is left is a useless, drifting shell.

The fundamental caution necessary aboard a supertanker to prevent this state of affairs is to ensure that its main boiler is never short of its fixed supply of distilled water for making steam. Without this water, the ship stops. The battle to maintain its balance is a ceaseless one, even in comparatively new ships such as *Ardshiel*, as the incident off the South African coast revealed; in older vessels it is a herculean task. 'This ship is two years old now,' Peter Dutton said. 'I'd say that within another two years we'll start turning her into a workhouse. When one of these ships gets a bit of age on her, everything starts to go. The biggest disadvantage is that you get the pipework going; the pipes start corroding. Once that starts happening, you find that the valves won't close down either; they're not steamtight. All the joints start leaking steam.'

The steam that leaks is all distilled boiler water, of course; the more it leaks, the less there is to serve the essential functions of driving the ship and providing its electrical power. The tremendous wear and tear that constant voyaging places upon these systems, which, given the prefabricated haste that goes into supertanker assembly, are not conspicuously robust anyway, means that the development of steam leaks is steady and insidious. It was practice aboard *Ardshiel* to stop once every four months and to lie idle at sea for a whole day simply to repair accumulated leaks. This was done while I was aboard. In ships less conscientious, I was told, the leaks after a while become so numerous that the atmosphere in the engine room is one of permanent steam-fog. When *Ardshiel* stopped to repair steam leaks her engineers felt that she had run matters very close. The ship was losing thirty-five tons of distilled water a day through the leaks, but her evaporator was producing only twenty-seven tons a day. The ship had two evaporators, which together were supposed to distil a hundred tons of seawater into fresh every day, but again, as always seems to be the case with technical achievement in a supertanker, their output and efficiency were a great deal less in practice. After all steam leaks had been repaired during our voyage the evaporators were producing fifty-five tons a day, against an overall daily consumption in the ship, including domestic use, of about fifty tons of water, which seemed to be somewhat narrow as a margin considering that the distilled water, in effect, was the lifeblood of the vessel.

It was the loss of any sort of margin in these water supplies that had in fact caused *Ardshiel*'s troubles when she had broken down. The ship had been losing distilled water heavily through steam leaks when her evaporators failed and she was incapable of producing water at all. 'If you can't make water and you're losing it all, well then you've got nowhere else you can get it,' Peter Dutton said. 'If you haven't the water, you can't flash the boiler. If you can't flash the boiler you haven't the steam for the engines, or for the alternators, which make the electricity. This is the chain reaction that leads up to complete disaster. If there's no water on this ship, the ship stops. It must stop. You've got no power because you can't make steam, and that's the end of it. You end up with a tug towing you in. Or worse.'

Aside from steam leaks and failure of the evaporators, contamination of the distilled water by seawater can wipe out a supertanker's reserves of distilled water, even when they seem fairly considerable. Such contamination is a fairly regular event in tanker life and is caused when a tube circulating cold seawater through the main condenser breaks or starts leaking, and then pollutes the pure distilled water inside the condenser chamber. In a tight situation this can provide the final step to disaster. The water in the boiler has to be kept pure (no more than thirty parts to a million must be salt), otherwise the high pressures and temperatures in the system quickly cause scale to form in the tubes through which it circulates. The water, hot as it is, helps to keep the boiler's furnace heat under control, rather in the way that boiling water in a kettle prevents the fire under it from burning out the underside. Scale becomes insulation, and the boiler can burn itself out, as a dry kettle on a flame would. The tubes also are heavily damaged when this happens. They expand and blister and crack.

'Even if you're down to your last reserve of distilled water and a tube breaks in the condenser, contaminating the boiler system, then you've got to clear the system out entirely, at once,' Peter Dutton said. 'You've got to dump all that water in there because it's no use to you whatsoever. You flush it out until you've got the chloride clear, back to good distilled water, and it might take fifty tons to do it. If you're already having problems because of steam leaks or faulty evaporators, your position could be tricky. But if another tube breaks in the condenser, which could easily happen – things always seem to go in pairs – then you are in trouble. On all ships you get tubes burning out in the system, but at least other sorts of ships have two boilers; they shut one off and repair it. That's not something you can do with one boiler.'

The vulnerability of a modern highly automated ship even with three boilers was well demonstrated by the breakdown of the new Cunard flagship, Queen Elizabeth 2, in the Atlantic south-west of Bermuda in April 1974. The QE2's boilers became contaminated when oil leaked into the steam system. The ship lost all power and drifted helplessly with 1,600 passengers aboard. Here, too, according to a Sunday Times report, the problem originally had been one of economics. 'When the QE2 was designed in the early 1960s, economic pressures forced Cunard to admit that they could not afford to build a sea-going Rolls-Royce,' the newspaper's correspondent said. 'The Queen Mary, for instance, had 27 boilers and 83 engineering officers. The QE2 has three boilers and 23 engineering officers.' QE2's celebrity as a ship and the large number of passengers aboard assured the sort of publicity that no supertanker ever gets when its boilers fail.

There is absolutely nothing that a supership sailor can do with a powerless vessel in which every flicker of mechanical life has died beyond hope of revival. Nor is there much he can do with a vessel whose weakening mechanical pulse is insufficient to control the vast inertial forces of its own hull. The one-boiler ships have a small auxiliary engine unit for emergencies, but its power is laughable against what it might be called upon to do. It is just strong enough to give the ship headway in fine weather, but incapable of doing so in the vile gales it might meet off Good Hope; and in any event it is not capable of providing the steam for both engines *and* electrical power. An official at Lloyd's Register of Shipping told me that he'd received a letter from a ship's master who told him that his vessel had actually been blown *backward* while using auxiliaries. At least one of the major oil companies, British Petroleum, has resolutely refused to have one-boiler ships in its fleet. 'I wouldn't have it. It's not worth the risk, for such a comparatively small added cost,' the director of the company's fleet, Commander Platt, told me.

A supership sailor might be excused under these circumstances if he did nothing but bury his face in his hands. That at any rate is the sense of helplessness, and of imminent hopelessness, that Basil Thomson had been trying to convey. It explains also why the bird's-eye view of a disabled, drifting supertanker is likely to be of the crew standing submissive and resigned on deck beside their packed bags, waiting for the inevitable helicopter while the ship drifts ostensibly untended toward doom on a nearby coast. There was a photograph of just such a sight published in the *Cape Times*, Cape Town's morning daily, after the 46,000-ton *Kazimah* had lost her power off the harbour and was slowly drifting toward the reefs of Robben Island. Where once it might have been the object of a special sort of maritime scorn, such a sight, at least so far as these ships are concerned, is entirely comprehensible.

Such vulnerability is ironic when considered against the apparent ultrasophistication of their automated technology. The wonder of their unmanned engine rooms with their self-driving devices, the vigilant all-seeing electrical eyes and instantly triggered alarms, and their clinical control rooms where the push of a button starts the ejection from a signals recorder of a tape printed with all relevant information, like a weighing machine that prints on a card one's weight and a brief message of good fortune, are all often held to be one of the great advancements and most excellent safeguarding virtues of supertankers, rather as though these of themselves make a vessel intrinsically better, sounder. The proper perspective on this is to remember that automation itself is an economy. 'Although he's going to spend a lot of money putting the equipment in, the shipowner hopes to get some of it back by cutting down on manpower, which is what automation essentially is for,' Alan Ewart-James said as comment upon it. He himself had been witness to the dangers of dependence upon automation when steaming up the North Sea in a loaded 60,000-ton tanker some time previously. When called for his watch he had been advised to 'bring your sea boots to the bridge'. Puzzled, he did what he was told. There had been good reason. Giant seas had put the bridge out of action. All the automatic equipment was out and the only piece of equipment working was the steering wheel. Spray and sloshing water had got into all the gear. Lanterns had to be rigged to see by.

From a safety point of view, all that automation can do is to cry havoc, which too often it does too late, or without an immediately ascertainable reason why.

Peter Dutton described to me an incident that had occurred aboard one of *Ardshiel*'s sister ships on its first night at sea out-bound from Japan after the ship had been accepted from its builders. The engine room was switched to automatic control and everyone went to bed. 'About two in the morning the general alarm went,' Dutton said. 'All the engineers pounded down there. The failure the signals recorder had printed out was that the main boiler had tripped, which in turn trips the main engine. When the boiler trips, the fires go out, so it's not generating any more steam. Whatever steam's left is used for the alternators, which gives them about twenty minutes of running time, of providing electrical power. That means you've got about twenty minutes before a blackout. The boiler had gone and the main engine had gone, and we hunted high and low to find out why the boiler had tripped, but we couldn't find anything.

'We got the boiler flashed again, so we had steam, and we had the engines back, and no blackout. But we still hadn't found out what had actually caused this. After six hours, we eventually found the reason. It turned out that the forced draught fans on the boiler had two flaps, which are held up by air. The air passes through a reducing valve which brings its pressure down from about seven kilogrammes to half a kilogramme. It's only a small valve, and inside it there's a half-inch-wide rubber diaphragm. This diaphragm had split, which in turn dropped the pressure just momentarily off the two flaps, or outlet dampers as we call them. This in turn signalled to the boiler that the forced draught fans had stopped, which immediately put the fires out, which stopped the engine, and the ship. A half-inch rubber

155

diaphragm had immobilised us, but no one could have foreseen that happening, and the computer couldn't have told us what actually had happened, or where it had happened. All it could do was to stop the ship and leave it up to us to find out for ourselves. It took six hours of hard detection work. If you're in busy waters, or off some coast, a situation like that is horrible.'

It is of course far more horrible, and damaging to the innards of the ship, if automation sounds its alarms too late, or not at all. The latter happened in November 1972 to the 250,000-ton British tanker *Fina Britannia*, which broke down off the East African coast while returning to Europe fully laden from the Gulf. The alarms had failed to warn of various electrical and mechanical defects that had occurred. A chain of overlapping faults led to a boiler explosion and the ship eventually had to be towed down to Cape Town for temporary repairs. *Fina Britannia* fortunately was well off the coast, and could safely drift until a salvage tug arrived. As a matter of interest, it was the failure of an automatic checking system, which should have rung an alarm bell and didn't, that caused such massive contamination of *Queen Elizabeth 2*'s boilers before her engineers realised what was happening.

One of the dangers of automation is that it undermines much of the old-fashioned vigilance that once was mandatory in ship's engine rooms. Engineers put too much faith in the electronic system and cut down on their investigative circuits around the engine room, which used to be an almost ceaseless activity in any vessel's machinery spaces. As a result, they begin to lose their occupational instincts as well. The value of these was well described to me by Peter Dutton, who was very true to an old-fashioned engineering sense, even complaining that his juniors for the most part were young men who'd never swung a hammer as he himself had done in the shipyards of the Tyne; he kept himself deeply attuned to the machinery around him.

'It often happens', he said, 'that when going round on the job I look at something and find that I keep thinking about it after I've got back to the control room. Invariably in those instances I've found something wrong when I've gone back to check. There was nothing there to tell me initially, but when I went back and went deeply into it, there was something wrong. It's just a feeling that builds up from experience and I've learned to act on intuition; if I don't, I've been the worse for it.

'On another ship of this class that I was on, before joining *Ardshiel*, one of our routines of a Saturday morning, before switching the engine rooms on to automatic control for the weekend, was to test the emergency diesel alternator. We had a lot of things to do one

Saturday morning and the diesel wasn't tested. On the Sunday morning I thought to myself, "I'm going to run that diesel." I told the others. "Ah, don't bother, don't bother," they said. "We don't want any noise." That diesel kicks up quite a racket. But I went down anyway. Lo and behold, the thing ran all right, but it wouldn't build up voltage. After that, the electrician worked all day on it to repair it. At half past ten that night we had a blackout on the ship. The diesel automatically took over. If I had not gone down and tested it, and it had not been repaired, we would have had no power on that ship.

'On these ships, losing electrical power is absolutely the main thing. If you lose your main engines, well, you're all right as far as safety goes. You've still got light, so you've still got fire-fighting equipment, but if power goes you have none of those things. So it's quite a problem if you lose the alternators that give you your electricity, which can happen even if they don't shut down because of lack of steam. Sometimes they just break down of their own accord. To quote just one ship of this company. They had one alternator break down: a gear came out and dropped among a lot of wheels that were spinning and smashed up the lot. So that was one alternator gone. Then they had a blackout and the second alternator tripped because of high back pressure. To restart that alternator they needed electrical power, which only the emergency diesel could provide. But, before they could get the diesel running, a connecting rod came off and smashed the gear box. That was the last source of power gone. They had to get tugs to take her in and that ship was lying up in the Gulf for six weeks.'

It seems always to be the same, that whenever one starts talking about these ships in this manner, the impression that forms is of things breaking and falling to pieces, of a shaky structure and an overall sceptical view of its chances. That is by no means the whole truth of these large crude-carriers, but the element of truth is large enough to make one fearful. *Ardshiel*, God knows, looked and felt solid enough; if the finish on deck wasn't what one was accustomed to in a vessel that was virtually a flagship, the quality and substance of the accommodation and the pains her owners had gone to there to remind one of the concern they felt for appearances more than made up for it. But the narrow margins of safety upon which it all travelled always recurred as a topic, whether in anecdotes such as Dutton's, or in Basil Thomson's morbid dwelling upon the rights and wrongs of calling up the salvage tug. It was invariably there, the constant presence of fearful possibility, largely drawn from the awareness that what propelled this size and apparent substance lacked a great deal by comparison with the real weight and measure of it all. James

Jackson and his engineers praised the quality of their Japanese engines and considered them as good as British ones. There was always such tribute for various components of the vessel, but seldom any for the ship as a design and entity and as a sound structural and mechanical proposition.

In an article titled 'Shipboard Automation. Is it right?' in the July 1973 issue of *Safety at Sea International*, the author, J. Bull, a member of the Nautical Institute, commented on the new ships and the danger of their dependence upon ever-smaller crews. 'Instead of installing expensive instrumentation to find defects, we should be bent upon not building in defects at all,' he said. What of the future? he asked. 'The shipbuilder is justly proud of his electronic marvel when he hands it over to its new owner, the ship has been constructed in accordance with the plans, and all systems function as required by the specification. But what of five years hence, ten years hence, when a few North Atlantic winters have taken their toll, and the fast runs and quick turnarounds have compelled maintenance to be minimal? Then the exposure to corrosion, vibration, ship motion, occasional pounding, and the day to day wear and tear will have produced failures in vital equipment.' The theory of preventative maintenance was sound, but the practice could be very different, when the skills were not available and breakdowns took precedence over preventative breakdown. It was difficult, the article said, to accept the idea that a ship was becoming another throwaway product of this modern age. Surely the capital cost was so great that it had to be made to last for as long as humanly possible? 'In the case of the modern ship, the shipbuilders' steelwork will be sound for many years to come, but the sophisticated equipment within it will cause increasing difficulties as time goes on.'

Whatever worries the VLCCs and all older generations of superships might be causing by the end of the seventies, those they provoke now are nasty enough and become of immediate regional concern as they crowd in ever greater numbers toward the North American approaches which, on the route they take from the Gulf, should bring them from the Cape directly off Maine and the Maritime Provinces of Canada, where as it happens the present deep-water ports exist and new ones are proposed, notably at Eastport, Maine. Those are foggy, troubled waters in winter, and not hospitable to either bad navigation or helpless, drifting ships.

Aside from the fundamental fact that two boilers would have been preferable to one in ships of such costliness and hazard, at the very least they should have had a permanent and adequate reserve of distilled water: a small part of their tank space could have been given over to this, to serve as a source to draw on in case the evaporators failed or were hard pressed to keep up the necessary supply in a crisis such as that in which *Ardshiel* found herself. The failure to provide this, as Alan Ewart-James explained to me, was just another of the economies that dictated the design of these ships.

What they also should have had, as a minimum concession to safety, was an emergency source of power capable of running both engines *and* electrical plant if steam were lost. As Peter Dutton said, 'I think they'll pay the price in the finish for putting too much emphasis on economy. When you consider the cost of these ships, they should have had a diesel alternator capable of taking the full load of the ship, which this one can't do.'

It seems extraordinary on the face of it that these ships should have risked themselves with power and propulsive systems that seem absurdly insecure and undependable given the range and consequence of potential failure, more particularly because of such strenuous service demanded of them, and because, when they entered service, facilities for repairing and dry-docking were almost non-existent along the routes they were to use, and still are very limited indeed.

Many doubted the wisdom of the ships, but no one scorned them. There was a strong curiosity to see how it all would work out; and from a shipping point of view it indubitably has. Most shipowners tumbled into VLCCs as fast as they could. Some of those who use their ships as they would high stakes on a gaming table, playing them on the charter markets according to hunch and hope, have lost big sums from time to time; by and large everyone has set himself up very well, however.

Automation *is* marvellous, a lot of it, perhaps even all of it: it has a pretty, animated face, what with its shiny futuristic air-conditioned soundproofed control rooms filled with coloured lights and flickering dials and marching digits and chattering tapes. One can spend beguiling hours there contentedly watching it all, soothed by its air of technological aplomb and the cool silent separation between one's self and the hot, pounding metallic turmoil that one sees through the plate glass windows. Here the engineers sit during the day shifts, chatting, drinking coffee, keeping an eye on this and that, rather like astronauts in a capsule, and occasionally venturing out into the noise and steam-leaked heat to climb one of the high ladders outside to look at something.

But aside from its diversionary pleasures, it is difficult to judge the real worth of it all while it remains so utterly and vulnerably dependent upon the ship's own by no means dependable power and propulsive systems. There are few things more terrible and bewildering to the supertankermen than watching the death of this robot of theirs when the steam starts to falter. To stand by and see all the arrows flicker to zero, and then to watch the radar screens one by one gather their intelligence into a single fast-receding pinpoint of light and go dark, is like watching the very soul of their ship fading into the ether.

NINE

WINTER! It was well apparent when I climbed to the bridge from the darkness of the lower decks at dawn the following morning. Alan Ewart-James and Cadet Davis stood out on the port wing, their throats muffled against the chill. The sea looked very wide and cold and blue, and its surface was massively creased by huge regular swells whose violent effect upon the ship had woken me. Around us lay mountains of cloud bank; they rose from the dark base of the sea at the horizon but their peaks touched a clear and unblemished sky so that they increased the feeling of space and width.

Davis was taking a bearing on a small point of light that shone faintly in a still-black corner of the sea. 'She's also on course for the Cape,' Ewart-James said. 'About the same speed, so we'll be keeping each other company for a while.' As the dawn spread over the water the single light became a ship which, as so often happens, seemed far less of a presence upon the visible sea than her light had been upon the dark. We held steady, companionable course together, and sailed on past the foot of the range of clouds, as though under the lee of an island, and on into a powerfully different ocean.

The quality of light, the smell and tone of the air, the denser flocks of seabirds, and the cold high-moving look of the sea itself already were indisputably 'Cape', even though we still were 1,400 miles north-west of Good Hope. We were in the great South Atlantic, which has a character all its own.

Sailing south, the impact of the South Atlantic is always pronounced because you enter it so suddenly from the tropics, where sea and sky melt together for days, limp and white both of them, misty from damp heat, and with no clearly defined horizon; so that, when you wake one morning to this fresher air, the sudden definition of sea and sky which it gives makes the ocean look immensely wider. It is widened still further by the swell which, like dunes in the desert, gives the eye its rhythmic measure of spaced and infinite distance.

I spent my boyhood and adolescence at the Cape, the adolescence covering the war years, so I recognised these South Atlantic seas at once and for a moment I even experienced that brief shock of reversion and time loss that the natural phenomena and apparitions of childhood can give when one re-encounters them after a long absence. It was a quarter-century since I had left the Cape, in a troopship, so I saw a wartime sea, which the South Atlantic really is to me: a cold sea with convoys of cold grey-painted ships coming in or sliding away from Cape Town; and the sight of the other steamer fixedly beside us, as though on convoy station, made the whole feeling of recall much stronger even. A mood of maritime discretion and wariness anyhow is a quality that goes well with this whole ocean, whose mood can be disturbingly equivocal.

Of them all, it is the true mariner's sea: more closely bound up with seafaring mythology than any other ocean because it holds all those mystic and morbid qualities that satisfied the sailor's superstitious, fearful nature, from which portents could be drawn, and from which myths and legends so easily arise. In this it is very different from the Mediterranean, whose maritime folklore and imagination have been much more involved with the historical processes of the shore than the salt-water deep itself.

The South Atlantic is a sea not sinister, but one where nothing is what it seems; and whose perversity begins with the deceptive serenity of its surface, where dead calm is placed upon the backs of the massive swell, which roll smooth and crestless under it: a ship can lie in boisterous tumult within this ocean's still and silent air and upon its rippleless surface, as storm-tossed under the hot southern sun as though weathering the North Atlantic. It is a strangeness that reminds one always of Conrad's eerily powerful description of the silken and ever-higher swell that battered *Nan-Shan* long before the typhoon enveloped her.

These swells are known as the Cape rollers, and they gain their size and momentum from their long journey up from the seas of Antarctica, the Southern Ocean, which is the main influence upon the South Atlantic. The Southern Ocean not only sends rollers into the South Atlantic but folds into it its own icy currents, making the South Atlantic a cold sea under a hot sun, and so adding to its perversity, and richness: enabling it to bring right to the tropics many of the curious creatures of the south polar sea, including the whale and the albatross, which were so much the symbolic preoccupation of the early sailors in these waters, and in addition seal, penguin, and a host of cold-sea birds.

Those frigid currents also account for the dense fogs that unexpectedly descend upon a day whose fierce sun has heated all the surfaces of the sea and sky to a coppery brightness. Steaming through such an ostensibly inviolate light a ship suddenly finds itself in an impenetrable mist; its decks grow wet and the deep chill of the seawater rises all around it, clammily penetrating the bones and enveloping the soul. It is an uncanny experience, even on large passenger liners, to stand peering into such a thick fog for the vanished sea and sunlight. How easy it is therefore to understand the impact of this ocean upon the imagination of the earliest seamen, so credulous and superstitious, groping their way toward Asia. Seamen never lost their respect for it, not even during the last epochs of sail when they knew all about these waters, least of all then perhaps, because they knew that these smooth rollers they met so soon after crossing the line were merely the messengers of the gale-driven far south through which they shortly had to pass to 'run their easting down'.

Once around Good Hope, their course took them straight on into the Southern Ocean, which is the only ocean that completely encircles the globe unhampered by any intervening land mass. The fierce westerlies that constantly blow over it, rotating from west to east, provide the legendary gales south of Cape Horn and in the 'roaring forties' (the area between Good Hope and Australia that lies between forty degrees and fifty degrees south) which dealt the nineteenth-century grain and wool clippers their most punishing, and often mortal, occasions. The Southern Ocean's seas have unrestricted freedom to build their power and size and are the most terrible on earth, with an estimated storm height south of the Cape of Good Hope of sixty feet, against forty feet in the North Atlantic. Deeper south, waves as high as one hundred feet frequently have been reported. *Cutty Sark* encountered the biggest sea in her career there and her master, Captain Woodgett, said in his log, 'An immense sea rolled up right aft. When I looked at it, towering up so steep, in fact, like a cliff, it looked as if it was about to drop down over our stern and completely bury the ship.' Captain Woodgett later told Basil Lubbock, the ship's historian, who gives an account of the incident in *The Log of the Cutty Sark*, that the ship ran down the advancing wall of water with her stern at an angle of forty-five degrees, 'whilst her bows split the side of the monstrous wave with a roaring hiss; the Cutty Sark ... probably never went faster in her life than she did on that sea'.

The considerable imprint that the southerly seas have made upon literature and legend reflects the extent to which they were regarded as the arena of true combat, the most fateful of all, and, as they descended toward them from the equator, sailors saw the character of the South Atlantic not only as forewarning but, with its rollers, fogs, calms, and odd sea creatures, as being very much of a piece with the baleful spirit of their true destination, the Southern Ocean. It was here, in this apprehensive peace of the South Atlantic, 'when all the waves rolled by like scrolls of silver', that *Pequod* first sighted the spirit-spout of Moby-Dick, and nobody describes better than Melville this descent through its derisive calm to the spiritual and physical terrors beyond. 'These temporary apprehensions, so vague but so awful, derived a wondrous potency from the contrasting serenity of the weather, in which, beneath all its blue blandness, some thought there lurked a devilish charm, as for days and days we voyaged along, through seas so wearily, lonesomely mild, that all space, in repugnance to our vengeful errand, seemed vacating itself of life before our urn-like prow. But, at last, when turning to the eastward, the Cape winds began howling around us, and we rose and fell upon the long, troubled seas that are there . . . and heaved and heaved, still unrestingly heaved the black sea, as if its vast tides were a conscience; and the great mundane soul were in anguish and remorse for the long sin and suffering it had bred. Cape of Good Hope, do they call ye? Rather Cape Tormentoso, as called of yore; for long allured by the perfidious silences that before had attended us, we found ourselves launched into this tormented sea, where guilty beings transformed into those fowls and these fish, seemed condemned to swim on everlastingly without any haven in store, or beat that black air without any horizon.'

That the souls of drowned and erring sailors inhabited the seabirds helped explain the abundance of the flocks that so inexplicably lived over those hellish seas, but the concept of the southern waters as a place of perpetual damnation was a natural one. Nothing on earth was as forsaken; nowhere else was there such a sense of the primordial rage of the earth when all of it was covered by a rushing sea. Nowhere else could the legend of the *Flying Dutchman* be quite as credible, or as inevitable. Van der Decken cursed that ocean and, in punishment for his blasphemy, was damned to sail the waters off the Cape eternally. Whether van der Decken existed or not, he was real enough to sailors for nearly three hundred years, the martyr and symbol of their inexpressible experience, the one whose desperation broke from credulity and God-fearingness and, in one anguished cry, damned God and his conduct of the universe.

> And still in the storm, as sailors say,
> Sere and wan and white as a bone,
> The phantom ship drives against the gale
> And an old man stands on her poop alone.

The sailors' need for this symbol has remained so strong or else the instinct and affinity for it is so charged by the general mood of those seas (or, who knows, perhaps it is true?) that sighting of the ghost ship has been officially logged on several occasions, and unofficially reported on numbers of others; and described by men, including Queen Elizabeth II's grandfather, King George V, who, in his published diary of a cruise aboard H.M.S. *Bacchante* in July 1881, described an encounter with the *Flying Dutchman* off the Cape: 'The look-out man on the forecastle reported her as close to the port bow, where also the officer of the watch clearly saw her ... a strange red light as of a phantom ship all aglow, in the midst of which light the mast, spars, and sails of a brig two hundred yards distant stood out in strong relief as she came up.' The validity of the apparition was confirmed for those on board by the fate of the ordinary seaman who first sighted it and who had hailed the officer of the watch: he fell to his death from the crosstrees twelve hours later.

The *Flying Dutchman* was believed always to appear in advance of severe storms off the Cape and, when sighted, bore down upon the ship near her as though to collide, only to vanish before impact. The last official sighting was in 1959, when the master of the Dutch freighter *Straat Magelhaen*, Captain P. Algra, reported on arrival at Cape Town that he and his second officer had seen the *Flying Dutchman* on the night of 7–8 October and that, true to tradition, she had headed straight for their ship, then vanished just as they thought that she would strike.

The momentum of the great westerly driven seas lies along a line slightly north-east beyond Cape Horn, so that they bear toward the other Cape, Good Hope, gradually lapsing into the big swells that become the Cape rollers and fan toward the whole South West African seaboard, and can reach as far as Ascension Island just south of the equator. After a particularly violent disturbance in the Southern Ocean, these rollers sometimes arrive at the island of St Helena, south of Ascension, like a sudden onslaught of minor tidal waves. St Helenans every so often have the unpleasant experience of finding that they must flee for their safety from the short promenade that fronts the seaward side of the narrow valley in which their capital, Jamestown, lies because a calm sea has suddenly hauled itself up into high slopes of advancing water.

To see any ship lying upon the Cape rollers was always as fine a measure as any of its line and general state of grace. Watching ships surge into Table Bay on the backs of the rollers or riding and plunging against them on their way out has always been a popular pastime at the Cape itself: as soothing and soporific as watching elephants browse the wild, and in fact offering the same satisfying enjoyment of vast bulk handling itself with prudence, tact, and great delicacy. Never more so than in the sight of the great battleships running out in line astern, as one so frequently saw during the war, forming immense pyramids of steel upon the water, tilting to alarming angles, so that one often seemed to be looking at their broad holystoned quarterdecks lying almost upright like white walls in the sea, yet never leaving any doubt about their imperturbable buoyancy and absolute manœuvrability.

This of course was much more interesting to watch than to experience. For some, the Cape seas were an unendurable ordeal. I remember the mighty *Ile de France* making an emergency stop at the Cape in 1945 while still serving as a troopship because one of her passengers was so stricken with seasickness that he had fallen unconscious. I remember too the case of Miss Wicht, whose great house stood empty on the seashore outside Cape Town from before the First World War until after the Second because, having satisfied a long-felt urge to visit Europe, she suffered so desperately from seasickness outbound from the Cape that she could never face the return home. Terror of the rollers supposedly held her in exile in Europe for thirty-two years, until her death in Switzerland in 1941.

During the war I occasionally sailed as a spare hand aboard a handsome sixty-foot ketch which had been taken as a prize in 1939 from some round-the-world-sailing German and sold to an invalided naval commander who, finding his way with her, liked to take her out in stiff weather. One of the occasions that this caprice beset him was during one of the worst north-west gales the Cape had seen in many years. This was an August Sunday in 1943 and I was in my early teens. We went out in the lee of the French troopship *Pasteur*, which was noted for an unusually high superstructure and funnel, even for a vessel of her considerable dimensions, just under 30,000 tons gross. To go out in that weather was a madness. The Cape breakwater, a solid nineteenth-century enterprise, was being hammered by combers of such ferocity that there had been some doubt whether *Pasteur* herself should sail, presumably because of the demoralisation that thousands of seasick soldiers would precipitate in the liner; but her mission must have been urgent and sail she did, and so did we. In fact we went out in her lee. Before we got beyond the breakwater, however, the pilot's tug, bearing away from *Pasteur*, on instructions from the harbourmaster ordered us in and gave us its own lee as the troopship drew away.

The *Pasteur* passed beyond the breakwater and almost immediately took a sea so huge that we wondered briefly whether she had been torpedoed, for the spray rose in such an explosive canopy that it flew white over her bridge and over that very tall funnel of hers. She must have put her nose right under.

It is hard to believe that we would have survived if our caustic and foolhardy skipper had not been ordered back. Strangely, a boy my own age and sometime companion died that very afternoon, unbeknownst to us, when his father, under similar compulsion, had tried to bring his yacht around to Cape Town from the small harbour of Hout Bay, which lies halfway along the peninsula on the way to Cape Point, the headland of Good Hope. The boat was lost within sight of Cape Town breakwater, more or less the time that we ourselves were setting out.

It never occurred to any of us on board, mostly boys, to question the wisdom of putting out in that weather. None of us would have dared step ashore, however frightened we were; nor did anyone say a word even when we saw the sort of seas that were smashing at the breakwater. It was only years later that I tried to fathom what made those two men, my friend's father and our own skipper, want to fling themselves to likely death in those horrible seas. Even if they were suicidally bent, one would not understand it. As Alan Villiers noted about the prospect of drowning off Cape Horn one wild night: 'To expect to die upon such a night in such a sea is a miserable sensation, and the longer the expectation lasts the deeper is the misery. There is nothing ennobling about it, nothing uplifting. The sea is too brutal and too cold.'

But there is a nihilistic force in such rage that always has its attractions, and even had for Villiers, who, in his memorable and perhaps undervalued books on the experience of deep-water sail in its last days, was always remarking on the horror but yet the challenge and uplift of it all that brought a man back. The southern seas never lacked challengers, those men who, in the clipper days, wanted the combat and drove ships in pursuit of limits. There was something about the elemental rage and power in the southern oceans that did strange things to men: often drew them to a point where the fantasies, enigmas, and demonology of those seas became blurred with reality, and created in them that peculiar sailor's fatalism that always seems to bear the desolate conviction of a lost and traceless cosmic self.

If I have digressed to this degree it is, in the first place, because the South Atlantic, especially that Cape fringe of it that lies brother to the Southern Ocean, obviously remains for me a very personal place. Its enigmatic qualities were marvellously suited to boyhood sensibility with all its demands for new areas of perception. I had a fourteen-foot sailing dinghy of a class called Redwing, so called because of the russet colour of the small jib and gaff-hauled mains'l they carried. Sailing that small boat around the perimeters of Table Bay left such a strong impression of the intensity of life, of the vivid surface and diverse nature of the South Atlantic that no other ocean has been able to match its power upon my imagination. I knew the Indian Ocean coasts north-east of Cape Point equally well and regarded them in fact more joyously because of their white, white sands, their sensual warmer waters and buoyant mood. But where the Indian Ocean was pleasure, the South Atlantic was experience. I have always felt that if you set me blindfolded upon all manner of shores I would at once know by smell and by its very air upon my skin which was South Atlantic: one was very close to it in a small boat, to the seal, duiker, gannet, penguin, and sea-lion that broke surface to regard one calmly, and to the exhilaration of that icy kelpy water exhaling into hot sunshine, such a cool impact, even in the most intense heat, like the clout upon one's nostrils of freshly cut water-melon.

I am therefore intensely concerned that its extraordinary qualities should remain intact; and here one really means its rich bird and marine life, because without these its dreadful temper and strange moods would give it the power only of a haunted house, which, if things go the way they are going, it may well become. The oil ships already have done great damage to it all, in some instances perhaps irretrievable damage, and, in doing so, as we shall see, they may be damaging Antarctica to a degree that we do not yet appreciate, and, as a result, much of the fundamental well-being of the globe itself since so many millions of us are dependent upon the resources of the Antarctic seas.

More oil probably has been wrecked, spilled, dumped, and slopped into the waters off and around the Cape than in any other single area of the world; almost daily, certainly at a rate so constant as to make no difference, oil and sludge are poured upon those waters in quantities both large and small, and the irony is that if man had to assess all the points in all the oceans that are upon this earth to decide which single place might be the one to guard with all his might from pollution and damage because of the larger consequences to himself, then this should be it; or if it is not, then Cape Horn. There is little general sea traffic around Cape Horn these days and the area remained wild, forgotten and untouched in its natural life, until *Metula* created her havoc in the Straits just beyond.

The modern curse of Good Hope is that every tanker that goes from the west to the Persian Gulf must pass that way twice; so must all the traffic to India and East Africa, as well as most of the shipping to Asia and to Australia. Before Suez closed, an average of sixty-two tankers rounded the Cape every month. The total now is something between five hundred and six hundred a month, half of them fully loaded, of course. On average two thousand two hundred and seventy ships pass the Cape every month and ordinary merchantmen make their own contribution to pollution of those seas by dumping their bilge sediments and oily ballasts, but the major havoc is from tankers and it is an appalling story of wreck, breakdown, collision, torn and leaking tanks, foundering, and wanton dumping. The pollution is steady and chronic; the total amount of oil spilled into southern African seas since Suez closed is incalculable. What we therefore must recall is that persistent spillage of oil in small amounts in one place causes far more havoc ultimately than the occasional major spill like *Torrey Canyon's* or *Wafra's*. This was the conclusion of Britain's Field Studies Council after studying the effects of refineries on adjacent waters. The final report of the Canadian scientific inquiry into the stranding of the Liberian tanker *Arrow* came to the same conclusion. 'It may well be', it said, 'that the smaller day to day spills have a far greater effect upon the ecology than catastrophic spills such as the *Torrey Canyon* and the *Arrow*.'

A major spill, once cleaned up, allows the shore and the sea to retrieve and heal their wounds. Constant spills allow no such chance. The water area afflicted becomes too bruised to breathe and succour itself, and slowly dies. Continuous spillage in large areas of open sea would seem to be an even bigger threat, though no one yet knows to what degree.

Oil dumped on a coastline at least remains stationary and can be dealt with there, but a slick keeps moving, and kills as it goes, often doing some of its worst damage far from the scene of the disaster. The *Arrow's* oil killed more seabirds (forty-eight hundred) around Sable Island out in the Atlantic, one hundred and twenty-five miles from the wreck, than it did in Chedabucto Bay itself. The damage a slick does as it travels is overall. It destroys all the way up from the foundation of sea life, the plankton, to the highest reach of it, the birds in the air. Plankton, the tiny plant and animal organisms that are responsible for the primary production of 90 per cent of the living material in the seas, must function in the upper light-penetrated levels of the oceans. They draw to the surface the fish that feed on them, and the rising fish attract the birds. This cycle ensures that they are all victims; destroyed too are the surface-floating fish eggs and fry, which need for distribution the currents upon which the slicks are likely to ride.

The most visible horror of oil upon the sea certainly is what it does to birds. Their agony is pathetic, as we have seen at Santa Barbara, and as we constantly see in British and South African waters where, because of so many converging tankers and general shipping, the incidence of slicks is high. The losses involved in a single big spill are the more appalling because the slicks that travel on beyond the scene of an accident extend the devastation by hundreds of square miles. This became apparent after the *Torrey Canyon* accident. Robert Spencer of the Council of the British Trust for Ornithology wrote in *Birds*, the journal of the Royal Society for the Protection of Birds, that of the fifty-eight hundred birds taken to rehabilitation centres fewer than five hundred survived, despite devoted attention. In assessing the total death rate, allowance had to be made for British birds that died off the French coast, and for those that died out upon the sea itself. 'We can fix a lower limit of not less than ten thousand victims,' he said. 'But what of the upper limit? Twenty thousand? Thirty thousand? Any figure I might give at this stage would be pure guesswork.'

Nonetheless, as indicated by the breeding survey conducted in the spring of 1970 by the World Wildlife Fund and the Royal Society for the Protection of Birds, the worst damage to the British seabirds has been done by slicks off the British coasts. The survey found that most of the damage to bird populations was done well before the drifting slicks reached or threatened shorelines. It is so persistent that it now threatens extinction to the British families of guillemots, puffins, and razorbills.

This documentation is available because of the traditional and special British interest in birds and the various institutions and centres devoted to this concern. It is much harder to find similar ready estimates elsewhere, but in the absence of them we must assume the same general degree of damage to birdlife wherever oil descends in quantity upon the sea. In the wilder, less accessible and bird-thronged waters south of the Cape census of seabird populations is much more difficult, but the damage that has been visible at the Cape itself has been dreadful and its implications are alarming.

The penguin family has been the first, principal, and most distinguished victim of the southern oil slicks. Already one species, the jackass penguin (so named because its call sounds like the bray of a jackass), is threatened by extinction in southern African waters, to which it is unique. Before the war it was found in millions in the area. The numbers are now down to an estimated forty thousand, the majority of which breed on Dassen Island, a small island just north of Cape Town, and which has not only been hit repeatedly by big slicks but is constantly assaulted by smaller bilge and ballast ones. The jackass, in common with other penguins, is more vunerable than sky birds because it *moves* in the water; and it is doubly vulnerable because it ranges far in search of food and therefore increases its chances of encountering travelling slicks. In any event, oil-crippled penguins are constantly coming ashore along the Cape coasts, even when no major oil inundation is known to have taken place on or off the South African shores.

None of this can be regarded as a local matter at the Cape because the marine life there is so intimately involved and interdependent with the life and ecology of the Southern Ocean and its offshoot currents.

Several tankers have gone down in the area, the largest of which have been the 45,000-ton Niarchos tanker *World Glory*, the 70,000-ton *Wafra*, and the 100,000-ton *Texanita*. Other smaller ships have also gone down. One tanker vanished without trace. Apart from the immediate damage they do at the time of accident, sunken ships, if they take a lot of oil down with them (*Wafra* still has more than 30,000 tons inside her), slowly leak from the seabed as they break up from the action of currents and sea movement, or disintegrate with time. That means that slicks are almost constantly present in the area, a situation that might last for half a century or more. Oil leaking from ships sunk during two world wars is a constant pollutant in European waters. The German cruiser *Blücher*, sunk in the Oslo Fjord in April 1940, for example, only began leaking in June 1969, from the huge bunkers she'd had aboard. After she had been hauled off her reef, *Wafra* was sunk by South African bombers in deep water off the coast where, as her tanks gradually collapse, slicks will be fed steadily into the Agulhas Current that flows above her. *Texanita* too lies under the Agulhas Current. As further evidence of the strength of the current portions of the wreck were found twenty nautical miles from the reported position of her sinking. She was empty when she went down but, as with all tankers her size, she had several thousand tons of bunker fuel aboard. Slicks have been forming on the surface above her since she sank. The *World Glory* also lies with most of her cargo still aboard.

The worst damage to those waters, however, is done by the continual occurrence of less spectacular spills, leaks from wrecked ships or ones whose hulls have cracked, from those whose tanks have ruptured for one reason or another such as going aground or striking submerged objects, from ships that callously dump their tank washings and sludge in the Agulhas or Benguela currents in the belief that these will swiftly remove all hope of detection from themselves, or from ships that lighten their cargoes in an emergency (when inexplicable oil slicks appear in those waters after bad weather it is generally assumed at the Cape that they come from cargo dumped by masters who were worried about the strength of their ships). And, of course, there is the general dumping by all shipping, tankers as well as ordinary merchantmen, of oily bilge water and oily ballast water. These are especially vicious in their effect upon marine fauna.

Oil leakage is constant inside any ship's machinery and bunkering spaces. Lubricating and hydraulic oils drip from worn gaskets and areas of heavy lubrication. Fuel oil can leak from valves and connections of the lines that bring it from the bunkers to the machinery. All of this accumulates in the bilges with whatever water has leaked into the ship and the lot has to be pumped out from time to time. Any master of a ship sluggish and perhaps even hazardous from heavy bilges who has been putting off the job of clearing them would be inclined to defer no longer if he were facing the prospect of heavy weather off the Cape. So out it goes – at night, because there now are heavy penalties – into the Agulhas and the Benguela and Mozambique currents.

It is the same story with the seawater ballast taken in after fuel tanks have been drained of their contents on a voyage. The fuel itself is used as ballast at the outset and, as the voyage progresses and tank after tank is emptied of its bunker oil, salt water is brought in as substitute ballast. That means that when a ship approaches a port where it must bunker, the ballast, which has meanwhile mixed with the sludge and cleaned off the residue from the sides of the tanks, is discharged into the sea.

On the long voyage to the Gulf, South-East Asia, Asia, or the Antipodes via the Cape, the South African ports have become a natural bunkering point for merchantmen, smaller tankers, and supertankers, and VLCCs in ballast; and quite inevitably their approaches have become a place of discharge for these thousands of tons of oily engine-room water.

The United States Federal Water Pollution Control Administration has estimated that 0.5 per cent of the bunker fuel would remain in a fuel tank after it had been emptied. A large, modern freighter might easily bunker two thousand tons at the Cape, which means that, if it dumps its ballast somewhere, it has put some ten tons of oil into the sea. If one made a conservative estimate and figured that in any given month only one hundred callers at South African ports took this amount of bunker fuel and made the equivalent discharge off the coasts it would mean a thousand tons of oil a month; in reality, the figure would probably be much higher.

A United States Environmental Agency estimate published in 1969 said that 1.3 million metric tons of oil were going into the sea every year as a result of bilge and ballast operations and that little more than one-third of this came from general shipping, the rest from tankers. With more than two thousand ships rounding the Cape every month, it cannot be idle speculation that Good Hope's waters see a most handsome share of this.

The international regulations as framed and approved by the Inter-Governmental Maritime Consultative Organization (IMCO) make it punishable to discharge oil in all areas within fifty miles of the nearest land, or within one hundred miles of special areas particularly vulnerable to pollution (the South Atlantic and Southern Ocean are not among these). But prosecution can only be carried out in the country of the ship's registry, unless of course she puts in at a port of the country whose seas she has polluted. In October 1972, a British ship, the 11,281-ton *Huntingdon*, carrying cargo from Quebec to New York, was inside the Canadian zone when a slick four thousand yards long trailing her wake was spotted by a Canadian aircraft. Her master subsequently was prosecuted at the Old Bailey for discharging a mixture of bilge water and oil and fined £250, under a maximum penalty of £50,000. The defence counsel in the case said that there had been 'no deliberate desire' to pollute. The captain had assumed that he was outside the prohibited area.

The *Huntingdon*'s master was unlucky in being spotted. The Canadians anyhow, since the *Arrow* disaster, have become extremely vigilant, actually as well as legislatively, and sailors are going to be much more careful in those waters in future. If they pollute, they'll do it at night, as they mostly do anyhow everywhere these days. Even when the entire sea becomes a prohibited area, who will be able to stop this sort of thing? What of a complaint laid against the master of a Liberian, Panamanian, or Honduran flag ship? Can one honestly suppose that he will face the processes of justice in those nations, which presumably he has never seen, nor ever will? And what about the Russians, who now have one of the largest merchant navies in the world? As recipients of a complaint they doubtless would give their own bland assurances of positive action, but even if they dock the master some of his monthly roubles, how does the state, the owner of the ships, then flagellate itself? The same might be asked of any of the many national fleets that have arisen in recent years and whose accountability is only to themselves. To police all such merchantmen in a busy seaway such as that off the Cape is almost physically impossible; in the end, all one can count upon is conscience and, judging by the amount of slick on those waters, there has not been too much of that since Suez closed.

The worst mischief occurs during the southern winter when tankers are bashed and battered by the Cape seas. Every winter season has its one or two major accidents, its breakdowns and its large, unaccountable slicks.

Pollution began an intensified assault upon all southern seabirds and creatures as soon as Suez closed and by 1968, when tankers were into their second southern winter, it already had reached critical proportions. Oil tankers began their own sequence of major disasters in February 1968, when the 81,000-ton French tanker *Sivella* ran aground off a Cape Town suburb, a few miles from the harbour and practically in front of the principal lighthouse in the area. Nine weeks later the 48,000-ton German tanker *Esso Essen* struck a submerged object near Cape Town. Her tanks were pierced and more than four thousand tons of oil flooded out onto the sea. Three thousand counted penguins and 500 gannets were hit, but local scientists hazarded that it cost the lives of an estimated 14,000 to 19,000 penguins and perhaps 3,500 gannets. Even as the *Esso Essen's* oil was floating ashore, a 16,000-ton fully laden Greek tanker, *Andron*, fighting a storm off the Cape, began to leak severely from cracks in her hull. She finally foundered seven hundred miles north of Cape Town, and continued to release large slicks from where she lay, in the middle of the South West African fishing grounds. While the *Esso Essen's* oil was causing disturbance in Cape Town and *Andron* was fighting for her life to the north, a third tanker, unidentified, was spotted off Dassen Island pumping oil into the sea. Four weeks later the fully laden *World Glory* broke up and went down north of Durban, and sent her own sixty-mile-long slick south to the Agulhas Current.

The damage done by that sequence of incidents during those few weeks (and they were by no means the only ones that season) has been matched by equally or even more damaging events every season since. Early in 1969 a tanker slick killed the penguin population of Dyer Island near Cape Agulhas, estimated at eight thousand; like Dassen Island, Dyer Island is an important penguin breeding area. When the 46,000-ton *Kazimah* went aground in Table Bay in November 1970 she spilled 200 tons of oil sludge into the sea. The resultant slick went mainly north on the Benguela Current and killed probably thousands of birds and penguins; 559 penguins were rescued and treated, and the unknown casualties are usually calculated by multiplying the number of those actually seen with a factor of between ×3 and ×5. The *Wafra* spill three months later killed between three and four thousand penguins. The casualties would have been higher were it not for the prompt action of South African Guano Island officials, who evacuated one thousand birds which had reassembled at Dyer Island. By the time the *Texanita–Oswego Guardian* disaster occurred in the same area in 1972 the South Africans had built fences around Dyer and other penguin islands off the coast, with gates to allow the birds access to the sea. After the collision, gates on all the islands were hurriedly closed, but the thousands of birds foraging in the sea were hit and hundreds of them came ashore, oil soaked, along a stretch of coast several hundred miles long. In August 1974 oil once more spread across those waters when the 60,000-ton oil–ore carrier *Oriental Pioneer* ran aground at Cape Agulhas after being disabled in a storm.

It is of interest to note that one of the most disastrous of pollution incidents around the Cape so far came, not from a ship in visible trouble, but from a huge unidentified slick that hit Dassen Island on 14 March 1972. Fishermen had spotted the slick on the sea several days previously and the subsequent conclusion was that oil had been dumped by a tanker somewhere to the south of Dassen Island. More than two thousand penguins were known to have been killed by the slick, and the actual figure therefore is probably much higher.

The impact of this upon such an important breeding colony can be judged by available population estimates. Dassen Island is the main southern breeding island for penguins. In 1930 a British naturalist, Cherry Kearton, estimated that the island had a population of five million penguins. In 1970 South African Guano Island officials estimated that the offshore Cape and South West African islands together had a total population of 137,450. Dassen Island's own population was estimated at 50,000. An independent scientific estimate in 1972 revised the total population figure upward to 250,000. Even so, the decline during the past forty years amounts to a clear drop of at least 95 per cent.

Such a colossal population collapse cannot of course be attributed to recent oil spillage. Penguin eggs have long been a South African delicacy and the collection of these eggs has been a major factor in the decline, as well as increasing human intrusion upon the breeding islands. At one stage, owing to complaints by fishermen, machine guns were actually turned on the birds. Egg collecting has been stopped, but it is the oil that may now prove to be the decisive factor in whether these Cape penguins are saved from total extinction.

After the first wave of havoc in 1968, women in Cape Town formed an organisation, the National Foundation for the Conservation of Coastal Birds, which established rescue centres around the Cape coast and to which birds could be delivered. The constant pollution of those waters means that birds arrive continually, but during major disasters the numbers are overwhelming. The rescue stations are patterned on those that were established around British coasts after the *Torrey Canyon* disaster and they have at least provided first-class observation posts for the effects of sea oil on birds.

Penguins suffer dreadfully from the oil, indeed all sea creatures do, but the penguin is large, mobile and, perhaps because he is upright and quaintly human, we are more deeply affected by his distress. His appearance and behaviour when harmed by oil are pitiful. Oil affects the balance of the birds when it enters their ears and they stagger drunkenly, or find it impossible to stand at all. Their eyes are infected or blinded. But they are most cruelly maimed by the diesel and other refined oils that are thrown out with the bilge water. These oils burn their skin and stomach lining, and affect their livers. There is usually little that can be done for them when they are in this state.

Penguins are vulnerable through their great range of foraging. In the course of their travels in those waters they are likely, if they dodge one slick, to encounter another elsewhere. A penguin from his base has a two-thousand-mile sighting east to west, and sixty miles seaward. But SANCOB has received birds which have picked up oil which was known to have been ditched 120 miles to sea. When a penguin has become oil-polluted its natural instinct is to swim to the nearest land where it will stand on the shoreline until it slowly dies of starvation and dehydration (a penguin in good condition can live off its body for two weeks, or even more, so there is no immediate concern for them when they are locked inside their islands during a spill). Those oiled too far from land die at sea.

In the case of all birds, oil destroys the natural waterproofing in the skin and feathers which insulates a bird from the cold and wet. Their ability to float properly and to catch fish is therefore affected; if they aren't poisoned by swallowing oil when they preen themselves, they are likely to die of pneumonia in those cold seas.

Thousands of penguins and seabirds have been restored to health by these British and South African rescue centres (indeed as was also done after the Santa Barbara spill in California in which four thousand birds died, which amounts to a mere fraction of the losses suffered in Cape waters every season since Suez), but the usefulness of such rescue, cleansing, and return to the environment has been questioned by some British ornithologists. Dr R. K. Gregory, director of the Oiled Seabird Unit of Newcastle upon Tyne University's Department of Zoology, said in 1971 when announcing the development of an effective method of cleaning oiled seabirds without damaging their feathers that his unit still had to establish that cleaned birds were able to return to a normal life. There was a possibility that the oil they had swallowed could prove poisonous or have long-term effects on their breeding. So too, doubtless, with the penguins of the Cape.

After *Torrey Canyon*, many British bird experts believed that the best course in the event of oil pollution was to discard sentiment and to kill all badly oiled birds outright because they had little chance of surviving when returned to their environment. John Barrett of the Dale Fort Field Centre in Wales, then responsible for the Skokholm Bird Sanctuary, told the *Sunday Times*: 'These bird rescue centres have been established because we haven't had the guts to say there is nothing we can do. It is only a public relations exercise.' So it may be, but it nonetheless represents one of the very few acts of resistance in which ordinary powerless people can indulge to avoid total despair over the havoc they see at their feet and the feeling that theirs is a complete surrender to the whole range of maritime folly that causes it all. Of those apparent follies one of the most curious and incomprehensible would seem to have been the decision by the Inter-Governmental Maritime Consultative Organization in 1968 to ignore the winter load limits in Cape waters.

Every ship has its Plimsoll line, or loading mark: originally the familiar red 'boot topping' that covers the vessel's bottom as far as her waterline. As a ship discharges, the red line rises until, especially in the case of tankers, which lie so deep in the water when loaded, it stands high above the sea. The ship is riding high, as sailors say.

This line was largely the work of Samuel Plimsoll, born in 1824, who made improvement of conditions at sea his life's work. His principal target was the flagrant nineteenth-century habit of sending unseaworthy and overloaded but heavily insured ships to sea in the hope that they would sink, enabling owners to collect on them. Even when they didn't go this far, overloading was so common that many ships were lost because of it.

The idea of a load line was hardly new. Any caveman loading his dugout must have had an instinct for how far he could go in putting things inside it; and every race that has ever dominated sea commerce for any length of time realised that overloaded ships were not only dangerous but slower, and therefore stood to lose not only their own timbers and freight but competitive advantage as well: the Hanseatic traders limited their loading, as did the Arabs in their dhows and the Venetians, who marked their load lines by the sign of the cross. And so of course did Britain after her commerce began its enormous nineteenth-century development, though not without an almighty struggle.

Plimsoll was elected to Parliament in 1868 and fought a long, hard, and frustrating campaign there for the mark that eventually took his name, and which finally was made compulsory by the Merchant Shipping Act of 1890: the legislation that still largely sets the standards for the British merchant marine. It penalised unseaworthy vessels and declared that it was compulsory for every British ship to have a permanent load line painted on the vessel's hull to indicate the depth to which it could be loaded.

The original load lines were worked out from tables provided by the then chief surveyor of Lloyd's Register. British shipowners had feared that the mark would put them at a disadvantage with foreign competitors, but the Plimsoll line was so sensible and desperately needed that by the time Plimsoll died in 1898 it had become universal. It has been the fundamental principle of marine safety ever since. It provides every marine inspector in every port of the world proof at a glance that a ship is not abusing its stability and that its freeboard is safe in the seas into which it will be venturing. He reads this from a diagrammatic marking at the waterline which gives the marks for seasonal loading.

At an international conference which sat in London from 1929 through into 1930 Plimsoll's line and other safety measures were modified into a modern code known as the International Safety of Life at Sea and Load-Line Conventions and these have served, with periodic additional modifications, as the international guide for the safe management of ships at sea. It would have been unthinkable for any responsible maritime power to sanction suspension of them or any alteration of their stringency. Or so one would have believed. In March 1966 however a new international load-line conference was held in London at which it was decided to amend the load lines for tankers passing the Cape during winter. The oil ships already had received permission to load deeper than usual but even so it was still legally necessary for them to see that when they rounded the Cape in winter they were not so deeply loaded that their winter marks were below the water. This further inconvenience was now to be removed.

The pressure for these changes arose, as earlier noted, from the fact that the age of the VLCC had begun and, loaded, they would all be using the Cape. While Suez was closed, and at that point it was generally assumed that it would remain closed as far as anyone could foresee, *all* tankers would be rounding the Cape if bound for anywhere in the Western Hemisphere with cargoes from the Middle East.

The argument in effect was that it was really quite unreasonable to demand that a ship carry a lot less oil just because five days out of a thirty- to forty-day passage required this lighter load. Yet those five days and the sort of weather and sea conditions they might bring were precisely what the rules were for.

Acceptance of these changes was built upon apparently sound and logical calculations. All deadweight calculations for tankers are based on the assumption that the temperature of a cargo of crude is sixty degrees Fahrenheit. In the Persian Gulf the temperature of oil being loaded can be much higher, and the oil therefore occupies more space than it would at sixty degrees. Allowance must also be made for its expansion in the tropics. Crude oil also varies considerably in weight; Middle Eastern crude tends to be much lighter than, say, Venezuelan crude. All this can mean that a ship can sail from the Gulf lighter than her cubic capacity allows. In *Ardshiel's* case, when we sailed from the Gulf on our return to Europe we were fully loaded, although the cargo occupied only 98 per cent of capacity. A 200,000-ton tanker leaving Bahrayn and steaming to the Cape at fifteen knots will burn up about 2,500 tons of fuel, which also helps lighten her. This would give her several inches on the spread between summer and winter marks, which is just under two feet. But when the rules were amended for the Cape the big ships were still a novelty, and experience of them was extremely limited. The weights loaded into their hulls were unprecedented; no one truly knew except theoretically what their fullest strain might be upon those huge hulls.

The appalling standards by which so many tankers are operated and their established proneness to accident and disability alone should have made such a move unwise. Many tanker operators, though not of course P & O, break enough rules on matters such as manning without providing them with official licence to break one of the most vital. Safety at sea has always been a question of standards, and the principle has always been that these should be inviolable. If there was to be latitude, where did it end? Some analyses of tanker losses under severe conditions conclude that the losses occurred principally because the ships had been poorly loaded, or because cargo and ballast had been badly distributed. Considering the inexperience, poor training and lack of proper credentials that so often come to light when tankers have been involved in serious accidents, it is not an unfair deduction that the confusions manifest in navigation might extend to other departments of these vessels, and that such men would not pay the proper, constant attention to weight distribution. Nor would it be an unfair conclusion to suppose that many of them might not even know what it was all about.

Anyhow, the request to amend the rules was swiftly responded to, and accepted not only by the governments of the principal maritime nations, that is to say by their responsible maritime authorities, but by the insurers and classification societies as well.

Possibly the most astonishing aspect of all this was the speed of its accomplishment. The background to this is especially interesting. To understand it one must know something about the workings of the Inter-Governmental Maritime Consultative Organization, or IMCO as it is generally known. It is the only international body with some nominal jurisdiction over maritime matters and thus, for form's sake at least, the only one that could have sponsored the two amendments, those of the deeper loading of tankers and of the lifting of winter load limits at the Cape. IMCO is a specialised United Nations agency and, like all UN specialised agencies, its organisation and ways of operation are by no means simple to understand.

IMCO was created by a United Nations maritime conference in 1948. It has its seat in London and is an autonomous body with a membership of eighty-six nations. Any member of the United Nations can become a member of IMCO simply by depositing a formal document of acceptance of membership. IMCO membership therefore consists of those who make the effort to join, and clearly most UN members do. They contribute to IMCO's budget on the basis of the tonnage of shipping they own. All members have a seat in IMCO's sovereign body, the Assembly, which meets every second year. A Council of eighteen nations acts as a governing body between those biennial sessions, but, as with any parliamentary government, the real work of IMCO is done by IMCO's secretariat and technical committees, who for the most part tend to be shipping men seconded from the principal maritime nations.

From the start, IMCO's special concern was safety at sea, but in recent years by far its biggest concern has become pollution at sea and the framing of laws to prevent it. Such laws of restraint as exist have been put up by IMCO. The way it does this, or does anything that needs to be framed as international law, is to call an international diplomatic conference. Invitations are sent out according to UN protocol lists, so that just about everyone gets one. Not everyone of course attends, and any sea law we have is by and large the work of those who do. One says by and large because here the matter becomes really quite complicated. The majority of the delegates who, as diplomats, may not know too much about maritime affairs, are inclined to defer to the advice of IMCO's technical committees, and to those among them who have shipping knowledge. The latter would inevitably be the delegates of the principal maritime powers.

The complications deepen when one considers how many of IMCO's international laws come into force. At the end of its sessions, the diplomatic conference adopts a so-called convention, which embodies its decisions. This has then to be ratified by domestic legislation in the parliaments of IMCO members. A convention becomes international law when two-thirds of IMCO's membership has deposited these articles of ratification. This usually takes years and years. Any IMCO law can, however, become effective in principle long before that. This is done by the device of allowing a diplomatic conference to stipulate in its final convention how many nations are required before the convention comes into *force*. A number is set, and when this group of nations has ratified the convention, it becomes law between *them*. This number is not a fixed one in IMCO's charter but is decided by every conference for every different convention. It must however include at least seven nations with at least 1 million gross tons of shipping each. Naturally if any edict is thus recognised as law of the sea between such a sizeable group of maritime powers then it is going to be accepted by anyone who finds it convenient to do so. The Load-Line Convention is one that might be said to have suited everyone's convenience. Conversely, even when a particular law is in force among a limited group of nations, those who aren't too eager for its principles can defer applying them if they wish until that far-off day when it actually becomes IMCO and world law. Such, unhappily, one might say is the case with most pollution laws, which have a hell of a time coming into force.

At the diplomatic conference called by IMCO in 1966 to amend the Load-Line Convention the suggestion to suspend the winter load lines for tankers rounding the Cape was handed to a technical committee of shipping experts, which saw no peril in the proposal. It then was sent on to the main body of the conference, accepted, and framed in its convention. That final convention stipulated that the load-line amendments could come into force once fifteen specified nations (Panama, Liberia, Britain, the United States, Russia, Tunisia, Trinidad, France, South Africa, Malagasy Republic, Peru, Somalia, Denmark, Israel, and the Netherlands) had ratified it in their domestic parliaments. It took the fifteen just a year to do this. IMCO rules decree that a convention comes into force twelve months after the last such acceptance, which was received on 21 July 1967. The convention therefore came into force in July 1968.

This whole business was remarkable not merely for its speed, which an IMCO legal expert admitted to me was 'relatively unusual', but also because at that point no one really knew the handling characteristics and response of big tankers in the sort of weather that was normally encountered off South Africa in the bad season. Worse, no one really was making any attempt to find out, or if they were their efforts were not then publicised nor have they been since.

One might have supposed that in July 1968 they would have considered that there was good reason to do so. The structural defects and unexpected strains and stresses of big tankers were at that point already a matter of great concern. Despite all this, the amendments meant that tankers would be much more heavily loaded as they rounded the Cape during the South African winter than previously had been considered safe or wise. If the designers of the amendments felt certain of the very biggest ships, as they said they did, and as they still say they do, they nonetheless did not appear to make any allowances for the smaller, older, conventional tankers, by far the majority, for whom the winter load lines previously had been considered absolutely essential off the Cape of Storms.

It could hardly be said that tankers were new to storm, or to southern African waters, that winter of 1968, when the load-line amendments came into force. But the closure of the Suez Canal brought to the Cape route hundreds of tanker masters who were accustomed to the fair-weather route through the Canal and the Mediterranean. Many of them had passed round the Cape during the first Suez crisis in 1956, but that had been brief and had occurred during the southern summer. The ships that came after 1967 included the new and bigger generation of tankers, such as *World Glory*, which during the fifties had begun replacing the old tanker fleets. Their masters might have thought that their occasional encounters with Atlantic or Biscay storm had provided them with sound and sufficient judgment of their ships, but they soon learned differently.

The shipping community is always more contemptuous of the outsider than most specialised groups. Yet, while one has always been inclined to defer to the sailor as master of our souls and destinies when we accompany him upon his unstable element, one might venture to say that no other transport industry has made more ludicrous presumptions about safety and has, at times, appeared to know less about the characteristics of its vehicles than shipping. When the *Queen Mary* set out on her maiden voyage in 1936 she was not fitted with the hand rails along her passages and decks that had always been considered indispensable for the safety of passengers in rough weather.

The absence of the hand rails in the *Queen Mary* might seem a trivial matter within our present context, but it has always seemed to me a good measure of the strange self-deceptions to which shipping has been prone. After all, if the directors of the Cunard White Star Line in 1936 after nearly a century of North Atlantic service and possession of most of the biggest ships ever built still didn't know what their ocean could do to a ship, then who on earth did? But they appeared to believe that the *Mary* was too big to roll excessively. Only a few voyages later when she hit bad weather and they took passengers off in ambulances did they acknowledge the strangeness of their omission and promptly fitted hand rails. As it happened, the *Queen Mary* actually rolled far more than many vessels afloat until she was fitted with stabilisers (as a reasonably frequent pre-stabiliser passenger aboard her I give my own witness to her capacity in this regard).

As with *Queen Mary*, and indeed as with *Titanic* and *Great Eastern*, they felt that mere size held its own guarantees. But even if that had been so and they had proved to their own satisfaction that a loaded tanker was the one thing afloat that was closest to being an imperturbable and relatively immovable object in violent weather ('the water just breaks over them', as I have so often been told by their sailors, operators, the insurers, and classification societies), then no one at the time that the Load-Line Convention was amended appeared to give any serious thought whether *that* fact of itself entailed new problems, for it did.

182

What was overlooked was actual wave impact upon such massive floating objects. That a loaded supertanker might have to be regarded much in the same light as a heavy *stationary* object in the water rather than as a floating buoyant vessel able to ride the waves and that it therefore represented a different pattern of response was a realisation that came only slowly. Perhaps the pertinent experience for supertankers lay not upon the sea but upon its fringe, with Victorian lighthouse builders, whose binnacles had to be placed at points of frightening exposure and yet endure. They, in order to understand their adversary, began measuring the force of waves upon rock. Thomas Stevenson found in 1843–4 that summer waves upon Skerryvore Rocks had a force of six hundred and eleven pounds per square foot, winter ones two thousand and eighty-six pounds per square foot. Much greater pressures were registered elsewhere. Bishop's Rock in a storm in January 1860 recorded a wave force of seven thousand and ninety-nine pounds per square foot. The Skerryvore measure, with its large variation between summer and winter forces, might be more apt in terms of tankers, however, as it indicates the great increase in battering power that a low-lying tanker faces in bad weather. Only recently have a few, a very few, tankers been fitted with actual automatic devices able to measure the mere impact upon the bows and to warn the masters oblivious in their towers a quarter of a mile back of dangers in the assault of the sea, which they were (and still are) inclined to ignore. When deeply laden, the waves fall upon tankers with the same impact they do upon rocks because the ship is not rising with them but bashing against them.

IMCO and the shipping men don't of course believe that they forgot or overlooked or underestimated Cape conditions. The load-line conference, I was told by IMCO, by Lloyd's Register of Shipping, by the Chamber of Shipping, and by others of similar weight and knowledge, had acted only after careful consideration of meteorological statistics for the area concerned. But the wild nature of the seas off southern Africa have quite as much to do with the currents running down the east coast as they do with the barometer. Meteorological records cannot possibly explain the phenomenon that makes the seas off the South African coast among the most dangerous and unpredictable in the world, perhaps *the* most dangerous.

The *Africa Pilot*, the Admiralty guide which every ship navigating round that continent's coasts would or should have aboard, provides a good hint of the serious trouble that waits for shipping south of Durban. 'In the event of meeting a southwesterly gale off this part of the coast a very dangerous sea will be experienced at or outside the edge of the 100-fathom line,' the *Pilot* says.

Even this is an understatement of what can happen. Ships sailing eight or ten miles off the shore suddenly find themselves falling into an apparent hole in the sea. Their bows plunge into an abyss, and they then lie at the foot of a wave of anything from forty-five to nearly sixty feet in height, which falls upon them. The wave effect is precisely that which the Queen Elizabeth met off Greenland during the war and which threatened to bear her down. A wave condition that elsewhere might be considered the once-in-twenty-five-years stress encounter that Mathewson of Lloyd's described here is common occurrence.

It is certainly this sort of wave that broke up the World Glory. Many passenger liners have had frightening encounters with these waves. Just a few weeks before we ourselves passed up from Cape Town toward Durban a British passenger liner, the 13,000-ton City of Exeter, also met such a sea. The force of the impact was so violent that, apart from damage to the ship, twenty passengers received injuries ranging from severe lacerations to broken ribs and broken collar bone. In the southern winter of 1973 a large and powerful new British cargo liner, the 12,000-ton Bencruachan, was nearly lost when one of these freak waves broke her back. The ship had suddenly found itself tilted forward over the edge of a hole in the sea and the wave that then loomed up high above her smashed down upon the decks with such force that it broke the hull near the bows.

Fortunately Bencruachan didn't sink and was taken in tow for Durban. A few months later yet another freighter, the 12,000-ton Neptune Sapphire, on her maiden voyage, was struck by the same sort of freak sea. She was less fortunate. The impact broke her in two. The ship's bow section drifted away and presumably sank. The crew remained on the after section and were rescued by helicopter.

When the British cruiser Birmingham fell into one of these 'holes' during the last war the impact was so severe and the ship plunged so heavily that crew below decks assumed she had been torpedoed and went to emergency stations. Since 1952, eleven ships are known to have encountered freak waves, the largest of which was the 28,000-ton Union Castle passenger liner Edinburgh Castle, which fell forward to an angle of thirty degrees when her bows hit the trough.

It was in this area too that the 9,000-ton British liner Waratah disappeared in 1909 to become one of the great unsolved mysteries of the sea. She sailed from Durban and that evening, within sight of the South African coast, spoke by lamp to a passing freighter. A violent south-westerly gale was rising and the liner vanished into its disturbance, never to be seen again. No trace of the ship or of its two hundred and eleven passengers and crew was found. The modern belief is that she was probably overwhelmed by a wave such as that

184

which descended upon *Bencruachan* and *Neptune Sapphire*. As a matter of passing interest, there was a strange extrasensory perception in connection with this disaster. *Waratah* had come from Australia and when she reached Durban a passenger, a Mr Claud Sawyer, left the ship because he believed she was unsafe and would topple over. He had had bad dreams to this effect during the voyage, he told the official inquiry in London, and had warned other passengers.

Those monstrous waves off the South African coast are created by a peculiar combination of seabed characteristics, the Mozambique–Agulhas Current, and weather.

The continental shelf ends abruptly a short distance offshore with a clifflike edge above the great deeps. The current passes along the edge of this undersea escarpment and, with its speed of four to five knots, creates surges similar to the effect of a gigantic flow of rapids. During the winter when the westerlies from the far south blow around the corner of Good Hope and become south-westerly up the coast, their own huge seas, which have accumulated their force over the long distance they have travelled, run into the surge of the Agulhas Current. The waves hurled into uproar by this powerful collision between current and gale are freak and horrifying in appearance and effect. The wave systems superimpose upon each other and thus frequently create a wave of extraordinary height and power at whose base lies a sudden deep gulf. A ship lurches into the gulf, and then receives upon its back the terrifying immensity of water towering above, as was the case off Greenland with the *Queen Elizabeth*, whose bridge ninety feet above the sea was flooded.

These waves are at their worst along the one-hundred-fathom line, which is more or less the course of the edge of the offshore shelf, where the main flood of the current runs. The hundred-fathom line runs offshore at a distance varying from eleven to twenty-two miles, which means that vessels getting into difficulties in the maelstrom there find themselves confronted as well by a perilous shore; from Charybdis to Scylla, as it happens in this instance. These, again, were the conditions which threatened *Ardshiel* when she'd broken down. Local sailors call this area the wild coast, and this general term seems a much more accurate description of the peculiar malevolence of the seas there than the pinpointed title, Cape of Storms.

Ships travelling along that coast are separated into two lanes, as they are in other busy waters of the world. This traffic-separation scheme was provisionally introduced by IMCO early in 1971 and, because it put loaded tankers on the inside lane, closest to the coast, it caused a lot of unhappiness at the Cape after the *Wafra* accident. The loaded ships, it was felt, should be running farther out to sea.

What especially alarmed the South African maritime authorities was the fact that the lane for loaded ships ran close to the hundred-fathom line. It is, unhappily, a route which the ship owners themselves prefer, and recommended. The Agulhas Current represents a major economy for loaded ships: assisted propulsion for two or three days at no cost. The two shipping lanes are only two miles apart but, bad as that whole stretch of water is, the seas at the heart of the race of the current are always visibly worse. Professor J. K. Mallory, head of the oceanographic department of the University of Cape Town, told the *Cape Argus* in an interview published in April 1971, two months after *Wafra*, that 'By standing farther offshore tankers would still benefit from the Agulhas Current, they would be less likely to encounter freak seas and would have little extra mileage to cover.' The South African minister of economic affairs, S. L. Muller, answering agitation about oil-tanker routing in parliament a month later said that South Africa had accepted the zoning with reluctance, but had little choice in the matter in view of 'the overwhelming majority of ships in favour of this rezoning'.

We therefore find ourselves watching a situation that often seems hard to believe. After having been allowed to load more than was previously thought advisable, and having then also adjusted the rules for their loaded winter passage through the southern seas, tankers passing through those waters chose to do so along the very narrow path that is the most destructive in that violent area.

The dismay that this has caused to South African port authorities is continually reflected in the reports published by the shipping editor of the *Cape Times*, George Young, who himself is an authority on those waters in particular and an internationally respected one on maritime affairs in general. In a report published on 15 June 1968, after the *World Glory* disaster and immediately before implementation of the IMCO amendment on load lines, Young said:

One of the greatest paradoxes in the international organization for the safety of life at sea has been the authority granted tankers of major western powers rounding the Cape in recent months to overload their vessels. And after July 21 the long-established rule for lighter loading of ships in winter in these waters is no longer applicable. After the closing of Suez the scarcity of oil in Europe induced controlling authorities to advise their shipmasters to ignore winter load-line rules off South Africa, and to come through these waters down to summer marks.

When associated with an earlier authority which allows tankers to operate with less freeboard – representing another five thousand tons of cargo – the tankers have been negotiating winter storms in half-tide rock condition. Some have sustained structural damage, another had a spare propeller on the deck break loose and threaten the ship's safety, and this week the World Glory broke in two. Two months ago another Greek sank off Luderitz.

Conscientious surveyors in South Africa who have apprehended ships for overloading, have had to condone the action when correspondence was produced from overseas authorizing ships to run in this condition.

Storms in those waters come not only in winter. In December 1969, the middle of the southern summer, Captain L. J. Tarp brought his loaded 102,000-ton Swedish tanker Artemis through a storm while travelling down the wild coast. One wave, he later told the Cape Argus, hit the ship and came rolling down the deck at such height that it hit the wheelhouse five decks up and flooded it. 'A ship of this size acts like a pier, unable to ride the swell,' he said. 'There are tremendous pressures.'

As he regularly does, always with disturbing evidence, George Young a few weeks later, on 9 January 1970, again criticised the overloading of tankers, and wrote in the Cape Times:

Two tankers have had to make a South African port with grave risk of their bows collapsing. In strong headsea, the buff-bowed ships suffered failure of frames in the forepeak which were proved by the elements to be entirely inadequate to withstand strain inflicted upon them. Longitudinals either fractured at the junction with verticals or buckled. And since strength of hull is composed of the composite framing throughout its length, one weak sector can imperil a ship.

A big Swedish tanker which put into Durban not only had internals buckled and broken by pounding into a headsea, but the shell plating after panting to the weight of the sea, disintegrated and fell off so that the water-tight bulkhead separating the first oil tank was withstanding the full weight of the sea.

Another Liberian tanker, rounding the Cape in a gale, had the bows fail in a similar way. There was an empty space between the stem plating and the first tank, so that forty-five feet depth of water was consistently being thrown against a blunt structure behind which was nothing but a series of steel frames. . . .

Characteristically, there is nothing that can be done about such an accident aboard a supership, no way in which the damage can be temporarily repaired or shored up. Merely getting to the bows is imposible. There is no interior access and no one would survive the journey forward over the decks in bad weather.

When *Queen Mary*, with 15,000 American troops aboard, cut in half the British cruiser *Curaçao* while travelling at top speed across the Atlantic during the war, her staff captain, Harry Grattidge, accompanied by the bo'sun and carpenter, could race to the bows along the working alleyway that ran the length of the ship from fore to aft to see whether the collision bulkhead, the water-tight reinforced steel wall that rises from the very bottom of the ship to the main deck, had been damaged. 'If that bulkhead were weakened,' Grattidge recounted in his memoirs, *Captain of the Queens*, 'I did not like to think of the *Mary*'s chances of survival. I sweated through my silent inspection. But finally not a crack. Not a break. The bulkhead had held intact.' His moment of anxiety was of course the very same experienced by Lord Jim staring at the collision bulkhead of *Patna*: 'You must remember that he believed, as any other man would have done in his place, that the ship would go down at any moment; the bulging, rust-eaten plates that kept back the ocean, fatally must give way, all at once like an undermined dam, and let in a sudden and overwhelming flood.'

Grattidge did what Lord Jim didn't do. 'I turned to the bo'sun and the carpenter. "Get every length of wood you can find, Bo'sun. Get it down here and strengthen that collision bulkhead as much as you possibly can!"' When the bo'sun had finished the job, *Queen Mary* steamed at twenty-four knots, with the bulkhead taking the full impact of the water. All that the officers aboard a supership can do in similar circumstances is watch and hope. They may not even *know* that their ship has been badly damaged. 'You never know what's happening,' Alan Ewart-James told me. 'I was in a sixty-thousand-ton ship that suffered severe structural damage off Durban. She must have hit a freak wave, but we didn't know it. We didn't realise the damage until maybe two days later. Quite considerable damage. The bow was pushed in by about four inches and the deck was set down. The bow was concertina'd upwards. I believe that when she went to dry dock at the end of that trip they dismantled the bow and rebuilt it.'

Part of the problem with supertankers is that they cannot ride a huge wave and must slam through it, therefore hitting the on-coming wave with a stubborn damaging impact. 'We were doing about twelve to thirteen knots at the time we hit that wave,' Ewart-James said. 'In any ship in very heavy seas it's always advisable to slow down. A lot of VLCC masters and officers don't. They just push through these Cape waves. Sitting all the way back here, a quarter of a mile or so from where the waves are breaking over the bow, they feel as though nothing's happening, that everything's all right. But you can't push through these waves like that. On this ship, I'd slow her right down in really bad weather, right down to a point where there's just enough to keep her steering.'

The day that *Ardshiel* sailed from Rotterdam I had sat in my cabin reading the latest batch of reports by George Young, no more than a few days old, concerning a storm that had just raged off the Cape. 'The weather along the South African coast has not changed, but the rules governing loading of vessels have,' he wrote, and began providing the same sort of evidence he'd proffered several years previously when the new rules had come into effect. In the gale that had just passed, the 60,000-ton *Texaco Venezuela* had been totally disabled north of Durban. Electrical blackout had immobilised the ship and she had been battered by the weather until taken in tow by a salvage tug. A P & O tanker, *Grafton*, had suffered hull damage and was making for Durban. The 18,000-ton British tanker *Blyth Adventurer* had had a particularly harrowing time of it. She had been in the same area as the other two ships and the storm when it appeared on the radar had seemed to be a rain squall. When it struck the wind increased rapidly to hurricane force and 'enormous cross seas and swell thundered down on the heavily burdened tanker'.

Speed was reduced, but even at three-quarters power the ship could make steerage way of only four knots. The force of the water tumbling over the bows flooded lockers and storerooms. Electrical cables had been ripped from their mountings and half the ship had been plunged into darkness. The living accommodation was without power and light and the navigation bridge had had to rig oil lamps. The forecastle deck fractured under the weight of the sea, pipe-guards were buckled and swept away, and so were covers on ventilators. One piece of equipment on the forecastle apparently had been wrenched from its steel sockets, flung the length of the main deck, right over the bridge, and had landed on the after deck! 'Two important factors emerge from the experience of the *Blyth Adventurer*,' George Young said. 'Firstly, the ship was on the recommended route along the seaboard which took her between 15 and 20 miles off the land which, some mariners feel, puts her right into the wildest weather. Secondly, the winter load-line having been suspended around these parts, the tanker was a half-tide rock in the wild weather. If the ship's steering had failed through electrical failure, and she had turned beam-on to the seaway, it is conceivable that she would have been lost from mountainous seas pressing down on her.'

'It's not surprising that they are reporting bows stove in,' an officer in a small tanker told George Young in a later edition, referring to VLCCs. 'One tanker which came up astern of us was colliding with the swell, and throwing water as high as her masts. There was not a dry spot anywhere along her decks and it was amazing that any floating structure could endure such punishment.'

They don't of course, as he knew, and as we know, and from their consequent cracks and fractures, or from their fatal wounds, they infect, season after season, the life and viability of those seas. Not a winter passes without disturbing incidents of the punishment suffered by these ships as they pass through the Cape seas. At the beginning of the southern winter of 1974 the foremast of one tanker, planted well inboard on the wide deck, was torn from its mounting by wild seas. While the actual difference of something close to two feet between winter and summer marks might not appear much it is by no means insignificant when one considers the extremely low freeboard of a deeply laden tanker. Anyone who has seen the incredible battering and bashing they take when shipping seas in heavy weather is bound to wonder whether, in such circumstances, even such a small difference might not sometimes be a fatal one. The tanker cannot rise as the conventional freighter does. When you stand on a VLCC's bridge you can see the crests rolling one behind the other against the long hull. Some pass just below the level of the main deck. Then come those just a little higher, no more than a foot or so, and the deluge they put aboard could kill a man if he were so foolish as to place himself in a position to be knocked down by it. Such is the case in a moderate blow. In a severe one the quantity and power of the water almost constantly on board is quite frightening; and, as we know off the Cape, the damage it can do in usual winter weather is tremendous, and in even heavier weather is excessive.

In this regard, nature has coupled the phenomenon of the freak waves off the South African coast with yet another phenomenon which, like the freak waves, is connected with the Agulhas Current and helps serve as a polluting agent of the southern seas. The Mozambique Current flows down the east coast of Africa to become the Agulhas Current off South Africa. Off Cape Agulhas itself, the current veers away from the coast virtually at right angles, and stands out to sea. Its course, south-eastwards, takes it toward the Southern Ocean's own circulating west wind drift.

The speed of the Mozambique–Agulhas Current, up to five knots, is important. What it grips it tends to hold, all the way south. Its tenacity and power are well illustrated by a remarkable and long-forgotten episode, one of the strangest of the sea's dramas and which very likely was the model for Conrad's tale 'Falk'. It concerned the 5,000-ton British steamer *Waikato*, which sailed from London for Australia in May 1899 and, after putting in at Cape Town, rounded Good Hope. Soon after, her propeller shaft broke and she lost all propulsion. *Waikato*, however, belonged to the age of transition between sail and steam and was rigged to carry square sails on her fore-mast and fore-and-aft sails on her mainmast. The sails were set, but she couldn't answer the helm. She was caught in the Agulhas Current and in fact was drifting *against* the wind. Over a four-week period, as food, water, and morale slowly diminished, the ship was carried steadily toward the Southern Ocean's winter, whose storms were likely to obliterate her even before cold and starvation finished off those on board.

The cargo was broken into and further supplies found, all of which were severely rationed. *Waikato* was too early for radio and was unable to call for help. After eleven weeks, at the end of August, she was sighted by a barquentine, which promised to report her plight to Mauritius. But she was later spotted by another steamer which, despite severe weather, took her in tow for Fremantle, where she eventually arrived three and a half months after sailing from the Cape. Her drift had set her steadily toward sub-Antarctic seas and, when found, she was on the edge of the Roaring Forties, halfway to Australia but on a course well south of it. It probably remains the longest steamer drift on record. It is interesting to note that ten years later, after the liner *Waratah* had been reported overdue between Durban and Cape Town, the warships sent out to search for her assumed that she might have broken down and, like *Waikato*, been caught on that southern drift, so they followed the course of *Waikato's* drift, but found no trace of the liner.

In any event, the way *Waikato* went, and the way the Admiralty thought *Waratah* may have gone, presumably is the way that much of the oil flung upon southern African waters now goes.

As we already have seen, all manner of slicks, whether from major accidents, sunken ships, tank cleanings, cracks, leaks, dumping, or the bilge deposits of ordinary merchantmen, are constant upon those waters. A quite small dumping at sea, the tank washings of a small tanker, can create a slick covering many miles of sea. Even in rough weather, a slick can be remarkably resistant to disintegration. It can travel long distances. When the 46,000-ton *World Glory* broke up the spillage from her cargo created a slick sixty miles long that travelled steadily down the coast and, since it didn't come ashore, apparently funnelled straight into the Agulhas Current and continued south.

All the major spills down there have occurred on or within reach of the Agulhas Current. The main slick from *Wafra* was more than thirty-five miles long and it too was borne away by the Agulhas Current. After the *Texanita–Oswego Guardian* collision, the latter jettisoned about eight thousand tons of her cargo which, together with four thousand tons of bunker oil that had been spilled in the crash and oil from *Texanita*, formed a slick sixty-five miles long and about ten miles wide. The slick eventually broke into smaller ones and most of them also vanished, like muck down a drain, down the Agulhas Current.

The Agulhas Current in effect acts as a funnel down to the Southern Ocean and swirls any oil it receives down to those latitudes, in daily spurts and driblets, and occasional wide blanketing sheets.

Much needs to be learned about the oceanography of the Antarctic so it is impossible to predict with certainty how such pollutants might disperse. What we do know about the Antarctic wind, current, and water movements indicates that the dispersion might be as wide subsurface as on the surface. Pollutants and tarry residues, if they continued along the drift of Waikato, would be borne along the rim of the Southern Ocean's west wind drift. They would pass through one of the richest of the southern marine pastures, a region of floating weed. Once upon the Southern Ocean, tar and pollutants would either go into circumnavigation, or return slowly northward. Drift bottles are believed to have made a circumnavigation of the ocean in about four years. But the most destructive effect will have occurred long before these remnants are set in permanent orbit around the Antarctic continent, or wash ashore upon the Australian or New Zealand coasts. An interesting recent example of this drift was provided by another tanker, the 73,000-ton P & O oil–ore carrier Heythrop, which suffered a violent tank explosion off the South African coast in November 1971. Fifteen months later, one of the ship's lifeboats, presumably torn from the ship's decks by the blast, arrived upside down in the western end of Princess Royal harbour, Albany, Australia, after a seven-thousand-mile drift. South of the Cape, the Southern Ocean's currents become deeply complex because of the surface winds and storms and the convergence of cold southern water with warmer northern water. All this is still little understood, but there is a great deal of interchange between the various layers of water, deep and surface, warm and cold. The area below Cape Agulhas is one of particular activity. There are warm eddies that are sometimes as much as one hundred kilometres across. Water appears to sink and spread southwards in a subsurface layer.

Any dissolved pollutants borne south of the Cape by the Agulhas Current at the outset are therefore guaranteed a good chance of a submerged and far-reaching penetration of the Southern Ocean. Less dissoluble and more buoyant fractions of any spilt oil will continue and attack upon the surface, borne upon an erratic and perhaps endless journey by the turbulence of that great sea.

Much of the world's oxygen, and by far the largest single portion of the life of the world's seas either exists or is dependent upon the

Southern Ocean, whose fauna and flora are the richest and most prolific of all. We are simply not yet in a position to know what we might do to our planet, to the life of *all* the oceans, to the viability of man's future existence, if we heedlessly, summarily, and destructively damage the Southern Ocean before we properly understand its functions. What we already know about its importance is quite enough to warrant the bleakest predictions should its ecosystems begin to fail.

The world's oceans are not uniformly productive. The major portion of the deeps, like terrestrial savannah, is relatively unproductive. The true richness of the sea's life is concentrated in a very few areas of high production, flourishing pastures if you like, where the density and variety of living matter are hugely in excess of what it is elsewhere. These thriving seas by and large lie either within the equatorial currents or are spread across the coldest flow of certain cold currents. But the layered cold-warm-cold Southern Ocean contains the biggest, most abundant, and most important of these areas. It is highly productive over much of its area whereas the other oceans are highly productive only in relatively small pockets. Indeed, several of those pockets of high productivity elsewhere are directly influenced by the Southern Ocean, notably the west coast of South America from Horn to the equator, and the west coast of Africa from Good Hope to the equator. The Antarctic richness is carried up the South American coast by the Humboldt Current, and along South West Africa by the Benguela Current.

Those two currents can be so fruitful that they have allowed Peru to account for as much as 10 per cent of the world's fish catch (by far the single biggest share of it), and make it worthwhile for trawler fleets to steam from the far corners of the world to the fishing grounds off South West Africa. The Russians and the Japanese are the principal of these far-ranging trawlermen. Most of the catch taken by Peru, Russia, Japan, and the other nations that fish the Humboldt and Benguela currents is processed into fishmeal, for use in fertilisers and animal feed. It would be difficult to say how many of the world's millions depend upon the direct and indirect results of these fisheries, but in face of the world's ever-increasing demand for food and sustenance the need is that they should continue to yield all they possibly can. It has been estimated that one-sixth of the world's fish comes from the South Atlantic off the South African coasts, which means that the Humboldt and Benguela currents together provide some 16 per cent of our fish.

The Southern Ocean, through influence upon its neighbouring waters, has had an involvement with modern agriculture and the feeding of new masses that is far longer than most of us might suppose. The world has forgotten that the Southern Ocean, through guano, has been an indirect and indispensable source of fertilisers for more than a century. Guano is the dried excrement left by millions of guano birds (mainly penguins, cormorants, gannets) on their breeding grounds, which are usually tiny rocky outcrops and islets scattered along the South African coast and the west coast of South America. Guano provided the base for the mass manufacture of the fertilisers that nineteenth-century agriculture required as it sought to improve production and to feed the rising populations of Europe and America and, while those brutal industries, whaling and sealing, drew Western man's first big plunder from the Southern Ocean and its related waters, guano probably brought the most profit. When first discovered, the guano deposits on those various rocky islets often lay twenty-five feet deep. At a price of nine pounds per ton in the mid-nineteenth century, guano represented one of the quickest of all roads to fortune: you bought or chartered a ship and sailed it out, and loaded it brimful without the cargo costing a penny. Guano claims on the South Atlantic islands were staked like gold claims in the Klondike and brought much to the lore and legend of the South Atlantic.

On Ichaboe, six hundred miles north of Cape Town, the guano rush brought some of the biggest gatherings of ships known, with as many as four hundred recorded on one day alone in the 1840s riding to anchor off the island. Their crews fought deadly skirmishes over claims, and their bodies, mummified by the guano, are found in a perfect state when sometimes exposed in their coffins by gales and high winds. The brutality of life on Ichaboe is a dark recurring tale in British maritime journals. A South African writer, Lawrence G. Green, who knew his African coasts and seas well, gives a typical Ichaboe anecdote in one of his books, *Where Men Still Dream*:

> Many years ago, there was a sailor working here; and after a storm this mad fellow found some of the graves with the earth torn away by the wind. Every morning he would go to the coffins, and lift up a lid and say, 'Good morning Jack – still here? You got a darn sight better shirt than mine. I think I'll take it.' He never took a shirt; but one day, after drinking rum from a ship, he went to one of these mummies with a jack-knife and cut off the head and came into the hut swinging it by the red hair.

In the 1930s, Ichaboe's gannet population was roughly estimated at 40 million. They still arrive in millions, and still leave behind the guano that the South African government now mines as a national mineral resource. The deep deposits have long since been borne away of course. A gannet eats its own weight in fish every day, and the colossal quantities of fish represented by this consumption give a fair idea of the harvests flowing with the Benguela Current.

This multitudinous and intermingling bird, fish, whale, seal, and sea-lion presence of the southern waters is the world's last and greatest natural preserve; only the Arctic itself can rival it, but the waters there are less rich and the distribution of life more confined, and the depredations, because of the area's relative proximity to civilisation, have been greater. The wonder of the south is that its species can be seen in such profusion three to four thousand miles from Antarctica itself, off South America and off Africa. As with the Arctic, man has seldom been admirable in his relations with the fauna of the great south. Whaling has been, and remains, a particular horror, with explosive harpoons taking from twenty to thirty minutes to kill the animal, which then might be pumped with compressed air before it is quite dead to make it easier to tow. The square-rigged sailors were neither sufficiently sentimental nor respectful of the albatross to prevent themselves from catching it by a metal hook for the fun of it. Whatever might be said about any of that, and other similar depredations, none of it, however brutalised and heedless of the magnificence from which all is sprung, can really equal the idea of the pollution and despoliation of the Southern Ocean and, as a direct consequence, of the other seas it directly influences.

Several of the world's major ocean circulatory systems draw their initial force of propulsion and much of their organic seed from the Southern Ocean. These systems provide the dominant currents of the South Pacific, South Atlantic, and Indian oceans. The Humboldt Current sweeps on to become, on the opposite side of the South Pacific, the warm South Equatorial and East Australia currents. The West Australian Current moves up from the Southern Ocean along the west coast of Australia and folds into the Indian Ocean's South Equatorial Current. In the South Atlantic, the Benguela Current curves past the equator to become the Brazil Current.

One of the reasons for the Southern Ocean's incredible richness is because it is so 'well mixed up', as Sir George Deacon, former chief of Britain's National Institute of Oceanography and a renowned authority on Antarctic oceanography, put it to me.

The Southern Ocean possesses the interplay of strong deep currents and surface currents of varying temperatures that induce such abundant fertility in the sea. Deep currents are essential for fertilising the sea's surface by swirling up nutrients, and vice versa, by bringing down for breeding in the colder depths many of the organisms that already have waxed on top. The gales and general turbulence of the south help stir and tumble the surface even more, and what we have there by and large is something akin to the original propagating circumstances of creation, the wet, wild stimulus of life. As we already have noted, those rushing circumpolar seas are indeed a vestigial reminder of when the entire surface was stormy water. The centrifugal currents that fly off from this, rather like the whirling streamers of a Roman candle, bear away the product or the seed, or both, and allow these currents to stimulate and enlarge other pockets of immense riches far from the rim of the Southern Ocean itself.

The greatest fruitfulness of those currents eventually proves to be where their cold flow gradually merges into a warmer tropical one. The cold water sinks below that which is less dense and the vertical swirl caused by this again raises nutrient salts from the sea bottom. The marine life stimulated anew by this helps account for the particular richness of the fisheries off Peru and South West Africa (in the northern hemisphere the same sort of conditions are created off Newfoundland, where the cold Labrador Current descends into the Gulf Stream).

At this point one might well ask to what degree does the Southern Ocean itself stimulate and help propagate the Gulf Stream and the North Atlantic? We are far from knowing. What we do know is that the seas are indivisible, they constantly exchange their waters. It is possible that cross-pollination of life in the oceans is far more complex than presently suspected; it would be a strange oversight in the normal checks and balances of planetary nature if it weren't. The Southern Ocean has a warmer more saline layer of water below its cold surface, and in the Atlantic sector of it some of the deep warm water can be traced to a Mediterranean origin, and some even almost to the other pole: to the boundary region between North Atlantic and Arctic currents.

We don't know how long water takes to move such vast distances. One of the fundamental difficulties of studying and truly understanding the effects of pollution at sea is this very absence of any clear idea of the speed of interchange of water between the various oceans, and of the role and function and long-term effects of it upon marine life. We can hardly suppose that a heavily polluted Atlantic or even Mediterranean for that matter could *not* have some effect upon the Southern Ocean, and vice versa. It is already widely known that DDT levels were found in Antarctic penguins a few years ago. In 1974 there was still no knowledge of how this had been transmitted to the birds, although several scientists to whom I have spoken are inclined to believe that the birds obtained it from the *air*.

In the face of such general ignorance it might not be unreasonable to suppose that they may have obtained it from water flowing south from an Atlantic where the plankton already possess high levels of PCB, an industrial pollutant related to DDT. But even if they *did* obtain it from the air, it means that the Southern Ocean is now vulnerable to pollution from every possible direction, whether undersea or above-sea, from the cold skies above, from the deepest-flowing currents bringing water from other oceans and seas, and, most directly, and perhaps most poisonously, from what it receives from the Cape.

It is sufficiently apparent alone from the great currents it propels and nourishes that the Southern Ocean's impact upon the body of the world's waters is probably greater than any other ocean's. Its global importance was scientific suspicion long before there was reasonable evidence to confirm it. The idea that all the tides were generated in the Southern Ocean was propounded early in the nineteenth century and remained common until well into this century. It was a logical proposal given the great power of such a mass of water continuously circling the world, driven by its fierce westerlies, and spinning off its strong currents into every other principal ocean. It has been disproved, of course, but the theory is a historic (one is inclined to say instinctive) recognition of the Southern Ocean's significance, and valuable as such because it allows no pretence that we are too recently aware and still too ignorant of its possible role in our destiny.

If, as we are frequently told, the seas are earth's last untouched resource and final frontier and a possible source of much of the food and nourishment that our overcrowded world will need, then it would be madness indeed if we allowed the Southern Ocean, the most fruitful of all, to be damaged even before we have had proper and practical access to it, or acquire any real and substantial knowledge of its true significance to all the salt waters of the world.

Although oceanographic research ships now go to the Southern Ocean and Antarctica a great deal more often than they used to, these waters have not been under close, consistent scrutiny by ordinary voyaging man since commercial sailing craft stopped using them to a marked degree forty to fifty years ago. There is no reason for steamers to go into those waters, except to supply weather outposts on isolated islands or at Antarctica itself. Most of the supplies for the latter go in by air anyhow. The whaling expeditions are now mercifully few and limited in range, the quarry being well on its way to extinction. There is no way of knowing, for example, whether the Southern Ocean is as distressingly oil-flecked and polluted on the surface as Thor Heyerdahl discovered the North Atlantic to be when he sailed his raft Ra from North Africa to the Caribbean in 1969.

It was a shock to hear from him that the midstream current of the Atlantic was so polluted that it made daily bathing unattractive. It was, however, symptomatic of our ignorance of the condition of the seas as a whole and what is happening to them that we should have found ourselves so unaware of the state even of the most accessible and, scientifically speaking, most intensively examined of all the major oceans.

In a radio letter sent to the Norwegian Ambassador to the United Nations from his raft, Heyerdahl reported that 'at least a continuous stretch of 1,400 miles of the open Atlantic is polluted by floating lumps of solidified, asphaltlike oil'. He himself believed that the entire ocean from the coast of Africa to the coast of tropical America was polluted. Some lumps were old enough to be covered by barnacles, others were smooth and fresh. There were whole areas where the water was discoloured and unclear.

Nobody had anticipated such findings from him; how then can we know from the random sampling of occasional oceanographic research ships what the true state of the Southern Ocean is? No one is going to sail those waters in a raft.

The Antarctic Treaty of 1959, to which sixteen nations (Argentina, Australia, Belgium, Chile, Czechoslovakia, Denmark, France, Japan, the Netherlands, New Zealand, Norway, Poland, South Africa, Britain, the United States, and Russia) are signatory, is regarded, justifiably, as a model of open-minded international agreement. 'It is the interest of all mankind that Antarctica shall continue for ever to be used exclusively for peaceful purposes and shall not become the scene or object of international discord,' its preamble declares. Special arrangements to protect Antarctica's flora and fauna were agreed to in 1964 and embodied in an Antarctic Treaty Bill, which has been ratified by the signatory powers. It unhappily excluded whales from its scope, but seabirds, penguins, and seals are of course fully embraced. A British expert on Antarctic wildlife, Brian Roberts, told the *Daily Telegraph* why this special legislative protection was considered necessary by the treaty nations. 'Most of the Antarctic fauna exists on what is believed to be a marginal basis of stability and human influences could easily tip the scale in critical cases,' he said.

Canada had the same fears in mind when it sought to protect its Arctic waters through the Arctic Waters Pollution Act of 1970 which, although not recognised by the United States, sets a hundred-mile safety control zone around the Canadian Arctic islands and is designed to prevent pollution of the waters of the Canadian archipelago. The bill, introduced when the north-west passage was under serious consideration as a route for Alaskan oil, set down precisely the standards of construction and operation of ships entering those waters, how they should be fitted, what qualifications their personnel should have, when they could sail and how and where. Speaking on the bill in parliament, the Canadian Northern Development Minister, Jean Chrétien, said: 'With this legislation, we are pioneers on the frontier of international law. This legislation goes beyond any previous action by the Canadian government for the control of pollution and is in advance of any action by the international community. Although we have taken this action unilaterally, we stand ready at all times to enter into international agreement which will provide for control over the dangers of pollution. Until this occurs, however, we must and will act now to protect the ecology of the north.'

In a radio broadcast on the bill, Canada's prime minister, Pierre Trudeau, amplified these comments by saying, 'Any maritime tragedy there would have disastrous and irreversible consequences. Such oil would spread immediately beneath ice many feet thick; it would congeal and block the breathing holes of the peculiar species of mammals that frequent the regions; it would destroy effectively the primary source of food for Eskimoes and carnivorous wildlife throughout an area of thousands of square miles; it would foul and destroy the only known nesting areas of several species of wild birds.

'Involved here in short,' Trudeau added, 'are issues which even the most conservative of environmental scientists do not hesitate to describe as being of a magnitude which is capable of affecting the quality and perhaps the continued existence of human and animal life in vast regions of North America and elsewhere.'

With some amendment, Trudeau's statement and the Canadian concern could be applied equally effectively to Antarctic and sub-Antarctic waters, yet with even more force because, given the global influence of Antarctic waters and currents and wildlife, the repercussions of failure there would be even more far-reaching in their influence and effects than failure in the Arctic.

In Antarctica, land and sea are ecologically indivisible. Antarctica is a continent but, since the interior is mostly a lifeless icy desert, it must be considered for all practical purposes simply a coast, along whose shores the various nations have set up their scientific camps. No continent is more wholly involved with its immediately adjacent seas than Antarctica is with the Southern Ocean; in effect, the sea is a natural extension of the continental Antarctic habitat. Much of the fauna that thrives down there is adapted to both land and sea, and it is the sea that feeds practically all of its varieties.

Large as it is, we cannot be complacent about the Southern Ocean until we have a reasonably exact sense of the possible damage that a slick thirty-five to sixty miles long can do to the surface of such a fertile sea and habitat. The real consequences of any pollution that already has occurred are quite impossible to judge. The damage done by *Metula* alone will take years to assess. To study thoroughly the effects of pollution upon the open seas, a most urgent need, would require tremendous international effort and outlay, which doesn't seem to be in prospect, and until it is, every possible caution would seem to be the wisest course. The general degree of our ignorance about the effects of oil in water was underlined by the Canadian report on *Arrow*, which recommended that urgent research and development projects were needed on, among other subjects, the life history of oil in water; the toxicity of petroleum products; long-term effects of petroleum products or mixtures on marine flora and fauna; the prediction of the movement of oil slicks on the surface; aerial detection, surveillance, and tracking of slicks; and the overall ecological, economic, and social consequences of major spills.

We know the heavy toll taken by various spills on the breeding islands off the Cape coast, and we know that the Agulhas Current must be delivering steady quantities of oil slick down into that part of the Southern Ocean just south of the Cape; and we also know, from the report of the British Field Studies Council, that it appears that constant pollution by small slicks is more damaging than one major spill. As we also know, a slick can blanket a big area of sea and throughout that area exude its toxicities, smother plankton, coat birds and fauna, and infect fish that rise to the surface. Natural seawater itself contains various bacteria and micro-organisms that can partly decompose crude oil, but the process is a slow one and depends also on the nature and state of the oil, on whether the slick is thick or thin or in droplets. And the asphaltenes, tars, and waxy components that compose as much as one-third of a typical crude oil are resistant to micro-organisms and can persist indefinitely in the marine environment.

Laboratory experiments in Britain and Canada have shown that the rate of natural decomposition of oil in seawater also depends on the temperature. It is much faster in warm water and falls virtually to zero at five degrees Centigrade. The surface waters of most of the Southern Ocean are icy, and therefore probably extend the life and toxicity of crude oil. We know from the investigations of the Canadians during the *Arrow* disaster, which occurred off Nova Scotia in winter, that the physics, chemistry, and microbial degradation of petroleum products on land and in water in a cold environment are still largely unknown and, in the words of the official report, 'need urgent research'. Canadian scientists, who are among the best in the world on cold-weather matters, found themselves so ignorant of the effects of cold weather on oil when called in to deal with the *Arrow* spillage that they resorted to the simplest of all experiments: a mixture of oil and water was shaken in a jar and put in the freezing section of a domestic refrigerator to see what would happen (the oil separated out before freezing occurred, and formed a layer on top of the ice).

The balances of the sea are delicate, mysterious and still largely incomprehensible. The herring, for instance, is the most prolific and familiar of fish. It was for centuries the commonest item of diet in Europe, often more staple even than bread. It is still the most sought after of all food fish, it is caught in greater numbers than any other fish, and as a result it is the most intensively examined of all fish. Nonetheless, the herring has succeeded in keeping most of its important habits and whims secret to itself. We do not really know why, time after time, it has appeared in particular regions in immense abundance and affected the fortunes of man to a historic degree, notably through the Hanseatic merchants in the Baltic and the Dutch in the sixteenth and seventeenth centuries, only to vanish and bring its human dependants down to a lesser state. What balance tipped its coming and its going? The physical state of the sea presumably, a condition of temperature and salinity and other related factors that probably pleases the fish and makes it thrive. We believe, for example, that the Atlantic experiences cycles of tidal pulls of varying intensity that mix different seawaters together. In certain instances these appear to have affected the herring. The greatest gravitational pull on the oceans occurs at certain rare conjunctions of the sun, earth, and moon. These come in periods of about eighteen hundred years apart and two of them have occurred during the historic span of man: the first between 600 and 400 B.C. and the other from the thirteenth to the fifteenth century. The great tides caused by the latter flooded the Baltic with cold Atlantic water, and probably brought in the huge shoals of herring that made the Hanseatics so rich and gave them the capital for their gilded cities and their commerce. Usually the Baltic is too warm for the herring, which is a cold water fish, to thrive well.

Such natural caprice recently led a distinguished team of marine scientists, headed by Dr Alan Longhurst, director of the Institute for Marine Environmental Research, Plymouth, to warn in the magazine *New Scientist* of 1 June 1972 that years, even decades, will be necessary to detect the biological effects of pollution in the open ocean. 'Two pitfalls await the student of man's influence of life in the oceans,' their paper said.

First, to consider any such effects in the open ocean as inherently improbable because of the ocean's vastness or, secondly, to regard populations of marine organisms as inherently stable and to assume any changes in them reflect the effects of man and his technology. Man's chemical invasion of the ocean does, we believe, pose a real and serious threat to marine life, despite the great volume of the oceans, despite their chemical buffering systems, and despite the probable elasticity of their complex food webs. Research on such effects must be pressed forward urgently, but unsubstantiated statements should not be made concerning 'ecocatastrophes'.

They conclude their paper by declaring that

there seems to be a real lack of understanding that pollution monitoring schemes, in the ocean or elsewhere, can only succeed if the natural effects of the changing physical environment are both understood and monitored continuously and indefinitely.

Natural fluctuations in animal populations have already been ascribed incorrectly to the effects of pollutants, and it would be easy for a serious impact on the environment to pass unnoticed through ignorance of natural population instability or a lack of monitoring of the oceans on a global scale.

The authors warn against crying 'Wolf' too often, lest warnings of marine ecocatastrophe be finally ignored. But can we afford to wait all those many years or even decades before the marine scientists gain sufficient enlarged knowledge of their subject to be able adequately to distinguish between nature's calamities and man's? By then, surely, one is inclined to think, the line between the two might be so hopelessly confused that no one will ever be able to know. In any event, in crying 'Wolf' in the case of somewhere such as the Southern Ocean one is doing so as much in face of ignorance of the short- and long-term effects of oil in seawater as ignorance of natural phenomena and their own afflictions upon the life of the sea.

There is a fear that fossil fuels already are affecting the balances of the sea from the air as well as through pollution in the water itself. A report in *Nature* in 1973 discussed the fate of the carbon dioxide gas released by the burning of fossil fuels, principally coal and oil. Dr A. W. Fairhall, of the Institute of Nuclear Sciences, New Zealand, reported calculations suggesting that the seas were absorbing appreciably more carbon dioxide than hitherto supposed, with consequent effects on marine life. There appeared to be a possibility that the extra carbon dioxide by the end of the century could alter the chemistry of the world's oceans in a way that might cause the calcium carbonate in sea shells and coral reefs to dissolve. Dr Fairhall's prediction was based on the assumption that present rates of consumption of fossil fuels would continue unchecked, in which case the danger point would be reached in just over thirty years, in the year 2008.

In their recent book *The Great Ocean Business* Brenda Horsfield and Peter Bennet Stone agree that we urgently need to know whether or not new pollutants can disrupt the balance of phyto-plankton and zooplankton abundance and the breeding success of animals all along the food chains. If we do sufficient damage to the chemistry of the ocean, they declare, it is not beyond us to wipe out certain species at the end of the line. Horsfield and Stone note that it already has been suggested that sublethal doses of pesticides as low as 0.02 parts may interfere with the essential 'imprinting' mechanism that enables a fish to recognise its spawning ground. Without the 'trigger' of this recognition breeding may not take place. Horsfield, an oceanographer, and Stone, senior information adviser to the United Nations Conference on the Human Environment, discuss the possibilities of 'biological magnification', whereby traces of chemicals, themselves too small to be directly toxic, nonetheless are so persis-tent in the food chains that they accumulate and concentrate from stage to stage until, finally, they are sufficiently concentrated to kill. This process, the authors remark, is exemplified by the case of pere-grine falcons, whose eggs became too fragile to be viable. DDT and other chemicals were found to affect the bird's metabolism of calcium and thus adversely affected the thickness of eggshells. The decline of the peregrine falcon was found out quite by chance at the Nature Conservancy's laboratories. 'But it is difficult to imagine this feat of biological detection being repeated in the marine environment,' Hors-field and Stone declare, and add: 'We can be sure therefore that pollu-tants which affect life in the oceans will only show up when they have done relatively far more damage.'

In fact, a case similar to that of the peregrine falcons already has been found in the marine environment. California sea-lions were dis-covered to be aborting their pups. When examined, body fat of the sea lions was found to contain high levels of PCB.

It has taken a good many years and widespread use of DDT and its related chemicals to bring us to these few glimpses of the effects they can have. How long before we ultimately know the damage that oil can do or, if you like, how safe it is, in the sea?

There is absolutely no data on the long-term effects of a major spill upon plankton, which is the most important thing of all to know because any effects upon plankton will be passed on throughout the marine environment. Nor do we know anything about the effects upon the marine environment of the dissolvable fractions of any spilled oil. It is *their* effect upon plankton and sea life that may prove to be the most serious, and of far greater concern than the actual smothering of plankton over a wide area by a spill. The dissolved hydrocarbons vanish invisibly into the body of the great sea while we, understandably, cry out in anguish over the visible blackness of the less dissolvable fractions. Yet those that dissolve are virulently toxic. This may well prove to be the most serious aspect of the persistent spills off the Cape. We might say that the Southern Ocean is big enough to absorb the remnants of those spills that finally reach it, the few thousand tons of drifting tar balls that must by now be circulating upon its surface, but, apart from the damage the oil has done on the surface on its way to the south, can the fauna and flora tolerate the steady invisible toxicity that constant spills suppose? We don't know.

What we do know is that if those fractions are in the water they will reach the south. By and large, water in the Southern Ocean appears to move in two principal routes, southward in a deep warm layer, and northward in cold surface and bottom layers. The south-travelling water is the warmer body of water from the north which, south of Cape Agulhas, begins to sink and spread southward in subsurface layers. This is a simplification of an extremely complex hydrographic system, but it helps indicate the widespread and destructive potential dispersion of any dissolved hydrocarbon fragments in the seas off the Cape. Plankton are borne in both directions on these north–south movements, travelling underwater as well as on the surface. The constant whirl of these waters may take them down from the surface into the subsurface currents and bear them back southward. At any rate, if infected, they carry their infection in all directions. The plankton, of course, provide the critical link throughout that southern environment. The birds that belong to the remoter reaches of the Southern Ocean are mainly of the petrel and albatross groups. They are not adapted, as are the gannet and other birds of the upper perimeters of the ocean, to catch fast-moving fish, and so they subsist mainly on the small squids and crustaceans known collectively as krill, which is also the whale's principal food. It would be hard to imagine any other food mass having such enormous economic and ecological importance. Seals, penguins, practically all the birds of the deep south, as well as Antarctic coastal and oceanic fishes prey on it. Its abundance probably exceeds that of any other living matter. Krill swarm so densely that they become virtually a single mass. These swarms remain so close to the surface of the sea that they can be seen from the decks of ships. They are part of the plankton, but by far the single most important part of it.

More than half the earth's food manufacturing by plants occurs in the sea and the biggest single portion of this happens in the Southern Ocean which, in terms of plant growth, must be the largest pasture on earth. Plankton are the grass, undergrowth, humus, and basic living tissue of this pasture. If they fail, so must the species dependent upon them. Damage to them is damage to all. There is immunity for none.

Nobody knows precisely where the line between damage and destruction in any species lies, that point where the balance slides inexorably and finally toward the latter: that point where the natural rhythm of the species has been shaken and fecundity impaired, or where a sudden onset of natural calamity has weakened its resistance and brought it to a point of critical diminishment. In the case of the herring, we have known since neolithic times how delicate and capricious this connection might be. But we nonetheless have always been able to assume that somewhere, somehow, some seed remained from which the fish might flourish again. As with the herring, so with the whole mysterious life of the oceans. Its species might appear to vanish, but somewhere, somehow, the substance of renewal remained, to be visited at some later date upon some other point when circumstances were right. But our own age and generation is the first that cannot make such assumptions because, if a particular species in these times finds itself at a low natural point of its fecundity, the new toxicity of the seas might render it a blow that shatters the cycle forever and leaves no fragile link to help connect it to some onward stronger period. We cannot yet know how this might be with fish and other deep-sea life, but we can certainly know how it might be with some birds.

In British and near-European waters the guillemots, razorbills, and auks have a very low fecundity rate. The southernmost colonies of auks here have been declining since the beginning of the century. They, like the guillemots and razorbills, are most susceptible to becoming oiled by slicks. It is quite clear that their own low fecundity rate requires only a relatively small increase in the mortality rate to wipe out the population. It does not seem possible that these particular groups can survive the repeated heavy contamination of British and European waters.

In the south, the jackass penguin similarly began a decline that appeared to make his survival problematical. The repeated slicks that now hit his breeding colonies and that assault him in the sea would seem to guarantee his demise. A South African authority on the gannet, M. F. J. Jarvis, in a paper presented at Cape Town University in 1970, said that the effect of slicks in the region of a breeding colony could be disastrous. The gannet still seems impregnable in its teeming millions, but so once did the passenger pigeon of North America. The bird populations astride the Humboldt and Benguela currents in any event rise and fall with the availability of fish. Off Peru, the bird population was estimated at 25 to 30 million before 1955 and before the start of the big anchovy fisheries there. Six years later the population had crashed to 6 million birds. Will the birds of the south in the future be able to withstand the combined intensive assaults of man and his fisheries and man and his oil? We can deduce the effects of damage to plankton, but we still don't know what a massive sustained loss of birds might do to the south. Some South African marine biologists have long believed that the birds, aside from helping to maintain essential natural balances in the fish populations, might well have a substantial fertilising role. Plankton are known to thrive on the excreta of the jackass penguin. Such an overall fertilising role would not be improbable if we consider the quantity of guano they have left and still leave on the guano islands, and the fact that man himself for more than a century has considered their droppings one of his own most valuable fertilisers.

Canadian Arctic biologists share with the South Africans this belief in the fertilising role of the birds in the sea. They believe that the huge colonies of birds which gather in Baffin Bay play an important part in the nutrient exchange of northern waters. The birds eat fish and through their droppings return the nutrients to the sea, where they travel down the Labrador coast and, when mixed with warmer waters off the Grand Banks of Newfoundland, help support the huge fish populations in that area. It was this belief that helped inspire the Canadian government to draw up stricter regulations for use of the Canadian Arctic, especially for the passage of oil ships using the north-west passage. 'No one can say what would be the effect of the loss of this nutrient caused by any accident which might wipe out a large bird population. No one, indeed, can put a value on the contribution of the birds to this cycle. All that it is possible to say is that it seems a lunatic idea to take any risk which might interfere with this finely balanced natural cycle,' Boyce Richardson, a New Zealand author and conservationist prominent in Canada for his defence of the James Bay Indians in their fight for their environment, wrote in the Montreal *Star* when tanker passage was proposed for the north.

It is a lunatic risk at the two Capes, Horn and Good Hope, as well. The fifty thousand tons of oil dropped by the *Metula* was not only the second largest spill so far but also the largest in the adjacent waters of the Southern Ocean. Her entire cargo very nearly went into those waters (a hurricane hit the area immediately after the ship had been emptied and refloated; had it descended earlier it would have broken her and made salvage impossible). The area is very far south, much further south than Good Hope, and the coldness of the water makes the task of clean-up and renewal so much more difficult. The terrible realisation here is that August 1974 very narrowly avoided becoming a month of historic calamity, for one week to the day after *Metula* ran aground in the Magellan Straits the 250,000-ton fully laden World *Princess* was drifting helpless in Table

Bay. She went to within about one and a half miles distance from the shore. Had the United States Coastguard not rushed technical experts and equipment to the *Metula* in time and had she spilled all her cargo where she lay, and had the *World Princess* done the same off Cape Town, the two Capes would have suffered simultaneously the two biggest spills on record and thousands of tons of crude oil would have gone into the adjacent seas of the Southern Ocean. If any alarm about infection of the Southern Ocean sounds far-fetched to some, I urge them to consider the horror that we very narrowly avoided.

The past few years of continuous delivery of slick from the Cape to the waters of the Southern Ocean might be considered serious enough, regardless of how big and turbulent that ocean is, but what is much more daunting is the prospect that it will continue indefinitely. An open and functioning Suez Canal will affect only smaller tankers for years to come. Even when Suez is enlarged to handle 250,000-ton ships in ballast, as the Egyptians plan to do, the job will not only take a long time but the big tankers that can now go through in ballast (before it closed in 1967, a 150,000-ton tanker managed the voyage through the canal in ballast) will still have to make their *loaded* passage round the Cape to North America or Europe. As some 70 per cent of the tankers now under construction in the world will not be able to use Suez loaded, and because of the miscalculation by the tanker operators in not building more intermediate and small tonnage, the Cape passage will remain in use indefinitely. American imports from the Middle East will increase, and will remain high through the seventies and perhaps even into the early eighties, however much the United States tries to control its energy consumption and whatever new oil finds are made off its shore. If, as has been suggested, America starts stockpiling oil, the traffic will be especially heavy. The same is true for Europe. So tankers will continue to take their extra heavy loads of oil through the winter gales off Agulhas and through the freak maelstrom of the Agulhas Current: and through the hazardous, gale-swept Magellan Straits.

The damage that their spilled oil in its accumulative effect can do during the next decade must be weighed against the value we put upon Antarctica and the Southern Ocean, as a natural habitat, for their importance to the other oceans, and for what they mean to man as a whole, particularly if we come to regard those waters, as well we might, as one of the great remaining nutritional resources of the world. Or will we treat it all with the scant sentiment and respect with which we have treated the whale?

The blue whale, the biggest of animals and the most desirable of hunted whales, is well on its way to extinction as a result of indiscriminate slaughter since the war. The Antarctic whales were in decline even before the Second World War, but in the Rushton Lectures at Birmingham-South College in 1952, Professor George H. T. Kimble of McGill University, Montreal, and a director of the American Geographical Society, could still say: 'In the Antarctic, the whale population, after the respite of the war years, is now said to be capable of providing the world with at least 40,000 tons of oil and 225,000 tons of meat annually, and in perpetuity if duly husbanded. The meat alone would supply a population of 350 million – equivalent roughly to that of India – with its entire protein requirements.'

That opportunity has gone: from 400,000 blue and fin whales thirty years ago, the Antarctic whale population has declined to some 35,000 or fewer, because of the stubbornly high annual catch levels set by the International Whaling Commission.

Ironically, the dwindling of the whale has left its principal food, the krill, as an alternative human food resource. The surplus krill left in southern waters because of the destruction of the whale was recently estimated as unlikely to be less than about 30 million tons. The Russians already have started fishing it and it is sold in Moscow as a nutritious paste. Considering that practically all of the deep south's fauna feed upon krill and that man now joins them to use up the whale's share, the biomass supported by it would make it a commodity to be preserved and defended at all costs from possible contamination and destruction.

There may be even more at stake than this. When the British Antarctic Survey returned to Britain in April 1974, after two years in the south, its leader, Dr Richard Maitland Laws, told the *Daily Telegraph* that an astonishing, and hitherto unknown, quantity of marine life had been found around Antarctica. It was too early to say how vital this discovery would be towards helping to feed the world's population, Dr Laws told the *Telegraph*, but he added that when the survey's findings had been analysed it was likely 'that man will turn to the Antarctic as a possible source of food supply'.

There is, finally, another factor to be borne in mind. As it degrades, oil draws a destructive amount of dissolved oxygen from the water. This involves the very air we breathe. We must therefore always bear in mind the consequences to the atmosphere of constant pollution in the south and the burden imposed by big loads of oil possibly sinking off the Cape.

Among the contributing factors that account for the density of fauna and flora in Antarctic waters are the intense photosynthesis induced by the long summer light and the high concentration of dissolved gases, carbon dioxide and oxygen, in the water; the carbon dioxide helps photosynthesis, and the oxygen gives energy. It was a common assumption among scientists and geographers until recently that about 70 per cent of the world's oxygen was produced by photosynthesis in the sea. Many of the most urgently expressed anxieties about pollution of the oceans have referred to this, the postulate being that if the seas die, so will the land.

This view has been rebutted by Dr J. H. Ryther of the Woods Hole Oceanographic Institution who has said that the amount of oxygen the atmosphere gets from the sea is much less than originally supposed, about a third. Even if all the photosynthesis in the sea were to stop, he said, it would take 1 million years for the amount of oxygen in the atmosphere to be reduced by 1 per cent. Although one feels relieved by Dr Ryther's assurance, no one can regard with equanimity the impairment of the sea's production of oxygen, which steady pollution makes likely. If the seas don't breathe, or if they breathe asthmatically and imperfectly, what else in our environment will struggle for breath? It is a simple-minded question that anyone rotating a globe two-thirds of which is marked as covered by salt water can't avoid asking himself.

TEN

THERE was trouble in the engine room as we approached the Cape and *Ardshiel*'s speed was cut from seventeen knots to less than fourteen. The trouble drew the engineers and the electrical officer away and pour-out was cancelled, but the evening before we were due to arrive at the Cape Basil Thomson came to ask whether I would join him in his sitting-room at the usual hour.

I found him still in the speculative mood of the night when he'd sat in the wardroom talking about *Ardshiel*'s troubles on the coast and, when Diaz had brought in the ice bucket and drawn the curtains across the lemon and pink glow of a lovely South Atlantic sunset, Thomson fell into a slow, steady grouse.

When he'd brought the ship into Rotterdam he'd already been on the bridge forty-eight hours practically without sleep. They'd raised anchor at one in the morning to come alongside. Two hours later they docked, and the agent, marine superintendent, customs and immigration came aboard. By the time these all had gone ashore it was five thirty. What was the use of sleeping then? Pointless. He had to be ready to check the supplies, see to the new people coming aboard, including our honourable writer friend, notice of whom he'd naturally got at the last minute thanks to our friends at head office, and on top of this he'd had to get through all the immediate paperwork. Then all day with the loading and the rest of the ship's business. Perhaps he'd got a couple of hours sleep all told. When the ship sailed again that evening, was he fit to take her out? That was the question. He, Basil Thomson, didn't think so.

It was the same when they flew you out to the Gulf. You went tourist economy when a master should travel first. A big man like himself, where did he put his legs? Impossible to sleep. After a journey like that, you boarded a ship in all that bloody stinking heat, and six hours later had to take her out. Everybody knew these days that executives when they landed should make no business decisions. By the same token was he fit to take the ship out? In his opinion, he was not. But apparently the company thought so.

I could sympathise with his plight on the airplanes for even in the wide chair in which he was sitting his arms and legs seemed to find no easy solution of his comfort and he slumped with the heavy passivity of a man who'd given up the struggle. He lay far back in the chair, at such an angle that he appeared to have no point of leverage upon it; his forearms lay like small timber upon the arms of the chair and his legs jutted at a high and awkward angle. When he'd delivered his tirade he seemed all the more captive to this unhappy position, as though of itself it represented some impossible and inextricable problem in his life. He stared fixedly, absently at an opposite corner of the room, and the expression he retained was of intense general dissatisfaction.

It was the idea of taking the ship into Table Bay that he hated, Thomson suddenly declared, rousing himself from his reflection, as well as from the position; he'd hoisted himself forward with a sigh to freshen the drinks. He was always relieved to be out of there, he said, and he would be even more so tomorrow because we were arriving after dark and going in there at night doubled the usual risks. In the past two years two tankers had gone aground in the bay. He didn't trust the efficiency of the South Africans, not when they couldn't even muster a tug to get him out of a jam off their coasts. They had a *mañana* complex. He would stay as far off as he could, that was the only sensible thing for any master on one of these ships to do.

'I hate going in there,' he said. 'I absolutely bloody well hate it.'

His protests might have seemed contradictory to his more usual complaint, often expressed during my time aboard, about the redundancy of modern shipmasters and the diminished dependence upon them in vessels as automated as *Ardshiel*. What he obviously was affected by, however, was the inequitable balance of the pressures felt by the master of a supertanker such as *Ardshiel*. The commander of a ship that moves frequently in and out of port and through busy waters accepts critical encounters with other vessels as part of the natural rhythm of the job and of his responses, whereas with tankers long weeks of monotonous uneventfulness separate brief periods of intense pressure.

When he is out on the open sea, which is practically all the time, the master of a tanker has little to do. He gets used to it. The strain of suddenly finding himself in the crowded waters of the Channel, off the Cape, or in the Persian Gulf, where the responsibility of command reverts to its full old-fashioned sense, is far more pronounced therefore than for a ship trading from port to port: nightmarish transition from placid, vacuous days to unrelenting pressure, strain, and fear. He is dealing with a severe practical problem, as well as a psychological one. He must summon atrophied instincts, and shake off the sloth of all his preceding days; it is an especially difficult proposition for a man who is getting on, in whom the weariness and cynicism of a lifetime have suddenly become cumulative, or whose health has begun to decline, as was the case of the master of the *Torrey Canyon*, who was found to be tubercular.

Boredom and the dulling of crew alertness is a major safety problem as far as these ships are concerned. It is, of course, never referred to when the oil companies and tankermen justify the advantages of VLCCs over smaller ships. Most tanker voyages are long and boring, whatever the size of the ship, but smaller tankers, through the very fact that they *are* more often involved with other shipping, and because they do relieve the boredom of their crews through some variety of route and destination, maintain in those on board better mental balance and responses. During my investigations I learned, through the most reliable medical sources, that at least one major oil company had become so concerned at evident general psychological deterioration among its VLCC masters that it had begun an intensive long-term study of the matter.

Some approaches have been made to the problem of strain aboard VLCCs returning to crowded sealanes. Shell, for instance, has adopted a policy of sending an extra chief officer to embark in its inbound ships at Las Palmas for the passage up the English Channel. The double-lane routing through the Channel, off the Cape, and in other similar areas of heavy traffic has helped remove some of the strain, though by no means all because there always are the so-called cowboys who ignore the lanes and go against the stream, either out of ignorance, for their own convenience, or, sometimes, just for the hell of it, a chilling instance of which was related to me by Alan Ewart-James. It was an incident for which full concrete testimony was available. The ship was a 200,000 tonner, fully laden, and inbound up the Channel, where inbound ships are routed along a lane off the French coast while outbound ships use another on the English side.

The captain of the ship concerned ordered his second officer to lay his course along the English coast, against the downbound ships. The second officer consulted his immediate superior, the chief officer, who told him to comply. However, he refused to do it without a written order from the master, who promptly and angrily plotted his own course, and 200,000 tons of ship and oil was set on a collision run to Rotterdam against every ship downbound through the Channel. 'It was just an act of rebellion,' Ewart-James said when he related the incident. 'There was nothing to be done about it except pray that there wouldn't be an accident.'

As tanker traffic thickens at the continental approaches and at the critical passage points such as the Cape, the Straits of Gibraltar, and Malacca Straits, some further and probably unprecedented safeguard will have to be installed to ensure that those seas, their adjacent coasts, and shipping itself are defended against the whim, fatigue, temporary unbalance, defiance, unsuspected illness, or miscalculation of one man. It will have to be some form of shore control that gradually takes over decision and course and direction from ships sailing within certain ranges of the coast, in the same way that aircraft are now controlled across the airways of the world, particularly as they make their approaches and departures.

Had the whimsical decision of the master who ordered his second officer to lay an improper Channel course resulted in a collision with another 200,000 tonner, or had some smaller downbound vessel crashed into and torn open its tanks, we now would have a far more disastrous measure of the consequences of oil spillage than *Torrey Canyon*. *Torrey Canyon* itself, and the stranding in the Gulf of the VLCC *Esso Cambria*, are among the examples from immediate experience of how a man's fatigue can bring calamity upon our shores even though he has all the background and reputation for sound seamanship. Commandant Oudet in his booklet for the Royal Institute of Navigation on *Torrey Canyon* attacks the Liberian Commission of Inquiry for trying to avoid deeper shortcomings aboard the ship by putting the entire blame of the accident upon the master. The master's mistakes and technical blame were self-evident, Commandant Oudet argues. 'How indeed could it be otherwise when we remember that he was on the bridge ... that he saw the whole picture, and was in complete control?' But the loss of *Torrey Canyon*, Oudet believes, may have been due, more than anything else, to the captain's health; had he been fit in body and mind he would not have made all the mistakes of error and omission he did. He had been on the ship for a year and a day without leave. He was sick, suffered from nervous exhaustion, slept badly, and his tubercular condition became apparent immediately after the accident. 'The immediate lesson from the accident', Commandant Oudet says, 'is that the health of crews and especially of captains should be more closely watched, particularly in those ships where the owners seem at present to take little interest in the matter.'

The case of the *Esso Cambria*, however, offers an instance of the effects of immediate temporary strain. Esso, a company with a good reputation for welfare and crew concern, had been experiencing a

214

spate of VLCC problems with *Esso Cambria*, including defective boilers; on top of this there had been a spillage of oil while loading at Mina al-Ahmadi for which the ship was blamed. All this, of course, devolved principally upon the chief officer, who is responsible for running a ship. There were other troubles in loading and then, after sailing, the ship experienced an electrical blackout and a man was seriously injured in the engine room. The strain of all these problems devolved upon the chief officer, the man who always bears the burden of the ship's handling and administration. On his early morning watch the day after sailing from Mina al-Ahmadi, as the ship was heading for the port of Bandar 'Abbas to land the injured seaman, the chief officer was so negligent of his navigation that he failed to make fixes and to put them on the chart; on top of this, he made several grievous navigational errors, which resulted in *Esso Cambria*, laden with 241,045 tons of oil, running aground, fortunately upon a shoal instead of rocks. Even so, her forepeak and No. 1 tanks were ruptured, and some 1,500 tons of oil spilled. 'The disturbing feature of this case', the British shipping journal *Fairplay* said in comment, 'is the fact that the navigation of this mammoth vessel was in the hands of a man unfitted, perhaps only temporarily, to have the control of the navigation. What would have happened if a close-quarters situation suddenly developed, and prompt avoiding action had to be taken, perhaps before the master could get to the bridge? An officer who fails to take the opportunities of fixing the position of the vessel for a period of many hours, and also makes alterations of course during that time, without recording them, and finally makes an error of such magnitude that the vessel is put ashore, could, on the face of it, be a menace to other vessels as well as his own.'

The suggestion of some fixed form of shore control of shipping in busy waterways would have been impracticable just a few years ago, not to say unthinkable; but the position has changed only recently, and the nature of the change itself makes a new and different system of traffic regulation upon the seas imperative.

Until recently, our sea commerce still ambled. It took its time because costs were relatively low, economic pressures less, and trained and responsible crew still not expensive, as well as being available and willing. Under these circumstances the principal sea traders, the United States, Japan, and the maritime nations of Western Europe, employed thousands of ships to carry their freight. These ships loaded a hotchpotch of bales, barrels, bags, and crates, crossed the sea, and then went from port to port on the other side unloading portions of cargo. But inflation has put up the costs of running ships, and prosperity in the affluent societies has made it difficult, and sometimes even impossible, to get men to go to sea. We therefore can no longer ship our freight in small parcels in the comparatively leisurely process of yesterday when the packages went down to the docks, waited on the quay, were stevedored aboard by manual labour or by winches and cranes, and then submitted to the same process on the other side. Under that system, a ship spent up to 80 per cent of her time idle in port. As a result, the economics of size have been swiftly applied to all manner of ships besides tankers: they help solve the problems of cost and crew because one ship does the job of several.

The principles of supertanker operation, of a ship scarcely ever idle, moving freight in enormous but quickly handled quantities, was applied to ordinary shipping through containers, shiny metal boxes in which commodities are prepacked and which can be stacked and arranged as simply as a child's play blocks. This reduces handling to such a degree that a containerised service employs a handful of ships where once hundreds were necessary. Container ships are growing as tankers once did and already are in the 50,000- to 60,000-ton range. One of the biggest, the 50,000-ton American vessel *Sea-Land McLean*, has a speed of thirty-three knots and a crossing time of the Atlantic of four and a half days, which was the speed and crossing time of the Cunard *Queens*. Aside from containerised general cargo, bulk cargoes such as grain and ore also now move in giant ships, including many of 200,000 tons or more, and the trend toward bigger ships is being applied as well to vessels carrying a host of noxious substances, principally liquefied natural gas.

As a result of the race into bigness, whole generations of conventional ships are being sold off or scrapped. Many are bought for continued trading by flag of convenience owners, or by nations of the Third World wishing to start their own shipping services, which most seem to want to do if they possess any seacoast at all. The industrialised seafaring nations have therefore virtually at a stroke thrown away their old fleets and replaced them with ones consisting of big, new automated ships while fleets of older, rundown ships have been formed by individuals and nations new to shipping.

The new oil, ore, freight, and chemical carriers with their standardisation and their advanced automated systems adaptable to satellite navigation and the new-outlook seamen who run them both represent an opportunity for a completely new approach to control and regulation of the seaways, and, at the same time, because of their vulnerability, awkwardness, and the potential dangers of mistakes made in their handling and navigation, underline the firm need for such a new approach. A world short of food and minerals cannot really afford to lose 250,000 tons of grain and ore, but such altruism is somewhat abstract against the visible and known damage caused by oil, which for the moment is the main worry at sea, although the carriage of chemicals and huge quantities of liquid natural gas is moving up fast as a companion fear. All this is aggravated by the fact that in busy waters and off the various continental approaches such vessels are increasingly surrounded by the inexperience, mistakes, disregard, and sloppy ship-management of older, smaller vessels bought by those new to the sea, or by those who have never cared about how they run their ships and never will.

We can deal here with one of the most common and, I believe, most fallacious of the reasons offered in defence of giant ships, namely that, in these days of declining standards at sea, the big ships by reducing numbers contribute to safety. There is nothing whatsoever to substantiate this. The accident rate for small tankers is virtually the same as for big ships. The most practical example of a smaller ship to use as a model would be the 50–60,000-ton class of supertanker, which could use American east-coast ports as well as practically all existing major European ports, and also pass loaded through the Suez Canal. One can consider the matter from the converse, the limited number of ports to which VLCCs have access: they in fact form their own congestion at these. After the big spillage at Bantry Bay, the Irish government ordered three giant tankers to leave the bay because it feared there was risk of collision. Furthermore, VLCC bases such as Bantry Bay operate upon the principle that the oil is transhipped there to fleets of smaller tankers, which alone makes a mockery of the argument. Smaller ships can be dispersed along a whole range of ports on, say, the American east coast or the north-western shores of Europe, so that they don't congregate at several limited points, as the VLCCs do. With less draught and greater manoeuvrability they are much less at risk in such dangerously crowded waters than the VLCCs.

What ultimately is visualised for this situation anyhow is that all shipping will be monitored by shore stations as it steams up to certain offshore limits such as the North American approaches, the English Channel, and the Straits of Malacca and that, as a vessel comes within a certain range, it will be given a number and a course which, fed into its own computerised system, will put the navigation under shore control; or, at least, that the ship will sail under explicit directions received over the VHF radio. A rudimentary system of this sort already exists in the English Channel where British and French radar, helicopters, and patrol craft try to police the routing system to ensure that no one goes against the stream. The United States Coast Guard and the Canadians patrol against oil slicks and sludge dumping. But the extension of all these measures into an overall electronic-guidance system for marshalling shipping on the airways model seems a long way off. The cynical view of this proposition is that it won't be broached or installed until one or two particularly severe accidents have forced public opinion to demand the security it provides. All the factors that make these ships such a risk – human frailty, their own frail systems, and the multiplying external risks from other shipping – will however require some firm alternative proposal in the near future for handling them in their numbers, until more sophisticated means arrive. One way would be compulsory pilotage provided from an advanced point out in the Atlantic, such as a helicopter carrier on permanent station, although this presents obvious difficulties for winter. Another, as a model for what might come in the future, would be for compulsory course and position reporting by radio with increasing regularity as certain limits are reached, until the ship touches an offshore point of pilotage. For narrow crowded waterways such as the Channel and the Malacca Straits, one solution would be a convoy system such as that operated in the Suez Canal before it closed. Ships went through in two daily convoys from each direction.

Every busy seaway has its own characteristics, and these have to be borne in mind but, as concern grows for the sea as a whole, it is going to become increasingly difficult in principle to separate control at the approaches from that on the deep and open waters. The supertanker run from the Gulf to North America is a case in point. These ships during the course of their voyage (24,000 miles round trip) will be risking the integrity of several of the main oceanic streams on the globe, the Mozambique–Agulhas Current, the Benguela, and the Gulf Stream.

As they round the Cape, the ships bear almost directly upon the north-east corner of the North American continent – Maine, Nova Scotia, Newfoundland – where, as it happens, the first deep-water supership ports have been established. The route keeps them well away from most of the North American east coast but it nonetheless cuts straight across all the heavy transatlantic traffic routes running in and out of the east-coast ports, as well as the southern ones from the Gulf. Any mishaps out there may be well removed from the coast, but they'll be inside the full flow of the Gulf Stream, which means that Maine and the Canadian Maritime Provinces face the double hazard of having these ships off their shores, and of being vulnerable as well to damage borne northward to their offshore fishing grounds by any accident that may occur even well to the south.

It was wet and cold off Cape Town the following evening, with Table Mountain not even faintly seen against the night sky, which hung low and misty. We went in around eight and were on our way again round the coast an hour later, all without any problems, although this didn't appear to appease Thomson's irritation, which kept him moving at a rapid pace to and fro across the bridge, and crying 'Speak up! Speak up!' to poor Stephen Tucker who, subdued by the large, dim, furiously moving frame of the master, had become inclined to whisper.

'Here we are, two hundred thousand deadweight tons of ship in a busy seaway and I want to know what Cape Town says but all I get from you is a mumble. Are you asleep, or did you hear what they told you?'

'The launch has just left,' Tucker cried, first clearing his throat for volume.

'It took you long enough to make that out, didn't it?'

'They've got funny accents,' Tucker said.

'Not any funnier than your mumble, Third Officer. Well, so they're on their way, are they? About time I'd say.' We were embarking two passengers for the Gulf, the principal of whom was Captain Harry Long, managing director of Marine Safety Services, a subsidiary company of P & O which originated a programme of strict safety procedure aboard tankers and sells this programme, as well as continuing advice, to P & O's own ships and other companies as well. I had never met Long but had been told that he would be likely to embark in *Ardshiel* to inspect its safety organisation, which in anticipation had been strenuously exercising itself all the way down from Rotterdam. The other passenger, David Owen, was an officer from another British tanker company, Athel Line, which had subscribed to Long's services and had sent their man along for instruction. They had suffered some delay in getting to Cape Town harbour, where the mail launch awaited them, and Thomson had found this a final test of his patience. 'Here we are,' he continued, 'waiting at a cost of two pounds a minute because our passengers haven't turned up. I wonder what excuse I'm likely to get from Captain Long and his mate. Couldn't finish their expense account dinner in time, I suppose. When I get to London and the marine superintendents are supposed to take me out all I get is a ham sandwich and a pint of beer in a pub, standing up. But you can be sure that what they put me down for is a slap-up dinner at the Great Eastern Hotel. Have you sight of them yet, Third Officer? Well, get those glasses to your eyes and let me know when you do!'

We were about ten miles off the city and, when they finally arrived, it took ten minutes to embark the two passengers and the various parcels and packages, and, even as Long and Owen were climbing to the bridge to pay their respects to the master, *Ardshiel* trembled back into speed and began following the coast around to Cape Point, and on into the Indian Ocean.

Predictably, the newspapers that came aboard carried headlines of tanker disaster. A laden Liberian tanker, the 18,567-ton *Alkis*, had started to disintegrate during the recent gale south of Good Hope. Battered by huge waves, the vessel had cracked amidships; deck-plating was bent and torn and, fearful that the ship would break up, her master had slowly headed for the only shelter available in that empty area, the lee of the island of Tristan da Cunha, where *Alkis* now had arrived.

'Stricken Oil Ship Threat of Disaster for Tristan,' said the *Cape Argus* in its front-page banner. It appeared that Tristan's crayfish industry (which supplies most of the rock lobster tails for the North American market), the only source of income for the island's 272 inhabitants, was under immediate threat if *Alkis* broke up at her anchorage. This was a strong possibility because the anchorage, while the best available there, nevertheless was extremely exposed and turbulent.

Tristan da Cunha deservedly has been called the loneliest island in the world. It lies on the edge of the Southern Ocean, a grey, clouded, and barren volcanic outcrop 1,500 miles south-west of Cape Town, far from the main shipping lanes and constantly hammered by the terrible storms of the Southern Ocean, whose flotsam and jetsam during the days of sail were bounteous enough to provide the islanders with most of their material needs and goods. Only since the last war have crayfish provided something more than subsistence and not so much more at that; the main profits go to the South African canners. Yet Tristan's few inhabitants cling to the island and to each other with desperate affection. When the island's volcanic core suddenly re-activated itself a decade ago and began blowing hot ash upon them, the entire population was evacuated to England. After two years, they asked to be returned to Tristan, preferring the risks there to the dissolution of their powerful communal ties and loyalties which, apparently, permissive Britain with its appeal to the young had swiftly threatened.

The *Cape Times*, a newspaper with a long and honourable history of liberal opposition to apartheid, offered a lovely, touching story about that aftermath which read like a scene from an early O'Flaherty documentary: 'Recently a youngster broke his leg on the island's rough ground and the next day a boat sailed into harbour to bring him here to Cape Town. As the boy lay on a stretcher at the harbour every other man, woman, and child appeared at the top of a nearby hill. Slowly they walked down to the harbour and each, in turn, went up to him, kissed him, and wished him luck.' This item was obviously written before the *Alkis* news was received, because the *Cape Times* writer wistfully concluded: 'So all is well on Tristan. It is comforting to know that there is at least one spot in the world where hearts are warm and where the old ethical precepts remain. There is no racialism or hatred. They want for nothing, eat well and sleep dreamlessly, unaware that they are so laughably behind the times. The best of luck to them.'

I was much affected by this account and its bitter postscript on the front page. With *Alkis* and its threat of pollution sitting off-shore, the Tristanites were no longer behind the times and, facing the possibility that they might very well want for a great deal if their one industry were to be damaged, they presumably weren't sleeping quite so dreamlessly. (South African-based tugs later got *Alkis* away from Tristan but she sank while under tow for Cape Town, where the port authorities anyway were undecided whether they would allow the leaking mess that she had become to enter harbour. So she lies now under the Southern Ocean itself, doing her bit for pollution right there on the spot.)

I had chosen the period of the Cape winter for my voyage as an opportunity of seeing a supertanker handling those seas, but the storms came just before and immediately after we rounded the Cape: a week after *Alkis* had sunk, the 70,000-ton Norwegian tanker *Moster* arrived in Table Bay with cracks to her shell, as well as in her forward and after tanks. Two weeks later (by which time we ourselves had arrived in the Gulf) the laden British tanker *Globtik Mercury* had to divert into Durban after her bow plating had been torn open by the sea.

Our own conditions were perfect. Twenty-four hours after clearing the Cape, *Ardshiel* was steaming over a calm, blue, and sunlit sea. 'Whites tomorrow?' Basil Thomson inquired on the bridge, and answered his own question by writing the order for inclusion in the noon chit. Now that the tensions of rounding Good Hope apparently were over, it was time also to welcome the new guests at pourout.

Harry Long, a neat, precise man in his early forties, had himself been a deck officer aboard P & O ships before going ashore and joining the executive ranks. He had in fact served on one occasion as third officer on a liner where Basil Thomson had been mate. The memory did not appear to be a nostalgic or sentimental one. 'Yes, and I put up with an awful lot of bollicking from you, Basil,' Long sharply remarked when Thomson reminded him of those days.

'Did I bollick you, Harry?' Thomson asked mildly, and, as usual, with a tone eager nevertheless for nostalgic recollection.

'Well,' he added, 'if I did then that's because you could never get the lead out of your pants.'

'You were never short of an excuse to bollick *anybody*, Basil,' Long said.

'Only when they deserved it,' Thomson declared. 'I've always run what some like to call a tight ship. That's the way it was in the P & O in those days. The juniors didn't get the world handed to them on a platter. Anyway, why should you worry at this stage, you're in the enemy camp, you've joined the other lot; you're among the brass, an executive.'

Thomson was in a good mood, however, and still determined to be nostalgic. 'Do you remember old Captain Allan?'

'I certainly do,' Long said.

'Talk of bollicking reminds me,' Thomson said. 'One day some of his officers came to him to complain about what they considered to be his high-handed treatment of them. He was sitting with his back to the door, playing patience.'

'As he always did,' said Long.

'As he always did,' Thomson agreed. "Well! What is it?" he asked when they knocked on the door, and without even turning round to look. He just sat looking at his cards. "Is that all, then?" he wanted to know when they'd finished saying what they wanted to say. "Yes," they said. "Well, off with you, then," old Allan said, still playing his cards and still not even bothering to look round. And that so far as he was concerned was that.'

'He had a pigeon,' Long said. 'Out-bound for Bombay one trip the pigeon got blown away in a gale so he turned the ship round and steamed back twenty miles, and all the officers were posted to watch for the pigeon. But they never found it.'

'How did he account for the extra forty miles of steaming?' James Jackson asked.

'P & O always put up with that sort of eccentricity in its master,' Long said. 'The eccentrics were good passenger men, they brought in the custom; the same people came back to them all the time.'

'These days a master gets no respect,' Thomson said.

'What gives you that idea, Basil?' Long asked.

'In the old days when a master went up to London the boys used to stand up at their desks when he went into the office. It was Yes sir, No sir, Three Bags Full. Not these days. I went in to Aldgate and the commissionaire said, "Do you have an appointment?" I said, "I'm Captain Thomson, and when you speak to me you call me 'sir'." '

'He probably didn't know who you were, Basil,' Long said.

'They should know who a master is. In the old days they did, they knew all the masters; and they were treated with respect.'

*　　*　　*

The chill wind into which we had been pushing on our way down the South Atlantic set itself behind us after we turned the corner at the Cape and warmed at once, and then grew steadily balmier as we moved north. It was still a strong blow, however, even though we didn't feel it: we lay behind the sound of it, and scudded along the crests, the whole ship softly enclosed by that mysterious stillness and peace of a following wind. The waves were so high that they broke level with the deck, their crests rustling as softly as the tearing of silk.

Hundreds of seabirds rode the wind as it flowed so silently and unfelt around us. Among them were the largest albatrosses we so far had seen. They floated motionless beside us, like stuffed birds inexplicably pinned upon the living sky; so close to the rail that one could read the colour of their fierce pink pupils. Their wings, stretched to their fullest span, nine or ten feet Stephen Tucker estimated, cast long shadows upon the sea.

The wandering albatross is the largest of all water birds, and its wing span is the largest of the entire bird kingdom, often measuring eleven to twelve feet. Its body is four feet long, but the whole bird is marvellously light, usually weighing about fifteen to twenty-five pounds, which helps it stay in the air day after day: the albatross doesn't fly so much as float upon the upflow created by wind striking the surface of the sea. He glides from one airwave to the next, and gets sufficient buoyancy to maintain flight with fractional effort from himself. The doldrums have effectively kept the albatross from the North Atlantic, where they are seen only very rarely. One was found on the British coasts in 1897 and another later was seen and shot in Denmark. Its skeleton is in a Copenhagen museum.

It is said that the coming of the steamship saved the albatross from extinction. Toward the end of the days of sail they were killed in particularly large numbers by sailors who caught them cruelly on hooks, sometimes just for sport, but usually for gain: the webbing of the feet was used for making pouches, the bones were sold for pipestems, the down was sold in Europe, and the bird itself, though tough, gave a change of diet. The beauty of these birds is so moving that it is hard to believe that anyone could ever have wished to kill them, or mock and tease them. But this is the cruelty that Baudelaire observed on his own voyage around the Cape and which he put into his poem on the albatross.

Conscience about that cruelty runs through many of the sailors' own memoirs of those days, and well it might. These birds were the most conspicuous company they had between landfalls on their long voyages. The albatross belongs to neither land nor even sea really; he is in the air 90 per cent of the time, settles on shore only long enough to breed, and stays off the water for days on end. Dr William Beebe told of one bird which was specifically watched and was known to have stayed in the air six days at least without landing on the water; he has also given an instance of a bird that followed one ship for three thousand miles.

Doubtless these observations could have been matched and probably improved upon by many in the days of sail. They watched their albatrosses attentively. The physical magnificence of the albatross – especially the pure white wandering one, largest of the species – and the serenity of its flight made it a natural symbol. But of what? The simple minds of the sailors told them that there was something ambiguous about the bird. Probably they feared and hated the albatross more than they ever could have loved it. The bird, as one watches him, does seem difficult to love. One feels a shiver: those pink eyes, so large, steadfastly alongside and effortlessly suspended above the sea and unceasingly watching! In their lonely and brutal struggles with cord and canvas on the Southern Ocean there must have been for those earlier seamen a disturbing suggestion of something strange and other-worldly about that indefatigable but aloof accompaniment of ships. The perpetual watch over their dispirited struggles upon precarious and constantly threatened decks from such a detached position must sometimes have aroused rage and resentment: easy to understand then why, when they got it on deck and saw its helplessness there (it cannot take off from a ship's deck), they felt moved to do what Baudelaire saw them do: 'One of the sailors torments his beak with a pipe,/Another mimics, limping, the cripple who used to fly.' At least when it was helpless and floundering on deck the bird could ridicule its own supernatural power and mythical attributes, and get weary like the rest of them.

The following morning, well out into the Indian Ocean, north of Durban, steaming over a blue and flat and sparkling sea, there once again occurred that strange business of two ships drawn to each other in perfect visibility and with nothing else in sight. When I climbed to the bridge after eight I saw a large freighter to port. Thomson was regarding her critically.

'How's she look now?' he asked Tucker, who was taking a bearing.

'She's closing toward the bow but the bearing's not changing appreciably,' Tucker said. 'The distance by radar is two miles. She's a bit too close for my liking, sir.'

'Well done, Tucker, because she's too close for me as well,' Thomson said, and jammed his finger onto the ship's whistle. He sounded one short fierce blast, and ordered the helm to be put fifteen degrees over and held. *Ardshiel* began a slow complete turn in her tracks.

'He should have altered course,' Thomson said. 'This happened to me in the English Channel once. The blighter stood on and on and on, and I had to alter course, a complete three hundred and sixty degree right around, to come up under his stern, as we are doing now. Miles and miles of bloody ocean, and he still keeps coming. It was his job to alter and pass under my stern, not for me to give way. But I did because you don't take chances with people like that. The bloody nut. He needs to have his mind read. Can you make out who he is, Third Officer?'

'Not yet' Tucker said.

Alan Ewart-James, drawn by the blast and manœuvre, had come up from below. 'What's happening?' he asked.

'Another cowboy' Thomson said.

'Not again? Bloody hell!'

'Bloody nut. On course for Singapore, I assume. You can steady up on her again as we line up, old Tucker,' Thomson said.

'Aye, sir.'

The steamer fell into its own distance and vanished; and Thomson returned to his cabin, still muttering 'bloody nut'.

'We would have cleared him if we'd kept on without altering,' Tucker said, 'though only by about fifty yards.'

'Probably an inexperienced third officer,' Ewart-James said and thumped a reminder upon Stephen Tucker's back. It had been a sobering, even shattering episode; it was precisely the sort of encounter that is likely to be the main danger when American-bound tankers cross the American east-coast transatlantic traffic lanes. It had been a lesson for other waters as well, however: 'You see, this ship's very good on the helm,' Ewart-James said, 'she'll answer very quickly when she has to. But when she starts to swing, when you've altered course for another ship as we have done, she will start swinging fairly rapidly. Especially when she's loaded. It's a lot of kinetic energy that's involved once you start a ship like this swinging and it's going to take a lot more energy in counter-helm to counteract it. If you make this manœuvre in the English Channel you have to be well aware that she can get out of hand and start swinging violently and end up in another and perhaps more embarrassing situation. You could find yourself banging up against something else.'

'It's at moments like this that I'm glad old Basil is around,' Tucker said.

'Yes,' Harry Long agreed later when we sat discussing the episode and tanker safety in general in his cabin. 'I don't think any amount of brains in a younger man can replace experience. No matter how academically experienced a young master or officer might be, he is still inexperienced, and experience at sea counts a great deal.

'In this regard, we have a relatively new situation because not only the junior officers but the masters of ships as well are now much younger than they used to be. Take this ship, there's twenty-seven years between Basil Thomson and Ewart-James, his second-in-command, who will certainly be getting his own ship relatively soon. P & O used to have a policy that no one was to be promoted to the rank of master until he had reached the age of forty-five. In fact, under that policy, if I were still at sea, I would still be a chief officer. But of course even experience is no guarantee of safety. It can create its own dangers. On one tanker belonging to a company that had subscribed to our safety programme, it was clear that the master didn't understand a lot about the basic theory of fighting fires, and we asked him whether he'd attended a fire-fighting course. He said he had, ten years ago. We recommended to the company that he be sent on a course, but when they phoned him and said they were arranging it he told them, "I also took my master's certificate ten years ago, do you want me to take that as well again?" and put the phone down. Well, as it happens, we *are* beginning to believe that masters *must* return for some sort of refresher course at certain periods.

'Then too,' Long added, 'in the case of tankers, the incidence of accidents due to carelessness or ignorance is increased in relation to the time the officers and men have spent on the ship. The longer they serve, the more careless they become. There's no doubt in my mind about that. Again, it all depends to some degree as well upon the age of the ship. Accidents appear to happen to older ships more frequently than they do to newer ships, and I think that is due to the fact that newer ships have better equipment and there's less deterioration. In the case of tankers, this can be a matter of just a few years' difference.

'The ten-year-old ships we've got now are extremely run down. There are a number of ships which the company built ten years ago which are becoming extremely expensive to maintain. And not only to maintain but to maintain to P & O's standards, and those still required by law. But the very high state of the tanker market has influenced them to recharter them time and time again rather than to scrap them as was their original intention. The influencing factor eventually will only be the cost of keeping the ship running in relation to the money it can earn against the present charter rates.

'Everything deteriorates. The machinery goes, not perhaps the main engine itself, but auxilliaries, generators, pumps, and in particular the boilers. The second point is the deterioration of the steel in the hull itself, and this is usually due to the sulphur content in a lot of the oil that is carried. Sulphur dioxide left behind by the oil in the tanks can condensate to form sulphuric acid, which is extremely corrosive. The average tanker loses two per cent of her steel every year through corrosion. This takes effect in local spots rather than spreading itself evenly over the whole steel structure. In other words, the corrosion concentrates in places. This is known as pitting. I have seen a ship less than five years old where more than half the steel plates have been eaten away by pits, and it reaches a state in either distance or depth where you have no alternative but to remove the plates, and this is extremely expensive. So, if you have been unfortunate in your tanker steel plates, particularly in the bottom of the ship, then you will be faced with very expensive steel renewal in three or four years' time when the next survey becomes due. What usually happens then is that they will run the tanker up to its special survey and they will take the opinion of the surveyor, and if he says that certain sections of the hull have to be renewed, they may be influenced to sell the ship to one of the owners who operate under a flag of convenience, and then she's not subject to survey, at least according to British or American standards, and she can continue to trade.

'As far as British ports are concerned, we require all ships sailing into them to maintain a certain standard, and we refuse them entry if they don't. But it would be physically almost impossible to survey every ship that comes into British ports, or any nation's ports. The procedure is that the ship's agent will ask the master the dates of his last survey certificates, and as long as he can produce a certificate which is in force, that's as far as it goes.'

Surely by the end of the seventies, I suggested, faced with an accelerated oil demand and the deterioration of ships such as *Ardshiel*, which, whatever its condition, would always find a buyer in an attractive tanker market, the world's sea lanes would be confronting an enormous safety problem?

'Yes, it could well be,' Long said. 'I think that basically what you are implying will be true. This will happen. Unless the governments of the flag of convenience countries enforce the same standards of survey and inspection that are now adopted in most of the West European countries and the United States, there will be a continued practice of passing on old ships to those countries, and they will continue to sail them in a dangerous condition. Probably at some time in the future IMCO, or some such body as IMCO, will require a certain standard, but it won't be easy to administer.'

*   *   *

The range of possible accidents aboard a supertanker is naturally large. In the case of the crew, the most common serious accident is gassing, usually in the pump room, and so far as the ship as a whole is concerned the most common alarm is for fire, which of course also happens to be the biggest risk. Most fires occur in the engine room, and are quickly doused as a rule. On deck it is another matter, and the biggest danger comes from spillage during loading or discharge when either vapour or oil drips and leaks can be ignited.

From his own experience, Harry Long said, he judged that the majority of tankers afloat had no organised safety procedure or fire drill. He supposed that most didn't even bother with lifeboat drill, yet there was no ship from which one might have to escape more quickly than a tanker, if things got out of hand. Crews had been known to be marooned in the lofty superstructure, left to watch the rising curtain of flame that would incinerate them.

In *Ardshiel*'s case, lifeboat drill was held twice a week and fire alarms were tested every day, and at least once a week, sometimes more often, an exercise simulating some common tanker accident or alarm was carried out. On the voyage to the Cape we'd practised rescues from the pump room and from one of the tanks as well as various minor emergency drills and these all had worked well and effectively, but Long's presence had brought some tension because he had licence on these shipboard inspection visits of his to sound alarms for a simulated emergency whenever he wished. Part of his own job was to study and correlate the experience of accidents aboard tankers and, as much as possible, to initiate exercises based upon these actual incidents. It was the fund of knowledge thus accumulated, and experience in the efficiency and deployment of safety-emergency teams aboard ship, that apparently made his salesmanship attractive to other tanker owners, who, faced by rising insurance costs, were increasingly aware of their own inadequacies in this regard.

Long finally sounded one of his alarms, just south of Madagascar, and he chose as his emergency situation an engine-room fire caused by a fractured fuel pump which, he said, was a fairly frequent and highly dangerous occurrence.

The whole exercise had the same tone. It was realistic and serious. It lasted thirty-two minutes, which was about as long as one could expect from a real situation of its kind, Harry Long said.

'You were bloody marvellous,' Long subsequently exclaimed in the wardroom when the officers and Pakistani warrant officers gathered there before lunch for a brief post-mortem. 'There are a lot of captains who unfortunately put on the exercise with enthusiasm when we are with them and then allow the safety programme to lapse when we have gone. They never fool me, and it was quite clear today that you were absolutely on your marks.'

'It's their effort not mine,' Thomson cried. 'It's the officers themselves who've made up the fire brigade. It's not anything to do with anyone but themselves, banding together, selecting themselves ... and doing all their practising.'

'The evidence supports that view,' said Long. 'Gentlemen, I also congratulate you.'

'Hear, hear,' Thomson cried.

Everyone looked pleased and happy, but euphoria began to vanish during lunch when Alan Ewart-James, James Jackson, Harvey Phillips, and Peter Dutton began talking about the three VLCC explosions and the continuing mystery about them, and, as an extension of this, about the risks of going down into the tanks and of how much they all disliked it.

Shell had spent hundreds of thousands of pounds on research, Phillips said, and they were no nearer the truth. It was all conjecture. It would never be absolutely certain. He himself saw no need for going down into the tanks; no need for tank inspections, and no need even for cleaning them. After the explosion Shell itself had gone on for a long time without any tank cleaning, which showed that it wasn't necessary every voyage, if at all. Some companies already were experimenting with a method of washing tanks with oil itself, and it appeared to be successful.

'Cleaning and inspection are P & O's policy, and that's why we go down. I see no other reason,' Ewart-James said.

'The company can do nothing,' James Jackson said, 'if the chief officer simply says "I will not go down into the tanks."'

'Nothing,' Ewart-James agreed. 'There's just no way of telling whether the tanks are safe. The explosimeters aren't an absolute guarantee. On one of the ships a party was down in one of the tanks for an hour and a half, working. They finished and were returning to the deck and, as they began passing up the ladder, three men were overcome by gas. On the way to the ladder they'd clearly passed through a pocket of gas. The gas can lie in pockets and one can be completely unaware of them, even though one has been all over the tank. Sludge lying just an inch deep on the bottom of the tank can release enough gas to blow up the whole tank. One takes one's life in one's hands every time one goes down.'

'But if one thinks of the risks involved one would never come on these ships,' James Jackson said.

'We're all here for the money,' Harvey Phillips said. 'Let's face it. If it wasn't for the money we wouldn't be here, at least I wouldn't.

229

You've got to look at it that way, we know what's involved and we've figured that the risks are worth the money.'

'You've got a point, Harvey,' Dutton said. 'But it doesn't stop a man thinking.'

'Oh aye,' Phillips said. 'That's for sure.'

But the matter obviously rankled because it reasserted itself that evening during a lecture on safety which Harry Long had announced as a corollary to the day's exercise. He delivered in careful, pedantic tones what was clearly a familiar and well-rehearsed talk on explosive gases at the end of which his listeners, invited to offer their own comment or ask questions, broke into impatient criticism of the risks of going down into the tanks and indicated the dismay most of them felt when called upon to do so. Several declared flatly that they would no longer go down. (Descent into the tanks is not in fact policy in all companies; British Petroleum for one will allow no one into the tanks of their ships, unless they have to go down for urgent inspection or repairs.)

When a man who had been gassed was being rescued, Long was saying at one point, artificial respiration was the best means of getting air into his lungs at once to save his life. Just two lungfuls could do the trick, but four would be best.

'If the gas is thick, who is going to be the lucky pigeon to take off his mask to apply artificial respiration?' asked Dave Haydon, the electrical officer.

'In the short time it requires to give the breaths, while taking in his own oxygen from the resuscitator, no harm can befall the rescuer,' Long said. 'The point I am trying to make is, suppose a rescue party finds someone lying on his face in the pump room and the gas reading is thirty per cent. The first thing the person in charge of the party is going to say to himself is, "Thirty per cent is not lethal in a very short time. This bloke has been down here for some time." At thirty per cent you can actually take your mask off and not suffer harmful effects for several minutes.'

'I don't want to seem arbitrary, but you rely on what I consider a very primitive form of assessment to make this decision,' Haydon said.

'Well, I'll put it to you another way,' Long said. 'If I were the chief officer in charge of the rescue party and I go down to the pump room and know that the measure of the gas at the bottom is thirty per cent I'll say to myself there is a good chance of reviving that bloke and I will persevere to do that. But if the chief engineer yells down from the top that the reading has gone over a hundred per cent, I know there's very little chance of reviving him. Anyway, gentlemen, if I may progress: it's never possible to be absolutely certain how much gas will affect any particular person. This depends on individual health, whether a person has a heart condition, suffers from asthma, whether he was on the booze the night before, or whatnot. So we have drawn up a table which is a guide as to how much gas will affect a normal healthy person: we think this information is necessary to the rescue team. It is my own personal opinion that people are not overcome by gas in the tanks unless the concentration is fairly high. Anybody who goes into a tank that is known to be full of gas will die. Nothing will save him.'

'On that graph you've got there,' Peter Dutton asked, 'is there any guide to one's sense of smell? Is there a position there that defines when you smell gas and it's dangerous, or when you smell it and it's not dangerous?'

'There's no position in the graph, Peter, where you can tell one way or another. Your sense of smell just vanishes.'

'Well, yes,' Dutton insisted. 'When you first go down you can usually smell gas. I want to know, does that smelling of gas indicate any particular position of safety? And when you no longer can smell it, does that mean any point of danger? Whenever you hear of someone being gassed in a pump room or tank one quickly thinks that it must have been so strong that they couldn't smell it. Whereas normally you can go in a pump room or tank and you can smell gas, and you more or less say to yourself, "Well, I've got a couple of minutes yet." So there must be some real guide lines.'

'Yes, there are,' Long said. 'When I was chief officer I used to do the same thing. I used to sniff and say, "That's all right for entry and now I'm going to take a chance." But these days I'm much wiser. Unfortunately hydrocarbon gas paralyses the sense of smell. Therefore the moment you breathe a large quantity of it your nose fails you and you no longer have any indication of how much gas there is.

'This reminds me of a story I was told by a man who sailed in a company where they didn't believe in providing explosimeters in the ships,' Long said, and smiled at his audience. 'I asked him how on earth they tested for gas, and he said, "Oh we had a bloke with a loose tooth which used to tingle. We sent him down into the tank and if his loose tooth tingled we knew there was gas down there." Gentlemen, even if any of you has loose teeth, I recommend you always use your explosimeters. That's your answer, Peter. Use your explosimeter, not your nose.'

'But why *must* we go down into the tanks?' Ewart-James suddenly demanded, with the force of someone who all day had nursed that one question. 'Why must I as chief officer do that general inspection after tank cleaning, which the company insists I do, when it can only be a cursory job? Nobody can pass through those tanks and give them a thorough survey under those conditions, just to see if there is a bit of corrosion.'

'Ah now, hold on a minute,' Thomson cried. 'That job is very important, even though you might not think so. It's not to look for corrosion so much but to see if the hull is fine, that there are no cracks. You're down there to see if the ship's structure is safe. If it isn't done, and there's something that we don't know about, we might crack in two.'

'Why then can't there be a sort of breathing suit for the job, some means for making it safer?'

'There is a suit,' Harry Long said. 'It is being introduced on Athel Line ships. The trouble about the suit is, will people wear it?'

'Let's debate that once we've got the suit,' Dave Haydon said.

'A suit might help,' Peter Dutton said. 'But it's still not an answer and it might not be a question of not wanting to wear it but of not being able to do so. Even now, just moving around those tanks at the bottom, going from bay to bay, is pretty difficult. You've got to squeeze through such a small aperture that you've scarcely got room for yourself, and you're not going to get through wearing a bulky suit and air bottles.'

Harry Long asked whether there were any more questions, as an indication that the lecture was over. There were none, but no one made a move to rise and go, and for a long moment they sat as they were, as if reluctant to give in yet on the subject and the matters that disturbed them: Long remained uncertainly beside his blackboard with its pinned-up graphs and diagrams, and scanned their faces expecting their silence to yield some verbal afterthought; but none came.

They sat on the black leather chairs and sofas wearing their beautifully laundered dinner kit, the girl Pat Allen in a bright red velvet dress, and in their hands were tumblers of eight-year-old Glenfiddich whisky which the barman Lawrence silently refilled at the briefest glance. The troubled look on each face, except Long's, flawed that atmosphere of consummate attainment and privilege; and the power of this feeling was stronger for the fact that each face held its separate and mysterious communion with the matter, so that there ran all around the room a frieze of pale and differing anxiety. And one was conscious of an older loss, themselves too worldly and disabused to retain in such moments the comfort even of a lingering instinct to rail against an albatross.

ELEVEN

CHANGE! It was what one was always aware of, and from so many points of view other than all those associated with the new species of ship that *Ardshiel* was, though these naturally impinged on everything one way or another. There was almost daily some deeper recognition that ships, sailors, and seafaring were casting away the past, and many of its traditions, to a faster degree than one could even suppose from shore.

In the wardroom after Harry Long's lecture, amid luxury and a free flow of expensive whisky, the melancholy faces reflecting upon the real price of the game were fairly typical in this regard. They were sailors very different from any previous generation of seamen, of which they were well aware, and a lot of their discontent grew from the fact that, like the ship, which for all its advancement still offered so many critical gaps in its own technology, they themselves were caught between the still-imperfect focus of the new maritime age and its innovations, and the past and its ways of thought and doing things; between Basil Thomson's world and theirs; as well as between the imperfect relationships of their own generation: between the designers and managers, and themselves, the operators and technicians. They knew the faults and failures and dishonesties of their vessel, but found it difficult to reconcile their own relationship to it, if any, other than to plead material advantage; and they knew that, while they still navigated more or less by the rules and principles of centuries, those who stayed at sea long before the end of their careers probably would be merely caretakers of push-button craft whose control was largely elsewhere.

The ship's own personality sometimes seemed as split as theirs. For one thing, she was a vessel confusedly caught at half point between British weights and measures and the metric ones which most of the world now prefers. All equipment put aboard by her builders in Japan was in metric units, but anything specially delivered to the ship from

Britain during her construction was in British units. As a result, an officer would move from one gauge showing pounds per square inch to another in kilogrammes per square centimetre; from one registering feet and inches to a dial marked in metres. Her load line was marked in feet, although metres are becoming more common because of a shift from the use of fathoms to metres in all chartwork. To her young officers she was thus an outstanding and even infuriating example of the British whim to hang on always to *something* of the past, even when leaping forward at a hasty pace. 'You get used to it,' Alan Ewart-James said, 'but it's ridiculous. If you're going to change over, you might as well change over completely; and none of this mucking around.' He felt the same way about the fathom and said, with his customary new-generation decisiveness, 'Oh it's got to go. It would be nice to keep it purely as sentimental value but a fathom's only six feet, so what!' And there, dismissed, went an immeasurable portion of the maritime past. There was, to be sure, little room aboard *Ardshiel* at any time for the nostalgist, or for the sentimentalist. If there was anything from the past that had to be abandoned, it went thus, one felt, quite unceremoniously and without much of a backward glance. It's the right attitude undoubtedly, but still....

A commission of the International Hydrographic Organization in Monaco decided during the sixties that the job of reproducing the world's charts to new metric specifications would be divided among various maritime nations, each of which was allocated areas of responsibility. It was division of a survey labour that the Royal Navy's Hydrographic Department had once undertaken almost single-handedly over much of the globe. Britain's trade and naval power after Trafalgar required a more reliable and proper knowledge of the world's seas and waterways and the Hydrographic Department, founded in 1795, spent the nineteenth century charting and surveying the seas and coasts. From this work there resulted a huge and embracing library of Admiralty charts which have remained the standard works on most of the oceans. Apart from the distinguished work that went into them, they had another distinction that makes them truly memorable: they were, after a decision in 1823, freely available for purchase to all.

Although constantly amended, many of the charts had had no complete revision since first produced and there was an urgent need for a sustained new effort to revise them, but it still required the special impetus of a world dependent upon the economics of super-ships and standing in fright of the havoc they might cause to stir itself to the task of systematically remapping all the world's seas. But who had accepted and approved the actual idea of getting rid of the

fathom? the writer A. P. Herbert demanded to know in the correspondence columns of *The Times* in 1969, and declared formation of
a Friend of the Fathom Society, with himself as president. Herbert
got his answer from Captain T. K. Treadwell, commander of the
United States Naval Oceanographic Office, who, also in *The Times*,
said: 'Who has approved and accepted the metric system? Practically
the entire civilized world, with the exception of the United Kingdom
and the United States ... only these two and Malaysia still cling to
the fathom in their hydrographic offices. The fathom-lovers are in
the insignificant minority, and in the interest of simple consistency,
not to mention economic, military, and scientific considerations, we
must simply face facts.' The United States Naval Oceanographic
Office, he added, already was publishing almost half its charts in the
metric system.

The Royal Navy's Hydrographic Department had begun its own
metric resurvey and charting programme in 1967, and in 1972 it
produced its first major new international chart from a projected
series of fifteen to cover the oil routes from the English Channel to the
Persian Gulf via the Cape, and between the Gulf and Malacca Straits.
Thus, for British sailors, more familiar with it than anyone, the
fathom finally began to die.

The fathom certainly has much sentimental value, and its loss, for
anyone who has had anything to do with the sea, is hard to bear if
only because of the associations it retains with the whole block of our
seafaring experience; it is probably the oldest computation in the art
of western navigation. As a measure, nothing could be more simple or
instinctive: a fathom of rope was the spread of a man's outstretched
arms. As this also was the natural gesture of a homecoming sailor
greeting his wife and family, it helps account for the word's Anglo-
Saxon derivation, *fæom*, meaning 'to embrace'. And perhaps even
ironically:

> Full fathom five thy father lies;
>   Of his bones are coral made;
> Those are pearls that were his eyes:
>   Nothing of him that doth fade
> But doth suffer a sea-change
> Into something rich and strange.

Fathom at any rate is one of those rare words that seems to com-
press a significant portion of both our practical and mystical
experience; and its sensibility is such that, whatever its philological
origin, it seems to explain itself, with the tongue falling swiftly
through the first shallow syllable like a sounding lead, and then
eddying down into the rounded depths of the second. As ambivalent

as the depths it serves, it has always met our sense of the finite, as well as the infinite, the noun 'fathom' being so precise a measure, six feet plain, while the verb 'to fathom' leaves the mind speculative upon something still without limit. 'Soundings in fathoms', the charts hitherto have announced, and they will be something less for the lack of that liquid and historic phrase.

Man fathomed his way, so to speak, along all the sea routes of quest and discovery. The unknown fathom was the symbol of risk and the fatal reef, the plumbed fathom that of safety upon which venture and survival depended; and the figure who for centuries embodied both was the leadsman, balanced right forward by the bows and skilfully casting his lead ahead, watching its line plummet and then stay, so that, as the ship closed up to it, and the lead line lay vertical, he could know by the marks on it (devised of bits of leather, cord, and different-textured cloth, so that they were identifiable by touch at night as well as by sight) how much he'd paid out, and sing that message of safety or caution or peril to the anxious ears above. It was the call upon which universal trade, naval penetration, and exploration depended, and became the salvation of thousands of seamen, and the epitaph for countless thousands of others. 'The waues being exceeding great they rolled vs so neere the land, that the ship stood in lesse then 14 fadoms of water, no more than sixe miles from the Cape which is called Das Agulias; and there we stood as vtterly cast away ... the shore so euill, that nothing could take the land, and the land itself so full of Tigers, and people that are sauage and killers of all strangers. The day of peril was the nine and twentieth of July.' Thus Hakluyt proffers Thomas Stevens, 1579, with the first English account of rounding the Cape, and of the turbulence there in winter. 'Taking deep-sea soundings was an all-hands job carried out when approaching the Channel in thick weather,' a retired Royal Navy commander, R. M. Reynolds, wrote in *The Nautical Magazine* in 1969, in a good description of the practice as it worked in sail in the early days of the century. 'The lead weighed about 14 pounds and was attached to some 70 fathoms of line; it was armed at the bottom so that if soundings were obtained the arming would show either sand or shells. Preparatory to taking soundings the ship was brought to the wind and the main yard backed. The lead was then taken on to the fo'c'sle head, and the men lined the rail each with a coil of line in his hand. The man who hove the lead cried out: "Watch there, watch!" and as the line slipped from each man's hand the cry was repeated until soundings were obtained or "no bottom" reported.'

The fathom thus was always close to fate, and somehow it seemed the more so for using the dimensions of the sailor's own body, that olden instinct to hold the world against our own measure. A subsidiary loss as the fathom goes is the magnificent nineteenth-century chartwork. The new metric charts look functional and bare by comparison. The old ones were works of art, a delight to handle, often beautifully illustrated, especially when the coast concerned was a wild and largely unfamiliar one and precise delicate drawings were provided of the offshore view to assist the mariner. I often found myself, at moments when I felt a need for diversion, ascending to the bridge and its chartroom section and there browsing among the charts and admiring them in their glory and variety for perhaps the last time. Stored in wide teak drawers and held there in fine white canvas holders, the act of retrieving them alone was a pleasure; I suppose that in another fifteen years they'll be auctioning these same canvas portfolios filled with the old charts at Sotheby's.

What we will not be able to retrieve at Sotheby's will be our living and romantic sense of ships. I was aware of this whenever I was beset by the urge to escape from the sealed-in mood of *Ardshiel*'s accommodation and sought brief relief outside from the structural exterior of the ship. Only at the few wooden rails aboard did one touch something of the old fabric of ships. One wandered among high walls of steel, and sometimes the various mathematical compositions of the functional decks piled atop each other held one's interest, but it looked as stripped of all but essential detail as a poster-painted ship.

One of the charms of the sea in our time, and for generations back, has been the continuous individuality of ships. They represented in the age of the ship-owning families, now rapidly expiring, the decorative fancies and often eccentric whims of the owners, who saw their ships as an extension of their own personalities, life styles, dreams, and ideas. Such men headed the North European dynasties modest or large which from the middle of the last century to the middle of this one commanded the bulk of world shipping from their stolid family seats near the Mersey, the Tyne, or the Thames, or at the head of some Norwegian fjord, on an island in the Gulf of Bothnia, or on the southern shores of the Baltic. Many of their fortunes grew from seafaring grandparents who, in the decades following the Napoleonic wars and the collapse of the East India Company monopolies, when the industrial base of Britain and the rest of Europe was rapidly expanding, owned a barque or brigantine and put the profits into a second and third vessel, and whose sons deployed the inheritance into steam.

While it wasn't always easy to identify every one of the hundreds of tramps and minor merchantmen that wandered the seas twenty, thirty, forty years ago, you could usually tell nationality or at least where a vessel was built, and, if she belonged to a major house, you could almost certainly name her owners by rake, colours, or just by the set of the superstructure, for there lurked in shipowners a strange assortment of memories of ships past, family traditions, and national tastes that always found their way into the look and composition of their ships. Each ship from a big house anyhow always bore the imprint of careful and often painstaking individual consideration because each was a new source of pride and pleasure in its time. And there wasn't a merchantman of consequence that one boarded that didn't somehow convey the whole overlay of shipping as it had been for the past century.

It was not just the lingering Victorianism of many of the interiors, but the many forms in brass and teak, the nooks and crannies that had no rhyme or reason for their existence any more than do the cupolas and alcoves of a garden gazebo, the very resilience of the white planking of the decks, and the look of the windows and scuttles and hull plates as they flowed in sheer, that ravelled together such a comforting presence. What we felt about ships was a mood drawn from the way they were inside and out, the way they sat upon the water, a curious combination of our then sense of distance, the time that it took to cross the seas, of the balance of the world, the way it connected and held together; not immutable, but slow-changing. Above all what one felt was the *soundness* of them, and the impression that they were put together with the best of everything.

Ships after all were, are, the buildings of the water, and they grew in much the same way and with much the same care and faddishness as the buildings of the land, from rough crude wooden structures into the feudal castles of the Armada's galleons, passing to the baronial piles of the East Indiamen, and on to the pleasure palaces of this century. At its finest, the architecture of the sea has often rivalled and exceeded the richness and splendour of the land's, even though perishable and, beyond its time, usually traceless. It is quite astonishing to reflect that in our own day we have seen many of the largest and most sumptuous structures ever built by man but which have had a life often of less than a decade. I am thinking of course of ships like *Conte di Savoia*, *Rex*, *Normandie*, *Bremen*, and *Empress of Britain*, all built in the thirties and which were casualties of the war years.

When the Andalusian caliph 'Abd-ar-rahman III in the tenth century began building what Gerald Brenan in his *Face of Spain* described as possibly the largest and most luxurious palace ever built in any age, the Mediterranean was ransacked for precious materials. In a similar fashion the entire globe was scoured for materials for the great liners, which were stinted nothing. The decorative woods for

Queen Mary included Indian white mahogany, Japanese chestnut, Australian maple, Canadian and Swedish birch, English pearwood, yew, and more exotic items such as betula, petula, avodire, papapsko, pomla, silky oak, figured teak, and weathered sycamore, to name only a few. The most grandiose rooms of this century have gone into ships. The two most notable of these were *Conte di Savoia's* baroque Colonna Hall and *Normandie's* dining-room, three hundred feet long, forty-six feet wide, and twenty-five feet high, and which provided the largest and most striking decorative use in one chamber of reflecting and illuminated glass, most of it Lalique, since the creation of the Galerie des Glaces at Versailles. Access to it was through a hall laid with Algerian onyx and through double doors of gilded ornamental bronze nearly twenty feet high. One of the principal features of the room, a bronze statue of La Paix, nearly eighteen feet high including pedestal, survives in the Fontainebleau Hotel in Miami. All the rest is gone, vanished as absolutely as the palace of ʿAbd-ar-rahman III, which, begun in 936 and destroyed in 1010, had a span not much longer than that of many long-lived ships.

Part of the mysterious appeal of great liners, of all ships, has been the fact that, however lavish and painstaking the concept and detail and craftsmanship involved, none of it has been built for posterity, though sometimes for eternity, as with the funeral boats of Cheops and those of the heads of the Viking clans at Oseberg and Gokstad. That quality of extravagant expendability has been heightened by knowing that, through the ages, ships not only have had the best but something even more, a flamboyant embellishment and excess of style that originally owed a lot to the ancient obligation to propitiate the unknown but which eventually was largely for its own sake, a lavish gesture, as it were, to transience. Perhaps too because water is elegant we simply like to be elegant upon it. Nonetheless, through the centuries comparatively few vessels shone through individually to lie illuminated upon the public mind. Those that did usually were the ones that carried explorers on their epic voyages or great admirals on theirs. It was rare for the ordinary merchantman to emerge from the plodding obscurity of its immensely long voyages. Life aboard ships anyhow was too brutal, and service in them too protracted, to allow much sentiment for them either from their miserable ordinary seamen, or from the public to whom the horrors of the conditions afloat persistently filtered and, eventually, made the press-gang necessary as a means of maintaining, at least in Britain's case, the strength of naval complements. It required an age of romantic public involvement with and affection for the whole body of shipping, complementary to mere pride and patriotism, to bring the view of ships and the feeling for them that we have retained until today, and this required a revolution in shipping itself, which the early decades of the nineteenth century provided.

Modern shipping and modern seafaring as we have known it as well as our feelings about it are mainly a nineteenth-century creation, and substantially British in origin. It is impossible to regard the commerce of the sea over the past century and a half in particular without finding the emphasis predominantly British in tone, and what one felt aboard *Ardshiel* was the gradual dispersion of many of those habits, codes, and sentiments which have so affected all of us, not only because they used to be the dominant way of seafaring but also because, in a world where Britain was strong, they seemed inseparable from the island's view of itself; and also because so much vital history turned on them; and because they so deeply affected the sea's literature, the principal body of which will always be nineteenth-century in focus and influence. They were largely formed by the ships and the men of that great post-Napoleonic period of mercantilism and change that was spurred by the industrial revolution and rising imperialism – in other words, by the very stuff that went into the founding of shipping lines such as P & O itself. And all of it created a sudden gulf between itself and the maritime world that had just been, that of the navy of Nelson's day with its dreadful brutalities and changeless ships and the slow East Indiamen laboriously winding their way to and from the east via the Cape.

The big changes initiated by the nineteenth century were prompted by speed, and they came long before steam established itself. The British and the Americans were the pioneers of speed in sail, which was mainly advanced by the clipper ship, in which cargo capacity was sacrificed to speed. The American clippers got some of their impetus from the gold rush of 1849, when there was big money to be made getting freight and prospectors to the west coast via Cape Horn as fast as possible, and the British clippers from the need to rush tea from China and wool and grain from the Antipodes. During the middle decades of the nineteenth century Victorian inventive zest and imaginative design streamlined sailing craft and gave them a speed that kept sail moving as fast as steam or even faster virtually to the end of the century, and just a hundred years ago precisely saw the heyday of the square-rigger, when *Cutty Sark* herself was establishing her reputation.

The improvement these square-rigged clipper ships brought to sea communications was comparable in effect only to the establishment of the world's airways systems in our own era. Voyages that normally took six months in the early decades of the century were reduced to two. Those ships made the other side of the world more accessible for trade and for the mass emigration that an overpopulated Britain required. Merchants could work with reasonably firm trading schedules for the first time: wool agents in Australia could stipulate to *Cutty Sark* that their wares should reach Britain in eighty days and be sure that the contract would be fulfilled. The annual races to land the first tea of the season from China and the first wool and grain cargoes from Australasia became public events. As Basil Lubbock remarks in *The Log of the Cutty Sark*, published in 1924, 'In the days of our fathers a racecourse was made of the mighty ocean itself, with the great capes of the world as the rounding marks...huge sums were wagered on favourite ships...whilst the stakes received by the winning owner represented a tidy little fortune, and his proud skipper, besides pocketing a very handsome douceur, knew that his reputation in his profession was made for all time.'

There were hundreds of ships which are largely unremembered now but which were widely famous in their day. Such widespread individual reputation was reflective of all that was new and different in the shipping world. Individual ships were publicly discussed to a degree that had never been known before. They were among the most satisfying emblems of the day, and the Victorians regarded them with much pride. They appealed to two of the most powerful British instincts of the time, patriotism and the sporting gamble. Wagering on the racing clipper ships, the Victorians were aware that they were putting their money on the lifeline of their empire and upon the standard-bearers of British ubiquity. Few things entranced the Victorian mind more than the apparently irrefutable logic of Britain's special destiny and greatness, and an impressive portion of this seemed shipborne.

G. M. Trevelyan notes in his *English Social History* that '...the oceans of the world were the highways of England'. In the second half of the nineteenth century a third of the world's seagoing ships were on the British register, including four-fifths of the world's steamships. So, if the ship had become the vehicle of the new mobility and increased expansion of the western world, it was a mobility and expansion that clearly was mainly British. And if shipping was making Britain great, then the ever-curious Victorian public needed to share the experience and the sailor's own sentiment, which it did vicariously through its insatiable demand for engraved prints of all manner of vessels and their storms and encounters, as well as through the thousands of emigrants and troops who were moving in such numbers to all parts of the empire and whose lengthy and detailed correspondence gave the main shipping lines and the units of their fleets a strong public identity and made the working sailor a closer and more intimate personal figure than he had ever been before.

The sailor himself had begun to share some of the public's attitudes.

Plimsoll had begun his agitation for reform, but conditions in the merchant navy were still bad. The great physical hardships and shipboard abuses of vile food and abysmal pay remained. Life hadn't got perceptively softer, nor would it even through much of the twentieth century, but it was different, and the difference made up for a lot.

The shorter voyages of faster ships meant the sailor could get away from a bad ship and mean officers and owners sooner and more easily than could have been imagined in the early part of the century; they gave him a better chance too of surviving the ailments and debilitations of sailing-ship voyages; and they meant that he could try his luck with several different ships in the time that it once took an East Indiaman for a single trip to India and back. Loyalties were created to particular ships, companies, and masters; the clipper ships especially were regarded with great pride and sentimental affection.

'Poor old girl, fancy finishing up on a crimson coast like this,' remarked a leading hand to his officer as they fastened mizzen topsails at the height of a gale which had driven their vessel, a barque inbound from Auckland and Tacoma, on to Cornish reefs in February 1915. 'No thought mark you for his own safety, just a valediction for his ship,' remarked the officer in question when recalling the incident more than half a century later in *Sea Breezes*, a British nautical publication that specialised in nostalgic recollection of the great days of sail, and offering it as reflective of the attitudes of the seamen of that whole epoch.

The incident might be purest Kipling, and indeed it was from this sort of romantic involvement and intensity of feeling that much of the new, more vigorous, and more authoritative body of literature about the seagoing experience grew during the nineteenth century; the maritime world that Joseph Conrad experienced and wrote about was that of the last quarter of the century, when sail finally had begun its full decline in favour of steam, mainly as a result of the opening of the Suez Canal. It was the greatest age of British mercantile pride, the sea had become the world, sailors were the kings, and we lean on Conrad, who wrote from and satisfied the seaman's viewpoint. There is nothing comparable; his writing placed into literature a virtual palimpsest of marine sensibility from which one could read, interwoven and overlaid, the greatest possible range of maritime experience that any sailor could know. English was an acquired language but, artist that he was, his creative mastery of it really was inevitable because, as the language of the sea, no other could possibly have fulfilled his sea experience at that time and more properly conveyed the poetic and idiomatic expression of it, or the precision of the sailor's own vocabulary. It is our fortune that he was there, within earshot of those who knew Nelson's navy and the East Indiamen while he himself watched sail in its glory and steam ascendant. Sail was finally dying, but as it went it offered its finest ships, *Cutty Sark* among them; and *Great Eastern*, aborted symbol of the splendours of steam to come, was still alive. Between them lay an astounding diversity of ships.

Neither Conrad nor Kipling, who gave the public in poetry the same highly emotional but exact view of ships that it bought as engravings, could have written about the sea quite as he did had ships and maritime experience, and British deployment of both, not existed in such great and ever-increasing variety. The diversity of ships that plied the world's seas and coasts as steam overlapped sail and gradually took over had completely changed the human as well as structural texture of ships; steam, with wider opportunities for the inexperienced, could more easily absorb the flotsam and jetsam of the industrial revolution and packed his fo'c'sles with a denser though not necessarily more atractive character; but it was the ships themselves that mainly carried the story of the sentiment, or the burden of the moral.

It is hard to imagine *Typhoon* or *Lord Jim* pivoted upon anything other than the precise character of *Nan-Shan* and *Patna* respectively. Only these ships could have sustained the tension of those stories in the way they did. Only a ship such as *Nan-Shan*, apparently fragile yet superbly founded, could have given such full effect to Captain MacWhirr's irresolution and the business of surviving the typhoon; and there is nothing more moving in *Lord Jim*, even without the subtle and powerful underplay of imminent fate, than Jim's feeling for the mood and detail of *Patna*'s decks, his innocent affection for the ship and the moment, while on watch before the mysterious impact that ruins his life.

Like Conrad, Kipling was obsessed with the nature and fabric and look of ships:

> There's a jaunty White Star liner
> and her decks are scrubbed and clean,
> And her tall white spars are spot-
> less and her hull is painted green.

He dramatised the aesthetics of ships as we have known them, but shan't much longer. Individuality is much too expensive. Aboard *Ardshiel* it was generally accepted that even the luxury of the living quarters marked her as a relic in a way. It could not be expected in future ships, which would be like the big Universe class ships, 'everything utility, all steel, no frills and fancies'. Instead of character of any degree there would be only functionalism. No texture. But did it matter, they continually asked, when it was clear that to keep people aboard these ships the period of service would have to be greatly reduced, with leave after every voyage? In that case, they agreed, they would willingly forego luxury and, instead of being served from silver salvers, would accept either cafeteria service or TV dinners taken from a slot, which was James Jackson's suggestion. The ship would become even more of a functional shell than it already was and more like a gigantic barge. 'Right now it's just a tank that's been fitted with engines and a place to live in and steer from,' Harvey Phillips said.

For those aboard *Ardshiel* the departure from the past already was complete, whatever further degrees of standardisation the future offered. None of them would ever return to the sort of ships they liked to remember from earlier days and talk about, which they did ceaselessly; they had sold out for the money as they themselves put it and this would keep them where they were, whatever their hankerings for the days of constant change and diversion in going leisurely from port to port. There was nothing in their present sea-going lives, one knew, that was ever going to make the stuff of nostalgic reminiscence. Any reference to *Ardshiel* or her class of ships bore no hint of real interest or affectionate involvement. This whole race of ships had been dismissed. They talked about them indistinctly, 'these ships', as though any clear identity for them was difficult to grasp. The only ships that lived were those that were gone. One could feel that they were actually talking about the remote past, reciting fragments of unpolished and unpublished Kipling, until one realised that, except for Basil Thomson, their recollections were all postwar and often no more than ten or twelve years ago; and, as in Conrad and Kipling, the strength and vigour of their memories were framed by the ships themselves, their colours and the look and way of them, and their different, stricter disciplines. It was such a discussion that brought us an evening of strange conflicting emotions while we were steaming up through the Mozambique Straits between Madagascar and the east coast of Africa, and which by tensing past against present in a sudden and initially innocent series of exchanges provoked a sadder, stronger glimpse of change than any.

The evening pour-out started well. Everyone was in good humour. It had been the first day of real heat and softness of air since leaving the tropics on the other side of Africa two weeks ago, and faces were fresh and rosy from hours spent at the swimming pool. James Jackson was talking about his apprenticeship in the Blue Funnel Line and his first deep-sea commission in the cargo-passenger liner *Hector*, 'a seven-hatch main-line ship'.

'You had more respect for the senior engineers there,' he said, as the company settled back with its drinks. 'The chief engineer on the *Hector* always did his rounds in an immaculate white boiler suit, with an immaculate white pair of gloves, his hat on, and with his number one Chinaman with him. In Blue Funnel main-line service the chief was a proper gentleman, a bloke in his middle fifties usually. Once he'd done his inspection he was up and away; he was never in the engine room unless required. But the machinery spaces were spotless, even on the old *Tyndareus*, and she was forty years old when I first saw her. All the brasswork shone like a mirror, everything just gleamed. She was on the pilgrim run then, up to Arabia. She used to carry two or three thousand pilgrims every trip and Blue Funnel paid a bonus of a penny a head on the pilgrims. If a pilgrim died you lost a penny; but you got it back if a baby was born.'

'Well, then, you did better than we did on the old Australian immigrant boats, the old *Bendigo* and *Ballarat*,' Thomson said. 'But we had our fun. They had the men and women separated, with iron rails between them. Two of you had to go down on duty inspection. If you went alone the women grabbed you and, well it was nobody's business what they did to you.'

'Blue Funnel had some of the best-looking ships I've ever seen,' Harry Long said. 'They had the tallest funnels in the world.'

'What a genius old Alfred Holt was,' James Jackson said. 'He gave his ships blue funnels because he got hold of a lot of blue paint cheap.'

'Typical shipowner's trick,' Harvey Phillips said.

'Hold on,' Basil Thomson said. 'That's not always the case, on those Israelite ships I sailed with they never spared a penny,' and he began discussing his experiences while serving with an Israeli company when he'd left P & O for a brief period some years previously. The ship in which he'd served had been an Israeli banana boat, plying between New York and South America. He had liked the Israelites, as he called them. They had been excellent chaps. Spoke immaculate English. His two cadets were twenty-five and twenty-seven years of age! The one had been a tank commander and had suffered ear injuries when a shell exploded near his tank. The other, a flying officer, had swooped down over his girl friend's home to drop her a bunch of flowers and been given the boot for it. That was the sort they were. The radio officer got ten thousand German marks every year as compensation for the loss of his mother, father, and sister in the camps.

On their independence day, to mark the British cession of Palestine, he had offered to stand all the watches on the bridge. At five in the afternoon he had to sound blasts on the whistle. After he'd done so the second officer came up and said he was wanted below. The Israelites had prepared a huge feast but they hadn't eaten until he came down. He was embarrassed and said, 'Here I am, British, and we were the ones whom you had to fight to become independent,' and they'd answered, 'Ach, Captain, forget it! It's all over! Sit down, eat!'

When a telegram came from P & O offering him a tanker command, he'd gone to the owners in New York and had shown them the telegram. They didn't have a replacement for him but they'd said, 'Of course you must go, Captain. Go back to your own people,' and they gave him a ticket to sail in the *Queen Elizabeth*. As he was a Royal Naval Reserve officer, before joining the Israelites he'd written to the Admiralty inquiring about the propriety of serving under the Israelite flag. But the Admiralty had replied that it made no difference. 'The Israelites are the same as us, they're on our side,' the Admiralty had said.

'We got three hundred gallons of enamel paint every year to paint the ship. No expenses were ever spared. She looked like a yacht. They had a most wonderful catalogue, with illustrations. You ordered from that. What you needed, you got, the very best always, but the point was that you got it, not the way it so often is with us here. You tell me, Harry,' he demanded of Long, on a sudden note of anger, 'why is it that we have to order double to get what we need? You want twenty-four pencils, HB, and so you get twelve. Then when you get to Cape Town you order another twelve. Those are the pencils you need for the chartwork. What can pencils cost that they make such a fuss about them?'

'That isn't quite the case, Basil,' Long said.

'Well, I can assure you from personal experience that it is.'

'When I was a marine superintendent you should have seen the orders that came in. People ordered wastefully, or didn't know what they were ordering. One officer ordered a piece of equipment for the bridge and when asked what it was answered that he'd ordered it because he wanted to find out,' Long said.

'That might be so, but it still doesn't cover up for the other foolishness, of trying to economise and ending up paying double, what with all the telegrams and so on,' Thomson insisted.

'I think you're exaggerating the matter, Basil,' Long said quietly.

The hands of the clock had reached seven thirty and Basil Thomson was on his feet, tightening his cummerbund, his expression firm and disapproving. We filed down silently and, as the menu was examined and orders given, Long suddenly remarked, as if to change the still-hanging subject, 'I've recommended to the Board of Trade that masters should make their own safety survey, what do you think of that, Basil?'

Thomson studied his menu afresh and made no reply. British ships carry safety certificates renewable every two years, when an inspector from the Department of Trade, the official arbiter of British maritime matters, inspects the vessel's safety equipment, including lifeboats and all the gear inside them. Anything faulty has to be fixed or replaced before the safety certificate, without which the ship cannot legally put to sea, is signed. Long's proposal was to transfer this examining authority and responsibility to the master.

'What do you think of that, Basil?' Long insisted.

'Well, like the matter of the indents, which I was accused of exaggerating, I'll have to take that under further consideration, Captain Long,' Thomson said, rearranging his cutlery, first alongside the plate and then above. 'I'd just like to think about that for a moment or two.'

'What if the captain makes his survey and decides that the ship isn't safe to sail?' asked James Jackson.

'The captain knows what's aboard his ship,' Long said. 'If there are any defects at sailing time, why didn't he know of them before?'

Jackson, normally a mild-mannered man, cried angrily, 'Is this another way of shoving something else onto the ship to save a penny? Soon the ships will be doing everything that the shore should do, except scrape the bottom in dry dock.'

'It's just niggle-niggle-niggle,' said Thomson, his plate pushed aside, his bulk shifted sideways in the chair – the attitude of a man whose scepticism already has propelled him a dismissive half-distance from the table.

'What do you think, David?' Long asked David Owen, who normally dined with the junior officers but had joined us for this meal.

'I don't see why not,' Owen said.

'Then you've got a lot to learn, Mr Owen,' Thomson said, advancing his body rapidly back to the table and leaning in Owen's direction. 'You've got something to learn about the whys and wherefores of this world, and the erring ways of some of our certificated brethren, who are not above getting away with murder if they can. In the first place I don't think you've been at sea long enough to be so assertive and emphatic about a matter of such importance because, if you had been at sea long enough, there are some questions you'd be wanting to ask right now.'

'I stand corrected,' Owen said.

'And so I think you should be,' said Thomson. 'All I want to say is that I consider the safety survey people our best friends. I believe that on a matter like that one must always have an outside opinion.'

'I don't see why,' Long said. 'I'm surprised that you should think so, Basil.'

'Why?' Thomson cried. 'You don't see why?'

'No,' Long said. 'Surely you're competent to be able to do it?'

'I might be,' Thomson said. 'But what about the others? What if a surveyor isn't available to assure the captain's own doubts, and for those who aren't so scrupulous about having doubts, it'll be just a quick scribble on a piece of paper and away we go, off to sea in a dangerous condition!'

The dinner happened to be an especially good one that night, mock turtle soup, halibut, roast pork with crackling and spinach, strawberries and ice cream, and it was symptomatic of Thomson's great agitation that he left untouched the deliciously crisp outside cuts which were always reserved for him from the roasts.

'You no like?' Diaz asked.

'Take it away!' Thomson cried.

Peter Dutton excused himself and left the table. Thomson himself now rose and went into the wardroom, followed by Jackson, Phillips, Haydon, and Ewart-James. Long and Owen, neither of whom had finished their meal, remained at table.

Dutton was at the rail when I went out on deck. I greeted him and he shook his head morosely. 'What did you think of all that then, in there?' he asked, in that soft and almost plaintive singsong tone of the Geordies. 'I tell you there are times when I wonder whether I can stand it a moment longer, marooned out here on this floating tank listening to a lot of grown men squabbling their heads off.'

We chatted about other matters for a while and then, on the assumption that Basil Thomson would have been to the bridge for his final check and gone, I ascended for my own nightly visit to Stephen Tucker. One is sightless as one enters the bridge house at night, even from starlight, unless one has taken the precaution of closing one's eyes beforehand. Even then one is left feebly groping. Someone passed me as I entered in that manner and the door leading down into the accommodation slammed.

'That was Bas,' Stephen Tucker said. He was at the chart table. In the dim light of the table's illumination he looked pale and strained. As a rule he was full of boyish larking, but there was no boy in him at the moment and his voice was tight with anger. He had been studying the Admiralty Pilot for the Indian Ocean as well as a volume of tables and had left these open on the chart table when he took a turn out to the bridge wing. One of Basil Thomson's strictest rules, however, was that books were to be consulted and then immediately returned to their appointed places. He had arrived on the bridge while Tucker was out on the bridge wing, seen the open volumes, picked them up and, from shoulder height, dropped them

248

with a crash upon the chart table. Tucker, hearing the noise, had hastened inside.

How many times did he have to tell him that he wanted a tidy ship? Thomson had demanded. Tucker had sailed with him as a cadet, so he knew what he wanted, why therefore didn't he conform with the instructions he'd received? 'You do on my ship what I tell you to do!' Thomson had cried.

'He called me bloody rubbish,' Tucker said. 'So I turned my back on him and walked away. Nobody's putting up with that sort of guff any more. Those days are gone. They're over. I heard he'd had a tiff down below, so he came up to take it out on me!' He went back to his charts, and I left him. Peter Dutton was still at the rail on the deck far below, staring down at the black sea. There was no one else in sight on that huge ship, which at that moment seemed like a ship of lonely and bewildered men, not the least of them being the angry bulky man in the suite of rooms whose lights shone faintly through the tightly drawn curtains as I passed. But ships have ever been so; sailors have always been great brooders, a natural consequence of their isolation, and shipmasters especially, after their long haul of introspection and responsibility, have seldom been regarded as a notably even-tempered race. What had just occurred on *Ardshiel*'s bridge was, in its own way, fairly mild as an episode of shipmaster's temperament, at least to anyone accustomed to the breed as it hitherto had existed, or for that matter to anyone who has ever listened, as in *Ardshiel* itself one so frequently did, to accounts between sailors about past ships and the temperate or intemperate masters aboard them.

The disciplinarian and/or intemperate ship's master is a stock figure of maritime mythology and the myth will continue to be enriched until ships have a structure of command and control very different from the one we so far have known. It is an extraordinary licence, but then it grew from an extraordinary situation: a fragile community set adrift from the rest of mankind on poor rations, with imperfect instruments and with frightening elemental odds against it in getting to where it was going. Through the ages right up to our own time these circumstances hardly changed. A master and his disciplines had to ensure that, whatever the conditions and the odds, the vessel *did* get there or, if it didn't, that it was not for lack of will or endeavour. His was the power that quelled the mutinous, or rallied despair. His was an absolutism matched on earth only by popes and kings. The authority that still attaches to command owes a lot to the lingering awareness that not so long ago it still held the right of life or death if the circumstances warranted, and a master's decrees are still touched by their former power and infallibility, as the bill of lading of any ship indicates, '... of whom is master, under God'.

Even when much of his way was charted and familiar and his vessel sturdier and faster and healthier, his voyage remained a challenge to fate, himself the immediate powerful delegate of that challenge. He could shoot dead anyone who threatened his own or the ship's safety. He could put recalcitrants in irons. The ship was his fiefdom, to do with as he wished within the prescribed limits of his voyage. He set his course, found his winds and currents, decided what his crew should eat and how much, what they should be paid and how often, and handled most of the ship's business himself. But, as the risks gradually lessened, the master's authority was increasingly admired and valued for its own sake, particularly by Victorian Britain.

It was inevitable for them to do so, given Britain's dependence upon her trade and shipping, but the shipmaster in any event embodied a great deal of the Victorian ethos. Unshakeable in his authority, indefatigable in his duty, profound in his natural knowledge, unmatched in his professional skill and, withal, necessarily credulous in his piety and faith, he met most of the heroic requirements of the day. Next to a vice-regal summons, none was more prized than the invitation to a seat at the master's table, most especially aboard a P & O liner outbound for Bombay.

On any ship, big or small, he was a man who should ask of no one what he would not and could not do himself. Alan Villiers, writing in 1963 in an issue of *The Nautical Magazine*, described the sort of example that belonged to those public expectations of the master, the man in this instance being a legendary sailing master, Finlay Murchison, and the incident involved being his courage and resource when the weather backstays on the main topmast of his barque *Wathara* were carried away during a vicious gale off Cape Horn:

The mast began to roll drunkenly. The yards were steel. If they came down they could pierce the wooden decks, let in the sea; within moments the barque could founder. Finlay Murchison called for volunteers to carry a stout preventer stay aloft, get it rigged with superhuman speed. To try such a job was to brush with death. How much could the mast stand? Was it any use to try to save it, and the ship? The whole watch on deck volunteered. The watch below came tumbling out. They volunteered too.

'I will name no man,' Captain Murchison said. 'I go myself. Bear a hand!'

And up he went, up, up, up the horribly swaying, weakened mast, which was steadily lurching the more heavily with each staggering roll. Up the shrouds, two of the seamen lighting the heavy line up to him; out over the futtocks, waiting for the swift roll to leeward that made them almost horizontal; up the swaying topmast rigging, step by dangerous step, as the severed black wire now slackened in writhing bights, now sprang steel-taut, all but parting with the violent, sudden strain, as if fighting to fling him off. If those few slight wires parted it was the end of Finlay Murchison – end of Wathara too ... it seemed hours while Finlay Murchison fought, staggered, clung on, hoisting that heavy monstrous hawser to the masthead, to fit the temporary collar there, rig a preventer stay strong enough to do its heavy work. And he won.

Example was indivisibly part of the shipmaster's authority, and nothing so enhanced it to the Victorian mind as the ultimate assertion of command, to go down with the ship. It is doubtful that any seaman saw that action in such mock-heroic terms: if a man deliberately went down with his ship it was usually because he was too broken by its loss to care. The active power and expression of command, however, was very real to all seamen; it had to be inviolable within the ship and defended if necessary through sheer physical prowess, as Basil Lubbock recounts in *The Log of the Cutty Sark*, and proffers a description given to him by an eyewitness of an incident in the late nineteenth century between Captain Tom Bowling of the clipper *Invercargill* and a powerful AB aboard his ship known as Brighton Bill.

Bowling said something pretty sharp, and Bill retorted, 'It is only your coat that protects you.' At which Bowling said sharply: 'Come on to the quarterdeck at four bells (six o'clock) and I will take my coat off.'
We were in the southeast trades and the weather was fine, so at four bells all hands came aft to watch the fight. Both men stripped to the waist and they fought for two hours, but Bowling was just a bit better than the other man, so he was considered to have won. It was a Homeric combat such as is given few men the chance to witness, for both men were as hard as nails (though Bowling was a man well over fifty at the time) and both knew something about handling themselves. But ever after that no man dared say a word against Tom Bowling whilst Brighton Bill was about.

If a master's word was law, his comportment therefore was the embodiment of it. There had to be a sense of distance; preferably awful distance, as well as humble approach and respectful withdrawal. Sometimes, however, withdrawal had to be hasty. Sir Benjamin

Chave, a commodore of the Union Castle Line in the period between the wars, once ordered thick soup for dinner and got thin. He was so angry that he rose among his dinner-jacketed first-class passengers, who ducked vainly as the plate and its contents flew in pursuit of the retreating steward.

That tradition of awful distance and humble respect for the master has never quite died in the British merchant marine. Not surprisingly it survives most strongly in the minds of the older rank of seamen. The British mercantile hegemony, always a staunchly conservative one, remained too set in its ways for too long. The family-owned companies that dominated British shipping clung to their own traditions and habits and customs, resistant to change, and they were served in this by that innate conviction of his own superior worth in maritime matters that had always given the British sailor his much-admired professionalism; and the comforting knowledge of indisputable supremacy through actual weight of numbers made it seem as well to generations of British seamen that their way at sea was the natural order of things, and always would be.

But there were unhappy social reasons as well for the firm preservation of those old-fashioned codes of discipline.

During the long period of their domination of the sea lanes the British provided the workhorses, the necessary reliability and the equally necessary example of steadfast standards, but as the present century progressed they fell well behind many others, notably the Scandinavians, Americans, Germans, and Japanese, who were their principal maritime rivals between the wars, in the conditions aboard their ships. The dark side of the nineteenth century lingered more persistently in the forecastles of a large proportion of the British merchant navy than it finally did almost anywhere on the island itself. It was a common saying of the depression thirties that slums of the sea were far worse than those on shore. British seamen had learned to live with a long tradition of slow advancement, bleak remuneration, and mean quarters, as well as their daily dose of strong discipline.

Not surprisingly, British sailors, besides their well-deserved reputation for sterling seamanship and courage, had another for anarchic hooliganism and precipitate fiendishness that was unrivalled; hard-case crews they often were called, and deservedly: when members of the *Queen Mary*'s crew decided they disliked their food on one occasion during the war they jammed the cook into his own main oven. He died of his burns. So the disciplinary code continued to justify itself, long after it had vanished elsewhere, and continued too to satisfy an unhappy aspect of the British view of things, that once-unshakeable requirement for social definition, an abiding sense of them and us, with all its mistrust of a fatal breach through familiarity.

Hardship, however, was not confined to the forecastles. Deck and engineering officers themselves had a background of bad pay, squalid quarters, and poor food. The depression laid up so many ships that some vessels were known to sail with their entire crew, including all deck and engine-room hands, holding officers' certificates. An average British freighter master in the early and mid-thirties could expect a salary of twenty-eight to thirty-five pounds a month, and long leave was practically unheard of. Promotion was scarcely a serious expectation for any junior officer, until many years had passed. A man like Basil Thomson, for example, comes from a particular generation. There is a quality of unhappiness, scepticism, and sometimes great bitterness, which one encounters among shipmasters of his generation: those who laboriously and arduously came up the ladder during the twenties and the depression thirties, and then went on to sail through the strains and hazards of the war as well. They were the last hardship generation.

As with so much else in contemporary British life, change came swiftly in the sixties. The shipping industry, confronted by decline and a loss of manpower, reorganised itself and discarded much of its old image. A junior officer now earns almost as much as a British cabinet minister did in those prewar days. His merest whims are swiftly responded to, just to keep him happy and at sea.

Although his writ over conduct and punishment has greatly diminished and only on the bridges and within the luxurious halls of the last of the great passenger liners does that former aura of vice-regency still attach somewhat faintly to his personage, the master of a ship nevertheless still retains a lot of power, which can only really go once responsibility has either been removed or radically redefined; until then, it remains his in full. In storm or stress, his is the final decision; safety and survival are still his gift.

The master is still the custodian and arbiter of his nation's laws and his company's regulations; and of course he imposes his own rules and whims. He can still lock up those who threaten the peace and safety of the ship, though he no longer carries firearms; he can however fine his crew by docking pay. He can decide his crew's form of dress, address, conduct, and civility. He can, as Basil Thomson does, make his own time by setting his clocks in ignorance of the sun. He can decide what liquor they drink, and what they eat.

It has always required a singular personality not merely to survive the strains of the rise to command and command itself but also to emerge relatively free of the megalomania which the position nourishes. In such a confined world as that of a ship a sense of proportion is easily lost. A strong wit and a blithe nature can help balance those corrosive forces of worry, exasperation, fear, despondency, loneliness, recrimination, and introversion that bind the boredom of a sailor's day. Or a strong portion or two of gin might be called upon to assist the defences. All too often, however, neither wit nor gin can offer any defence against the paranoia ranging from mild to feverish that distorts the reason of so many who have spent their working lives at sea, and it was disturbing to ponder that it was probably no mere coincidence but reflective of their incidence that I heard recounted aboard *Ardshiel* two of the strangest cases I have ever heard of shipmaster's unbalance. David Owen had told me of one supertanker master whose hobby was to write long rambling letters to his company's head office.

In one of the letters the master wrote to say that a parrot had come aboard the ship in the tropics. He knew that keeping a parrot was against company regulations, he said, but he had nevertheless felt a need to care for the bird in his cabin. Subsequent letters described in great detail the circumstances of the parrot's capture, its care and provision and state of health, while continuing to express concern about the contravention of the company's regulations. Finally, in a letter of equal and companionable length, he described in great detail how he'd strangled the bird.

Alan Ewart-James provided the other example, of an 'old man' whose first action on coming aboard ship was to throw out all the furnishings of his cabin – sofas, carpets, tables, desks, and whatever – leaving only one chair in a corner, with a naked bulb rigged over it and a radio set beside it. There he spent the voyage, listening to the radio, not switching on even his single naked bulb, so that, when one entered the cabin at night to make a report, the only hint of human or any presence was the low murmur of the radio and the dull red gleam of the illumination inside it. One somehow was not surprised to be told that this was the same man who had ordered his second officer to lay course improperly against the downbound traffic in the English Channel.

Intemperance very often is not so much a case of eccentricity as one of barely controlled despair. For a master with thirty to forty or more years at sea most of the summers and winters of his life have been merely different states of water. His wife has aged beyond his view, his children grown into strangers. 'My wife doesn't want me home,' Basil Thomson joked once or twice, when the subject of leave came up. 'I upset her life and arrangements. She's got her life all worked out, and then I show up and upset it all. I can't expect her to give it all up when I get back. So I just sit in a deck-chair in the back yard and feel bored.' 'Bas never really wants to leave his ship. He doesn't really like going ashore,' one of the present complement aboard *Ardshiel* who'd sailed with Thomson on several occasions remarked. For many such masters the life they lead on board and the form of command that they build for themselves in a ship become the principal structure of their lives, and they guard it jealously, with an intense dislike and intolerance of any assault upon it, however minor the infraction, such as Tucker's delinquency in failing to return the books to their shelves even for the few minutes during which he went off to scan the night horizon.

To a sceptical generation without any built-in terrors about its own security and lacking any notions about the value of discipline for its own sake, much of Thomson's behaviour and many of his rules and dicta seemed merely whimsical or absurd. For his part, the apparent insouciance of his juniors angered him. They had the self-assurance and easy blandness of humour of the period, which might have galled any man who remembered how he'd had to keep his own place and restrain his own cockiness. When the lights in the wardroom were low at night and the noise of the tapes high, they had an air not so much of shipmates in any conventional sense but of young courtiers self-indulgently at play in some reigning pop star's shiny plastic penthouse. The noise alone must have been an affront to Thomson's disciplinary instincts, but he only asked for it to be turned down when he came into the wardroom for coffee after dinner, which, except for special occasions, was the only moment of the day he appeared there.

When they occurred, his rages anyway were petulant, never murderous, perhaps because when he was angry it propelled him ceaselessly to and fro, so that his bulk was distributed everywhere at once instead of being summoned into a stationary attitude of menace and intimidation. Perhaps also because his temper long since had lost any real physical power of projection. It was more querulous than vehement, and he sounded quite wistful when, during pour-out, he described the days in the passenger boats when he had had to 'mix in' and break up fighting drunken Australian passengers whom, he related, he sometimes threw down the stairs to cool them off. He had a quality moreover which they all appreciated; he never sought provocation. He remained in his luxurious eyrie, to emerge only at times ordained by himself and on inspections and rounds that were part of a fixed schedule, unless of course there happened to be an emergency, or a report from the bridge that he felt required his attention. He was, above all, a careful, scrupulous seaman.

Shipmasters all differ in the way they handle their ships and, if there is to be any simple classification of them that disregards personal idiosyncrasies of character, then it must always be whether they are good and scrupulous seamen or not. Even in this too there are great variations of conduct. Thomson was a traditional man of the rules. 'He does everything by the book,' the ship's radio officer, whom Thomson had reproved for wearing white socks in the wardroom one evening instead of the P & O-prescribed dark ones, remarked afterwards, ruefully adding, 'That's why he's always right.'

Thomson himself preferred to be regarded as a traditionalist of the old school and had served in British ships since his youth. He liked to talk about the way things were done in the 'old days' and was a stickler on the need for all information to be passed down to him from the bridge. If naval craft passed, he would appear on the bridge, with his cap on, to stand at the bridge wing while *Ardshiel*'s flag was solemnly dipped in salute. Discussing a master whose style of easy-going command he admired, Stephen Tucker said, 'He's on leave now and it's going to be strange if he relieves old Basil at the end of this run because I'll be staying in the ship and will still be automatically obeying Bas's instructions to call him on absolutely everything. It's already happened to me that I've served under the two of them one after the other, and the other captain got irritable, and said, "Okay, okay, use your nut, old chap, I don't want to know about every gull and bit of seaweed you see, just call me when you think you should."'

'Ah yes,' Alan Ewart-James said in reply to this. 'I've known a lot of what you call "good" captains, sociable chaps, easy to get on with, good to have a drink with and a chat in the wardroom, but the crunch comes when you're in a crisis, then you often find that the man's a poor seaman or navigator, or, worse, that he's not there: he's gone to hide and left it all to you. Then you've got no one to turn to but yourself. At least you know where you are with Basil.' Ewart-James had been aboard *Ardshiel* with Thomson when the ship had started breaking down off the South African coast and Thomson had faced his difficult decision on whether to summon the salvage tug or not. 'During those few days of crisis Basil was a completely different man,' he said. 'All his little mannerisms and fastidious regulations were forgotten. The matter at hand was too big for them. As soon as the crisis was over, however, they all came back.'

So long as Thomson's temper was not actively directed against them, the junior officers were inclined to regard him with the amused ribaldry boys have for a stern headmaster. Any collision with the master seemed to pass away entirely within a day or so. Recrimination did not appear to be much a part of the new generation's character. Thomson in any event was constantly undermining resentment. He always brought aboard ship a small store of gifts for special occasions such as birthdays and anniversaries, as well as chocolate eggs and cards for Easter, and presents and cards for Christmas.

'He is always at the gangplank to say good-bye to all those going on leave, as he did at Le Verdon,' Ewart-James said. Patricia Allen remembered his thoughtfulness aboard another ship in which she had travelled with him when, after being provided with a limousine for his own use in one port by the ship's agent, he placed it at the disposal of the wives on board for sightseeing and shopping trips.

Thomson had not much time to go before retirement, and within a very few years few of his generation will still be at sea. Perhaps the definitive view of him and of his ways was provided in an acrostic ode written by *Ardshiel*'s Steward-in-Charge, Wilson D'Costa, a Goanese, after Thomson had left *Ardshiel*, and which was published recently in P & O's house magazine, *Wavelength*:

C aptain, Oh Captain Oh my captain,
A *rdshiel* is forever yours, your name has it
P en writes well, your words are very sweet,
T errific looking man, but always smiles and keep talking,
A ll the same and equal, these are your words,
I ndian, Pakistan, Chinese and European makes you no difference,
N o men on earth can forget you.

B asil Thomson, your name is framed on board the ship *Ardshiel*,
A lways punctual at work, time is always fix,
S trict as you're, that's your duty,
I nspection day, all that you like best is glittering and attractive,
L oving words you whisper when some one is found guilty.

T ime is fixed to all daily routine,
H alf a minute not more, bells goes just in time,
O n hearing bell everybody run to bring their caps,
M uster on deck to one's respective boats,
S tewards worked with you, will have you well in mind,
O n every Sunday, they look forward for the beer to come,
N ow we want you back to give us the beer.

TWELVE

AFTER the domestic upheavals I had gone to bed as grave and sober-minded as everyone else, but I woke with an embarrassing feeling of elation the following morning, as though the previous evening's business had incited in me a perverse and indecent pleasure that I would have to account for to my conscience. There was no other explanation for the desire to shout, or even sing, until I suddenly realised that, when I opened my eyes at five thirty, the cabin had been filled with light, which was gradually strengthening. It was the first early light since leaving the European summer on the other side of the world, rather of Africa. The eastern tropics had defeated Basil Thomson's clocks and their imposed obedience to Greenwich Mean Time, and, in wonder and disbelief, I went out and swam slowly, pleasurably around the pool under an equatorial dawn of pale greens, yellows, and blues – all the warm, beautiful, and special colours of heat to come. The colours of early Deccan light.

As a further bonus, the Comoro Islands lay around us, volcanic upthrusts, blue upon a green sea, and their sheer rise from the water offered that diffident look that tropical islands always seem to have as a ship closes in toward them from a wide, flat sea: humidly, mysteriously self-contained, peering upward into their clouds instead of out across the sea, and completely inattentive to any vessel's approach.

I remembered that I had passed through here twenty years ago in Messageries Maritimes mailboats, when Madagascar was still part of the French empire (the Comoros still are) – delightful ships, panelled in rare woods and filled with colonial servants, whose luncheons and dinners had an air of interminable tropical leisure. Those mailboats had many mornings such as this, when they passed into a lagoon or inlet or a small bay, ringed with white buildings with rusty corrugated-iron roofs, where the hottening sun filtered through a hazy odour of tropical mould, cloves, coconut oil, curry, coffee, and over-ripe fruit. From *Ardshiel*, it all still looked the same: a memory, seen again through clear glass, but unreachable.

The previous evening's explosions had not dented Stephen Tucker's humour. He seemed in better spirits if anything, for the fineness of the day had touched off an urgent wish for an outing somewhere, so he decided to check the equipment of the lifeboats. We climbed into Number One boat, which was the one to which I myself was assigned in case of emergency, and one did feel that one had taken an outing to somewhere different; sitting virtually outboard from *Ardshiel*, there were new and interesting views of the ship, which one saw whole, as though it were steaming away beside us. But Tucker had little time for this; holding his inventory card, he checked his way methodically around the boat, item by item.

Lifeboats are marvels of forethought or, more accurately, of the result of generations of tragic experience, especially during the two world wars. *Ardshiel* had two boats, each of which could hold sixty-one persons, more than the entire ship's complement. They were made of fibreglass and were motor-driven, but lacked the fireproof canopies that many tanker lifeboats now have. They were provisioned for only one week: one pound of barley sugar, one pound of biscuits, six pints of water, and sixteen ounces of condensed milk per person. This is considered adequate for civil times, especially since a powerful radio is kept handy inside an adjacent doorway and becomes the first item put into the boat as soon as it is lowered to deck level. Aside from the rations, which were stowed in heavily greased tins under the boat's thwarts, the amount of equipment provided was considerable: four rowing bars and a steering oar, mast, rudder and tiller, sea anchor, compass, boat hook, wave oil to prevent choppy seas from splashing inboard, an oil bag stuffed with oakum for dragging behind the boat to achieve the same purpose, a lamp, trimmed, and with sufficient oil for twelve hours; waterproof matches, axes, buckets, fire extinguishers, various flares, including four parachute ones for long distance at night, two smoke floats for sighting by air during the day, six hand flares for close-by sighting, helio mirror, with a signal card; knife, tin opener, manual pump, a boarding ladder for entering the boat from the stern, and very necessary for an exhausted swimmer unable to hoist himself up; waterproof flashlight with spare bulbs and batteries, a floatable first-aid box, sharp-pitched whistle, tow lines, graduated drinking cups, marked in half-ounce, ounce, and two-ounce measures; toolbox and instruction manual for the engine, fuel for twenty-four hours of continuous running; and a brilliant orange canopy for shelter and for attracting attention. Everything was attached to the boat itself by rope so that, if the boat overturned, or was flooded, none of it would sink or float away.

Tucker worked with an air of boyish lark and adventure, as though he'd plunged himself into a game of Robinson Crusoe, with whistles of surprise, cries of 'ho-ho', grunts, and a medley of shipshape phrases as he came across faults and deficiencies or a bonus of tidiness he had not expected. He was clearly proud of the boat and its general order, and restowed things that already seemed a model of neatness, coiled rope and wires, replaced lids, or straightened this and that. 'Just in case we go down in the monsoon,' he said.

The south-west monsoon awaited us in force at the equator and the first whisper of it lay on the water as we steamed north beyond the Comoros – the barest whisper, though, for the ship was enclosed in a warm still softness of air that seemed at that moment incapable of any temper whatsoever. *Ardshiel* appeared to be skimming across the surface of the water, which was full of expression and colour, green-blue, but of such a delicacy of tone that one could scarcely take one's eyes from it. The water looked so inviting, so easy; it could take hold of you, Patricia Allen suddenly remarked from her chair at the side of the ship's pool. She meant the sea, at which she had been steadfastly gazing. 'I can understand why some officers suddenly jump overboard,' she said. 'It becomes irresistible.'

Alan Villiers in *The Voyage of the Parma* recounts a classic instance of this, of a sailor who, 'seated calmly on the rail one day in good weather, asked the mate for the loan of a steel snatchblock so that he could tie it to his legs and jump overboard. The mate, thinking it was a joke, said he could have the block, and all hands looked on with amusement while he tied it to his legs. Then the sailor slipped over the side and went down like a stone. No one knew any reason why he should wish to commit suicide; and nobody was amused then.'

This strange invitation from the sea and the curious, calm response to it persists. 'I heard of a third officer who ditched himself like that,' David Owen said, in response to this story. 'He was on the eight to twelve and he called down to the master and asked him to come up to the bridge at ten, which he did. "I've marked our position on the chart. There it is," the third said. "Yes?" said the master, wondering what it was all about. He couldn't figure why he'd been called to the bridge just to be told this. While he was standing there looking at the chart, the third turned and walked out of the wheelhouse. The master thought he'd gone out to the bridge wing to check something. The next moment the quartermaster outside came rushing in to say that he'd jumped overboard. The ship was put about, but they never found him.'

'Yes,' Ewart-James cried. 'I knew the third who replaced him.' The sea is a small neighbourhood.

'He was always talking about it,' Ewart-James said, 'because he was flown out to the ship and hadn't been aboard her long when, on the same watch, he felt ill one night, so he called down to the old man to tell him he wasn't well. Seconds later the captain was on the bridge, put an arm lock on his neck, grabbed the phone, called the mate, and yelled to him to come to the bridge. He wasn't going to have it all happen again.'

'Every trip we hear a couple of calls at least from other ships who've lost someone overboard,' the radio operator said.

'Stop!' Patricia Allen cried. 'You're all getting morbid on such a lovely day.'

'You brought it up,' her husband said.

'I know,' she said unhappily.

There was in any event a one-reel silent Chaplinesque diversion. Through the long lazy afternoon a Pakistani seaman had been painting the rails and steel deckwork of the bridge deck high above us. He had first wiped all of the steelwork, very slowly, thoroughly; even tenderly. It was a reflective, sunshine job, not meant for haste. Then he fetched his paint pots and, with equal tenderness, began to paint. It was Sunday and Basil Thomson's blue ensign had been proudly aloft since eight. The cleat to which the ensign's halliard was tied intruded upon the seaman's scheme of work. He untied it, to paint properly; painted; then retied it, but presumably not in a seamanlike manner, for it soon came adrift.

The line paid itself out very slowly, waving gently as it began to catch the breeze, and the flag began travelling from its smartly secured position at the head of the jack and out into space, where it flapped wildly in the funnel's windstream. The Pakistani stood a long while regarding this phenomenon and, finally, with the broom he'd used for sweeping clean the scuppers, he made motions to retrieve the end of the errant cord. In the background now there appeared the figure of Basil Thomson, who had taken over his daily portion of the second officer's watch and was passing to and fro the length of the bridge doing his walking exercises. With his arms swinging, his eyes were, in these preliminary moments, directed toward the bows and the horizon on each quarter there. The Pakistani regarded the passing, still-oblivious form of the master, and, after a moment of apparently tense and frantic thought, turned and vanished. He reappeared inside the funnel itself, above the jack, where he crouched, gazing down at the flag, which was quite impossibly out of reach; his expression wished it back, but it trailed steadily further astern, its blueness flapping with truant indignity. He looked down briefly, wishfully, at us, his audience, and, with a faint defeated smile, retreated.

Basil Thomson had finally noticed the deposition of his banner and *his* expression bore the furious astonishment of a knight-errant whose coat of arms has been sullied upon ceremonial occasion. The fierce, wild snapping sound of the ensign as it sailed loose on the wind had probably drawn his attention to it. He bore down angrily upon the scene and the disapproval upon his features became distinctly angrier as he glanced down at the supine, sun-soused, and apparently indifferent forms of his off-duty officers; he seemed on the point of bellowing reprimand to the pool in general but then quickly, deftly began doing the obvious. He paid out the line so that the flag gradually sank lower. It became entangled in the radio wires but Thomson, using his height and long reach, played and manipulated the line until he finally got it free. As it sank, the Pakistani, rearmed with his broom, chased it hither and thither, like a man with a net about to capture an absurdly outsize butterfly. It finally sank low enough for him to grab it by hand, and, timidly, he brought it back to Thomson, whose mouth opened and shut upon a torrent of words that mercifully flew away upon the same stream that had caught the flag in the first place. Thomson snatched the ensign and began securing its halliard, berating the seaman as he worked at his own knots. Then the blue ensign sailed upward once more, and unfurled at its proper station. With final angry gestures at his knots, Basil Thomson turned and walked away.

The Pakistani remained dutifully at attention, as though this respectful atonement was required on his part until the master regained the bridge and, as Thomson resumed his progress there, with swift angry watchful glances at the flag, the Pakistani himself happily returned to his painting; and we who had watched the small skyward drama intensely performed against the high black funnel and the higher blue sky, suddenly had no further distraction, except the deep-sinking heat, the sea kicking behind, the clear empty horizon, and the steadily freshening caps on the sea as we began to run with the monsoon.

The Indian Ocean's monsoon is one of the great and crucial winds of the world; the south-west monsoon is the summer wind, blowing northward from the equator along a south-westerly course from April to September, after which it reverses itself and becomes the north-east monsoon and blows southward toward the equator.

The monsoon's complete reversal of direction from season to season made it a natural propulsion for commerce to and from the east from the earliest times. No other wind has been more consistently used by seafarers, and probably none has had greater influence upon the commerce of the world and relations between the hemispheres. It possibly drove the first sails to be set upon the sea: Mesopotamian river craft venturing beyond the sheltered waters of the Gulf. The sea routes between the Indus and the Persian Gulf and the Red Sea became one of the principal bridges for the trade of the ancient Middle East; Mesopotamia had a sea route to India through the Persian Gulf during the second millennium B.C.; but it took almost two thousand years more before the trick of regulating trade entirely by the monsoons was learned by a Greek captain, Hippalus, whose discovery is generally set in the reign of Claudius, A.D. 41–54, but may have been later, during the Ptolemaic period. Hippalus at any rate realised that the monsoons not only allowed exact trading schedules that offered big economies in time but, with the compass still unknown, helped deliver ships to the Indus with pinpoint accuracy.

The south-west monsoon starts along its course in spring with such exactness that it arrives at each place approximately the same date every year, and brings torrential rain to the Indian continent when it reaches there. By picking up the wind when it arrived off the Red Sea, Roman trading ships sped to India, where they loaded Indian and Chinese luxuries such as pepper, perfumes, ebony, ivory, pearls, silks, and drugs. They waited for the north-east monsoon in January to carry them back to the Red Sea, whence their wares travelled overland to Alexandria for shipment across the Mediterranean.

If we argue that for most of his civilised existence man's practical concept of immense distance has been the measure between his different hemispheric selves and that, in the case of the west, history constantly has been framed or driven or moulded, directly or indirectly, by the aggressive greedy obsession to link the hemispheres and derive power and material benefit from the process then the trading schedules devised by Hippalus were the first major consolidation of the impulse, and initiated the true expansion of the modern world, for they brought its first significant contraction through speed, and remained the pivot of east–west trade and contact for almost fifteen centuries. They created on the one hand the strategic leverage of the Levant and all the implications that this would hold for the future, and on the other the rise and greatness of the Mediterranean city-states such as Venice.

The Romans rightly named the monsoon after Hippalus: ' ... they sail with the wind called Hippalus in forty days to the first commercial emporium of India,' Pliny says in his *Natural History* when describing navigation from the Red Sea to India, adding, ' ... they commence the return voyage from India at the beginning of the Egyptian month of Tybis, which answers to our December (or thereabouts). Thus it comes to pass that they return home within the year.' With the monsoons serving as such a reliable and fixed-direction propulsive force, the Indian Ocean became the most intensely navigated ocean in the world; and its moods and humours became as familiar to sailors in the early centuries of the Christian era as they are today. In the first century, between A.D. 50 and 80, an unknown Greek mariner wrote the *Periplus of the Erythraean Sea*, a handbook of commerce and navigation on the Indian Ocean between the Red Sea, the African coasts, and India and the East Indies. But the Arabs became the true masters of the Indian Ocean, and their lateen-rigged dhows rode the monsoons in fleets. They established their power down the eastern coast of Africa and, with a head start of a thousand years upon their European counterparts in west Africa, started the trade in black slaves, which, still in operation until just a few years ago, was perhaps the oldest continuous deep-sea trade in the world.

One of those early monsoon voyagers was Suleiman the Merchant, whose accounts of his ninth-century voyages created the epic of Sindbad. Even after the Portuguese had discovered the sea route to India round the Cape, the monsoon schedules remained as necessary and effective for their East Indiamen as they had been for the Romans. The advantage of the Cape route was that, although longer, it evaded the crushing transit levies of the Levant, as well as the political uncertainties of the area. Nothing changes, it seems.

Ardshiel passed into the monsoon overnight. At dawn one morning we were in the thick of it, and it continued to gather its force behind us, driving at the ship, which surfed along upon the backs of very large waves. There was no horizon. The light and the sea were silver from humidity, spray-blown haze, and heat, and one felt the depressive weight of all that airborne moisture around us as it whirled toward its ultimate descent in deluge upon the Indian subcontinent; but the racing sea brought an immediate sense of imminent destination. The ship, which for weeks had seemed like a maritime form of fly in amber, a grotesque insect stuck inside the water, now appeared to be advancing fairly rapidly after all to where it was going.

At noon, the wet air and haze were so bright from the fierce penetrating sunlight that one's eyes hurt from the glare. The rails were slimy to the touch, and one felt that one would choke upon that dense atmosphere.

We passed Socotra, once a staging post for the east–west trade, but it remained unseen in the haze; it was difficult to imagine, however, how any small and primitive craft could have survived the ferocity of those seas which, relatively, must have been as intimidating to them as they piled up astern as the great waves of the westerly gales were to the clippers in the roaring forties. The waves tumbled beside *Ardshiel* and, even sealed inside the ship, one could hear them crash and thunder as fearsomely as though we lay upon a reef, which, what with the violent shaking and vibration of the ship, one sometimes felt one did.

Sailing in from the Cape, or Suez, the Gulf is approached by rounding two corners, Ras al Hadd, the cape where the southernmost coast of the Arabian peninsula turns sharply northward, and the Quoins, at the Strait of Hormuz, which form the very entrance to the Gulf. Ras al Hadd however is generally considered to be the true point of arrival or departure.

Inbound or outbound upon a tanker, the name of Ras al Hadd is always uttered as an implied threat. 'When we turn the corner' is the recurrent phrase, and attached to it comes some solemn warning. Inbound, they were talking of the heat: 'Tomorrow you'll be able to fry eggs on the foredeck, I've seen it done. Just wait, the heat hits you like a wall when you turn the corner.' Outbound, the dread expressed was of the force of the monsoon as one bashed into it instead of running with it: 'Wait until we turn the corner, you won't be able to stand up on deck.'

In neither case, as it happened, was the extreme confirmed, but the sense of it was: Ras al Hadd is one of the natural divides of geography and experience, a traverse between worlds, another of those places that make seamen's mythology comprehensible, as in Sindbadian or Homeric fantasy when sailors cross from one exotic realm to another with that illogically swift transition that usually strikes one as merely one of the marks of the ancient imagination. Ras al Hadd makes it all very real, however, and one can see how early voyagers, when flying in upon the wings of the monsoon gale, might have been astonished and bewildered to find themselves quite suddenly drifting with almost empty sails upon a still hot sea whose barren shores hinted of new and terrible perils.

In the way these sailors speak of it today, nothing of the old essential experience seems to have changed. Ras al Hadd is a sea corner as real to the VLCC men as it was to those in the dhows. The south-west monsoon blows up from the equator and hits the high mountainous wall of the southerly Arabian coast, which neatly deflects it, so that at Ras al Hadd, where the southerly coast ends, the wind is diverted straight across the mouth of the Gulf of Oman, which is really just the hot antechamber to the deeper oven of the Gulf proper. You cross a line from turbulence into sweaty humid silence as you round the cape, and it is uncanny. But there is the curious thought as one rounds this most ancient headland that for so many of the centuries that it has served navigation the principal freight bearing upon it has been energy. In the millennium before the outward flow of black crude began, Ras al Hadd was the point to which the dhows inbound from Africa on the monsoon delivered themselves and their cargoes of slaves: black human fuel to make the olden wheels of Araby turn.

A light breeze lay behind *Ardshiel* after we'd turned in past Ras al Hadd. The whitecaps had gone but the air remained pearly from humidity. There was still no horizon. It was impossible anyway to see out from the cabin: the windows were thickly encrusted with salt blown upon them by the wind.

As we sailed along the coast Basil Thomson went to the bridge and broadcast to the ship: 'Attention please, your attention please. We are going to Hallul Island to part load, and then to Mina al-Ahmadi, Kuwait, to complete loading. We will then go to Taranto, Italy, for full discharge.'

It is the announcement upon which all tanker life pivots. Nothing else is more eagerly awaited or more joyfully received. Life suddenly had definition: three destinations, including the ultimate one. A mysterious, formless voyage had unity and pattern. You knew where you were going. The difference upon the mood and spirits of everyone was remarkable. Luncheon was an animated meal. Hallul Island and Mina al-Ahmadi were familiar to all, but who had been to Taranto? No one, as it appeared. Harvey Phillips had known someone who once had and, as far as he could remember, he believed that the discharge point there was a sea-berth, miles from shore, so there would be no shore leave for those not getting off the ship to go home. As most expected to get off, these dismal tidings bore no great impact.

The news had, however, brought new worry to Alan Ewart-James. This was his first voyage as first officer and as the ship approached the Gulf he had become increasingly aware of his responsibility for the proper loading of the cargo. The news that *Ardshiel* would be loading at two points, which meant two different types of oil, was an unexpected complication in a problem that is not as straightforward as it appears.

The two principal types of strain upon any ship are known as the shear force and the bending moment, the former being a vertical force and the latter basically a horizontal one. The shear force itself is produced by the interplay of two other forces, gravitational pull of the ship into the water and the buoyancy that thrusts it up: the ship floats where these two meet.

The more weight you put aboard, the more gravitational pull you have and, in the case of tankers, this would be a serious matter if one huge tank were full and one beside it empty. In this instance you have the force of the full tank going downward at the bulkhead between the two compartments and, on the other side, the force of the buoyancy going upward. These two, working against each other at the point where the two tanks divide, comprise the shear force. Expert loading is therefore a vital safety factor in supertankers. Careful adjustment of the weight of their huge cargoes is essential to avoid uneven stresses that could lead to hull fractures.

All these forces in turn interact with the bending moment, which roughly speaking is what it sounds to be: the limit of the pliability of the hull. A ship's hull is rather like a thin plastic ruler, flexible if toyed with. It must be able to bend upon the waves, and the circumstances that require this usually are when the vessel is supported at both ends by different waves, with no support in between, or when it is supported by a single big wave at the centre of the hull and the bows and stern are hoisted beyond support from the water. Obviously, because of their length, it is the former rather than the latter circumstance that matters most for supertankers. If a tanker is wrongly loaded, with too much weight in the middle, its pliability is affected and it lies brittle upon the seas, liable to be carried beyond its bending moment into a splintering crack, and thence to disaster. And unless the oil is pumped into its tanks in an even and well-balanced distribution, it might even crack at its berth, or start a weakness that could pass unnoticed but spring disastrously into play in bad weather. Undoubtedly this has been the cause of many of the tanker disasters.

These complicated calculations are too much for a man working under pressure, as any first officer is during loading, so superships are fitted with computers programmed to each ship's specifications. The loading computer aboard *Ardshiel*, known as a Lodicator, was a Swedish machine that allowed the mate to find in a few seconds the figures for the proper trim of his ship. His working material is the weight of the ship in its various degrees of loadedness and he feeds into the Lodicator the weights of the cargo, water, and fuel in the different compartments of the vessel. The Lodicator gives the shear force and the bending moment of the ship at set positions along the length of the hull. Ewart-James believed that the machine was an absolute safeguard against all strains and stresses; if it was properly used, they simply could not arise. There nevertheless had to be an exact, well-timed plan of loading, especially when two grades of oil were involved; the Hallul oil would have to be evenly distributed over the ship to avoid any list or stress, and the actual inflow of the oil through the intricate pipe system also had to be carefully planned to avoid Hallul oil from contaminating the Mina oil or vice versa, and thereby spoiling the integrity of both grades, which would be an abominably costly mistake.

As a result, Ewart-James was to be seen standing for long periods beside his Lodicator, as he fed it questions and waited for the answers with a tense, anxious look, for all the world like a young man playing a pinball machine in hours-long expectation of an elusive payoff. He found his plan, but then, on sudden hunch, he plunged into the voluminous documented paperwork that earlier in the voyage he had so firmly deplored and to his joy discovered there that the ship on its maiden voyage had had exactly the same loading plan. The old plan, worked out by an experienced mate, confirmed his plan, but also allowed him to improve it, and he kicked up his heels and drummed them on his desk, and declared himself to be 'chuffed', which is an old Royal Navy expression for being very pleased.

As in an airliner, one is never wholly unaware aboard a supertanker of the potential dangers of the ship. I myself am an early riser and therefore inclined to be weak-minded at night, so it was usually then that any reservations occurred, but only as a perverse delight in the comfortable business of going to bed in my delightful state-room. Sometimes, when returning to my cabin from the cinema, I found myself regarding the steward's scrupulous preparation of the room for the night: superb P & O butlering, with the curtains drawn, the quilt turned back and the pillows fluffed, all the day's paraphernalia sorted and put away or neatly arranged, thermos of iced water beside the bed, a bowl of fruit, the overhead lights off and only the reading light by the bed casting a gentle confined glow. No A-deck steward on the *Queen Mary* could have done better. And then, as I switched off the light, drew back the curtains to show the starlight, and got into bed, there to lie pondering the bliss of its ample comfort, the nervous thought possibly would occur. How ghastly to be turned out of all of this in a matter of moments and to be cast out upon those dim, raging, monsoon-driven seas, assuming one was lucky enough even to reach them. But there is a marvellous false security about luxury, rather like eating one of those dinners from Maxim's in the front cabin of a transatlantic

269

airliner. Surely, one would avow, champagne and caviare have their own immunity? Fate could never be so scornful. Alas!

It was therefore of some comfort at least that the first serious alarm we had during the voyage aboard *Ardshiel* occurred during the afternoon, moreover within sight of the Quoins, which we were then fast approaching.

'Fire in the boiler room!' said the ship's speaker, after the bells had jangled with nerve-piercing clamour, followed by the hoot-hoot-hoot-hoot of the ship's whistle. The response was instant. Doors crashed open and there was the sound of people running. I caught a glimpse of Patricia Allen with a towel around her head dashing for the stairs. I picked up my typewriter case, filled with all my notes and which I'd kept handy at the door since the first days on board, and followed her to the bridge, our emergency station. Was it an exercise? I asked when I joined her. No, the real thing, she said. This was clear too from Thomson's expression, which was serious in a way different from usual. Stephen Tucker, who'd been in the swimming pool and was still in his trunks, dripping, was beside the master, who was talking to the engine room. Except for the terrible clamour of the klaxon, the mood was very cool and calm and controlled. Then Thomson said into the speaker, 'Stand easy, stand easy. Situation normal.'

Something had happened in the engine room which had quickly been brought under control. But the alarm had shaken everyone. Graham Allen had been shaving when the alarm sounded and he returned from the emergency headquarters with his face still covered in shaving cream. They all stood talking outside their doors with an air of nervous release. I regarded my own cabin with some surprise, as though I had not expected to see it again.

THIRTEEN

INSIDE the Quoins, tankers become the most political of ships in the most political of waters.

The Persian Gulf, as it mostly has been known, or the Arabian Gulf, as its sheikdoms and sultanates now insist that it be called, or the Gulf, as we ourselves henceforth shall call it, has never for long absented itself from its historic role as the strategic fulcrum of the world. No one with an instinct toward global supremacy has ever been able to ignore the Gulf, from Alexander to Stalin. It has always been a prize among prizes, and indeed it rightfully has been regarded by many as *the* prize of all. None of the great empires of the West or the Near East has avoided either reconnaissance of it, an attempt at subjugation, or actual lodgment there; and as the destinies of Occident and Orient became increasingly enmeshed no one with any sort of presumption to control the way between could do so without control of the Gulf. Rear-Admiral Mahan regarded the Gulf as being of far more value to Britain than any Far Eastern possessions because it controlled India and the Indian Ocean, which after all meant controlling the way to everywhere else, and he saw Russia's abysmal naval forage against Japan in 1904 as very much in Britain's interest because it exhausted Russia's surplus energy and 'will withdraw her from the Gulf'.

It is a view that in one form or another recurs through history, expressed by action when not by words. There was, as it were, a constant urge, in the West at any rate, to reclaim the stones and middens of the hemisphere's earliest civilisation; nice as such a thought seems, the motivation was, and is, the extraordinary leverage that the Gulf gives over the passage to India and the east, and its domination over Arabia and the Middle East as well. The trade either through it or which it controlled has never been less than the single richest in the world, whether in pepper, pearls, and frankincense or crude oil. No empire since the Middle Ages particularly has felt secure without it, and none of the Near Eastern hegemonies, whether Ottoman or Tsarist, ever stopped manœuvring for it, toward it, or in and around it. But the European ones, the Portuguese, Dutch, and British in succession, as they gained ascendancy over one another, made certain that it was one of the first things they grabbed; that is, if they could, for the Arabs and Persians who lived upon its shores have always been tough-minded, independent, and adamant – and commensurately fierce – about their territory. Of all the outsiders, it was only the British who managed to hold any sort of effective suzerainty for an extended period. Theirs was a good and, on the whole, commendable showing.

East India Company interests and Arab piracy had brought an increased British naval presence into the Gulf during the eighteenth century, and the nineteenth century confirmed the British presence and protectorate, even though it was ceaselessly challenged by the locals, and Russia beyond.

Aside from the obvious strategic value of the Gulf, the British gave their position there the moral sanction of putting down the slave trade, at which they were determined but never wholly successful; ten years ago, in the early sixties, the slaves were still going in, according to the Anti-Slavery Society of London. But what really mattered so far as they were concerned was what Lord Curzon told the chiefs of the Gulf's Trucial States in 1903: 'We found strife and we have created order. It was our commerce as well as your security that was threatened and called for protection ... we saved you from extinction at the hands of your neighbours. We opened these seas to the ships of all nations, and enabled their flags to fly in peace. ...'

This civil presence and military control was practically the last of Britain's former great imperial and strategic garrisons to withdraw as the empire folded. It did so in 1971, long after the bugles and pack drill had stopped elsewhere and broken forever the linkage of that immensely extended range of influence or possession that Kipling called the dominion over palm and pine.

But the rising oil production in the Middle East and the increasing demand for the crude in Europe, the United States, and Japan, as well as elsewhere in the industrial world, could not keep from the Gulf its traditional share of intense international pressures. These established themselves far sooner than anyone expected, during the Indo-Pakistan War at the end of 1971, just before the deadline for the British withdrawal, and which by involving the United States, Russia, and China set the pattern of the future; thereafter the modern manœuvrings and power plays for command in the Gulf began in earnest and the fourth Arab–Israeli war of October 1973 hastened the inevitable, shifting the focus of the postwar Middle Eastern political crisis from the Suez Canal to the Gulf.

Tankers and their cargoes have been an integral part of all the Middle Eastern wars of recent times; they were after all the very reason for the war of 1956. Egypt's nationalisation of the Suez Canal struck the British and French as a direct threat to the passage of the oil tankers upon which they had become dependent.

In 1956 and in 1967, the involvement of the Gulf itself was nominal. The Middle East as a whole did not yet hold the decisive balance in oil production which it now does. In 1967 even, Middle East production was 505 million metric tons against a total Western Hemisphere production of 737 million metric tons. By 1972, these production figures were 913 million metric tons and 801 million metric tons respectively.

In the 1956 and 1967 wars only Britain and Western Europe stood to be serious losers outside the main arena of conflict, because of the closure of the Suez Canal. In neither case however were they as deeply affected as they feared they might be. The oil remained available. In 1956, British control of the Gulf ensured it anyway, and in 1967 there was only a perfunctory and soon-relaxed embargo against Britain and the United States. The problem on both occasions was one of logistics, of distance, haul and numbers of ships, all of which the supertankers and VLCCs were intended to solve. Anyway, after 1956 the Egyptians, under a brilliant young engineer, Mahmoud Younes, ran the Suez Canal far better and more efficiently, and showed more willingness to spend money on improvements, than the old Suez Canal Company ever had done.

What should also be remembered of those crises is that Japan herself, far from suffering as she did as a result of the war in 1973, which threatened to bring the country down and in any event stopped the postwar boom, was actually a major beneficiary of the 1956 and 1967 wars. The provision of the VLCCs, the economic alternative to the Suez passage, helped make her export fortunes. And, as a result of the VLCCs, the 1967 war was far less traumatic for Europe than 1956 had been; to such a degree that the shipping prepared itself to live entirely without the Suez Canal, and revealed no visible regret over the fact. Suez lost its critical importance, and the effortless manner in which this was achieved gave everyone as false a sense of control of circumstances as that which led Britain and France to Suez in 1956, and prepared no one for the real shock, which was that, finally, Suez had nothing to do whatsoever with the delivery of oil.

The six years between the June war of 1967 and the October one of 1973 had set in motion circumstances that began to polarise the Middle Eastern tensions at the Gulf, and, after the October war, when oil itself finally became *the* weapon after many predictions and threats and long deferment, the dominating role of the Gulf was indisputable, and such it will remain, even with Suez open. After all, it is the opening and shutting of the taps in the Gulf that now controls the movement of that fluid, not the politics of the passage home.

The pertinent fact in all this of course is that Middle Eastern oil, and Saudi Arabian oil in particular, has become indispensable to the developed world. At the beginning of this decade Shell Oil predicted that the world would burn more oil during the seventies than it had in all previous history. The senior geologist of British Petroleum, Harry Warman, in 1970 expressed his belief that by the mid-1990s, half the world's known and discoverable oil would have been burned.

Between 1920 and 1971 the world consumed 200 billion barrels of oil (there are about 7.3 barrels to a ton); between 1971 and 1985 it supposedly will use some 300 billion barrels more. At those predicted rates of consumption the world has enough oil for the next twenty to twenty-five years at least, which also is the span, it has been suggested, that is the minimum required for the advanced industrial nations to produce an alternative source of energy. These consumption estimates were made before the October war and the higher oil prices it brought and the new awareness of a need to conserve energy. The upheavals and the economic uncertainties that those factors precipitated everywhere will make it difficult for anyone to issue predicted consumption figures during the next few years but, whatever it does, oil consumption is not likely to decrease in the industrial world nor is it even likely to stand still, so the pre-October-war predictions on consumption still give a fairly good idea of where we are so far as oil requirements are concerned.

Nobody of course knows how much oil there really is anywhere, but we do know that most of what there is lies in the Middle East, mainly in Saudi Arabia.

The Saudi reserves are by far the largest in existence. At the beginning of 1973 Saudi reserves were estimated to be 138 billion barrels against 65 billion barrels held by Iran and 64.9 billion barrels in Kuwait, the next largest sources in the Gulf. Altogether, Middle East reserves amounted to 355.9 billion barrels out of known world reserves of 667 billion barrels.

Saudi reserves may be as much as double the present estimates, and we don't know yet what lies in the offshore waters of the continents, or in the ocean deeps, or in much of the Arctic and Antarctic. Further major finds such as Alaskan and North Sea ones are confidently expected. Substantial as these fields are, they make little difference to the overall position. At best, they help cope with annual increases in consumption, either in the United States or Europe, but they do not, so far, create independence. It is quite clear therefore that unless this position changes, and until alternative sources of energy have been developed, dependence upon Middle Eastern and Saudi oil in particular will remain and will be the centre of the diplomacy, strategy, and economic calculations of both hemispheres and of all power blocs. But whatever outside diplomacy and strategy envisages or attempts by way of influence events in the Gulf will be controlled increasingly by local circumstances.

The situation among the Gulf states themselves has been a precarious and disturbed one for some time. At its simplest, local problems in the Gulf have to do with the contentions involved with the very name of the place. No Arab state will accept the name Persian Gulf. The Iranians (or Persians, as the British still prefer to call them) for their part regard the name Persian Gulf as historic evidence of their own title and, although they have repeatedly declared that they have no territorial ambitions beyond what they rightfully possess, which is the entire north-eastern shore of the Gulf, they nevertheless seized the Greater and Lesser Tanb islands in 1971, one day before the dateline for the official British withdrawal, and have since fortified them. Through these islands Iran holds effective control over the tanker routes passing through the entrance of the Gulf. This in fact was one justification Iran gave for their seizure, the other being simply that they originally had been hers anyway.

Much of the oil wealth of the Gulf belongs to a hotchpotch of tiny independent sheikdoms, sultanates, and emirates such as Kuwait, Bahrayn, Abu Dhabi, Dubayy, and Qatar, and the larger Gulf states of Iran, Iraq, and Saudi Arabia have at one time or another laid claim or asserted rights against one or the other of these. Or against each other.

These have all been relatively minor storms, but the fears and suspicions they provoked linger and the biggest consequence of it all has been an arms race in the region the extent of which has been overshadowed by the Arab–Israeli issue but which, even before the 1973 war, was bringing to the Middle East a whole new set of perils. These turn upon the question of who is to be the local dominant power in the area, how it construes its roles and to what degree its self-delegated functions are acceptable to the rest.

As Iran at this point clearly is the dominant power and determined to stay that way, the pertinent questions apply to relations between her neighbours and herself.

Whatever the confusion of quarrels and claims and counter-claims among fellow Arab states and sheikdoms in the Gulf, these tend to become secondary to the divisions between themselves and Iran.

By seizure of the Tanb islands Iran had shown her strength in the Gulf, and she continued to show it in many ways, notably by giving her navy powers to stop and search ships within fifty miles of her coast and which were suspected of causing pollution. This in effect extended her territorial waters to cover most of the surface of the Gulf itself and adequately covered the approaches to the Strait of Hormuz, where a large new naval base has been built at Bandar 'Abbas, which in turn is backed up by an air and military base at Chahbahar near the Pakistani border and almost opposite Ras al Hadd.

Iran's gift to herself of stop-and-search powers in 1973 may well prove handy against potential polluters, and the Gulf certainly suffers its own steady rate of tanker accidents and spills, but they do equivocally declare as well who it is who for the moment commands the right of entry at the gates of Hormuz.

If she realises her present intentions, Iran will not only dominate the Gulf but become as well the principal military power in the Middle East. Her military budget for 1973 was two billion dollars, most of it for arms from America.

Aside from Iran and Iraq, Saudi Arabia and the other Gulf states have not lagged in the arms race. Unfortunately, arms races anywhere have a propensity to get out of hand, by generating a great deal more trouble than that which they presumably were intended to cure. This is especially true in unstable and unpredictable political climates, where a lot of weaponry suddenly placed in unfamiliar hands can have consequences either unforeseen or too casually discounted by the military salesmen and their strategy-minded promoters, as well as by the customers themselves. In many Gulf states, dissidence has grown with literacy, and reached its majority with militarisation; feudal desert nations, accustomed to patriarchal acquiescence and those two biblical components of civil serenity, summary justice in the market-place and the protracted sibilant courtesies of a tented hospitality, find that among the many things their black treasure has brought them is a generation released from traditional respect and obligation into incoherent wishfulness, dissatisfaction, and unstable ambitions. It is not the entire basis of change in those sort of countries, but it represents much of the framework of it. The sort of men who arise to meet these dissatisfactions, whose model we perhaps saw in Colonel Gadafi of Libya, are the ones who may give the Shah more problems than he counts upon, either by challenging his power in the Gulf, or by offering themselves as surrogate for other more powerful forces behind them.

The Shah indicated even before the British left the Gulf at the end of 1971 that he did not wish to see any active superpower presence in those waters, which are heavily patrolled by his own destroyers, frigates, and naval hovercraft (the Iranian navy has the largest fleet of British-built naval hovercraft in the world, ideal vehicles for the normally tranquil surface of that sea). But that was being wishful. Where the oil is, and where the tankers sail, is where modern power-play is going to be.

The American and Russian power game is serious enough, with both determined to cover the Gulf by holding positions of strength for their navies in the Indian Ocean, thus competing for the pre-rogatives abandoned by Britain. But China's involvement in the Gulf, motivated by her support of Arab revolutionaries and guer-rillas, fear of Russian menace and, by no means least, of a remilitar-ised Japan, brings a far more dangerously unpredictable complexion to it all. And then there is the equally unpredictable element of American and Japanese competition for the Gulf's oil and what this might mean to their own hitherto special postwar relationship.

Japanese self-interest can certainly be expected to be sharply advanced to assure the maintenance of her future oil supplies, Middle East crises or no. All this returns Japan to a position of in-dependent strategic thinking and self-advancement of a sort that she has not known since before the Second World War; and it is uncom-fortable to remember that it was the prohibition of petroleum ex-ports to Japan in 1940 that helped make war her choice, and launched the strategy of Pearl Harbor. Her absolute dependence upon hundreds of tankers rotating between her home islands and the Gulf is far more vital to her survival than Roosevelt's petroleum ever was. China's prime minister, Chou En-lai, is well aware of this and, in an interview with the *Sunday Times* in December 1971, he de-clared that tankers transporting oil from the Middle East to Japan had to pass through the Malacca Straits and the excessive passage of them polluted the water there. 'Japanese militarists claim that the Malacca Straits are Japan's lifeline,' he said. 'This causes dissatisfac-tion in Malaysia and Indonesia. They have not forgotten the havoc Japanese militarism did them in the Second World War.'

Japan's dependence upon the Malacca Straits is so important that one doesn't have to quote militarists to make the point, but the asso-ciation in Chou En-lai's mind is what matters, and anyway the dis-satisfaction he referred to is very real, for the Malacca Straits too have their constant tanker accidents, oil slicks, and groundings, much as the Cape of Good Hope does. One of *Ardshiel's* sister ships was in collision there and the shallowness of the seabed also means that loaded tankers often touch bottom, which is granite.*

As a result, Malaysia and Indonesia have made angry noises and taken points of principle. They have ensured their complete control of the Straits by imposing twelve-mile limits to their territorial waters. Malaysia proposed a toll on ships using the Straits, and Indonesia even went so far as to suggest a total prohibition on ships of 200,000 tons or more, which would mean a twelve-hundred-mile detour through the Lombok and Makassar straits. Neither has gone so far as to put these proposals into practice, perhaps because they fear that such action might precipitate more ominous consequences than those of pollution, or perhaps because the Thai government has suggested that one way out of the problem would be construction of a Suez-type canal across the Isthmus of Kra, the narrowest point of the Malay peninsula, and which they control. The Japanese themselves have suggested a pipeline across the isthmus, with the oil transhipped from tankers at a terminal on the Andaman Sea to tankers berthed on the Gulf of Siam. But whether the oil goes across the Isthmus of Kra or through the Malacca Straits is not going to make much difference politically or strategically; the point is critical dependence upon such a supply line and the need to maintain it against all eventualities. It does not seem likely therefore that Japan will long be absent as an important entry in *Jane's Fighting Ships*. China already has begun a new programme of naval construction and it is quite likely too that her concern with Russian and Japanese intentions will lead her eventually to the sort of enlarged naval expansion that Russia undertook after the Cuban crisis of 1962.

So, in the final analysis, it always comes back to the tankers and, indeed, to the Gulf, because even the pressures that might be exercised against the ships at a point such as the Malacca Straits are obviously less than those able to be applied at the point of loading. North America and Europe also have long vulnerable routes connecting them with the Gulf. They, like the Japanese, might individually or collectively feel free to exercise considerable power, deployment of forces, or even actual intervention along the way, in the belief that they would get away with it. The Gulf allows no such options or opportunities. Any aggressive or punitive action there to protect the oil ships or to ensure the oil certainly would blow up the oil installations and thus kill the goose, apart from the fact that it very likely would blow up the world. The way things are, that's not to say it won't be tried.

* *Publishers' note.* As this book went to press in January 1975 the Japanese supertanker *Showa Maru* lay grounded in the Straits, having spilled 844,000 gallons of oil.

As the oil embargo after the October war indicated, however, oil is always likely to flow from some producer dissident with the rest. Neither the Iranians nor the Iraqis shut their taps, though for very different reasons. A lot of oil continued to leave the Gulf for destinations under Arab embargo, although by no means sufficient to reduce the impact of the embargo. While Egypt imposed a naval blockade on the Red Sea against Israeli-bound ships, no one tried to impose a similar one in the Gulf against, say, any American-bound oil from Iran. The idea however must have occurred to many and will certainly arise again in any future crisis centred upon the Gulf and its oil. By then on the other hand the Arabs themselves probably will be heavily engaged in the tanker business, as they indicate they will be, and they might create the same effect simply by withdrawing their ships from the market. But the shape of future crisis in the Gulf is unpredictable, except to say that there probably will be one.

In the light of all this, the Anglo-French landings at Suez in 1956 might now be viewed more properly for what they really were, not the last convulsive kick of militant imperialism, as we have been inclined to regard them up to now, but as the first of the energy war-crises that, enlarged to universal proportions, now involve our entire future, not only our politics, diplomacy, and strategy, but also our alignments, posturings, loyalties, and perfidy.

Aside from these matters, there is another grave issue to ponder as one enters the Gulf. Everyone wants Middle Eastern oil, and, in an emergency, they'll pay any price, cash, moral or otherwise for it, as we saw in the October war and after. But should they be allowed to have it at the rate they want it? Of all the moral problems raised by oil, this perhaps is the greatest and the least debated.

In the first place, the human, legitimate problem for the Saudis and the other Gulf states is their recurring question of what is to become of them when all the oil has been siphoned from under the sands and every last drop has been borne away by supertanker to the furnaces of the developed world. No one then will give a fig for them or their well-being, any more than they did before, and, wrenched from the feudal past by oil, they will be hurled back into it from the twenty-first century by those whom they have helped to riches, and the desert will blow over their lives and the monuments that sudden wealth has built, as it has done repeatedly in the past when entrepôt trade between east and west raised city after city in the Gulf to riches and luxury only to abandon them upon some accident of chance and arms. Apart from diversified investments abroad and in their own countries, their only security they feel is to leave something under the ground for posterity. It is not

279

an unreasonable wish, and it is sound planning from their point of view: the oil accumulates value underground faster than money in unstable currencies or even gold does in vaults and, even if the big economic powers of the industrial world find their alternative sources of energy, there are many who may never be able to afford those, so that at the very least oil will always be required in some measure by the future, just as coal has remained in demand. But this view of oil simply as an energy source, so well reflected in the gleeful belief that once the industrial world found an alternative form of energy the Arabs wouldn't know what to do with their oil, shows the incredible underestimation of its value as a resource that is perhaps the most notable fact of our present-day association with it. It is a view for which posterity may well hold us in high contempt, and even abomination, because it has been and still is responsible for dissipation of the most extraordinary of all natural commodities.

Nothing else does more for man. Oil is the cornucopia from which flows not only his transport, heat, and light, but much of his clothing, most modern shoes, fertilisers and insecticides, detergents, candles, long-playing records, ointments and face creams, medical drugs, roofing, drainpipes and guttering, furniture and curtains, household utensils, paints, to name only a few. Oil is the indispensable source of our plastics, artificial fibres, and many of our chemicals. If we no longer required it to drive our cars and industry, we certainly would need it for countless items of daily use. More important, through a remarkable job of discovery, research, and development by scientists working for British Petroleum, it could become the principal source of protein for a hungry world.

By the year 2000 the world population will have doubled. To feed it properly, the production of high-quality protein will have to be trebled to at least 60 million tons a year. The production of conventional animal proteins, meat, milk and fish, cannot possibly meet an estimated shortfall of 20 million tons of protein necessary to meet the requirements for the year 2000. These in any event are likely to prove too expensive for the majority of humans. As the world nutritional problem is essentially a question of proteins, protein poverty looms as one of the most pitiful prospects of the future. According to BP estimates, the present world production of petroleum is sufficient to allow the potential production of at least 20 million tons a year of petroleum-derived proteins, which of course represent that estimated shortfall of protein in 2000.

What BP's scientists have actually produced is a dried yeast rich in biologically valuable protein. It is known at Toprina and can be cultivated during the dewaxing of certain oils. It draws on oil's former animal–vegetable origin and is as natural, BP says, as the yeasts with which bread is baked and beer is brewed. It already has been extensively tested and used in animal feeds. Its greatest potential role, in man's own diet, awaits it in the future. That is, providing there is sufficient oil left from which to cultivate it.

Under their barren sands the Arabs now hold, it seems, the greatest potential source of nutrition in a world whose cultivable land already is strained to the limit and whose seas are being exhausted. We cannot even begin to suppose what other magical uses our future scientists might wrest from oil, but this one is enough to be grateful for at the moment; it should not surprise any of us, however, given the disposition of the times, if this future succour of mankind instead is entirely consumed within the next couple of decades by the internal combustion engine, on the highways of the Americas, Australasia, Europe, and Japan.

FOURTEEN

THE Gulf's oil, which we had come to fetch, is by no means a modern discovery and presence. The Alexandrine geographer Eratosthenes of Cyrene (276–194 B.C.) is quoted by Strabo three centuries later as saying that 'asphaltus is found in great abundance in Babylonia'. Strabo also quoted Posidonius (135–51 B.C.) as describing springs in Babylonia that produced both white and black naphtha, 'the second or black naphtha is asphaltus, and is burnt in lamps instead of oil'. Pliny described the perpetually burning 'apertures' of Babylonia, where oil and gas presumably broke the surface in natural wells. 'The plain of Babylon throws up flame from a place like a fish-pond, an acre in extent.' Actual oil production in the modern sense however is a very recent business. Before the Second World War, Iran was the main producer. The entire area produced less than 20 million tons a year in 1939. As we have seen, it took a whole new circumstance of demand to bring in the big-bellied ships such as ours. But, come and go as they do, their view of the Gulf scene seems as scanty and mysterious as that of Eratosthenes' or Pliny's.

We were off Hallul Island at breakfast, but it took a long morning's fine manoeuvring to tie up at the loading buoy and to pick up the pipelines, bright orange, which drifted on the surface. Hallul Island itself looked brown, arid, and forsaken, with a small cluster of white administrative buildings and a group of bright silver tanks. Once the pipes had been picked up and connected, the ship drifted at its moorings as the taps were turned on and the oil flowed in, and *Ardshiel* began, hour by hour, to sink lower in the water.

The line between monotony and difference was a profoundly appreciated one. The ship had changed completely. She was still: and, after nearly five weeks, silent. Footsteps seemed to be in an untenanted mansion. No swaying, wind whine, cracking of plastic timbers, or vibration. After so many weeks, it was as good as going ashore or being in another place. The air-conditioned atmosphere inside the ship was cool and fresh, and, as the day advanced, the heat lay thick and dense and glaringly white against the windows; even with the curtains drawn, the light that broke through was as piercing as a thrown lance, and one regarded its quivering presence upon the carpet as one would a weapon that falls spent in one's presence. The window glass was as warm as a live coal to touch, and the gunwale of the lifeboat immediately outside shone with a white-hot fierceness.

Darkness when it fell removed the glare but didn't alter the temperature, and on deck the night air flowed thickly hot upon one's skin as though from an intense but black and invisible sun.

The ship lay surrounded by high barbaric torches flaring against the night; they were fireballs from the burning waste of sea rigs many miles away, offshore in the middle of the sea, which had been hidden in the thick haze of the day. They now bloomed everywhere, giant night flowers, and cast a ruddy loom across the entire horizon as they reflected off the surface of the humidity, so that the sky overhead was one of graduated flame right down to the horizon. One walked the deck as if in a terrible garden, in a corner of which, bathed in the red glow of those primeval gases, Peter Dutton sat listening to Charlie's pipes, as he seemed to like to do for at least a part of each evening.

Charlie unfortunately was having difficulty with his pipes. The wind off the water was stiff and got into them, whichever way he turned, and the notes couldn't emerge whole. He played 'Auld Lang Syne' and what sounded like other Scottish airs, but with great difficulty. He turned his back completely to the wind, but it was no use. He was giggling, and finally said, 'No good,' giggled again, and vanished, presumably to play somewhere below, cloistered and unseen, like Pan.

Dutton was musing, as he so often did, about the worth of this seagoing life against what he might have been doing on shore, where he probably would have been in social work, to which he would have preferred to have given his life. 'In all modesty,' he said, 'I feel I could have done that sort of work. Once when I was on leave I applied for a social job and, while I waited to hear, I got a job on a building site. It was marvellous. I could labour all day with a shovel or a hod, and I could just be a thousand miles away. I could think to myself, *You've been a chippie, a bricklayer, all your life.* One never even knew one had been an engineer. Anyhow, the cruel twist of fate was that this woman who gave me the interview said I wouldn't be able to cope with married people's problems because I wasn't married. Me in my shortsightedness didn't realise to say that I would be married soon. It's incredible that I didn't realise to say that. I was told the other man was going to get the job. I'd been on about two thousand a year as an engineer, and this job I was going to take on was about twelve pound ten a week. My fiancée was working and they give you a council house with the job, so we would have got by. It would have been a hard game, but, you see, it would have been a vocation, like.

'I'm not a natural engineer. Oh, I'm conscientious, I get along all right; I'm strong. The other day when a joint needed hammering I knew that I would get a hammer and go down there and hit it and hit it and hit it until I was physically exhausted. But I know that if by some God-given chance I left tomorrow and I could be an instructor in something like a Borstal, I would quite easily never go near an engine again. I know my job, because I should know it. But it's true, I'd be quite happy not to come near an engine again.

'The one hope and joy I get out of this job is to be responsible as I am for the young junior engineers and their training; to get them up and talk with them. Thankfully, I do seem to get on with them. But I'm sorry that I didn't get that social work job.'

Dutton was a recognisable northern British type. A powerful physical frame carried an earnest, even fervent, but soft nature; it was the material of which armies of nineteenth-century missionaries were made. His Bible was always beside his bed. His place was marked. He, Peter, took comfort from his Christianity when, on his voyages, he looked at the miseries of the world and wondered why it all had to be. He sank on his knees by his bed every night and prayed, and he didn't see how he could get through life without doing that.

Well, he knew truly that he would stay at sea, Dutton continued, after a brief period for reflection during which we had sat silently regarding the lighted sky above us. It was best for him, but he missed his family life. His old people too were getting on and they wanted to see him as their life drew to a close. Family ties in the north were very strong. His father used to be a wild man, with a taste for the beer, very much for himself, but then his mother fell ill. Now the old man was very changed. He did everything for the old lady, who was probably better but putting it on a bit because she liked the old man doing things for her. He bought the groceries, cooked the meals, looked after her every whim. And, of course, Peter missed his own wife. It was impossible to say how much. He had a big double bed here in his cabin like everyone else, but he didn't like sleeping in it. A double bed was a terrible place in which to lie alone, thinking thoughts. So he slept on his sofa every night of the voyage. He set his back to the back of the sofa, closed his eyes, and stayed in that position until he woke in the morning.

We sailed from Hallul during the night and, after steaming up the Gulf the whole of the following day, we arrived off the Mina al-Ahmadi sea berth at dawn. Tankers lay upon the sea all around us, like the assembly for a huge wartime convoy. They were of all shapes, sizes, and periods, but mainly VLCCs and supertankers of the immediately preceding generations. Their colours were indistinct in the heat mist, and one saw practically nothing of the coast, which was nine miles away, except patches of hard whiteness whiter than the haze; the desert shore.

The sea berth was a very large man-made island capable of handling two VLCCs, or four smaller ships. The water around it and as far as one could see in that hazy bay of Kuwait was smooth and iridescent from oil. Oil slick spectra lay as thick as confetti upon its sullen surface. The opposite berth was taken by a big Onassis tanker, *Olympic Adventurer*; its cool white sides and green-painted decks seemed to cool and cleanse the air, and, moving around on them, was Mediterranean man with his different, compelling use of energy and ease: total mobility as he worked at precisely the same tasks that we worked at, and total leisure in his stance when he didn't. Everyone regarded the other ship with great interest, and someone commented upon the pleasure of sailing with green decks such as the Greek's: so refreshing for the wide and bare spaces of the main deck, like grass.

The rising heat gradually drove everyone inside, however, and humidity drew a curtain of haze between the two ships. A smell of gas grew strong throughout the accommodation, and smoking was allowed only in the wardroom, not even inside the cabins. Covers had been laid over the carpets, to protect them from oily boots, and the decks grew dusty from sand blown in from the desert.

The loading of a supertanker is an invisible and largely automated business. There is a never-never quality to the whole connection, as Alan Ewart-James remarked: 'The oil is piped out of the desert well into tanks, then it comes out from the shore in pipes under the sea and passes straight into the ship's own tanks, from where eventually it is discharged into storage tanks, later into the refineries, and finally passes through a hose into a car's petrol tank, all without being seen or touched by anyone.'

Automation means that even what work there is escapes the touch and sight of man. A Japanese VLCC that had preceded us to the Hallul Island mooring had loaded itself without anyone doing anything at all. Her chief officer had punched out a programme and fed it into his computer, which had opened and shut all necessary valves at the right time, taken the ballast out of the tanks before starting to load them, and, as the oil poured in, taken the tanks' ullages: that is, kept measuring the space between the rising oil and the top of the tank, a precise and vital task as a proper space must be left for expansion of the oil in the tropics.

Ardshiel was by no means so fully automated, but Ewart-James, standing in his control room and surveying the banks of dials and gauges around him, held complete push-button control over the inflow of oil. 'It's like Clapham Junction,' he said, and gestured at the control panel with its diagrammatic representation of the ship's pipeline system. Tiny red and green lights glowed at various points upon the diagram. 'From his signal box the signalman can watch his trains passing along their various lines while I stand here imagining the oil pouring through the various valves. It gives me complete visual aid to what's going on in the ship. A red light means a valve is open, a green light that it's shut. I can tell from other panels whether a pump is running, its suction pressure, its speed, and so on. I can slow them down or speed them up, as required.' Dials known as Whessoe gauges showed the ullages in the various tanks, which were loaded to 98 per cent capacity. Theoretically none of the tanks can overflow as it is filled. The loading valve is automatically shut when the 98 per cent mark is reached. At this point the surface of the oil should lie six feet eight and a half inches below the deck and, in quaint mistrust of the automation that had filled and measured them, the officers passed along the decks after each tank was loaded to take the final ullages with an old-fashioned dip stick.

The oil gushed into the ship through two pipe systems, each with two outlets, known as Manifolds, on the main deck. The Hallul cargo had used one pipe system and at Mina we loaded through the other, at a rate of 7,800 tons an hour. If she was loading through both pipe systems *Ardshiel* technically was capable of loading oil at a rate of some 20,000 tons an hour, which was more than the capacity of the largest tankers afloat at the end of the Second World War.

Harry Long was to leave us, together with David Owen. They'd had a farewell party the evening before but good-byes as they prepared to go ashore were stiff. There had been, alas, a final brush between Long and Thomson as the ship approached Mina. Long had woken with a painful foot and had called to the bridge at dawn and, when Thomson answered the phone, he asked whether 'Alan' could step down briefly and bring his box of medicaments. If Mr Long was referring to the first officer, he Thomson sought to inform him that this was the first officer's watch and he could not attend to supernumeraries in their cabins while on duty, Thomson said. In that case, Long asked, could the keys to the dispensary be sent down to him and he would go there himself. 'On my ship, Mr Long,' Thomson answered, in deliberate, measured tones, 'I don't allow the dispensary keys to be given to any Tom, Dick, or *Harry!*'

I myself had been delegated to accompany the film boxes ashore and to make the best choice from what was available among new films there. Journey's end after a long, slow chug through the haze and slick of Kuwait bay was a steel pier and an establishment run by NAAFI. It was a barracks-like restaurant–reading-room–cinema–shopping complex, whose only occupants were five sailors from a British tanker nearby, one of whom asked what ship we were from.
'*Ardshiel.*'
'British?'
'Yes.'
'Got any spare knives and forks?'
'Don't know.'
'Got a crew bar?'
'No. The crew is Moslem. They don't drink alcohol.'
'A lot of use, aren't you!'

'A lot of use, aren't you?' repeated Basil Thomson when he came to the wardroom to see what films we'd brought back. The general selection at the NAAFI had been poor, but the three boxes with which we'd returned included *Paint Your Wagon* and *Far from the Madding Crowd*, which had appeared to be the best features available. Thomson was the only man on board who'd seen both. 'I might have known', he said, 'that you'd mess it up.'

We sailed the following afternoon at four fifteen; by four thirty the sea island had vanished in the haze. It was not anyway something to which one would look back with any sense of interest.

To those sailors who now spend their careers sailing to and from the Gulf, it remains, and is likely to remain, a name not a place; or rather, a series of names, these being the various points at which they collect their cargoes: Mina, Hallul, Kharg Island, Abadan, and so on. These are voyages without shore memories. The sailor's memory was once defined by his ships and their ports of call, and it was always the latter that enlarged the former. Ports fostered the only kinship they had with each other outside the narrowly prescribed relationships within the ship itself; friendships at sea are seldom long-lasting, if they exist at all. But shore-going at least provided the brawls and excursions that gave them something to remember each other by apart from the faceless months at sea.

Tankers arrive nowhere. After a month's voyage we came to a sea berth off a desolate and unreachable island. Hallul provided our only landscape within the Gulf itself, except for the Quoins. Everyone was attentive when one of the Hallul pilots spoke of nice coves with soft sand and beautiful shells. He could have been speaking of some exquisite Pacific atoll, so desirable and worthwhile did this paltry description make that barren, sun-baked mound appear. After Hallul Island, there was even worse: the black-painted steel of the Mina sea berth, dust coated, blistering hot, and nine miles from shore, only another ship and its different men to look at. When I had come back from fetching the movies people had asked, 'How was it on shore, then? Did you see anything?' as though in forlorn hope that there had been something pleasantly evocative there as well, such as soft sand and shells, which they could vicariously touch.

Distance or impersonality has claimed every aspect of the job, and there was a real horror when, as we sailed away, someone remarked in the wardroom that Liverpool also was to become an off-shore berth. 'Can you imagine what it will be like?' Harvey Phillips asked. 'Smelling the British fog and not even able to get across those few miles of water to spend half an hour in a pub enjoying a pint of bitter!'

Loaded, *Ardshiel* had become a serene ship. The propeller was now buried deep, deep under the water and not a tremor or hint of vibration touched the stillness of the vessel – so still that on several occasions after sailing from Mina I got up to look out in the belief that we had stopped. Outside, the sea was closer to the deck and, eventually, doubtless would bring a pleasant intimacy; but not in the Gulf, which is infested with sea snakes, noisome creatures, as long and yellow and fat as king cobras, and as deadly. They drift on the surface, so prolific that one saw one of them every few seconds. When a British liner, *Dara*, caught fire and sank in the Gulf a few years ago some of those who leaped from the flaming decks met their end from being bitten by these ghastly serpents.

We rounded Ras al Hadd and the monsoon blew fierce, steady, and warm; spray hung in the air like a permanent rainstorm over the bows and the ship was bound by rainbows, as if in celebration. We were riding home, it seemed, in a bright cloud of colour. The refraction was so intense that the whole air and its wet tropical light around us was grained with spectra, which floated like coloured dust and which thickened day by day as we drove deeper into the wind; and the wind brought a special luminosity even at night for, sailing through the dark, a white shore, as vivid as a floodlit surf, appeared dead ahead and, moments later, *Ardshiel* ran into it: into a soft pale burning sea, the tone of moonlight, except that there was no moon or other celestial light, only an eerie inexplicable brightness upon the water that seemed to shine up from under the surface. We had run into a 'white sea', a phenomenon peculiar to the Arabian Sea and the northern Indian Ocean. The sea was dark only where the ship broke it, and the spray itself was a small dark cloud against the bright surface beyond the bows. In the morning the decks shone blindingly, as though from remnant fragments of this light, but it was the salt left by evaporation of the pools of water formed by spray. Black footmarks ran paths across the dried salt, like prints in the first snow of winter.

If there was a sense of celebration in all this air and light, it was perhaps because of the feeling inside the ship itself that this was the beginning of the last stage, the homeward passage at the end of which was home itself for most of them, not turn-round for another voyage to the Gulf and back. The wardroom lights shone until later in the night than had been usual, and there was a frequent sound of singing, mainly of the songs from *Paint Your Wagon*, the score of which had been taped and thereafter ceaselessly resounded through the ship at shattering levels. It played from the wardroom machines, and in the cabins, and out at the pool; in the cinema, the film seemed to be in almost continuous performance. It had struck a mood, and outburst reached its natural crescendo with the number 'There's a Coach Comin' In', with all its pronounced pleasure in an imminent arrival. They crowded the wardroom floor in an impromptu square dance, or whatever, shouting the words, swinging, wheeling, circling, leaping. 'I feel like tearing up telephone books,' Ewart-James said, and the feeling appeared to be general.

'Well,' Thomson said, as if in benediction, 'now that Harry Long and his mate have gone, we can relax again.'

'Well,' Graham Chalmers, the junior engineer, said, 'live and let live.'

'What's that? What's the matter with you?' Thomson demanded.

'I'm happy, Captain,' Chalmers said simply, and offered to buy the master a drink.

'Well, thank you, young Chalmers,' Thomson said. 'I'll have a Mars bar instead.' Chalmers brought the Mars bar on a silver salver, said, 'Cheers, Captain,' and Thomson himself said, 'Cheers, bless you, my boy,' and Chalmers went off to join the dancing, which had resumed to the tune of 'Hand Me Down a Can of Beans'.

We lost in the monsoon the only pet *Ardshiel* had, a pigeon who'd come aboard at Le Verdon and stayed with the ship all the way to the Gulf. He had appeared each day for his rations at the galley door and, in the Gulf, had brought with him a mate. But the winds had proved too much for the birds, and we never saw them again. *Ardshiel* had not, so far as I could gather, ever had any other pet. Some tankers do have pets, but on ships such as *Ardshiel* the turn-over is too frequent and the absence of animals becomes another de-humanising touch. It was impossible to imagine that, as with ships of other days, generations of animals could make the vessel their residence. When the *Aquitania* went to the scrapyard in 1950 the cats that were brought ashore were the descendants of those which originally went aboard when she was built in 1914.

Ardshiel sailed back into the tropics, and out of them again into the southern winter; Durban passed as a faint smudge of high-rise buildings on the horizon, sunrise and sunset wheeled around the ship to opposite positions as we rounded the Cape and began ascending the Atlantic toward Europe; and they began to count their very last steps home, some more soberly than others. 'After the trip home and all the excitement of looking forward to it, there is a sense of anticlimax when you arrive at the front door,' Dave Haydon said. 'You've built up in your mind something that really isn't there. The only thing is my wife, well she gets a lot of excitement out of the fact that I've arrived home, but it takes me, to be quite honest, about fourteen days to get used to being with her again. You go home into a woman's world, and therefore you feel a bit of a stranger. An outcast in a bit of a way, a misfit. Because she has the home the way she wants it, her things; the house after a while quite definitely takes on a feminine look. Because she's there all the time, which is quite natural. Your things are hidden away. I'm not saying on purpose; you have to go and search for them, or ask for them. They've been put in a box and shut in a cupboard, and you have to go and get them, to sort of give you the atmosphere that you are home really. But if you're in the mood for something, you can go and have it. One of my great joys is to go to the fridge and take out a bottle of fresh milk and drink a glass. Things like this are the be all and end all.'

'I know every step at the end of the trip,' Peter Dutton said. 'The plane comes down over Newcastle, and I get a taxi, and I'm not in a particular hurry to get home. I want the guy to take his time, and I look at all the familiar things, and I soak it all in; and it all happens always the same: you drive up the road, and you turn at your street, you see the neighbours, and you see the kids, you see the same kids but they've all grown an extra six inches, you know. You look around, and they're pointing; and the women cleaning their windows there, they turn. Oh yes, Jolly Jack's home again, they seem to say. At home, when the car pulls up, I get out of the taxi like, I don't want to hurry, because it's all so lovely, and it always happens the same way: our front door has glass in the door, a frosted glass door, and I stand by the side of the door, and I can see the light from the back kitchen. I can see my wife as she comes to the door, and she's sort of running; she's got her apron on. It's going to happen, it's going to happen like I say, in just two weeks' time. She's dressed, and she's just as nice as she can be, and she's coming, coming down the passage.'

I got off the ship at Las Palmas instead of Taranto. South of the Canaries, *Ardshiel* had received a message from P & O to say that the ship was to make for Las Palmas to embark two Japanese technicians who, on the run to Taranto, would check various engine-room troubles she had been experiencing. It seemed a good opportunity to cut my own voyage short by almost a week, and permission to land was obtained from the various authorities concerned, so that, to my surprise, I finally confronted the end of my experience.

It must be said first that there seemed to me now to be a certain unfairness in having framed the whole drama of superships through the voyage of *Ardshiel* which, to a degree, would suffer through association, or by inference, when, at least so far as her standards of safety, navigation, and general well-being were concerned, these were of the highest order. She was after all virtually a flagship in the biggest and proudest and most traditional of British shipping companies. Her master, according to P & O tradition, was a first-class seaman and he ran his ship according to older precepts, regardless whether they made him popular or not, which is what counts, because it is first-class seamanship and conscience that will help us save our seas, not polish and affability. If there were a Basil Thomson in command of every flag of convenience tanker afloat there would perhaps not be so much to worry about, except of course the very structure of the ships themselves, and in this regard *Ardshiel* certainly provided a sound enough measure and basis for concern.

She was absolutely typical of her generation and class of ship, the first generation of 200,000 tonners, and she was in fact indubitably better than most because of the care and attention that P & O put into her, in their pampering of their crew and in their rigid concern for safety. Nonetheless, whatever the splendour of her quarters, the style of living, and the standard of the men who ran her, she required the constant weight of everyone's concern, effort, and physical ability to keep her in shape. What of the others in lesser hands, with less scrupulous standards?

In one way at least the voyage had been far more shattering in its impact than I could possibly have anticipated, and this was because of the range of fearsome incident touched merely in the experiences recounted on board which had nothing to do with our own voyage. I mean stories such as the account of the master who'd ordered a potential collision course up the English Channel, the sight of the collective breakdown of tankers off Ceylon, and Peter Dutton's various accounts of alarms and failures, to name only a few. If one added to this only one episode from *Ardshiel's* present voyage, the near-collision situation with the freighter in the Indian Ocean, and then brought together as well those many tanker disasters and accidents that occurred along our routes during the general period of the voyage – the breakdown of the *Simfonia* and *World Miracle*, the partial disablement of the *Texaco Venezuela*, *Grafton*, *Blyth Adventurer*, *Moster*, and *Globtik Mercury*, and the sinking of *Alkis* in the Southern Ocean – then one felt quite simply that if one voyage could involve so much, what truly could be the aggregate of these failures and failings at any given moment on the world's oceans? Whichever way one looked at it, one confronted the knowledge of disastrous shortcoming on every level of ships and seamanship, and not much apparent prospect of retrieving the situation, least of all under the flags of convenience.

Aside from their constant faults, misdemeanours, and delinquencies, the influence of the flags of convenience upon the sea has been felt in three particular ways of importance. They have advanced by their casual standards on even the most modern of ships a disrespect for and indifference to a ship and the ways of the sea whose influence has become widespread, mainly by creating a body of seamen which is well on its way to being the single largest in the world and whose view of the sea and ships is entirely that of the vessels in which they have trained and served. They have brought the credentials of the sea into disrepute by making them easily available through minimum standards or modest purchase, or even not necessary at all. By removing themselves from accountability, they have virtually suspended law upon the sea, and diminished the oldest concept of international collaboration and responsibility in the world.

The best standards are no guarantee against accidents, but they create a better climate of vigilance and responsibility, and responsibility itself is ensured by accountability. Any British, American, or

Scandinavian seaman knows that his errors, if they have resulted in mishap, must be accounted for to a formal board of inquiry and that they could cost him his ticket, or put a permanent stain upon it; but that inquiry he also knows will be impartial, and incorruptible.

In 1971, Liberia announced that it would establish its own marine survey and inspection service to check on vessels flying its flag; it was the first practical gesture it had made toward the sort of legal stringency that governs safety, maintenance, crew training, officer certification, and working and living conditions in American, British, Japanese, and most European merchant navies. What the effect will be remains to be seen. But a year after the announcement a Liberian tanker, *Tien Chee*, collided in the estuary of the Plate with a British freighter, *Royston Grange*, which was incinerated in a fireball blaze similar to that which created the black rain upon the Spanish towns of Panjón and Bayona after the *Polycommander* fire. Eighty-one persons died in the *Tien Chee–Royston Grange* disaster and, because of the heavy loss of life, the circumstances were never completely clear; among the facts the inquiry did reveal however was that three officers aboard the *Tien Chee*, including the third officer, lacked certificates. The tightening up had obviously not yet caught up with her.

These questions become of increasing concern as the Liberian and other flag of convenience fleets continue to grow; the Japanese, with the second largest merchant fleet in existence, have begun to advance the same arguments as the Americans for putting their ships under the Liberian flag. What is obviously required in face of this phenomenon is an international authority to which such vessels are accountable. Under the supervision of the Inter-Governmental Maritime Consultative Organization, which is the only international organisation we now have dealing with matters of the sea, accountability is still a national concern, and that, so far as one's fears for the present and future state of the sea are concerned, is next to useless, at least until the world has achieved a uniformity of punitive code and of alacrity to apply it, and *ability* to apply it, which can scarcely be a serious proposition where the flag of convenience countries themselves are concerned. It is quite impossible to visualise any sort of international authority with real teeth which in the immediate or even foreseeable future would have the means and administration and executive power to control the seas. If nearly half the world's tonnage did not consist of tankers, it would not perhaps matter so much; unhappily, tankers themselves are now only part of the matter.

The fear, danger, and social and environmental havoc that tankers have brought to the seas is now enlarged by the ships carrying poisonous substances and liquid gas of various kinds. These ships too are growing in size. In an article on this matter in the periodical *Safety at Sea International*, Captain W. L. D. Bayley, the publication's editorial consultant, discussed the range of chemicals and noxious materials now being carried at sea, and said:

> After research into brand names and the same chemical under different names, it was found that 250 varieties were shipped in bulk by sea, being manufactured by 80 British and 10 foreign companies. The truly mammoth task of collecting data on these chemicals was sometimes frustrated by the unwillingness of manufacturers to co-operate, and eventually 230 chemical data sheets were compiled. What the other 20 non-listed horrors were must be left to the imagination and, I sincerely hope, future legislation at the international level.

However, as Bayley himself pointed out, there is at present no legislation forbidding pollution by noxious substances other than oil, although the matter has been raised by IMCO.

Chemical tankers used to be small ships, usually in the 500- to 1,000-ton range, gross, but they already are up to 24,000 tons. The products they carry vary in danger from being highly inflammable to being highly toxic to touch and inhale. Defoliants for Vietnam were carried in such vessels. In February 1972, an American chemical carrier, the 21,000-ton *V. A. Fogg* whose last cargo had been benzene, exploded and sank off the Bahamas, killing 39 men. The ignorance about the full effects of crude oil dumped in the sea must be small change against our ignorance of what such chemicals can do if deposited in the mainstream flow of a major current such as the Gulf Stream – indeed, if deposited *anywhere*. At a maritime symposium attended by Captain Bayley in Liverpool to discuss the handling of pollutants, it was admitted that there were no laws to stop chemical tankers from dumping their slops into the sea, as doubtless they do when they clean tanks. 'Obviously much remains to be done, with pilots and port authorities having great responsibility for the safe movement of the chemical carrier,' Bayley said. 'Should all other traffic stop when such a vessel is moving within the port limits in reduced visibility? Or at all times? ... As an extreme safety measure, should this trade by sea be permitted at all?'

It is the liquid gas carriers, however, that form the most conspicuous of all dangerous developments, after the emergence of the supertanker. Natural gas composes about one-third of the world's hydrocarbon reserves and is rapidly becoming a basic fuel. The

United States accounts for about 60 per cent of world consumption, and formerly piped all its gas straight from the wellhead into a consumers' distribution system. The expense and difficulties of transporting gas meant that in remote areas of the world such as the Middle East and Borneo gas was simply burned at the oil well-head to dispose of it. Kuwait alone burns in this manner the equivalent of a year's gas consumption in Britain. The energy crisis in the world has brought a natural disinclination for such waste, either of energy or of profit, and has finally justified the enormous expense of building ships to transport the gas in liquefied form. They are the most expensive civilian ships afloat, with a cost apiece of between $80 million and $100 million. Their capacity is immense: 75,000 cubic metres of liquid gas which, when regasified, expands some 600-fold in volume. Less than a decade ago, there were only two of these ships afloat; the world fleet still consists of fewer than thirty. By 1985 a fleet of from 200 to 250 of these ships is expected to be in service, each carrying the energy equivalent of a 250,000–300,000-ton oil ship.

The gas is piped from the fields to a refrigerating plant where it is liquefied, and this liquid flows into the ship's tanks, where it is held at a steady chill of minus 160 degrees Centigrade. In effect, the liquid gas ships are floating thermos tanks containing this deeply chilled liquid. Experience has shown that the liquid is so cold that the smallest drop of it is enough to cause a ship's decks to become brittle and fracture, and, as a result, survey techniques are so thorough that they enable detection of a hole in the pipework the size of the head of a pin. Theoretically, if one of the big tanks were breached in a collision the surrounding sea at first would freeze, until the liquid began to evaporate, whereupon it would become a lethal cloud close to the surface of the sea.

The gas is lighter than air, and most experiments so far suggest that it would quickly disperse. Tests carried out in the United States indicated that a spillage of one large tank from one of these ships occurring off Staten Island could result in a gas cloud extending from seven to twelve miles from the point of collision. It would, it was said, swiftly disperse. On a subzero windless day? 'No details were given of the actual amount of liquid discharged,' the British shipping journal *Fairplay* said in comment upon a report published by Shell about experiments undertaken in the Bay of Biscay on jettisoning liquid gas, 'but the tests indicate that the dangers are less than was at first feared – providing the dumping is carefully controlled'. The purpose of the test was to determine whether a stricken gas-carrier could lighten itself by dumping its cargo, without further endangering itself. But the gas was dumped in calm weather with a wind speed of six knots and at a rate fractional compared to what might occur in an accident. Need one add that the conditions of an emergency dumping, or of a collision, might not be so precisely favourable.

Liquid gas brings an entirely new factor to collision and shipwreck anyway, apart from the explosive risks; a heavy escape of the chilled liquid would make the hull of the ship so brittle that any damage already suffered might be swiftly enlarged by cold-induced cracks and fractures, perhaps leading to the cracking and breaking of other tanks.

Experience is the only guide and there is one particularly disturbing experience with a liquid gas carrier, as recounted in his article in *Safety at Sea International* by Captain Bayley. In the autumn of 1968 a small Swedish gas tanker named *Claude*, carrying 900 tons of liquefied butane gas, was sailing down Southampton water in foggy weather in the charge of a pilot. The *Claude* collided with an inbound British ship. 'Seconds after the collision,' Captain Bayley writes, 'the pilot of the *Claude* found himself alone on the bridge of the stricken ship, the rest of the crew having jumped into the fog-shrouded water. The gas tanker's engine was left turning with slight reverse pitch on the propeller! The pilot knew nothing of the cargo beneath him, but figuring that the crew knew what was best for their own skins, he too abandoned ship.' The abandoned *Claude* drifted back the way she had come, assisted by her propeller and the tide, and went aground. The drama however did not end there. The ship was towed to a refinery and a Portuguese gas ship was chartered to take off *Claude*'s cargo. During the transfer operation one of the hoses sprang a leak and a 'vast cloud of gas was carried on the wind towards the refinery and the city of Southampton.

'In a fine display of panic,' Captain Bayley writes, 'the Portuguese tanker steamed away, ignoring the rupturing of hoses and pipelines, inestimably increasing the risk of explosion. The rapid evaporation of the liquid gas caused ice to form and volunteers working without gas masks ... had a hard job to close the valves left open by the departing gentlemen of Portugal.'

What is particularly distressing in this regard, and in regard to supertankers, is that as ships get bigger and more technical and difficult to handle, and as they simultaneously set afloat upon the waters quantities without precedent of dangerous and damaging substance, they are being sailed by unskilled or improperly trained or uncaring men whose minimal terms of employment are part of the basis of a profit for the shipowners and operators gross beyond any previous calculation of avarice.

If there was one simple conclusion to be drawn from my own

survey of the tanker problem alone it was that, whichever way one sees it, the world's seas cannot be expected to survive the oil ships if they continue to be built to and operated and sailed by the sort of standards that now largely prevail. At any rate, what is left of the seas by the time they have done with them might not be worth the having. As this basis of management is transferred to chemical ships, the outlook becomes even bleaker.

If a battle is to be fought, however, it must be fought with tankers; if anything is achieved, the benefits will transfer as a matter of course to the other vessels. For the moment, therefore, it is the tankers that must engage our fullest interest. We might be expected to control the effluence that we ourselves directly pass from our cities and rivers into the oceans, and it would be pointless to single out tankers unless we do, but it is they that principally distribute pollution and destruction out upon the deep sea; and there is no law on earth at present that can be effective against them there. All that we can do is to hedge them with accountability: that is, ensure that those men who profit from them should be held accountable for making these ships as fail-safe as possible; that they should also be held accountable for the health and standards and efficiency of their crews; and that they should be held accountable for every drop of oil that goes on board. If we hold them to account for these things, we will still have no guarantee of absolutely clean seas, because ordinary merchantmen will still be dumping their bilges where they wish, but the main offenders will be under a programme of chastisement, and the difference will bring us closer to survival of the oceans than to the possibility of their dying.

Two groups that might have made a conspicuously stronger contribution to this situation are the insurers and classification societies and the major oil companies in their role as charterers. The insurers exercise a punitive range of premiums against some operators, so they say: those with consistently bad records. But one is left with the strong impression that it would take the shock and incalculable impact of a fully laden VLCC totally wrecked, as *Torrey Canyon* was, in an area sensitive to public opinion and political reaction, and the incalculable claims that this would involve, before the insurers establish a code of acceptance based on something more than mere seaworthiness of a vessel. The view of the insurers and classification societies appears to be that so long as owners and operators meet their standards for seaworthiness and fire fighting, the rest is up to the owner. That is, no attempt is made to lay down a code of design or back-up systems. There are high standards for hull and engines, that is to say for *condition*; but no code that specifies how an owner should design his ship, nor what equipment or machinery should be in it. These, according to the traditional view, are strictly the owner's business. That is how a whole race of one-boiler ships with insufficient back-up systems comes to exist.

In a paper titled 'Technology and Safe Navigation' read by J. A. H. Paffett, head of the Ship Division of the National Physical Laboratory, to the Institution of Engineers and Shipbuilders in Scotland at Glasgow in 1971, the author considered the various responsibilities of owners, builders, classification societies and underwriters. 'Safety costs money,' he said, 'and in such an intensely individual and competitive business such as ship-owning one must appreciate the reluctance of even an enlightened owner to "go safe" while his competitors take risks and prosper. The owners naturally prefer safety rules to be set by an impartial body, and to be imposed equally upon all so as not to upset the balance of competitiveness...' The shipbuilders, he said, are technical innovators in constructional techniques, but in matters affecting navigation – steering equipment, sensor installations, bridge layout and so on – they fit what the owners ask for. 'The classification societies are concerned mainly with the structural strength, the mechanical equipment and the propulsion machinery of the ship; while these directly affect survival after a mishap, they have little bearing on its prevention. The builders or the Societies cannot be looked to to initiate technological development work aimed specifically at preventing casualties.' One would expect the underwriters to take a close interest in matters of ship safety, Paffett said, and to have some influence upon such matters as navigational equipment and crew training. 'It seems that for the most part the underwriters exert their influence by adjusting the premium rate in accordance with the owner's claims history.' The owners in fact would appear to have conspicuous influence upon the underwriters. Discussing marine insurance in an article in the July 1974 issue of *Tanker and Bulk Carrier*, E. D. Rainbow, chairman of the Institute of London Underwriters, wrote: 'When the first 200,000-tonners appeared, several of us who took part in technical studies of the problems involved foresaw difficulties which seemed to justify a rate structure much higher than we were applying for smaller vessels; but the reaction of shipowners led us to accept the proposition that we ought to accept a lower level of premium unless and until our forebodings were proved to be correct.'

For their part, the major oil companies appear to exercise little or no control over the standards of the independently owned ships they charter. In the case of P & O, of course, this is not necessary. The oil company ships as well are run usually to the highest standards, yet they allow to crawl in and out of their terminals, under the eyes of their marine superintendents and managers, vessels of deplorable condition and standards of operation, on charter to themselves. Only when these ships get into trouble does it emerge on whose account they were carrying oil.

IMCO should be credited with the single biggest achievement so far against pollution by oil ships, represented by its new international convention for the prevention of pollution of the sea. This was adopted at a special international conference called in London in 1973. The new convention, which supplants all previous legislation on sea pollution, includes a provision to limit the sizes of tanks in big ships, so as to reduce spillage in an accident; and it stipulates that every new tanker of 70,000 tons and over must be equipped with segregated ballast tanks. This means that ballast water no longer will be pumped into cargo tanks to give the ship stability after it has unloaded its cargo. The deposit of oily ballast water in the seas is thus brought under gradual assured control, at least so far as tankers and chemical ships are concerned. These steps represent the first powerful international attempts to control the design of superships. But the convention also takes the first important step toward avoiding dependence upon the conscience of ship's crews by requiring that all tankers be fitted with an approved oil discharge monitoring and control system. The system will have a device to produce a continuous record of the discharge. Unfortunately, these requirements don't apply to existing tankers until three years after the convention comes into force, which may not be for years. One must always remember that it took eight years for IMCO's first major postwar anti-pollution legislation, the convention of 1954, to be adopted. At any rate, such a serious start is certainly better than nothing.

Meanwhile, no future tanker of VLCC class, and certainly none of Ultra Large Crude Carrier size, should be built and be allowed to operate without twin screws, a stronger rudder system (the British have developed a new rudder that not only helps big ships to manœuvre with remarkable facility, but also improves their stopping), a double bottom, and a major auxiliary boiler of sufficient power and independence to handle fully the ship's entire electrical and automatic system as well as its engines. No VLCC of the present generation should be allowed to change hands in the future (the very act of sale can be assumed to be an admission of advanced deterioration and costly upkeep) and accepted in operation on the seas unless it has been surveyed by the most exacting standards, especially for hull corrosion and the condition of its engines. As we have seen, corrosion in these tanks can eat away the metal with the same intensity that shipworm could devour the timbers of wooden ships. Moreover, its effects upon large tanks are not yet fully appreciated. Undetected corrosion could have very serious consequences on the vessel's plating. The buckling strength of the plating is proportional to the square of its thickness. This means that a 10 mm.-thick plate corroded down to 7 mm. may have its resistance to buckling reduced to 50 per cent. Ships in such condition are not going to handle bad seas, whether off the Cape or off Maine, without fearful danger to themselves. A United States Coast Guard analysis of tanker accidents for the period 1969–70 found that nine of the largest tanker accidents causing pollution involved structural failure; altogether structural failure accounted for half the accidental outflow from tankers in that period. The evidence suggested that the nine ships concerned had deteriorated structurally; all were lost at sea and were believed to have broken up under extreme weather conditions.

If airline pilots are compelled to undergo health examinations, why not the masters of supertankers? The state of health of Captain Rugiati of the *Torrey Canyon* alone would seem to have made that an indisputable requirement.

Nor should any master take command of a supership without intensive simulator training of the airline sort, which is now provided at Delft; and, in model ships, in France.

So far as crew is concerned, one of the reasons given by the tanker operators for building outsize ships has been the difficulties of getting seamen in the rich industrial nations, where men no longer are tempted by the sea life. This has served also as a reason for going under a flag of convenience, when they can hire so-called third-world sailors. There was a unique opportunity here to bring a technical skill of great value to the world at large to the under-developed nations, as well as providing employment. It would have cost the oil and tanker companies very little jointly to establish maritime training schools in those nations from which they recruited their seamen, and in which sailoring could have been taught according to rigorous standards. Instead, those sailors have mainly learned on the job, often without even knowing English, the language of the sea.

That tankers and the exemptions they gain by operating under flags of convenience have changed completely all accepted ways and standards of the sea was acknowledged and discussed in a paper prepared for the Royal Institute of Navigation in 1971 by two Netherlanders, Dr F. J. Buzek, a master mariner and doctor in international law, and Captain A. Wepster, a master with the Holland America Line and the Institute's gold medallist for 1970. What had emerged, the authors said, was a new and heavier responsibility for the master, namely his responsibility to society and the environment, and this in turn required a new standard of education and safety in training. 'In order to take care of this newly defined responsibility towards "the environment", masters may have to concentrate their activities more on safety than ever before,' their paper said:

> Education for the seafaring profession should be especially directed towards this goal. . . . At present after a period of prolonged fog, a number of foreign vessels, equal to approximately 10 per cent of all vessels waiting for entry before the [Rotterdam's] New Waterway, cannot be reached for anchoring and pilotage instructions via the shore-based radar advice system, because even the simplest conversation in English proves to be impossible. Vessels thus manned are a danger to society. In the air transport industry such conditions are not accepted, because environmental and personal danger were recognised right from the start. This is only one example where education and certificate requirements no longer meet even today's requirements.

Buzek and Wepster recognise the need for a new international authority and plead for the establishment of an international court of marine justice with jurisdiction over standards and codes in all marine matters. Such a court, they believe, should be founded under the auspices of IMCO. It is a wise goal, indeed the only practical and possible one for the situation, but it is a pipe dream. Only someone supremely wishful could believe in its creation within any foreseeable future; and by that time it probably will be too late, if one assumes that one of its main intentions would be to save the sea and the environment. Only ruthless arbitrary unilateral action can do that. Nothing else can possibly be effective.

Such unilateral action is relatively simple because the major tanker terminals are in relatively few countries, and principally in the main consuming areas, North America, Europe, and Japan. If tankers are forced by the nations between which they mainly sail to maintain rigorous standards of safety, operation, and crew health at risk of being severely penalised or even shut out from the ports they serve, there can be no doubt that they will comply. The way to force them would be to make them subject to scrupulous examination upon arrival. They should be compelled to discharge their tank washings on arrival under supervision, as tankers using the west coast Alaska route will do. Inspectors of the American or Canadian coast guards, or the British Department of Trade, or the equivalent, should check the survey and safety certificates of the ships, the state of all essential equipment, and the certification and conditions of service of the crew, with authority to impose summary fines, penalties, or cautions for obvious delinquencies and shortcomings. In the case of survey, certificates should be acceptable only if the issuing authority is one whose standards are accepted by bodies such as the British

Department of Trade and the United States Coast Guard. As we insist upon examinations of flocks, stock, and crops, to prevent the entry of disease which may damage the national health, why not do so as well for the prevention of damage to the coasts and coastal waters and *their* shoals and life and vegetation?

There is another powerful precedent for this sort of unilateral action. At the urging of the United States, IMCO approved a new and severe code of structural and safety requirements for the prevention of fire aboard passenger liners a few years ago. Without waiting for other nations to ratify the amendments, the United States passed a law requiring that a liner calling at an American port to pick up passengers had to conform to the coast guard demands. There was much consternation among foreign ship operators, but it was a question of either complying or pulling their ships off the North American run. In effect, because the American market is so important to passenger tonnage, the coast guard requirements forced worldwide compliance. No new passenger ship was built without fully incorporating the new standards. Ships too old to be expensively rebuilt and adapted to the rules were withdrawn from service, or put on routes where the rules were easier. Tankers, like cruise liners, are switched from route to route as business requires. Any code imposed by one major oil importer would soon make its impact felt upon *all* new ships, and upon all older ships that justify the expense of reconstruction. If the United States made such a demand from shipping on behalf of American tourists, a comparatively small group, then the same demand on behalf of its coastal populations would seem warranted.

The Canadians already have embarked upon such a unilateral course. Their Arctic Waters Pollution Act serves as a precedent which is gradually being extended to all waters; ships entering Canadian territorial seas are increasingly being forced to offer themselves and their standards of operation for examination according to Canadian rules. Nothing less than such action will make the tanker operators part with more of their profits to give their ships the sort of overall safety and seaworthiness that they should have had in the first place; and it goes without saying that if such measures strenuously enforced bring a respite for the coasts and inshore waters, then they will bring one for the deeps as well.

The oil is running out; as a resource it is finite, and always was. The seas were infinite, and should have remained so. We'll find something else instead of oil to light our lamps and to turn our too-many wheels. The seas we shan't replace. During the past two decades we have undone much of the structural gift of the eons; by the end of this very decade we might have destroyed it altogether;

and so have brought to extinction the only truly eternal feature of this planet. Why should we allow this unspeakable depredation, when so much of it is no more than an aspect merely of the dedicated unhindered greed of a few unscrupulous and unprincipled tycoons, companies, and corporations, and, in turn, of the companion immorality of their abused and uninterested sailors? There is no good technical reason why we should. For those on shore, shipwreck was once not an unwelcome event; it drew the plunderers from far and near. It was talked about for generations, with wistful recollection of the drama and the spoils; but shipwreck, once feared principally by those on board, has become in our own time the more solemn dread of those on shore than of those on board. For the first time we on land have more to lose, and nothing to gain. Helicopters get the sailors off, we clean up the muck. That is why the responsibility for ships has become ours, and is no longer the sailors'; and why they are beholden to us, not each other.

'So you're off,' Basil Thomson said. 'If we go on the way we're going, this ship is going to need a passenger licence. First we got you, and then Harry Long and his mate; we got rid of Harry Long and his mate, but you stayed, and now that we get rid of you, we get those two Japs, who'll be bowing and hissing all over the place tonight, I suppose.'

The Japanese came up the ladder and I went down, into the tiny launch that had brought them out. *Ardshiel* lay like a mountain above us, and then we parted. Basil Thomson gave me a couple of toots on the ship's whistle, and everyone waved, but the big ship was already out of sight when we entered Las Palmas harbour. I found myself sitting soon after on my hotel balcony listening to birds in pavement trees, watching the traffic and people, and ardently smelling that characteristic but not especially distinguished Spanish *calle* odour of bad oil, cheap perfume, poor petrol, stale crushed gamba shells, unflushed bar toilets, and strong coffee. It all had the impact and flavour of paradise regained, and I became aware that I was contentedly humming to myself, 'There's a coach comin' in . . .'.